Teaching Science
for All Children

third edition

Teaching Science for All Children

Inquiry Methods for Constructing Understanding

Ralph Martin
Ohio University

Colleen Sexton
Ohio University

Teresa Franklin
Ohio University

with
Jack Gerlovich
Drake University

PEARSON
A B
and

Boston ✦ New York ✦ San Francisco
Mexico City ✦ Montreal ✦ Toronto ✦ London ✦ Madrid ✦ Munich ✦ Paris
Hong Kong ✦ Singapore ✦ Tokyo ✦ Cape Town ✦ Sydney

Series Editor: Traci Mueller
Editorial Assistant: Janice Hackenberg
Executive Marketing Manager: Amy Cronin Jordan
Editorial-Production Administrator: Annette Joseph
Editorial-Production Coordinator: Barbara Gracia
Text Designer: Denise Hoffman

Photo Editor: Katharine S. Cook
Electronic Composition: Omegatype Typography, Inc.
Composition Buyer: Linda Cox
Manufacturing Buyer: Andrew Turso
Cover Designer: Kristina Mose-Libon

The material in this textbook is based upon work supported by the National Science Foundation under Grant No. 91-47392. Any opinions, findings, conclusions, or recommendations expressed in this publication are those of the authors and do not necessarily reflect the views of the foundation.

For related titles and support materials, visit our online catalog at www.ablongman.com.

Between the time website information is gathered and then published, it is not unusual for some sites to have closed. Also, the transcription of URLs can result in typographical errors. The publisher would appreciate notification where these errors occur so that they may be corrected in subsequent editions.

Library of Congress Cataloging-in-Publication Data

Ralph Martin E., [et al.].
  Teaching science for all children: Inquiry methods for constructing understanding—3rd ed. /
Ralph Martin, . . . [et al.].
    p. cm.
    Rev. ed. of: Teaching science for all children: Methods for constructing understanding, 2nd ed. /
Ralph Martin, . . . [et al.]. c1998.
    Includes bibliographical references and index.
    ISBN 0-205-43153-4 (pbk.)
    1. Science—Study and teaching—Methodology. 2. Science—Study and teaching (Elementary)—
Methodology. 3. College students—Training of. 4. Teachers—Training of. 5. Constructivism (Education).
I. Sexton, Colleen M. II. Franklin, Teresa III. Teaching science for all children IV. Title

Q181.M17782 2005
372.3'5044—dc21   20040

Printed in the United States of America

10 9 8 7 6 5 4 3 2 1   RRD-IN   09 08 07 06 05 04

Photo Credits: Photo credits are on page 430, which is considered an extension of the copyright page.

For Jen, whose passion for the environment is educating today's youth, our next generation of leaders and policy makers. Your intuitive grasp of authentic teaching and learning inspires Dad.—R. M.

For Jimmy, my friend, whose energy, enthusiasm, and passion for life help me see science in things I would have missed, and for Sarah and Celeste, my daughters, who continuously motivate and inspire me!—C. S.

This book is dedicated to my best friend and husband, Doug. Keep sailing!—T. F.

To the elementary science methods and science safety students at Drake University, for their tolerance and their inspiration.—J. G.

contents

Preface   xiii

chapter 1

What Is Science?   3

chapter 2

Learning Science   33

Inquiry for All Children   65

Planning Inquiry Lessons   109

chapter 8

Integration—How Can I Do It All? 259

chapter 9

Safety: Creating a Safe, Efficient, Inquiry-Based Science Classroom 283

Using Educational Technology to Enrich the Classroom 341

Resources for Best Practices 365

How do you prefer to learn? Do you believe you learn more from what you hear, what you see, or what you do? Certainly all are important, yet if you feel confident learning directly from what you do, then you are like most school learners. Wouldn't it be nice if you, the teacher, and your younger learners could actually learn together in many of the same ways? If you agree, then this book is for you. In the third edition of *Teaching Science for All Children: Inquiry Methods for Constructing Understanding*, we have expanded our approach to constructed learning. We demonstrate how to help learners "make meaning" through firsthand experiences, using inquiry to form discoveries about the natural world.

Our mission is to help you understand the importance of teaching in ways that learners prefer to learn, and to help you use the National Science Education Standards (NSES) and National Education Technology Standards (NETS) in effective and natural ways so that you can help all of your learners excel in learning science and benefiting from it. This textbook will help you to do this in a seamless way, with interactive pedagogy and multimedia features. Each chapter contains a number of learning tools to help you access the relevant research, see classroom teaching examples, learn from the voices of experienced teachers, and think deeply about your chosen profession—all within the context of modern science and standards.

We feature many teaching skills and methods, but most important is our distinct and robust learning cycle model for planning, teaching, and learning. While there are many effective ways to teach and learn science, one of the most effective and enduring is the 4-E learning cycle: *Exploration, Explanation, Expansion, Evaluation.* As verified by numerous sources of science education and brain research, experience is an important foundation for the processes of inquiry if a learner is to be successful in making meaning out of the unique experiences that science can provide. Our learning cycle is rooted in a history of substantial research, which supports that using the learning cycle approach has improved student science achievement and development of process skills. In this edition, the 4-E learning cycle has been refined with specific strategies to provide learners with the essential experiences that help them to understand specific science concepts and expand what they understand by precisely addressing the new NSES content areas in each lesson. Evaluation or authentic assessment is embedded throughout each lesson.

The text provides, in short, an opportunity to accumulate science teaching experiences by applying the methods and techniques described in this book.

New to This Edition

This text has been reorganized into a format that helps users understand what science is, how children learn science, and how children may experience standards-based science through inquiry, integration, and uses of popular science texts, and supplementary science resources. A 4–E feature lesson in each chapter is based on the main concept of the chapter.

Each chapter is written to stand alone so that you may easily choose how you wish to use this text. We often teach the text out of order when we use it for our own classes. Users of previous editions will find familiar material. In addition, we have expanded science for the primary grades and offer the following new items.

Pedagogy

+ **New! The Video Explorations VideoWorkshop Student CD-ROM** is included free with each copy of the text. Over 60 minutes of brief, interactive video segments feature classroom footage, insights from future teachers, and safety demonstrations. These clips are integrated into the text via a corresponding two-page Video Explorations feature in each chapter that includes discussion questions and activities to help students understand the video material and instructors to integrate the video into classroom assignments.
+ **New! Chapter on integrating the content areas.** Chapter 8 discusses integrating science teaching with math, language arts, and social studies teaching, with examples as to how teaching across the curriculum may be accomplished.
+ **New! 4-E Lesson Plans** have been incorporated into each chapter. Each lesson describes hands-on, classroom-tested activities.
+ **Updated Build a Portfolio or E-Folio** now provides suggestions on how to keep a portfolio electronically and what to include.

Updates

+ Chapter 1, "What Is Science?" is a sharper focus on modern science teaching and learning, and reports changes that have occurred in elementary school science teaching with updated research from the National Assessment of Educational Progress (NAEP).
+ Chapter 2, "Learning Science," includes the latest brain research and discusses misconceptions and conceptualization, while it maintains a constructivist teaching and inquiry learning approach, including the 4–E learning cycle.
+ Chapter 3, "Inquiry for All Children," gives greater attention to exceptional learners, illustrates how all children can benefit from the 4–E learning cycle, offers suggestions for involving parents in school science, and builds a foundation for the importance of scientific literacy for all children.
+ Chapter 4, "Planning Inquiry Lessons," focuses on designing and using concept maps and on using National Science Education Standards for planning effective 4-E learning cycle and authentic inquiry lessons.
+ Chapter 5, "Assessing Student Performance: How Can You Assess Student Learning?" is a completely revised chapter that promotes designing opportuni-

ties for authentic assessment using the 4–E learning cycle as a primary model. Numerous examples are given of how teachers can assess and evaluate student performance.

+ Chapter 6, "Inquiry for Scientific Literacy," demonstrates many different appropriate methods for teaching by inquiry, such as scientific method, Suchman's inquiry, playful discovery, and an expanded section devoted to the 4-E learning cycle for developing scientific literacy.

+ Chapter 7, "Questioning and Inquiry," builds effective questioning skills with up-to-date research; user feedback supports the importance of this chapter in performing well on the PRAXIS II principles of teaching and learning test.

+ Chapter 8, "Integration—How Can I Do It All?" is a new chapter demonstrating teaching and learning science through integrated subject planning and teaching of science in mathematics, language arts, and social studies.

+ Chapter 9, "Safety: Creating a Safe, Efficient, Inquiry-Based Science Classroom," focuses on safety and classroom management with increased emphasis given to the early childhood years.

+ Chapter 10, "Using Educational Technology to Enrich the Classroom," underwent a dramatic revision and sharply focuses on effective uses of appropriate classroom technologies.

+ Chapter 11, "Resources for Best Practices," elaborates on the concept of best practices, offers practical tips for selecting and using science texts and trade books effectively, and features a wide range of high interest, best practice science resource supplements, including a feature lesson from Project Learning Tree modified into a 4–E learning cycle.

+ The Appendix is thoroughly revised and supports the reform efforts advocated by the National Science Education Standards.

Video Explorations VideoWorkshop Student CD-ROM

Bound with the text, this CD-ROM, produced by the authors, consists of 22 original videos, featuring up to 60 minutes of brief, interactive digital video correlated with in-text learning exercises and critical thinking questions. Each video illustrates important chapter principles and concepts and includes classroom footage, safety demonstrations, and interviews with teachers. Classroom footage provides the authentic, unrehearsed efforts of experienced educators and preservice teachers. Two longer videos feature edited versions of programs on concept mapping and the 4–E learning cycle. Each video has a specific message supported by engaging scenes of classroom learning that exemplify chapter concepts. The custom videos provide unique experiential learning opportunities. Videos may be used selectively by instructors to supplement lectures, create presentations, or assign authentic classroom projects, and may be used individually as study guides or tutorials. Videos can also be a colorful and effective complement to web-based courses.

Supplements

Instructor's Manual and Test Bank

Prepared by the authors, this manual contains five parts:

✦ *Teaching Suggestions*—A model syllabus with assignment guides and grading rubrics for field experience, draw-a-scientist, concept mapping, learning cycle lesson planning, peer-taught demonstration lessons, self-analysis of teaching papers

✦ *Chapter Outlines*—Capsule descriptions of the material and concepts for each chapter; useful for lecture preparation

✦ *Test Item Bank*—Hundreds of test items; when used with the test generator, provide custom quizzes and examinations

✦ *Concept Maps*—Multiple uses as exemplars for each chapter, study guides, and presentation graphics

✦ *Transparency Masters*—PowerPoint files are provided on the companion website and in the Instructor's Manual in hard copy as student handouts.

Companion Website (www.ablongman.com/martin4e)

Our new companion website contains several helpful learning and teaching aids, such as:

✦ *Chapter objectives* for quick summary of each chapter's mission

✦ *Concept maps* that provide a visual graphic story of each chapter's concepts

✦ *Practice tests* that support study and preparation for examinations by giving instant feedback

✦ *Additional readings* that contain annotations for further reading and study on the important topics of each chapter

✦ *PowerPoint* slides for teaching and learning about the main features in each chapter

✦ *Resources,* as exemplars of best practices, that include modern or historically significant examples of innovation in science teaching and learning

✦ *Sample 4–E lesson,* created using an activity from the "Project Learning Tree" environmental science curriculum

mylabschool New! Allyn & Bacon "mylabschool" Web Resource

Free when packaged with a student access code. Contact your local representative for more details!

Discover where the classroom comes to life! From video clips of teachers and students interacting to sample lessons, portfolio templates, and standards integration, Allyn & Bacon brings your students the tools they'll need to succeed in the classroom—with content easily integrated into your existing course.

Delivered within Course Compass, Allyn & Bacon's course management system, this program gives your students powerful insights into how real classrooms work and a rich array of tools that will support them on their journey from their first class to their first classroom.

Related Text

Teaching Science for All Children: Inquiry Lessons for Constructing Understanding, **Third Edition,** provides a wealth of lessons and activities that follow the learning cycle. The two introductory chapters provide information on the learning cycle, specifically the "4 E's"—*exploration, explanation, expansion,* and *evaluation*—and on science safety, as well as how to integrate educational technology tools into each of the lessons. Each lesson is then matched to specific grade levels according to the National Science Education Standards. ISBN: 0205431526

Acknowledgments

In addition to our author team, many important people supported the project and turned our dreams and ideas into a reality. Indeed, it is an understatement to say we are grateful to these talented people.

We are indebted to Traci Mueller, Allyn and Bacon's education editor, whose vision shaped the project into a comprehensive product, and her able assistant Janice Hackenberg, who assured first-class support at every stage of the publishing process. Erin Liedel's quick study, commitment, and uncommon good sense seamlessly marched us through deadlines, and her awesome talent restructured this edition and helped to distinguish this book from its competition. Annette Joseph, as production administrator, steered us through the complexity of textbook production, and packager Barbara Gracia assured the book's accuracy and completion.

Other support was provided by Chris Mayer and Kasey Snyder, who proved to be dedicated, persistent, and talented researchers.

Our special thanks go to the reviewers who offered substantial suggestions that helped shape the fourth edition. They are Bonnie Bailey, Ohio University, Lancaster; C. David Christensen, University of Northern Iowa; Ravider Koul, Pennsylvania State University; Barbara Rasco, State University of New York at Buffalo; Dorothy J. Sluss, Clemson University; and Debby Todd, Ohio University.

Finally, we are grateful to our spouses and children for their encouragement, support, and understanding, especially during the tense moments that always accompany the deadlines for such a project. Knowing that we could help our children's teachers gave inspiration and helped to shape our mission. There will always be a special place in our hearts for Marilyn, Jennifer, Jessica, Jonathan, Sarah, Celeste, Doug, Matthew, Pat, Jacque, and Kelly.

Teaching Science for All Children

What Is Science?

*O*ne of Jessica's first assignments was to observe two different grade levels of children. Her science methods course was designed to immerse her into teaching so that she could form several snapshots of science teaching and impressions about the factors that impact learning, then use these experiences as a platform for constructing the main concepts of the course. Jessica selected Dawn from the prekindergarten class and Jorgé from the fourth-grade class. She decided to shadow the two students and to record her observations about the types of things each child did while learning science. She also had discussions with the children and used her field notes to write a summary for her methods course portfolio. Here is her account:

Today Dawn's teacher asked why some things float and why other things sink. She encouraged children to explore and discuss their ideas. Dawn played with a small plastic boat at the water table. I observed her push the boat down into the water until it filled and sank. Dawn did this several times and then the teacher suggested that Dawn try some investigations with marbles and wooden buttons of a uniform size. Dawn spent about five minutes putting the marbles and buttons into the water and watched the marbles sink immediately and the buttons float. She pushed the buttons down into the water, released them, noting that they floated to the surface each time. I suggested she put the objects into the boat to see what would happen. Dawn put six buttons and six marbles into the boat and the boat slowly began to take on water until it sank to the bottom with the buttons floating to the surface.

Dawn persisted by piling six marbles into the dry boat. The boat began to take on water and Dawn quickly added the buttons. The marbles went down with the boat and the buttons floated to the top. "Pop!" exclaimed Dawn for each button that jetted to the surface: "Pop! Pop! Pop! Pop! Pop!" Dawn continued to investigate the boat's sinking and floating with different numbers of marbles and buttons, and she returned to the water table after snack time to try different objects in the boat. Dawn mentioned that she thought the heavy things always sank, but she seemed unsure.

Jorgé had missed some school because of illness and the teacher asked me to "tutor" him in electricity so he could catch up with the rest of the class. My heart raced because I knew nothing about electricity, but having observed earlier lessons on electricity, I gave it a try and asked Jorgé what he thought it took to make a bulb light. Jorgé remembered the concept of "circuit" from a prior class. Today's challenge was to use a variety of materials to construct a flashlight: a cardboard tube, a bottle cap, metal paper fasteners, a metal paper clip, batteries, a couple of short wires, and a flashlight bulb. Jorgé had to construct the flashlight using these materials and what he knew about circuits and make it work at least one time. He dove right in, but *I* felt the pressure. To me, the minutes turned into hours and I wondered if we would succeed. The task had become our project because Jorgé was teaching me about conductors, insulators, and a series circuit. Jorgé needed help putting the bulb in place and was a little frustrated because the parts and connectors kept slipping and loosening. Finally, when all was hooked up, Jorgé turned the paper clip switch and the bulb lit. "You did it!" I shouted, attracting the attention of the whole class. I immediately turned scarlet; I couldn't help myself. The shouting came as a natural release for me and a nice reinforcement for Jorgé. He beamed. The teacher didn't frown or scold us as I expected. Instead, she winked as if this type of reaction happened all the time in her class.

Before this field experience, I dreaded having to take a science teaching course. Science was not one of my favorite subjects, but I think I can already see that it is important and the children seem to like it. I am aware now that asking a pertinent question can help children to explore, find evidence, and offer explanations for the questions. Thinking seems to improve when children are encouraged to communicate and justify their answers. I wonder, though, what kind of difference I can make. I don't feel confident or competent in science. What kinds of things should I do or teach to help children have a better impression of science than I had before I started this course?

Introduction

Jessica's prior experience in science (or lack of experience) influenced her perspective, attitude, and self-confidence. Our perceptions, attitudes, and confidence influence our teaching decisions and what we expect from our students. Our expectations also influence how students will perform. Jessica's two questions are very fair. What kind of difference can one teacher make in a science program? What things should be emphasized in science classes? We suggest adding another question: What factors help to make effective lessons?

From Jessica's notes we see that Dawn and Jorgé's teachers made a difference. Each child demonstrated interest and persisted with their task by reaching meaningful conclusions. Four-year-old Dawn explored the concepts of floating and sinking—at her own pace—and she demonstrated several important skills such as observing, comparing, and investigating. These skills helped her to form rudimentary conceptions of cause and effect as she began to accumulate some factual knowledge through play. In Jorgé's case, he appeared more systematic, had a firmer grasp on cause-and-effect relationships, and had a repertoire of scientific attitudes to help him persist with thorny problems. Most likely, Jorgé acquired and developed his attitudes and skills from an early science program and from teachers who had a clear vision of what students should know and be able to do in science. Both children benefited from teacher expectations and programs that were built upon a strong foundation of science teaching.

Both teachers followed five key actions to make their lessons effective:

1. *engaged students* in the content with purposeful interaction,
2. *created conducive environments* that provided respectful and rigorous learning opportunities,
3. *ensured access* for all learners by adjusting instruction,
4. *used questioning* skillfully to promote and assess understanding,
5. *helped students to make sense* of their experiences by making intellectual connections among important science ideas (Weiss et al., 2003).

What is science? In this chapter we explore answers to this crucial question and develop a strong foundation for understanding the challenges of teaching modern science by introducing you to

1. children's perceptions of science and scientists as well as their science achievement,
2. the nature of science,
3. the essential elements of investigative and interactive science, and
4. the aims of standards and research-based reform in science education.

How Do Children Perceive Science?

Jessica's professor assigned her to interview children in the next school on her field experience rotation. She was to find out what they thought about science and scientists. The professor suggested that the insights she gained would help her understand the readiness and needs of the children and prepare her for the challenges that lay ahead.

Science Is . . .

Jessica obtained permission to interview children of different ages. She used the question: "What is science?" Some children simply shrugged off the question or chose to talk about something else. Jessica presumed that was because they were unfamiliar with "real" science given that little time, she had observed, was devoted to it. She reported to her professor a sample of her findings*:

> "Real hard. Harder than reading. We aren't allowed to have it in kindergarten." (Antonio—kindergarten)

*These replies are direct quotations from a sample of children (distributed across race and socioeconomic status) in urban and suburban settings when asked the question "What is science?" (Wagner, K., 1988) and from children interviewed by the authors' preservice teacher through 2003.

"The weatherman. He gets to choose the weather each day and he gets to color on the wall." (Mary Beth—kindergarten)

"It [science] is what brainy people who know a lot do." (first grader)

"After lunch sometimes when there is nothing else to do." (Shawna—grade 1)

"I don't think we have science yet. I'm not a good reader." (Jeremy—grade 1)

"Mostly rocks and leaves. We put them on a table." (Lyn—grade 1)

"Computers and moving things with buttons you push. Also, anything with batteries or that plugs in. Rockets are my favorite part of science." (Carl—grade 1)

"When you smoke cigarettes and get cancer it is because of science." (Nancy—grade 1)

"Children can't be scientists until they are older." (first grader)

"On TV sometimes. *NOVA* is my favorite." (Alex—grade 2)

"When you go up in the space shuttle and you are an astronaut. Girls can be astronauts too, you know. I'm going to be in science when I grow up. The only thing is—I don't know if I will have enough money to buy a space shuttle. You have to be rich to be an astronaut." (Andrea—grade 3)

"The opposite of social studies." (Luanne—grade 3)

"Children can be scientists, and *really* good ones, too!" (third grader)

"We just read a book. I think you get it [science] in junior high. My brother is in junior high, and he has science." (William—grade 3)

"The same old stuff. I've seen the same filmstrip on erosion three years in a row." (Joshua—grade 4)

"It depends on what grade you're in and who your teacher is. If a teacher doesn't like science, then you don't get it very much. Once when the principal was coming, Mrs. — did this experiment with a tin can and a candle and a balloon—but that was the only time." (Greg—grade 5)

"Supposed to be about learning how we learn about the world and how to use the scientific method in thinking. I know because my dad is a scientist and he keeps asking me when we're going to learn that in science. I just tell him that we haven't gotten to it yet." (Doreen—grade 6)

Jessica pored over the messages and wrote a summary to report back to her methods class. Jessica was not certain how much she could generalize from the interviews. The children described science as something that usually was not given much time in the primary grades, and was reserved for the more advanced grades, or when children could read well. Children also had several misconceptions about what science is and isn't; for example, one child opined that science is responsible for causing disease or illness. Overall, the children did not seem to value science or perceive it as useful. Some thought it was repetitive or something to be watched, and implied that teachers used it as a time filler, or might not have felt comfortable or prepared to teach it adequately. On the positive side, Jessica noted that some children viewed science as a career opportunity for women, though access to science careers was believed to be limited, and some parents expected the science curriculum to help the children develop important cognitive skills.

Scientists Are . . .

When Jessica's professor urged her to probe a bit more into the values and stereotypes the children revealed, she decided to try the Draw-A-Scientist Test (Barman, 1996), which she had read about in several articles. This test was simple; it required only that she ask students to draw a picture of a scientist without prompting the students to do the drawing in any particular way. Jessica selected a new sample of students and hoped to get a fresh, unbiased perception. She collected dozens of drawings and compared them to find similarities. Then she selected two to put into her science methods class portfolio.

The first drawing (Figure 1.1) illustrates a composite view and was a common perception among several drawings. She wrote in her summary: "Scientists are middle-aged, white males who wear lab coats and glasses. Their facial features are indicative of their generally deranged behavior. They work indoors, alone, perhaps underground, surrounded by smoking test tubes and other pieces of technology. An air of secrecy and danger surrounds their work" (Flick, 1989, p. 8; Barman and Ostlund, 1996).

Jessica based her summary on the fact that most scientists were depicted as white males (Barman, 1997). Overall, only about 8 percent of the scientists were drawn as female—close to the reality of the 6 percent women in the engineering and scientific workforce (Kahle, 1983). Only 1 percent of the students drew minority scientists, mostly African Americans; in reality, Asians "make up 5 percent of the scientists and engineers (in comparison to 2 percent of the population)" (Fort & Varney, 1989, p. 9). When they drew the scientists, the children reached back into their own experiences. Some drew the scientist by race and gender as a self-image; some took their images from television and movies; some were honoring a significant person who had affected them; and, of course, some knew only the general stereotype that is perceived to fit the look of most scientists (Sumrall, 1995). However, only a small number were drawn as fictional characters (Barman, 1997).

Jessica was now curious about why the children held these particular attitudes and beliefs about science and scientists and how the children's perceptions might reflect the beliefs of others, such as teachers. As she reflected on her findings, she decided to try to see a snapshot of the field of science teaching. Given all of the research and attention placed on improving science programs and teaching over the past several years, Jessica was motivated to ask what changes have occurred in elementary science.

FIGURE 1.1 Children's Perception of a Scientist

What Changes Have Occurred in Elementary Science?

For more than thirty years the National Assessment of Educational Progress (NAEP) has been the only continuing assessment of U.S. children's achievement in grades K–12. This test was mandated by the U.S. Congress and attempted to measure what students know and how they perform against agreed on expectations in science and other subject areas. NAEP scores denote the levels of student performance: (1) *Basic*—partial mastery of knowledge and skills that are fundamental for performing proficient work at each grade; (2) *Proficient*—solid academic performance over challenging subject matter, application to real world situations, and ability to use appropriate analytical skills; and (3) *Advanced*—superior performance. NAEP science tests use multiple-choice and constructed-response questions and hands-on tasks to measure knowledge and performance of three science themes: systems, models, and patterns of change.

The test has changed over time and longitudinal comparisons across 25 years of test scores are not possible. Comparisons of prior tests using the "old forms" revealed substantial increases in achievement during times of active experimentation with science curricula and decreases in scores during the "back to basics" era of the late 1970s and early 1980s. The following list shows the changes in science according to *The Nation's Report Card: Science 2000* (O'Sullivan et al., 2003):

Achievement
+ Achievement in grades 4 and 8 is largely unchanged from 1996 to 2000.
+ For grade 4, only 29% of the pupils in 2000 achieved at or above the proficiency level established by the National Assessment Governing Board, compared to 32% of 8th graders.
+ Students in the 8th grade scoring in the 90th percentile have achieved modest significant improvements.

Gender
+ Males in 2000 achieved higher average scores than females in grades 4 and 8.
+ Between 1996 and 2000, the average scores for 8th grade males increased.
+ Between 1996 and 2000, the achievement score gap between males and females widened, favoring males by three points in grade 4 and five points in grade 8.

Race/Ethnicity
+ In 2000, the average scores of white students at all grades were higher than those of their black, Hispanic, or American Indian peers.
+ The gap in scores between white and black students and between white and Hispanic students has not grown since 1996.

Teaching and Learning

An independent national study of K–12 science education in the United States offers additional insight that may help to explain why more children do not score higher on the national assessment. This study also may help us to understand better the key factors necessary to improve teaching and learning.

Led by Iris Weiss et al. (2003) of Horizon Research, numerous teams of researchers observed more than 360 lessons in mathematics and science. Based on findings from this national sample, only 15 percent of the observed lessons were judged to be of high quality and 27 percent of medium quality; 59 percent were low quality. Low-quality lessons are unlikely to help students understand important science content or to develop essential skills in doing science. High-quality lessons are planned with structure and taught in a manner that engage children with important concepts, and strive to help learners construct meaning and connect their understandings in ways that develop their capacity to do science successfully. High-quality teaching will stimulate powerful learning over time. High-quality lessons will

- include content that is significant and worthwhile (standards-based),
- be taught with confidence and accuracy,
- require strong intellectual rigor,
- use skillful teacher questioning to enhance conceptual understanding, and
- emphasize sense-making that is appropriate for the learners and the purposes of the lesson.

The second drawing of a scientist that Jessica put in her portfolio appealed to her for its special message (Figure 1.2). A female student who had drawn a picture of her younger brother explained: "This is my brother and I think he is a scientist. He is very curious, like this time when he threw our cat down the stairs. He always wants to know

FIGURE 1.2 Children as Scientists
Children are great examples of scientists. Their curiosity motivates them to act on their ideas.

why things work and what will happen when he tries a new idea." Jessica doubted that the sister was advocating violence or cruelty toward animals. Rather, her remarks seem to suggest that the brother was following his natural curiosity. This caused Jessica to ponder what science is and what it means to "do" science.

The Nature of Science

The word *science* originates from the Latin word *scientia,* meaning "knowledge," as in possessing knowledge instead of misunderstanding or being ignorant. In fact, one of the authors distinctly remembers having to memorize a definition from a junior high textbook (long since forgotten, along with almost everything else in it!) that defined science as an "organized body of knowledge." Following that were the steps of the scientific method, also to be memorized: (1) identify the problem, (2) examine the data, (3) form a hypothesis, (4) experiment, and (5) make a conclusion. Textbook definitions and memory exercises are helpful only to a point in learning *about* how some of the ideas of science were developed, a process that was often the subject of large posters adorning walls in science classrooms.

Eventually most science classrooms abandoned the posters and the scientific method as something to be memorized, perhaps because the mechanistic certainty of the steps did not reveal the true nature of science, its history, and its implications for society. For example, George deMestral did not set out to invent Velcro. However, he was curious about why some burs stuck so tightly to his clothing (Roberts, 1989). By recognizing that the commonplace provided an important insight, deMestral developed a product that has a wide range of uses. Charles Townes too saw the commonplace in a special way, and his vision helped him to invent the laser. He said: "The laser was born one beautiful spring morning on a park bench in Washington, D.C. As I sat in Franklin Square, musing and admiring the azaleas, an idea came to me for a practical way to obtain a very pure form of electromagnetic waves from molecules" (Roberts, 1989, p. 82). Who among us does not use Velcro in some way? And consider how much the laser has changed whole fields: medicine, electronics, merchandising, and defense among many others. These examples of serendipities—accidental discoveries made possible by a mind receptive to scientific thinking—are typical of many sudden breakthroughs in science and help us to understand that not all of what is learned through science is orderly and predictable. Robert Hazen and James Trefil help us to see this a bit more clearly:

Science naturally stimulates positive attitudes, enhances inquiry skills, and elevates understanding of our natural world.

There is a temptation, when presenting a subject as complex as the natural sciences, to present topics in a rigid, mathematical outline. . . . In the first place, it does not reflect the way science is actually performed. Real science, like any human activity, tends to be a little messy around the edges. More important, the things you need to know to be scientifically literate tend to be a somewhat mixed bag. You need to know some facts, to be familiar with some general concepts, to know a little about how science works and how it comes to conclusions, and to know a little about scientists as people. All of these things may affect how you interpret the news of the day. . . . Finally, . . . [science] is just plain fun—not just "good for you" like some foul-tasting medicine. It grew out of observations of everyday experience by thousands of our ancestors, most of whom actually enjoyed what they were doing. (Hazen & Trefil, 1992, p. xix)

A definition or a description does not always give a sufficient impression of what and how science should be taught for maximum effect. Consider Jessica's recollections of her classroom experiences with science and its effects on her. It seems fair to assume that Jessica's teachers carried an image and feeling about science that contributed to their beliefs and affected their teaching of science. This teaching then influenced Jessica's beliefs. And when Jessica teaches, she will continue the cycle by influencing her own students' beliefs. Perhaps this is not a desirable picture when you consider the influence Jessica could have on children—that is, *before* she acquired new impressions about science.

How does a child receive information, construct knowledge, and gain meaning from what is experienced? Hazen and Trefil's view of science offers some useful clues for answering this question. From their description, we may infer that human curiosity is important and that certain types of mental and physical skills are needed for learning: skills for acquiring useful information that has practical value and carries real meaning for learners, meaning that is constructed from the learners' experiences. Therefore, science

- ✦ is a human construct and human activity,
- ✦ is bound by history,
- ✦ changes over time,
- ✦ has theories that are underdetermined by empirical evidence,
- ✦ has a knowledge base that is not absolute,
- ✦ has methods and methodology that change over time,
- ✦ deals in abstractions and ideals,
- ✦ has research agendas that are influenced by social interests and ideology, and
- ✦ in order to be learned, requires that children be attentive and intellectually engaged. (Matthews, 1998, p. 166)

Children are naturally curious (remember the brother who threw the cat down the stairs). Their curiosity motivates them to discover new ways to unlock the mysteries of their world. Therefore, when we consider what science is and make decisions about what to teach children and how to teach them, three parts of what science actually is must be remembered and put to use:

1. *Attitudes.* Science encourages humans to develop positive attitudes, including their powerful curiosity.
2. *Skills.* Science stimulates humans to use their curiosity to construct new ways of investigating and understanding.
3. *Knowledge.* Science consists of what humans learn—knowledge for practical learning and everyday living—the meaning humans construct for themselves (Flick, 1993, pp. 3–4).

The new things children learn tend to stimulate curiosity and motivate them to investigate further. When children are given a complete experience with all that science is—whole science—a cycle is established that continues to build under its own momentum. Whole science thus consists of three parts: development of children's *attitudes* and *skills* and children's construction of useful ideas—*knowledge.* Children's experiences can stimulate their curiosity (*attitudes*), which can motivate them to develop new ways of processing ideas or solving problems (*skills*); these are used to construct the *knowledge* of science. Successful learning enriches the experience universe of children and stimulates further inquiry. Teachers provide children with a whole science experience when they are immersed in all of science's essential features.

Three Essential Features of Science

Three features of science are necessary for a wholesome, productive learning experience: development of children's attitudes, development of their thinking and kinesthetic skills (gross, fine motor, and eye–hand coordination, as well as training of the senses), and development of knowledge that is constructed from experiences in natural settings.

Science Attitudes

What Are Attitudes? Attitudes are mental predispositions toward people, objects, subjects, events, and so on. In science, attitudes are important because of three primary factors (Martin, 1984, pp. 13–14). First, a child's attitude carries a mental state of readiness with it. With a positive attitude, a child will perceive science objects, topics, activities, and people positively. A child who is unready or hesitant, for whatever reason, will be less willing to interact with people and things associated with science. This readiness factor occurs unconsciously in a child, without prior thought or overt consent.

Second, attitudes are not innate or inborn. Contemporary psychologists maintain that attitudes are learned and are organized through experiences as children develop (Halloran, 1970; Oskamp, 1977). Furthermore, a child's attitude can be changed through experience. Teachers and parents have the greatest influence on science attitudes (George & Kaplan, 1998).

Third, attitudes are dynamic results of experiences that act as directive factors when a child enters into new experiences. As a result, attitudes carry an emotional and an intellectual tone, both of which lead to making decisions and forming evaluations. These decisions and evaluations can cause a child to set priorities and hold different preferences. In the scenario, Jessica's attitude toward science and the way she values it shifts from a negative to a neutral and to even a positive viewpoint. In time, with continued positive experiences and adjustments in her attitude, Jessica may become more open to science, think differently about it, and accumulate more useful ideas and skills—all products of her learning. But all of this begins with her attitude.

Emotional Attitudes. Young children's attitudes often are more emotional than intellectual. Curiosity, the natural start of it all, may be accompanied by perseverance, a positive approach to failure (or acceptance of not getting one's own way all the time), and openness to new experiences and even other people's points of view (tolerance for other children's ways of playing a favorite game). These are fundamental attitudes useful for building specific scientific attitudes that are necessary for success and the continuation of the science cycle.

Intellectual Attitudes. Attitudes based on intellect or rational thought develop simultaneously with science process skill development (a second feature of science) and with the discovery or construction of useful science ideas (the third feature of science). Teacher guidance, learning materials that can be manipulated, and interactive teaching methods help encourage formation of intellectual attitudes. Examples include skepticism and the development of a desire to follow procedures that increase objectivity. (See Table 1.1.)

Importance of Attitudes. Younger children tend to have positive attitudes toward science and display many of these attitudes as they explore and interact with classmates. However, over time these initial positive attitudes may decline.

TABLE 1.1 Attitudes of Young Scientists

Emotional	Intellectual
From children's natural curiosity for learning and acquiring new experiences, we can encourage them to develop • more curiosity • perseverance • a positive approach to failure • open-mindedness • cooperation with others	From children's positive learning experiences we can encourage them to develop • a desire for reliable sources of information • skepticism; a desire to be shown or to have alternative points of view proven • avoidance of broad generalizations when evidence is limited • tolerance for other opinions, explanations, or points of view • willingness to withhold judgment until all evidence or information is found or examined • refusal to believe in superstitions or to accept claims without proof • openness to changing their minds when evidence for change is given and openness to questions about their own ideas

Video Explorations   Science Is . . .

Video Summary

Science seems a mystery to many, but when examined closely there are three interactive components: attitudes, processes and knowledge. Understanding these components helps to unlock the mystery of effective science teaching. This chapter is represented by three videos. Each video briefly portrays a component of science. Young children naturally demonstrate many of the emotional attitudes about science, while older learners have learned to use intellectual attitudes. Science processes are types of thinking skills, beginning with the basics of observation and measurement, and advancing to the design of investigations and development of models. The knowledge (that many mistake as the essence of science) exists on several levels ranging from seemingly isolated facts to complicated theories. Real science includes all of these components, as does modern science teaching.

Tips for Viewing, Objectives, or What to Watch for

Keep in mind the following as you watch these videos:

+ Review Table 1.1 "Attitudes of Young Scientists" and refer to it.

+ Read "What Research Says" and consider how attitudes fit within the nature of science.

+ Review Table 1.2 and consider the range of process skills that are age appropriate for children.

+ Note the expressions and postures of the children in the videos.

Questions for Exploration

1. What types of attitudes seemed to be visible? What did the children do or how did the children behave that suggest these attitudes?

2. What processes were visible and what activities verified that these skills were used?

3. What action in the video suggests that science knowledge is formed? How might what is learned be related to attitudes and processes?

Activity for Application

Consider the visual images collectively seen in the three videos and consult Table 1.3. How do the behaviors of science support or enhance a child's development in reading skills? How do the three components of science relate to form a rich, holistic learning experience for children? Select a science activity from a favorite source and examine it closely. How does the activity explicitly nurture science attitudes? How does it encourage process skills development? What types of science knowledge are explicitly learned? What could you do to this activity to transform it into a robust lesson that helps children to benefit from a whole science experience?

Children's natural curiosity for learning will lead them to scientific discoveries.

One way to maintain and improve positive attitudes is to help children develop appreciation for the role science plays in their daily lives. They can realize the value of science when attitudes and practical value become teaching goals. Consider, for example, the influence science has on all aspects of life: on food, clothing, leisure time, entertainment, and the higher quality of life technology provides us. Is there any career that is unaffected by science? Appreciation for science and recognition of its value accumulate as the intellectual attitudes of science are emphasized. Guide children through the science process skills—ways of doing and learning science—to stimulate and develop intellectual attitudes.

Science Process Skills

Perhaps you remember hearing about the *scientific method* in your science classes. At one time people believed that scientists used a specific, step-by-step method in their research. But when scientists were questioned about how they actually went about their work, it soon became clear that there were numerous ways to approach problems. It was also obvious that several processes are common to most forms of inquiry, and these became known as the *science process skills*. These processes also apply to other subjects of study as well as to science, and you probably have been using some of them most of your life. What sets professional scientists apart from you might be little more than the skill to use these processes to solve problems. We think you will recognize the process skills as you review them and realize how important it is that children learn to use them to solve their own problems.

The mission of elementary and middle school science is not to persuade all children to become scientists. The mission is to help make science more accessible to *all* children. One way this can be done is to help children discover how science can be important to them. Therefore, consider the process skills rooted in science that young children must develop and the ways children can use these skills to solve problems of learning and life.

Learning How to Learn. Some people refer to developing process skills as "learning how to learn." Children learn how to learn by thinking critically and using information creatively. Children continue to learn how to learn

> when making discriminating observations, when organizing and analyzing facts and concepts, when giving reasons for expecting particular outcomes, when evaluating and interpreting the results of experiments, and when drawing justifiable conclusions. [Also, children] . . . should be able to predict what will happen when the conditions of a phenomenon in nature are changed. (Victor, 1985, p. 47)

Attitudes and the Nature of Science

The importance of attitudes was recognized in science teaching and learning more than 40 years ago during the 1960s. The Educational Policies Commission issued a document titled *Education and the Spirit of Science.* The writers urged schools to promote "understanding of the values on which science is everywhere based." Those values represent essential attitudes:

1. Longing to know and to understand
2. Questioning of all things
3. Searching for data and their meaning
4. Demanding verification
5. Respecting logic
6. Showing consideration for premises and consequences

These values can help us in our quest toward an important standard from the *National Science Education Standards:* The History and Nature of Science, which is best learned through experiences that arise from activity rather than only superficially on an intellectual level. The idea that scientific knowledge is always subject to change may be difficult for children to grasp. However, the standard for grades K–4 and 5–8 requires that as a result of activities, all students should develop understanding of science as a human endeavor, the nature of science, and the importance of history to science.

The challenge for us is to create an educational system, beginning with our own classrooms, that exploits the natural curiosity of learners. Curiosity is the motivation and inspiration for doing science in pursuit of this standard and motivates learning during school years and later life. Curiosity is a fundamental emotional attitude and the science teacher is the key person for successful promotion of positive attitudes and affective attributes in children. Convince fellow teachers and parents that children's "Why?" questions are important. Science teachers must have good knowledge of the nature of science and must be good role models so that children will emulate these valued attitudes. Demonstrate question-asking, hypothesizing, prediction-making, record-keeping, and making conclusions based on results. Enable children to perform experiments and solve problems that require use of the thinking skills involved in scientific inquiry so that they rise to the proficiency levels demanded by modern reform.

Source: Compiled from Patricia Blosser, Bulletin Editor, *Attitude Research in Science Education,* Columbus, OH: ERIC/SMEAC, 1984, pp. 2–3; Lawrence Lowery (Ed), *NSTA Pathways to the Science Standards,* Elementary School Edition. Arlington, VA: National Science Teachers Association, 2000, p. 103; and *National Research Council, Inquiry and the National Science Education Standards,* Washington, DC: National Academy Press, 2000.

Types of Process Skills. In science, the ways of thinking, measuring, solving problems, and using thoughts are called *processes. Process skills* describe types of thinking and reasoning and may be divided into two types: basic skills and integrated skills (Arena, 1996). Table 1.2 on page 18 suggests the grade levels at which these skills are appropriate.

Basic Skills. If children show they can observe, classify, communicate, measure, estimate, predict, and infer, they are showing understanding of basic science processes.

Observation is the primary way children obtain information. This does not mean that children benefit solely from watching someone else and listening to what others think. Children observe by using all their senses. For example, how do you observe a concert? Can you close your eyes and recreate it by recalling how your senses were stimulated?

TABLE 1.2   Science Process Skills

Basic skills can be emphasized at the primary grades and then serve as a foundation for using integrated skills at the intermediate and higher grades.

Basic Skills	PreK	K	1	2	3	4	5	6	7	8
Observation	X	X	X	X	X	X	X	X	X	X
Classification	X	X	X	X	X	X	X	X	X	X
Communication	X	X	X	X	X	X	X	X	X	X
Measurement	X	X	X	X	X	X	X	X	X	X
Estimation	X	X	X	X	X	X	X	X	X	X
Prediction	X	X	X	X	X	X	X	X	X	X
Inference		X	X	X	X	X	X	X	X	X
Integrated Skills										
Identifying variables					X	X	X	X	X	X
Controlling variables					X	X	X	X	X	X
Defining operationally					X	X	X	X	X	X
Forming hypotheses					X	X	X	X	X	X
Experimenting					X	X	X	X	X	X
Graphing					X	X	X	X	X	X
Interpreting data					X	X	X	X	X	X
Modeling					X	X	X	X	X	X
Investigating					X	X	X	X	X	X

Can you see the lights and special effects? Can you smell the odors unique to the crowd and those special effects? Can you feel the vibrations of the bass and drums? Can you hear the music and vocals—really hear them with all of their rhythm? Can you taste the popcorn or the Junior Mints? Teachers stimulate useful observation through the five senses when they ask children questions that cause them to identify properties of objects, changes, and similarities and differences; and to determine the difference between an observation and an inference. Example: *The object is hard, gray, round, and the size of a baseball*. Instruments such as thermometers, volt meters, balances, and computers help to add precision to observations.

Classification requires organizing observations in ways that carry special meaning. Teachers can encourage children to classify when they ask them to group objects by their observed properties and/or to arrange objects or events in a particular order. An example is: *Place all rocks of the same size, color, and hardness into the same group.*

When *communication* is emphasized, children use language (spoken, written, and symbolic in many forms) to express their thoughts in ways that others can understand. Development of useful communication skills is to ask children to define words and terms operationally, to describe objects and events as they are perceived, and to record information and make data tables, graphs, and models to show what they have found. Example: *Describe observed changes in a river over time through speaking, writing, or making a graph or data table.*

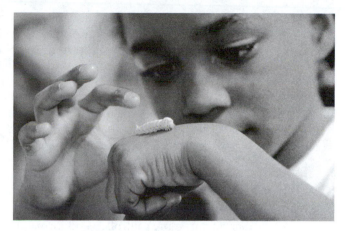

Observation is a basic science process.

Measurement adds precision to observations, classifications, and communications. Children can be encouraged to measure by using standard tools like rulers, meter sticks, balances, graduated cylinders, calibrated liquid containers, clocks, calculators, computers, electrical instruments, and even arbitrary units such as marbles, paper clips, and so on to measure quantity or distance. Example: *Use a meter stick to describe the height of a child.* (Note: The metric system is *the* measurement system in science.)

Estimation involves judging an approximate amount or value. The estimate is based on knowledge of measurement, but is not a direct measure. Estimation is useful for quick observations for which precision is not necessary. Example: *I think the chair is about 1 meter high,* or *the glass looks as if it contains about 300 milliliters of water.*

Predictions are best guesses based on available information. Meteorologists, for example, predict the weather. Their predictions are made in advance of the weather's actual occurrence and are based on accumulated observations, analysis of information, and prior experience. Similarly, children can be encouraged to make predictions before they carry out an act, such as grouping different objects into classifications based on a prediction concerning whether they will float when placed in water. A teacher can stimulate predictive thinking by asking children to review the observed properties of objects or events and asking them to tell what they think will happen when a change of some sort is made, such as our sink-or-float example. Example: *Predict the size and shape of an ice cube after heating it for 10 minutes.*

Inferences are conclusions about the cause of an observation. Consider the sink-or-float example again. Children may observe that all lightweight objects from their collections float in water and infer that the light weight was the cause of floating. Of course, this could be disproved by items not included in the children's limited collection of objects. Therefore, it is necessary to help children make better inferences by guiding their thinking in ways that help them make conclusions about an observation based on the prior knowledge they have. Example: *A person is happy because she smiles and hums a song.*

Integrated Skills. Integrated science process skills rely on the students' capabilities to think at a higher level and to consider more than one thought at a time. As the word *integrated* implies, several basic process skills are combined for greater power to form the tools to solve problems. The basic skills are prerequisites for integrated skills—those necessary to do science experiments. These skills are identifying and controlling variables, defining operationally, forming hypotheses, experimenting, making graphs, interpreting data, forming models, and investigating.

Identifying and controlling variables requires students to identify aspects of an experiment that can affect its outcome and to keep as many aspects constant as possible, while manipulating only the aspects or factors (variables) that are independent. Example: *Vary only the amount of fertilizer used on similar plants while keeping soil type, amount of sunlight, water, and temperature the same.*

Defining operationally occurs when using observations and other information gained through experience to describe or label an object or event. Example: *An acid is a substance that changes bromethymol blue indicator from blue to yellow.*

Forming hypotheses is important for designed investigations and is similar to prediction, but more controlled and formal. Hypothesizing is using information to make a best educated guess about the expected outcome of an experiment. Example: *The more fertilizer is added to plants, the greater their growth.*

Experimenting requires using many thinking skills to design and conduct a controlled scientific test. This consists of asking a research question, forming a hypothesis, identifying and controlling variables, using operational definitions, conducting the experiment, and interpreting the data. Example: *The entire operational process is investigating the effects of amounts of fertilizer added to plants of the same type.*

Graphing is converting measurements into a diagram to show the relationships among and between the measures. Example: *Construct a graph to show the heights of the plants, experimental and control, for each day (or week) of the experiment.*

Interpreting data is collecting observations and measurements (data) in an organized way and drawing conclusions from the information obtained by reading tables, graphs and diagrams. Example: *Read information in a table or graph about the growth of plants in the experiment described above and form conclusions based on the interpretation of the data.* The interpretation could help to "prove" that *more fertilizer added to plants causes greater growth.*

Forming models requires creating an abstract (mental) or concrete (physical) illustration of an object or event. Example: *A model shows the best amount of fertilizer to use on a plant and the consequences of using too little or too much.*

Investigating is a complex process skill that requires using observations, collecting and analyzing data, and drawing conclusions to solve a problem. Example: *Complete an investigation to evaluate the fertilizer dosage model as a way of deciding on a plant feeding routine for the class's garden.*

Importance of Process Skills. Basic science skills expand children's learning through experience. Beginning with simple ideas, these ideas compound and form new, more complex ideas. An accumulation of ideas is valuable because of assisting children to become decision makers and problem solvers. Emphasizing science process skills helps students discover meaningful information and accumulate knowledge by constructing understanding within and beyond the science classroom.

Science process skills are remarkably similar to those skills used in reading comprehension (Table 1.3 on pages 22–23). When children are doing science, following scientific procedures, and thinking as scientists, they are developing skills that are necessary for effective reading and understanding (Padilla, Muth, & Lund Padilla, 1991). A creative lesson planner can have students working on science and developing the skills useful to other subjects simultaneously. Science experiences can help preschool children develop their intellect and get an early start on fundamental reading and thinking skills. Primary school students can become motivated through science activities and their natural interests to work on vocabulary development, word discrimination, and comprehension. Intermediate and middle school youth develop their communication abilities to identify and control variables, make meaningful conclusions, and express ideas clearly.

Science Knowledge

Importance of Science Knowledge. Children construct important ideas and discover much for themselves when they use science process skills. They gain knowledge by accumulating and processing information and by forming concepts about their natural world, humans' use of natural resources, and the impact of this use on society. Children also discover, in time, that knowledge provides power and carries with it a responsibility for its proper use. Perhaps most important, children can understand that much of science is tentative, changes over time, and is subject to future change. The content of science is not absolute, and research findings may be interpreted differently by different people, depending on their values and experiences.

Scientific knowledge consists of concepts, principles, and theories.

Examples of Science Knowledge. The knowledge base of science is often referred to as *products*. New discoveries that add to the base of scientific information are the products of curiosity and experimentation. An interesting thing about science knowledge is that new discoveries often lead to more questions, more experiments, and more new discoveries. Indeed, the solutions to scientific problems can create new problems. Science cycles move under their own momentum, propelled initially and again later sustained by human curiosity and a desire to explain natural phenomena. The effect is an exploding accumulation of new information that is added to the knowledge base. Scientific knowledge consists primarily of facts, concepts, principles, and theories.

Facts are specific, verifiable pieces of information obtained through observation and measurement. For example, during a class project Jessica observes over the course of two weeks that she produces an average of 1 kilogram of solid waste each day: cans, bottles, paper, plastic, and so on—a fact of her living habits.

TABLE 1.3   Relationship of Science and Reading Skills

Science Skills	Reading Skills	Examples
Observation	Discriminating shapes, sounds, syllables, and word accents	Break words into syllables and list on chalkboard. Class pronounces new words aloud. Teacher mispronounces some words and rewards students who make corrections.
Identification	Recognizing letters, words, prefixes, suffixes, and base words	Select a common science prefix, suffix, or base word, define it, and list several words in which it may be used. Example: *kilo* (1,000): *kilometer, kilogram, kiloliter.*
Description	Isolating important attributes and characteristics	Ask students to state the purpose of an activity.
	Enumerating ideas	Construct keys for student rock collections, etc.
	Using appropriate terminology and synonyms	Play vocabulary games. Use characteristics to identify an object or animal.
Classification	Comparing and contrasting characteristics	List in order the steps of a mealworm's metamorphosis.
	Arranging ideas and ordering and sequencing information	Construct charts that compare and contrast characteristics.
	Considering multiple attributes	Put concepts in order.
Investigation design	Question asking	Use library resources and design an experiment from an outline. Write original lab reports.
	Investigating possible relationships	Outline facts and concepts.
	Following organized procedures	

Source: The comparisons are drawn from Glenda S. Carter and Ronald D. Simpson's "Science and Reading: A Basic Duo," *Science Teacher* (March 1978): 20, and from Ronald Simpson and Norman Anderson's *Science, Students and Schools: A Guide for the Middle and Secondary School Teacher* (New York: Wiley, 1980). M. Padilla, D. Muth, and R. Lund Padilla (1991) continue to clarify the similarities between science process skills and reading comprehension skills.

Concepts are abstract ideas that are generalized from facts or specific relevant experiences. Jessica's class project may help her form the concept that her habits of consumption yield considerable solid waste over time. She believes her habits are typical of other young adults and she forms a concept about the amount of solid waste some people generate within a specific amount of time. Concepts are single ideas that may become linked to form more complex ideas.

Principles are complex ideas based on several related concepts. Jessica's example: "The reason people recycle solids is because they create a lot of waste." Jessica's principle is based on three concepts: creation, waste, and recycling.

Science Skills	Reading Skills	Examples
Data collection	Note taking	Prepare bibliographies from library information.
	Using reference materials	Use tables of contents, indexes, and organizational features of chapters.
	Using different parts of a book	
	Recording information in an organized way	Have students compare and discuss notes.
	Being precise and accurate	Use quantitative skills in lab activities.
Interpretation of data	Recognizing cause-and-effect relationships	Discuss matters that could affect the health of an animal.
	Varying reading rate	Teach students to preview and scan printed text.
	Organizing facts	Have students organize notes in an outline.
	Summarizing new information	
	Thinking inductively and deductively	Have students construct concept maps, flow-charts, and new arrangements of facts.
Communication of results	Arranging information logically	List discoveries through a time line.
	Sequencing ideas	
	Using graphs	Ask for conclusions from graphed data or *tables and figures.*
	Describing clearly	Describe chronological events.
Conclusion formation	Generalizing	Ask "What if?" questions.
	Critically analyzing	Have students scrutinize conclusions for errors.
	Identifying main ideas	
	Establishing relationships	
	Using information in other situations	Use case studies to develop conclusions through critical thinking.

Theories consist of broadly related principles that provide an explanation for a phenomenon. The purpose of a theory is to provide the best explanation based on evidence. Theories are used to explain, relate, and predict. After some added observation and consideration, Jessica may theorize that commercial marketing practices and convenience packaging are responsible for much of the eastern United States' landfill problems. She may use her theory to urge lawmakers to develop regulations and to persuade city leaders to establish recycling programs to ease the pressures on their landfills.

Throughout history, scientific thinkers have found that the accepted hierarchy of facts and ideas cannot answer certain important questions. As scientists struggle to

(text continues on page 26)

4-E Feature Lesson

Air

Inquiry Question: How do we know that air is real?

Concept to Be Invented: Air takes up space.

National Science Education Standards: K–4 Physical Science—Properties of objects and materials. Objects have many observable properties, including size, weight, shape, color, temperature, and the ability to react with other substances.

Science Attitudes to Nurture: Open-mindedness, curiosity, perseverance, positive approach to failure, cooperation with others

Materials Needed: Balloons, clear plastic bags, plastic party horns, Styrofoam cups, soap bubble solution, drinking straws (bendable), clear plastic cups, large plastic tub or aquarium, scrap materials

Safety Precautions: Wear goggles to avoid chemical eye splash. Avoid sucking soap solution into mouth.

Exploration *Which process skills will be used?*

Observing, identifying, comparing

Set the stage for exploration by demonstrating how to blow a balloon and to make "music" with the escaping air. Engage the children by asking: "What do you think is inside the balloon?" "What do you think makes this music?" Answers may differ, but most will refer to breath or air in the balloon. Pose the question: "Do you think air is real?" "Why?" Use the students' variety of answers to convey the need to investigate in order to find out if air is real. Avoid discussing the concept at this point.

Investigate by filling large plastic bags with air, closing the open end of the bag over the small "blow into" end of a party horn. Hold the bag closed against the horn and gently squeeze the bag to blow the horn (kind of like a bagpipe). Pose open-ended questions to the children about what they think makes the horn sound, what filled the bag, where the air came from, etc.

Investigate by giving each child a Styrofoam cup and have him or her punch a hole the size of the diameter of a straw 1 inch from the bottom, invert the cup and dip into soap bubble solution, and then insert a straw into the hole. Encourage the children to blow through the straw. Larger bubbles will result when the cup is inverted.

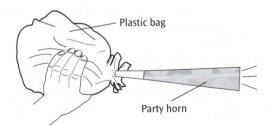

Plastic bag

Party horn

Caution the children to avoid sucking up the soap solution and demonstrate how to change their breathing to make the bubbles larger and smaller. Question: "What do you think is inside your bubble? How do you think the air got inside the bubble? How do you think you could remove the air from your bubble?"

Straw

Explanation

Demonstrate how to fill a plastic cup with water and invert it in a water tank or a clean aquarium (you can use a large plastic tub or classroom's water table, if available). Ask the children prediction questions, such as: What do you think may happen to the water in the cup if you blow air into it? Demonstrate how to use a bent straw to blow air into the filled cup while it is in the water and inverted.

Water level   Bent soda straw

Ask the children to explain what they observe. Invite some of the children to try the same demonstration. Discuss what happened in each of the investigations and how air behaved the same as in this demonstration. Use a sentence starter and invite the children to offer ideas to complete it: "Air takes up _____." The desired answer is *space*, and the sentence represents the *concept* common to each investigation in this lesson. Ask children "How do we know air is real?" Relate the question to the concept statement and use the concept statement throughout the rest of the lesson.

Expansion   *Which process skills will be used?*

Classifying, communicating, and predicting

Permit all children to practice the demonstration (described in the Explanation phase). Encourage all children to describe the property: Air takes up space.

Set up an additional investigation that will be used for *Evaluation.* Partially fill several clear plastic shoeboxes or small clean plastic aquaria. Have several small potted plants on hand with dry soil. Immerse one plant into the water and observe the air bubbles as they emerge from the dry soil. (You can substitute a small cup of dry sand for the same effect.) Discuss: "What do you think causes the bubbles? Where do you think the bubbles come from?" Answers should reveal that the children understand the lesson's concept, are able to use it in their spoken communication, and can use it in a new setting. Continue to question and encourage children to communicate their findings as they investigate the following dry objects.

(continued)

small pieces of wood	pieces of brick or fish tank gravel	crayons
small rocks	leaves	paper
pine cones	side walk chalk	clay
Popsicle sticks	classroom chalk	cloth
sponge pieces	aluminum foil (flat, folded, crumpled)	paper

Use cooperative groups to predict and investigate what happens when the objects are immersed in water. Use a pictograph to classify objects as having air or no air. Pose the question again: "How do we know air is real?"

Evaluation

Upon completing the activities, the students will be able to:

◆ observe changes to the balloons and water in the cups, and predict what they think will happen when changes are proposed, and communicate their observations;
◆ describe and illustrate examples of objects or conditions where "air takes up space";
◆ classify objects as having air or no air;
◆ give a response to the question "How do we know if air is real?" and a reason for their answer.

refine the theories and principles in an effort to answer these questions, they sometimes come up with a radical new idea that seems to solve the problem better. If the new idea answers the questions as well as the old ways of thinking did, the scientific community will eventually throw out the old ideas in favor of what Thomas Kuhn (1970) called a *new paradigm.* The work of Copernicus is a good example of what Kuhn called a *scientific revolution.* Copernicus was trying to explain the orbit of Mars using Ptolemy's geocentric theory of the structure of the universe, but he was having no success. As he tried to refine Ptolemy's system, it occurred to him that it would be a much simpler problem to solve if only the sun were in the center of the universe rather than the Earth. He came up with an idea that, on further examination, explained the orbits of the other planets as well as Ptolemy's theory did, and a new paradigm was born. It was many years before Copernicus's heliocentric theory was widely accepted by the scientific community as the basis for a new hierarchy of theories about the relationship of the Earth to the sun and the other planets (Prather, 1991).

It is important for science teachers to help learners realize that scientific theories are based on the best information that scientists have been able to collect, but that many theories have been discarded as the result of new ideas that provide greater problem-solving power. Therefore, many of the theories and principles that scientists believe today may be discarded by the discovery of new and better ideas. At first, this concept may seem confusing to learners. They may ask why they should bother to learn about such things as Newton's laws or the theory of evolution if it might be imperfect and replaced by another view. At this point, a teacher might use the history of science to help learners gain an appreciation of the nature of science and its worth. For example, Ptolemy's system was used for navigation for centuries, and Arab camel drivers used it with confidence to navigate the otherwise intolerably hot deserts in the cool of night. Also, it was Ptolemy's astronomy that Magellan's sailors used to sail safely around the Earth—nearly a quarter of a century before Copernicus published his new astronomical theory (Prather, 1991).

Scientists are very aware of the limitations of their knowledge, but they are also aware that, based on the strength of evidence, it represents the best information available to them at the time. Therefore, it is useful to learn about the theories of science, even if they might be replaced later. Theories are the best explanations that scientists have. Scientists possess a holistic view of science. They use scientific attitudes to identify and define problems and scientific skills to inquire, and they contribute what they learn to the knowledge base of science, which makes it possible for the scientific community to attempt solutions to many important problems that can benefit us all.

Children construct science knowledge for themselves.

The Aims of Standards and Research-Based Reform in Science Education

The aims of modern science education exceed the simplicity of understanding the three essential features of science. The primary aim is to provide pupils with experiences that will help them become *scientifically literate.* Literacy is more than commanding a list of ideas and demonstrating selected skills. Modern views of scientific literacy include mathematics as well as technology and the social sciences as well as the natural sciences.

We are tasked by standards to set higher expectations for students and ourselves in order to achieve literacy. The standards and research-based reform expect us to develop and practice expertise at

- ✦ guiding learners as they investigate, engage in meaningful content and construct sense from their experiences by focusing on understanding and using scientific ideas, skills, and attitudes;
- ✦ sharing with children the responsibility for what is learned;
- ✦ adapting the curriculum, budgeting time and managing inquiry, perhaps for lessons that span multiple days or weeks;
- ✦ assessing progress in multiple ways to discern what learners know and can do;

How Do Science and Real Life Connect?

by Phyllis Frysinger, Retired
Grades 7 and 8, Miami View Elementary, South Charleston, Ohio

Remember the first time you learned that spiders have book lungs, sponges have spicules, oak trees have inadequate abscission layers, and two round bacteria existing together are called diplococci? I thought that was really interesting, too, and I couldn't wait to tell kids all of this neat stuff. I found myself presenting discovery lessons on the value of spiders, natural carnivores, as possible pest controllers in soybean fields; on how strong sponge spicules would wreak havoc on populated beaches; how oak trees that keep their leaves longer would also lose more water in the fall; and I didn't teach that diplococcus business, but rather demonstrated the subtlety of bacterial contamination.

Today's students are much more demanding that you as a teacher justify why you are teaching what you are. Be prepared: If you are using a text, don't try to cover all of Chapter 2 by Friday. Instead, sit down, read Chapter 2, and pretend that there is a student sitting beside you asking, "Why do we have to know this?" If you can't come up with an answer, then leave

it out. Develop a list of outcomes or test objectives that you want to obtain from material to be studied. Give this list to the students at the beginning, develop a way to teach each of your objectives, and show them how you plan to present each of these goals. If you cannot come up with a way to teach a particular goal or objective without standing in front of the class and telling them about it, then leave it out.

Once you have decided what is important and how you are going to teach it, sit down and write the evaluation for the chapter. Yes, right now, not the night before so that you only have time to reproduce it. This way you can justify in your own mind how you will evaluate an objective or your evaluation technique. Newer evaluation techniques are being proposed, and I have used all sorts of things through the years. You will, too, if you keep up with the times.

Oh yes, keeping up with the times. This does not mean rapping the latest hit while you are dissecting a frog, but developing viable alternatives to dissection in general. I used dissecting for a long time and even

* providing essential materials and equipment and maintaining a safe environment;
* questioning to excite and to motivate, and to sustain intellectual inquiry; and
* supporting learning science for all children by understanding and responding to individual student interests, strengths, and needs.

Science for All Americans—Project 2061 (Rutherford & Ahlgren, 1990) and the *National Science Education Standards* (National Research Council, 1996) are significant reports, and *Benchmarks* (AAAS, 1993) is a curriculum effort based on many years of collaboration among several hundred scientists, mathematicians, engineers, physicians, philosophers, historians, and educators. These efforts offer a comprehensive and valid view of modern scientific literacy, the prime aim of science teaching. We learn from them that

the scientifically literate person is one who is aware that science, mathematics, and technology are interdependent human enterprises with strengths and limitations; underdeveloped anatomy lessons to use with my eighth-grade earth science classes.

By promoting science as an important part of the life of students, you will promote a positive attitude toward science and encourage students to develop science skills they will use for the rest of their lives.

To be more specific, I taught in a multidisciplinary situation with a pod scheduled time in which three teachers had all of the seventh-grade students in the morning and all of the eighth-grade students in the afternoon. During this time we taught science, English, and literature.

We presented a lesson in which the science classes had been working on chemical reactions. We had mixed together several chemicals including starch, sucrose, ovalbumin, ethyl buterate, and triglycerides to note a chemical reaction. The product was a cake. In literature class the students were reading *A Christmas Carol,* by Charles Dickens. In a combined class we mixed the ingredients for a traditional plum pudding, noting the chemical ingredients and the importance of accurate measurement, as in the science class. The English teacher made the point that there were no plums in the plum pudding and discussed the origin of the word. The literature teacher reflected Mrs. Cratchit's anxiety over the preparation.

After the concoction was properly steamed and the traditions closely followed, including the stirring and wish making by each student, the pudding was flamed with orange extract, and we all enjoyed the feast.

With this approach, the students were presented the opportunity of learning the importance and the interrelationship of each of the disciplines involved. There really was an answer to "Why do we have to know this?" We write journals each day, and it was certainly rewarding to note the number of times that we read, "I'm going to take this recipe home and make plum pudding for my family." When the students want to take your lesson home and share it with others, then you know that you have taught science.

One more thing: Don't forget to join all the professional organizations that are available, and participate in them. You will not only learn the latest that is available in your field but will also have a great deal of support in your professional years. That's how I ended up taking physics almost thirty years after I entered the classroom when I didn't even teach physical science.

stands key concepts and principles of science; is familiar with the natural world and recognizes both its diversity and unity; and uses scientific knowledge and scientific ways of thinking for individual and social purposes. (Rutherford & Ahlgren, 1990, p. ix)

The National Science Education Standards (NSES) (coordinated by the National Research Council of the National Academy of Sciences and the National Academy of Engineering) provide direction toward our national vision. *NSES* advocate a less-is-more philosophy for developing science curriculum, teaching approaches, and appropriate forms of assessment. These standards support practical learning experiences and problem-solving opportunities for children. The standards are based on a holistic view of science. These standards can help us progress toward our national aims and to do our part, as teachers, to fulfill the national vision.

The chapters that follow present additional standards, offer specific examples for using standards effectively, and offer support from the research base.

Chapter Summary

The nature of science must be viewed holistically and its essential features understood. Science is more than knowledge and scientific names and facts. Assumptions about science that focus only on treating it as a body of knowledge are incomplete and incorrect. Science is possible because it is inherently human. Human attitudes provide the curiosity to begin its study, the perseverance to continue, and the necessary qualities for making informed judgments. Science process skills make it possible for children to accumulate the factual information they need to construct concepts, form scientific principles, and comprehend theories. Children are able to construct their own understanding when encouraged to inquire by exploring, questioning, and seeking.

Science has the most impact on children when they value it and are exposed to all of its essential features. Science programs, science teaching practices, and assessment techniques must provide experiences that will help children to value and use science by making important discoveries for themselves. These experiences must engage learners with meaningful content in an environment conducive to learning where all have access and are exposed interactively to rigorous expectations. How children construct ideas and learn is a topic explored in Chapter 2.

Discussion Questions

1. Think back to your primary and middle school years. What do you remember about your science classes? How do your memories compare with those of your classmates? In what ways do your recollections represent holistic science?

2. To what extent did your teachers teach science according to our definition? What do you remember about the emphasis given to attitudes, thinking skills, and science content? Why do you think your teachers emphasized (or did not emphasize) each of these parts?

3. Think about developmental differences observed between first-, third-, and sixth-grade students. In each grade, how much emphasis do you think should be given to emotional and intellectual attitude development? Give reasons for your answer.

4. Review the differences between basic and integrated science process skills. What is the connection between these skills and the types of science information children are expected to learn?

5. The attitudes we carry with us are linked to experiences we have accumulated over time. Both help us form images that we treat as our personal sense of reality. Sometimes these images represent stereotypes. For example, when you hear the word *scientist,* what image comes to mind? Draw a picture of a scientist.

6. Compare your picture of a scientist with other class members' pictures. Classify them according to such features as age, gender, amount and types of hair, eyeglasses, lab coat, laboratory apparatus, appearance (weird, out of control, and so on), and other factors. Tally the features and compute percentages to develop a class profile of a scientist. Treat this as a pretest and do the exercise again at the end of the course to look for any possible differences in stereotypes.

Build a Portfolio or E-Folio

1. Try a version of the projects described in the discussion questions with elementary school children. How do their pictures compare with your own or those of your college class? Develop a summary of the children's views and speculate about reasons.

2. Interview children and ask questions:

   a. What is science?

   b. Is science important? Why?

   c. What is the most important thing you have learned in science?

   d. What types of people (children included) make good scientists?

   e. Are you a scientist? Why? or Can you be a scientist? Why?

3. Try this exercise with different age levels. What similarities or differences do you detect across ages?

Learning Science

After teaching for some years, Jessica from the scenario in Chapter 1 has developed routines to manage her classroom duties. Her teaching methods are consistent. In math, she presents the topic, demonstrates models, explains functions and steps by giving examples, and involves some children in board work. Drill and practice come next and are followed by assigned seatwork, which is reviewed the following day.

For science, Jessica explains the point, provides a demonstration, and gives step-by-step instructions for completing the corresponding activity. She always uses visual models to help students understand complicated concepts. Each learner follows her recipe, and her methods are similar for all subjects.

Jessica is regarded as an outstanding teacher and has received several commendations. But although her students perform well on the school's standardized tests, they do not fare well on the obligatory statewide performance assessments. Jessica is frustrated. Her fifth graders do well only on memorization. They return to their own ideas when confronted with problems or questions that are not an exact replica of what they have studied in class. What can Jessica do to develop deeper, lasting understanding?

Jessica pondered this question during her vacation as she supervised the play of her two children. Her daughter, her older child, was having difficulty using a pump to inflate her bicycle tires. As she struggled with the pump's plunger, she exclaimed: "Ouch! Why is this so hot?" She had touched the plunger that she had been rapidly moving up and down to inflate the tire. Jessica's nine-year-old son, Jonathan, was close by, riding his skateboard, and offered an explanation: "It's hot because of friction."

"What's that?" inquired his sister.

Jonathan attempted to explain: "See the wheels on my skateboard? Listen as I turn them quickly. Hear this one squeak? Now let me put a little oil on it like Uncle Gary showed me." Jonathan retrieved the oil can from the garage workbench and put a few drops of oil on the wheel's bearings. "What do you hear now?" he asked.

"I hear the wheel turning, but I don't hear the squeak," his sister replied.

"Exactly. The wheel squeaked because of too much friction. I put on oil to take away some of it. I think there is still some friction here. That is why we hear this rolling sound of the little balls in the wheel," hypothesized Jonathan. "Let's try something. Feel the back wheel on your bike to see how cool it feels. Then hold up your bike so the back wheel is off the floor so I can turn the pedal really fast. Then hang on but drop it so the wheel hits the floor." This was done with a skidding sound and jerking motion that left a black mark on the concrete floor. "Now quick, feel the tire. How does it feel now?"

"I think it's hotter, but I'm not sure," ventured his sister.

"Yes, that's because the tire rubbed against the floor and the friction heated it. Now try this. Press your hands together so the palms are flat. Press a little and then rub them back and forth. How do they feel now?"

"A little bit warm," replied his sister.

"Yes. Now press harder and move them faster. How do they feel now?" asked Jonathan.

"Hot!" exclaimed his sister.

Jessica was intrigued by this conversation and startled that her young son seemed to understand the idea of friction, although he did not define it exactly. "Jon, how do you know about friction? Did Ms. Glock teach you about it in school?"

"Well, I think she tried," offered Jonathan. "We studied machines in third grade, and I remember reading about friction in the book. Ms. Glock talked about it, but I can't remember much."

"Then how did you learn so much about friction?" persisted Jessica.

"Uncle Gary taught me."

Jessica encouraged Jonathan to explain and eventually uncovered his story. Jonathan had helped his uncle build a storage shed for lawn tools. His uncle had put a board in place with long screws as a temporary support, then rapidly removed the screws with his cordless drill when the support was no longer needed. Jonathan's job was to pick up the screws and put them away. His uncle had warned that the screws would be hot and that Jonathan should let them cool for a few moments. Jonathan did not understand. The screws had been cool to the touch when he had handed them to his uncle, *before* they were driven into the board. Instead of explaining, Jonathan's uncle drove some cool screws into a board and then removed them quickly. They both carefully touched the screws and noticed that they were quite warm. Uncle Gary then explained that the surface of the screw threads rubbed quickly against the wood and that the rubbing heated the screw. He showed Jonathan how to understand what happened by rubbing his hands together, as Jonathan had done with his sister.

Uncle Gary used the word *friction* to represent the idea they were investigating. He also demonstrated the same idea with a sabre saw. Jonathan carefully touched the blade of the unplugged saw and felt that it was cool to the touch. Then Uncle Gary cut a board, unplugged the saw, and touched a piece of tissue paper to the blade. The saw blade scorched the paper. Uncle Gary asked Jonathan to explain what happened by way of friction. He also asked Jonathan to get his Cub Scout book, and they looked at ways to make campfires with primitive methods that used a bow and friction. They continued their discussion of friction by trying to stand on marbles in a box and noticed that it was difficult to do since friction between their shoes and the floor was reduced, and they speculated what it would be like to try to run on slick, wet concrete with smooth-soled shoes. They discussed why oil and coolants are important to an automobile by reducing friction and removing excess heat from the motor that is caused by friction and why cars skid off rain-slicked highway curves or on snow and ice. Jonathan and his uncle worked together to identify times when friction is helpful, such as a fast-moving biker trying to cycle around a sharp curve, or a basketball player driving to the basket. The firsthand experiences and discussions had helped Jonathan understand the basic idea of friction and expanded his understanding by applying the idea in new situations, such as with his sister and the bicycle pump.

The story was serendipitous for Jessica and signaled a connection to her teaching. She decided to change her way of learning and developed a vision for presenting lessons during the upcoming school year. She consulted her college texts and journals to review the principles of child and brain development. She changed from teacher-explainer/student-receiver to teacher-guide/student-constructor. Jessica was determined to see her students through new eyes, and she considered various perspectives on how children learn and possibilities to help them form mental connections. She resolved to try different teaching approaches that would guide her students' learning—helping them learn how to learn rather than telling them what they needed to know.

Introduction

How did you learn science? Was it similar to Jessica's typical way of teaching it? Was your experience based on the teacher's instructions and explanations, vocabulary development, and memorization? Or was your experience more like an adventure, where the exact steps to follow were as unknown as the consequences of your decisions? Did your teachers emphasize the facts, symbols, labels, and formulas of science? Or were the general ideas—concepts—developed in a way that helped you to discover the connections among the many ideas and fields of science?

How do you view science and how do children learn to share related consequences? If you view science as a discrete body of information to be learned, you will probably bring that assumption to your teaching, which will be much like Jessica's routine. If, after reading Chapter 1, you view science as a dynamic opportunity to help children develop essential attitudes, skills, and knowledge that can benefit each of them, you will likely bring that assumption to your teaching, which may resemble Jessica's new vision. Your view of how children learn has been shaped by your teachers, and in turn your beliefs will affect the children you teach. With a little imagination you can see the consequences or benefits of this cycle.

Jessica's routine methods did not produce the results she wanted. She decided to experiment and try other methods and in doing so changed her beliefs about learning. In this chapter how children learn will focus on four areas:

1. the brain's unique structure and the function it plays in learning,
2. the role that children's prior ideas and misconceptions play in their learning,
3. the dominant contemporary perspective on science learning and how it helps children to become self-motivated and sustain independent learning,
4. the essential techniques important for constructivist teaching.

What Role Does Brain Development and Processing Play in Learning?

Simplified Brain Anatomy

The adult brain is about the size of an oblong grapefruit, weighs about 3 pounds, consists of about 78 percent water (10 percent fat and 8 percent protein), and is covered with a one-quarter-inch-thick, wrinkled covering, resembling an orange peel, called the cerebral cortex. If unfolded, the cerebral cortex would be about the size of a newspaper page. The cortex is divided into lobes. Each lobe has a specific task with some functional overlap between lobes (see Figure 2.1). The occipital lobes process visual stimuli, the temporal lobes process auditory stimuli, the parietal lobes interpret and integrate sensory stimuli, the frontal lobes process high-level thinking such as problem solving and future planning, and deep somewhere within the cortex's lobes exists the capability to reflect and have awareness about what one thinks and does (Wolfe, 1998). The human brain also contains the largest area of cortex (of all animals) that has no specifically as-

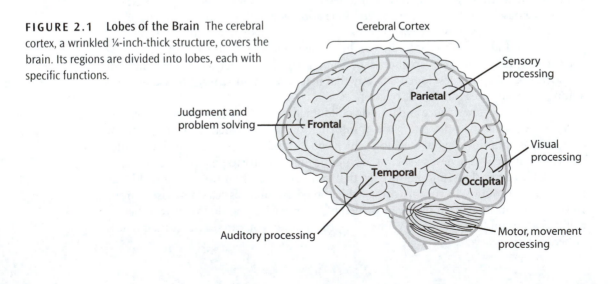

FIGURE 2.1 **Lobes of the Brain** The cerebral cortex, a wrinkled ¼-inch-thick structure, covers the brain. Its regions are divided into lobes, each with specific functions.

signed function, giving humans extraordinary flexibility for processing information and plasticity while learning. To assist in rapid and thorough processing, the brain's nerve cells are connected by about 1 million miles of nerve fibers (Jensen, 1998).

Simplified Brain Development and Function

Although the brain is about 2 percent of body weight, it consumes 20 percent of one's energy (enough to light a 25-watt lightbulb). Brain energy comes from nutrients in the blood, and people need eight to twelve glasses of water each day to assure optimal electrolytic balance of brain chemicals. Dehydration is a common problem in schools and can impair learning (Hannaford, 1995). A brain uses 20 percent of the body's oxygen. Air quality and lack of exercise can affect the oxygen richness of the blood, which can impair learning. Many worry that schoolchildren do not exercise enough to ensure oxygen-rich blood (Jensen, 1998).

About 10 percent of a brain's cells are neurons, and these are used for thinking and learning (see Figure 2.2). Adults have about 100 billion neurons, plenty to get through a lifetime, about half the number found in a two-year-old (Howard, 1994). Young children's brains are like sponges, thriving on enriched stimulation. Human newborns begin to form synapses at rates far in excess of adults, so that by about age four, synaptic densities have peaked and are about 50 percent greater than adults. Around puberty, a process that prunes away excess synapses and continues through adulthood begins, in which losses of cell neurons and synapses can occur every day through attrition, decay,

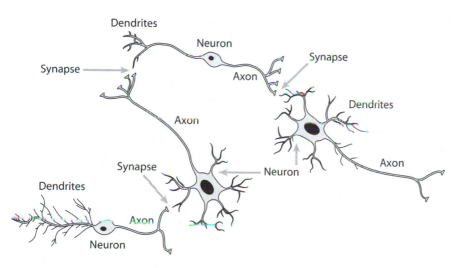

FIGURE 2.2 **Neurons Make Connections; Connections Define Learning** Neurons connect to other neurons via multiple pathways. Axons trail outward from neurons and connect with dendrites from other neurons. The connecting point is called a synapse—a space gap—across which electrochemical signals travel. Learning is believed to exist at these connections. A single neuron can connect with many other neurons.

and disuse (Bruer, 1998). As well, sufficient challenges and mental stimulation can increase and improve connections.

Signal Processing

Neurons have a compact cell body. They process information by converting chemicals into electrical signals and by conveying signals back and forth between other neurons; normal neurons constantly receive and send signals. Dendrites and axons are attached to the body of the neuron cell. Dendrites are like branches and extend outward from the neuron. Enriched learning environments stimulate the growth and number of dendrites, helping to afford each neuron multiple pathways for processing signals. Similar to alternative traffic routes used as detours around clogged highways or closed bridges, multiple pathways provide bypasses for each neuron; this helps learning. Axons grow out from each neuron and connect with the dendrites of other cells. Each axon helps to transport the brain's chemicals and conducts the electrical signals received by the neuron (see Figure 2.3). Each neuron receives signals from thousands of other brain cells, depending on the number of branches grown.

FIGURE 2.3
The Synaptic Gap
An electrical charge is received by a neuron and travels to the tip of the axon, where electrical energy is converted to chemical energy by chemicals called neurotransmitters, which send a signal across the synaptic gap to the receptors on the dendrite of another neuron. The chemical signal is converted to electricity and travels through the axon of different neurons to the receptors of other neurons' dendrites. A network is established with multiple pathways for signals that travel at speeds of about 200 miles per hour.

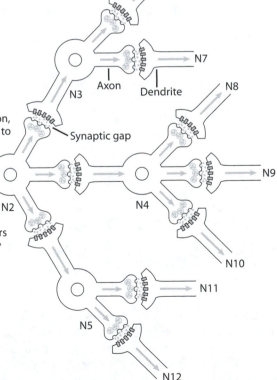

Dendrite from receiving neuron has receptor sites that receive signal and transmit to axon, which relays signal to other neurons.

Synaptic gap

Axon   Dendrite

Neuron 1
N1

Tip of axon receives electrical charges that stimulate neurotransmitters to release chemical energy across the synaptic gap.

Electrical signals speed along at about 200 miles per hour. Each brain cell behaves like a small battery, generating electrical impulses from the potassium and sodium concentrated in cell membranes located at the synaptic gap—the small space located between the end of the axon and the tip of a dendrite. Some of these electrical signals may be new stimuli, requiring more neurons to be involved in the processing beyond the well-rehearsed pathways already conditioned to respond to stimuli. New stimuli encourage the growth of new synapses, which are regarded as evidence that the brain grows new connections as a consequence of learning. When the transmitted signals are related to what we already know or can do, they move along previously established neural pathways. Accumulations of pathways with recognizable patterns enhance memory retrieval and application of "remembered" (stored) material to new experiences (Krueger & Sutton, 2001). This allows the processing to be more efficient and uses fewer of the brain's neurons, but it also reinforces and makes connections stronger (Jensen, 1998). In brief, learning occurs when synaptic efficiency is enhanced.

Making Connections Makes Learning

Jensen (1998) distinguishes between learning, what we have described so far, and behavior, which is more likely governed by emotional states and memories. The brain is a soup of floating chemicals, mostly peptides, and Pert (1997) estimates that at least 98 percent of the brain and body's internal communications occur through peptides, and control behavior such as attention span, levels of stress, and drowsiness.

Experienced educators today often remark that children seem less well prepared for learning in school. There is some evidence to suggest this is true. A developing fetus is extremely sensitive to stress from chemical and emotional effects and from poor nutrition. The effects can be huge if these stresses occur and interface during embryonic development, a time when brain cells develop at a rate of 250,000 a minute.

Experiences using tools help to develop and strengthen neural pathways.

Researchers report that emotional intelligence begins very early, and the early school grades may be a last opportunity to nurture emotional literacy (Goleman, 1995). Troubled early relationships can cause the brain to consume nutrients essential to cognitive functions and divert them to dealing with stress or violence. The brain can become reorganized, and the child more impulsive or aggressive in school or social relationships (Kotulak, 1996).

Unstimulating playgrounds, car seats that limit visual stimulation, sedentary activity while in day care, and lengthy exposure to television can impede the development of early motor skills by restricting vestibular stimulation, which can impact the brain's readiness for reading, writing, and attention (Hannaford, 1995). Restricted stimulation has been linked to learning problems such as dyslexia (Cleeland,

1984). Early stimulation in enriched environments can help the brain develop visualization (Kotulak, 1996), thinking skills (Greenfield, 1995), auditory skills (Begley, 1996), and language (Kotulak, 1993). Inadequate sleep, poor nutrition, and dehydration also impact the developing (and the developed) brain's ability to function properly in school (Jensen, 1998).

What does brain research suggest we can do to improve learning? The first thing is to focus on helping learners to grow more synaptic connections between brain cells and to strengthen, rather than lose, existing connections. Connection-making is central to learning, and enabling brain cell connections helps learners problem solve, a key to modern scientific literacy. Connections are made among and between ideas and experiences. Children will learn science more effectively if we consider their prior ideas and nurture their connection-making through constructivist principles of learning.

Where Do Children's Ideas Come From and How Do They Influence Learning?

Rosalind Driver (Driver, Guensne, & Tiberghien, 1985) and her fellow researchers have studied this question extensively. Consider the following classroom example involving two 11-year-old students.

Tim and Ricky are studying the way a spring extends as they add ball bearings to a plastic drinking cup that is attached to and hangs from the spring, which is suspended from a clamp on a stand. Ricky carefully adds the bearings one at a time and measures the change in the length of the spring after each addition. Tim watches and inquires, "Wait a moment. What happens if we lift up the spring?" Ricky clamps the spring higher on the stand, measures its stretched length, and continues after he is satisfied that the length of the spring is the same as before the change in position. An observer asks Tim the reasons behind his suggestion. Tim picks up two bearings, pretends they are pebbles, and explains his idea about weight changing as objects are lifted higher:

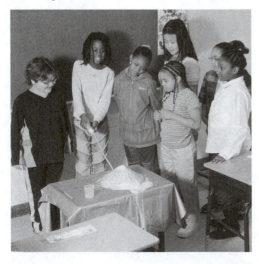

Children form their own science ideas through direct experience.

> This is farther up and gravity is pulling it down harder the farther away. The higher it gets the more effect gravity will have on it because if you just stood over there and someone dropped a pebble on him, it would just sting him, it wouldn't hurt him. But if I dropped it from an aeroplane it would be accelerating faster and faster and when it hit someone on the head it would kill him. (Driver, Guensne, & Tiberghien, 1985, pp. 1–2)

Tim's idea is not scientifically correct. The object's weight decreases as height increases. However, the idea is not irrational if you consider Tim's reasoning: He seems to be referring to what scientists call gravitational potential energy. The ideas children bring with them often influence what and how they learn.

Preconceptions

The ideas from prior experiences that children bring with them have been called a variety of names: alternative frameworks, children's science, naive theories, and preconceptions. We prefer to call them *preconceptions* because children's ideas are often incomplete preliminary understandings of fundamental science concepts that explain their everyday world. These preconceptions are influenced by hands-on, minds-on experiences, such as direct physical experiences, emotional experiences through social processes, and thoughtful efforts to make sense of the various things that exist in a child's world. Preconceptions that are brought to a new learning opportunity are important, even for adults, because the process of learning is the human activity of making connections in the brain.

Adults and children can have a type of bias that is influenced by expectations that fit patterns already formed in the brain from previous experiences. Young children may have limited or incomplete experiences. Bias inherent in preconceptions can influence concept formation. A well-known paleoanthropologist, Donald Johanson, recognized the importance of this when he wrote: "There is no such thing as total lack of bias. . . . The fossil hunter in the field has it. If he is interested in hippo teeth, that is what he is going to find, and that will bias his collection because he will walk right by other fossils without noticing them" (Kinnear, 1994, p. 3). Another scientist, David Pilbeam, illustrates this point by explaining how his original interpretation of a particular fossil was affected by his prior expectations: "I knew . . . [the fossil], being a hominid, would have a short face and rounded jaw—so that's what I saw" (Kinnear, 1994, p. 3). Additional discoveries and further investigation revealed that the fossil did not possess the features that Pilbeam described and that it was not a hominid.

Misconceptions

Misconceptions are alternative understandings about phenomena that learners have formed. They are scientifically incorrect interpretations that learners believe or responses to problems that learners provide. "Misconceptions do not simply signify a lack of knowledge, factual errors, or incorrect definitions. Instead, misconceptions represent explanations of phenomena constructed by a student in response to the student's prior knowledge and experience" (Munson, 1994, pp. 30–31). For example, through reading and participation in class activities, including gamelike simulations, a learner may form the misconception that the top of a food chain has the most energy because it accumulates up the food chain (Adeniyi, 1985), whereas a correct scientific conception maintains the opposite: Available energy decreases as one progresses up a food chain (Munson, 1994). Students commonly believe that gravity results from air pressure (Minstrell, 1982) or that light from a candle travels farther at night than during the day (Stead & Osborne, 1980).

Despite sincere efforts, even some of the best students give correct answers using words they have memorized but do not fully understand. If we question them more closely, we can often discover misconceptions that are based on lack of understanding about the underlying concepts. Misconceptions represent a liability that affects students and their teachers. The Committee on Undergraduate Science Education (1997) described several categories of misconceptions that shed light on the basic reasons behind misconceptions and the lingering liability associated with them.

Conceptual misunderstandings may occur when learners are taught in a way that does not allow them to examine the differences between their own beliefs and "real science." For example, adults may tell growing children that the "sun rises and sets," which gives children a mental image that it is the sun that moves around the earth. In school they are taught that the earth moves by rotation and revolution, and now children face the difficult task of removing one mental image and replacing it with another. This is not easy to do and it is not a trivial task to rearrange mental schema.

Vernacular misconceptions can arise from the word choices that we use during explanations. For example, perhaps a teacher remarks that glaciers "retreat." As a child, could you imagine a glacier stopping, turning around and going back in the opposite direction from where it had come? Simply substituting the work "melt" could avoid or correct this misunderstanding and help children to understand that glaciers can melt faster than they advance (this is what is meant by "retreat").

Factual misconceptions often occur at an early age based on false statements, such as "lightning never strikes twice in the same place." Lightning can strike the same place twice and nothing prevents this from occurring; lightning does not have a mind of its own to decide where to strike.

William Philips, an earth science teacher, discovered some interesting but depressing facts about what his students knew about science—or rather, what they really did not understand. What was most troublesome was that his students thought they were correct.

Guided direct experiences help to reduce misconceptions.

Misconceptions are rarely expressed aloud or in writing and, therefore, often go undetected. Twenty years ago, shortly after I began teaching science, I encountered an outrageous misconception (or so it seemed at the time). While I was using a globe to explain seasonal changes, one very attentive eighth grader raised her hand and asked, "Where are we?" Thinking she wanted to know the location of our school, I pointed to Delaware and resumed my lecture. She immediately stopped me with another question. "No. I don't mean that. I mean, do we live inside the Earth or outside it?" The question caused several students to laugh, but most appeared to be waiting for an answer. It was all I could do to hide my astonishment. (Philips, 1991, p. 21)

Philips cites a survey in which second-grade teachers estimated that 95 percent of their students knew the earth is a sphere. Later, the teachers conducted interviews with the children and discovered that the students actually believed the Earth is flat. Misconceptions are common, and once formed, they are held a long while. Misconceptions are linked to intuitive ideas, beliefs, or preconceptions. It is not unusual for students to go through school providing correct answers when the teachers ask for them but believing otherwise, much like the second graders mentioned above. When students give science facts correctly to questions and on tests, it does not mean they have replaced the misconceptions they formed much earlier.

Examples of misconceptions Philips uncovered are given in Table 2.1. Misconceptions seem to occur as students construct knowledge; they may be linked to incomplete or insufficient experiences, faulty explanations, and misperceived meanings. Joseph Novak (1991), a professor of science and education, reminds us that students must construct new meaning from the foundation of the knowledge they already possess. This means that teachers cannot afford to overlook student misconceptions because of the negative learning cycle caused by misunderstanding the simplest point. Novak also states that students can create new meaning only by constructing new propositions, linked concepts that are usually formed through discovery learning. This requires expansions of their neural networks.

TABLE 2.1   Common Earth Science Misconceptions

More than ten years' worth of research on misconceptions yielded the following list for children. Adults often harbor the same misconceptions.

The earth is sitting on something.	Empty clouds are refilled by the sea.
The earth is larger than the sun.	Clouds are formed by vapors from kettles.
The earth is round like a pancake.	The sun boils the sea to create water vapor.
We live on the flat middle of a sphere.	Clouds are made of cotton, wool, or smoke.
There is a definite up and down in space.	Clouds are bags of water.
Astrology is able to predict the future.	Stars and constellations appear in the same place in the sky every night.
Gravity increases with height.	
Gravity cannot exist without air.	The seasons are caused by the Earth's distance from the sun.
Any crystal that scratches glass is a diamond.	
Coral reefs exist throughout the Gulf of Mexico and the North Atlantic.	The moon can only be seen at night.
	The Earth is the largest object in the solar system.
Dinosaurs and cavemen lived at the same time.	Gas makes things lighter.
Rain comes from holes in clouds.	Batteries have electricity inside them.
Rain comes from clouds' sweating.	Things "use up" energy.
Rain falls from funnels in the clouds.	Wood floats and metal sinks.
Rain occurs when clouds are shaken.	Liquids rise in a straw because of "suction."
God and angels cause thunder and lightning.	Boiling is the maximum temperature that a substance can reach.
Clouds move because we move.	
Clouds come from somewhere above the sky.	Air and oxygen are the same thing.

Source: Excerpted from the list provided by William C. Philips, "Earth Science Misconceptions," *Science Teacher* (February 1991): 21–23. Bill Weiler. (1998). University of Illinois [Online]. www.amasci.com/miscon.opphys.html

What Do We Know About Children's Ideas?

Children bring many ideas to class. Their ideas represent the interpretations they have formed about the dilemmas and phenomena they have encountered. Many of these experiences occur out of school and are not connected to formal teaching, including play, conversations, and events observed through the media. Recent research on children's ideas reveals three important factors: (1) children's ideas are personal constructions, (2) the ideas may seem incomplete or contradictory, and (3) the ideas are often very stable and highly resistant to change (Driver et al., 1985).

Children's Ideas Are Personal. Have you ever been with a group of friends and witnessed a remarkable event, such as a concert, championship play-off, or auto accident? Or have you participated in a heated debate about a topic important to you? How did your perceptions of the facts or the event compare with those of your friends? Was there complete agreement on each detail? "No" is not an unusual answer. Consider children in a class, each participating in the same science activity. It is likely that the children will report diverse perceptions of what happened during the activity. Each child has seen and experienced the activity, but each has internalized the experiences in his or her own way. Our perceptions and descriptions depend as much on our original ideas as they do on the nature of the new experience or lesson. All readers do not receive exactly the same message, even from written words.

Learners construct their own meanings. *Constructed meanings* are based on new experiences that are accumulated and compared with and processed from old ideas. Constructed meanings arise from the expanded and cross-referenced neural networks formed in the brain. The preexisting ideas are the basis for observing, classifying, and interpreting new experiences. In this way, each learner, even a very young one, continually forms and reforms hypotheses and theories about natural phenomena. We call on the mind's existing ideas to help us understand new experiences (Harlen, 1992, p. 11). What is remarkable is that although ideas are constructed independently, the general interpretations and conclusions are often shared by many (Driver, 1983).

A Child's Ideas May Seem Contradictory. Natural science is blessed with many intriguing discrepancies. Touch the flat bottom of an uncoated paper cup with a candle flame, and predictably, the paper burns after a brief time. But add water to a cup and the cup will not burn even when heated by a stronger source for a much longer time. This result challenges the mature mind to identify a coherent reason that explains the behavior of the candle and cup under all circumstances. The younger mind may see no problem and simply use another, even contradictory, explanation, unconcerned that the explanation is inconsistent with what was previously said. As Driver (1983) reminds us:

> The same child may have different conceptions of a particular type of phenomenon, sometimes using different arguments leading to opposite predictions in situations which are equivalent from a scientist's point of view, and even switching from one sort of explanation to another for the same phenomenon. (p. 3)

A child does not have the same need for coherence as an adult or a scientist, nor does a child have a mental model to use to unify a range of different perceptions that relate to the same event. Furthermore, a child usually does not see the need for a consistent view. The constructed ideas work quite well for the child in his or her classroom practice, even though the ideas may be based on prior false conclusions.

Children's Ideas Often Resist Change. It is not simple for teachers to change children's incomplete or flawed ideas about scientific events and phenomena. Additional activities, comparative discussions, and even direct teacher explanations may not cause children to modify their ideas. Changing ideas is a slow process, and the necessary changes may never be complete. Children may only feel that they are to provide a certain correct answer to a teacher's questions but choose to turn off the academically correct answer in favor of the previous independent ideas once the test is over. Counter evidence presented to the child seems to make no difference. Interpretations often are based on prior ideas. Personal, if contradictory, ideas have tremendous stability and endurance (Driver, 1983, p. 4).

What Is the Dominant Perspective About How Children Learn Science?

Constructivism is the general name given to the dominant perspective on learning in science education. A constructivist perspective on teaching and learning is unlike traditional views. A teacher who embraces constructivism supports a different view of science, regards the roles of teacher and learner very differently, and selects and organizes teaching materials with particular care. A constructivist perspective emphasizes the role of the learner, regarding the role as active—physically, mentally, and socially—rather than passive. The constructivist teacher seeks ways to challenge and stimulate mental connection-making in order to enhance the active participation of learners in lessons and encourage learners to construct their own understanding of their reality, which arises from their experiences. Jessica's efforts toward change illustrate a constructivist attempt.

Jessica: A Constructivist Attempt

Based on her experience with her son, Jessica was determined to avoid her usual demonstration and recipe instructions. Now she distributed the materials for the science lesson *first:* clay, scissors, cardboard, rulers, string, and so on. She asked small groups of children to work together in teams to design and construct a landscape—any type of landscape *they* chose. Jessica wanted to avoid mimicry and to encourage the students not to get fixed on the definitions of a landscape, since that was not the point of the lesson. Therefore she did not define "landscape," nor did she show particular examples. When students questioned her about the task, she encouraged them to use their intuitive understanding about landscapes—their preconceptions—to think about their experiences and use what they already knew.

Brain-Based Learning

Much has been written about hemispheric brain dominance, and these ideas have influenced our views on learning and teaching even though they do not apply to normal learners. Although it is true that our brains benefit from abundant varieties of stimulation, prescriptions are difficult and risky because we are still learning how our brains function. Researchers have summarized important principles from the brain-based research on teaching and learning that may help you to find effective ways to stimulate learning:

- We should stimulate all of the senses, but not necessarily all at once.
- Science curricula should repeat concepts in a new manner or context; avoid mere duplication.
- Previous experiences and meaning affect how the brain processes new experiences and organizes new knowledge.
- Our emotions and our learning share an important relationship.
- Emotion enhances memory—a reason to include personal examples and social materials into the science curriculum.
- Learning is more than exercising the brain like a muscle. It is a true physiological experience that involves a sophisticated set of systems.
- New material will fade from short-term memory unless learners can connect it to already familiar material.

- Our brain processes and organizes many stimuli and ideas at the same time, even though we may focus on only one thing at a time.
- The significance of subject matter content depends on how our experiences are arranged and fit into patterns.
- We should present a series of novel challenges that are appropriate for development.
- Our brains process peripheral stimuli consciously and unconsciously.
- Parts and wholes are processed simultaneously by our brains, not separately or in isolation in a particular hemisphere.
- We possess spatial memories that help us to retrieve experiences rapidly and easily; for example, we might have a detailed memory of an important event even though we made no special attempt to memorize details.
- We need more practice to recall facts and to establish a level of skill when these facts are not embedded in our spatial memories.
- Our brains respond positively to problems and challenges but are less effective under duress.
- We should allow social interaction for a significant percentage of activities.

Ernst von Glasersfeld, philosopher and regarded leader of the constructivist movement in science

The groups did not begin smoothly, perhaps because the children were not accustomed to vague instructions. However, the puzzled expressions and occasional off-task behavior associated with the newfound freedom quickly subsided as Jessica maintained consistent contact with each group and challenged their thinking by asking guiding questions: "How else could you do that?" "What other features could you add?" "Where have you seen landscapes like this?" Jessica also lifted up the unique examples from single groups for all of the other groups to examine. These examples stimulated many to say: "Oh, now I see!"

After a bit more exploration, Jessica challenged each group to draw two-dimensional maps of their three-dimensional landscapes. This proved difficult until the concepts of

education, provides the following implications for teaching and learning:

- Whatever a student provides as an answer to a question or problem is based on what made sense to the student at that time. The response must be taken seriously, regardless of how odd or "wrong" it might seem to the teacher. Otherwise the student will be discouraged and inhibited. Also, understand that the answer may be a good one depending on how the student interpreted the question.

- A teacher who wishes to modify a student's concepts and conceptual structures must try to build a mental model of the student's individual thinking. Never assume that a student's way of thinking is simple or transparent.

- Asking students how they arrived at their given answer is a good way of discovering something about their thinking, and it opens the way to explaining why a particular answer may not be useful under different circumstances.

- If you want to motivate students to delve further into questions that they say are of no particular interest to them, create situations in which the students have an opportunity to experience the pleasure inherent in solving a problem. Simply being told "good" or "correct" does not help a learner's conceptual development.

- Successful thinking is more than "correct" answers; it should be rewarded even if it is based on unacceptable premises.

- A teacher must have an almost infinitely flexible mind to understand and appreciate students' thinking because students sometimes start from premises that seem inconceivable to teachers.

- Constructivist teachers can never justify what they teach by claiming it is true. In science, they cannot say more than that it is the best way of conceiving the situation because it is the most effective way at the moment of dealing with it.

Sources: Renate Nummela Caine and Geoffrey Caine, *Teaching and the Human Brain* (Alexandria, VA: Association for Supervision and Curriculum Development, 1991); Diamond, M. & Hopson, J. (1998). *Magic trees of the mind: How to nurture your child's intelligence, creativity, and healthy emotions from birth through adolescence.* New York: Dutton (pp. 107–108). Ernst von Glasersfeld, "Questions and Answers about Radical Constructivism," in Kenneth Tobin (Ed.), *The Practice of Constructivism in Science Education* (Washington, DC: AAAS Press, 1993), pp. 32–33. Alice Krueger and John Sutton (Eds.), *EDThoughts: What We Know About Science Teaching and Learning* (Aurora, CO: Mid-continent Research for Education and Learning, 2001): p. 91.

contour and interval were constructed. Jessica guided her class in defining what these words meant and figuring out how the ideas were important to the lesson. Soon each group was applying basic math and measurement skills to construct a contour map of their own landscapes to scale. Later, the children took actual contour maps and recreated different landscapes they had never visited, again to scale.

Jessica did continue to use typical testing methods and noticed a deeper understanding of the children's learning. When she asked questions or when the children wrote answers to her tests, the responses were more detailed and appeared to be more thoughtful, and the children seemed able to use their ideas in new situations. The children seemed happier and excited about science, and this satisfied Jessica—for now.

Constructivism

Jessica also appears to be guided by the notion of constructivism, an emerging consensus among psychologists, science educators, philosophers of science, scientists, and others who are interested in improving children's learning. This view of learning maintains that learners (young and old, and professionals such as scientists) must construct and reconstruct their own meaning for ideas about how the world works (Good, Wandersee, & St. Julien, 1993). In a very simplified way, an ancient Chinese proverb encapsulates the intent of constructivism: "I hear and I forget; I see and I remember; I *do* and I *understand*." A lot of wisdom is packed into these three phrases. One type of sensory experience alone is insufficient when we strive for understanding. Experience requires substantial stimulation of all senses and each child's mental processes if meaningful learning is to happen.

Childhood educators Connie Williams and Constance Kamii (1986) recommend that we strive to accomplish three things when we encourage children toward understanding:

1. Use or create learning circumstances that are indeed meaningful to the learners.
2. Encourage children to make real decisions.
3. Provide children opportunities to refine their thinking and deepen their understanding by exchanging views with their peers.

Williams and Kamii (1986) remind us that what is important is "the mental action that is encouraged when children act on objects themselves" (p. 26). Mental action is the planned or guided metacognitive activity of cognitive constructivism, a mental state influenced by physical and social interaction with the learner's world.

Constructivism Defined. Constructivism is a theory that assumes knowledge cannot exist outside the minds of thinking persons. This theory capitalizes on the brain's natural curiosity as it constantly seeks to make connections between the new and the known (Wolfe & Brandt, 1998). Joseph Novak (Novak & Gowin 1986) defines constructivism as the notion that humans construct or build meaning into their ideas and experiences as a result of an effort to understand or to make sense of them. Novak explains that this construction

Constructivism enables each learner to build understanding.

involves at times recognition of new regularities in events or objects, inventing new concepts or extending old concepts, recognition of new relationships (propositions) between concepts, and . . . major restructuring of conceptual frameworks to see new higher order relationships. (p. 356)

Constructivism emphasizes the importance of each pupil's active construction of knowledge through the interplay of prior learning and newer learning. "Learning is a process of active construction by the learner, and an enriched environment gives the students the opportunity to relate what they are learning to what they already know" (Wolfe & Brandt, 1998, p. 11). Connections are sought between the prior and newer learning; the connections are constructed by the learners for themselves. Researchers and theorists maintain that the key element of constructivist theory is that people learn by actively constructing their own knowledge, comparing new information with their previous understanding and using all of this to work through discrepancies to come to a new understanding (Loucks-Horsley, 1990; Harlen, 1992; Peterson & Knapp, 1993; Yager, 1991).

Consider the possible vast difference between a scientist's ideas and those of a child. A scientist's perspective might be, "A plant is a producer." In contrast, a child's perspective might be as follows:

> A plant is something that grows in a garden. Carrots and cabbage from the garden are not plants; they are vegetables. Trees are not plants; they are plants when they are little, but when they grow up they are not plants. Seeds are not plants. Dandelions are not plants; they are weeds. Plants . . . have multiple sources of food. Photosynthesis is not important to plants. (Osborne & Freyberg, 1990, p. 49)

Some concepts are correct but not inclusive. Other concepts are incorrect and merit thoughtful attention and eventual correction.

Constructivism is a synthesis of several dominant perspectives on learning. It is not entirely new. Contemporary researchers from Great Britain, Australia, New Zealand, and the United States have updated theories and methods to capture the synergy of legendary psychologists, philosophers, and researchers.

The constructivist perspective is grounded in the research and theories of Jean Piaget and Lev Vygotsky, the Gestalt psychologists; Jerome Bruner; and the philosophy of John Dewey, and is a natural extension of applied brain research. As you may imagine, the very nature and meaning of constructivism is open to interpretation; there is no one constructivist theory of learning. Some perspectives embrace the social nature of learning (Vygotsky); radical constructivists do not believe the world is knowable (Ernst von Glasersfeld); and more conservative views advocate using constructivist principles to help learners construct accurate and useful conceptions and webs of conceptual understanding. The continuum in Figure 2.4 illustrates degrees of difference in viewpoints among constructivists and constructivist views in respect to traditional views on teaching and learning (Shapiro, 1994). Radical constructivists place greater emphasis on the individual's active participation in knowledge construction and are located at the farthest point on the left of the continuum. Conservative constructivists use activity-based and problem-based learning experiences and teacher intervention to promote conceptual constructions, and they attempt to correct student misconceptions by helping learners construct understanding based on concepts embraced by the scientific community. Traditionalists, at the extreme right of the continuum, assume more passive learning roles for students.

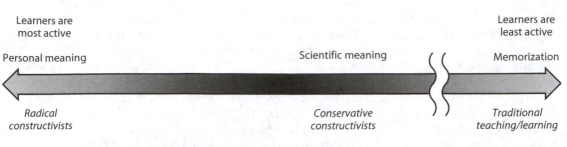

FIGURE 2.4 Teaching/Learning Continuum of Mental Operations

Jean Piaget's research and his cognitive development theory are regarded as the foundation of conservative constructivists' views. His contributions to constructivism arose from his theory about mental equilibration and its interplay with assimilation and accommodation.

Equilibration. According to Piaget's theory, learning is an active mental process in which each learner must construct knowledge by interacting with the environment and by resolving the cognitive conflicts that arise between what is expected and what is observed (Driver, 1983, p. 52). Each new interaction or conflict creates a dilemma in each learner's mind about how to maintain mental equilibrium.

Equilibration is a process by which each learner compensates mentally for each dilemma. Each new attempt at restoring equilibrium helps to create a higher level of functional equilibration; higher mental structures are formed. (See Figure 2.5.) However, equilibrium is not a static point at which the mind rests as if on a balance beam. Instead, equilibration is like a cyclist's maintaining dynamic balance with each new challenge on the touring course. "The brain is continually seeking to impose order on incoming stimuli and to generate models that lead to adaptive behavior and useful predictions" (Yager, 1991, p. 54).

Assimilation. Assimilation is one way the mind may adapt to the learning challenge and restore equilibrium. If the stimulus is not too different from previous experiences and mental actions, it may be combined with or added to existing mental structures, like filing a new letter into a preexisting folder containing the same or similar information.

Accommodation. On those occasions when no preexisting mental structures (or file folders) are available to assimilate, the mind must adapt by changing or adding to its mental structures. This process of adaptation is called accommodation. The learner's thinking is adapted to accommodate the dilemma.

In practice, assimilation and accommodation are related and do not occur in isolation; each process complements the other. A rational, thinking learner is mentally active. When losing equilibrium and trying to restore it, the learner develops structures through the continuous interaction between the person and the external world. Again, rich, stimulating experiences—physical and mental—feed the learner's development.

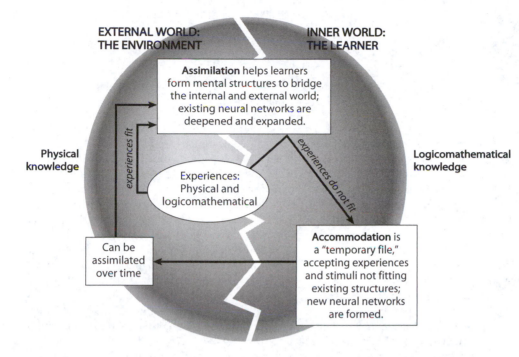

EXTERNAL WORLD:
THE ENVIRONMENT

INNER WORLD:
THE LEARNER

Assimilation helps learners form mental structures to bridge the internal and external world; existing neural networks are deepened and expanded.

experiences fit

experiences do not fit

Physical knowledge

Logicomathematical knowledge

Experiences: Physical and logicomathematical

Can be assimilated over time

Accommodation is a "temporary file," accepting experiences and stimuli not fitting existing structures; new neural networks are formed.

FIGURE 2.5 Equilibrium Model Based on Piaget's Theory When disequilibrium occurs in each learner's universe of experiences, the learner attempts to restore equilibrium through assimilation and accommodation.

Jessica: The Novelty Wore Off

Jessica used learning groups to undertake the class's new approach to science learning. The students were very excited and cooperative—for about a week. Soon, what had been discussion, sharing and playing roles, and collective searches for meaning degenerated into arguments and stalemates over who would get materials and clean up. Normally, class time devoted to positive human relations, genuine regard, and time management would not concern Jessica. As the weeks passed, what bothered Jessica most was the growing number of students who seemed to have persistent ideas and misconceptions unchanged by the effort of problem- and project-based group work. Several individual students complained that they preferred to work by themselves rather than be a part of a group.

Concurrent reading that Jessica was doing as she experimented with her new class arrangements led her into a deeper investigation of cooperative group learning processes, constructivism, and learning models. Students wanted a flexible grouping arrangement and job assignments; they also wanted opportunities to leave a group structure. Poring over how to structure and manage all of the requests for changes, Jessica became mildly embarrassed by the sudden realization that the true spirit of constructivism would be, for her, to let the *students* decide how to solve their problem. The class decided to vary

How Can You Teach Skills Now, Content Later?

by Charlotte Schartz
Grade 6, Kingman Middle School, Kingman, Kansas

The year is 1977 and time for sixth-grade science class. There will be a unit on, let's say, the cell. We'll do lots of worksheets, with a large amount of reading. I'll lecture, assigning much vocabulary to memorize, and maybe I'll do a demonstration or two. The students are listening, I think. Individual seat work is the norm. Talking to your neighbor is out. I am on stage telling them what to learn, what to memorize. The emphasis is on content.

That was then, this is now, and I'm learning. My evolving theory on how an adolescent learns is based on a conglomeration of articles that I have read, behaviors that I have observed, and experiences that I have had. I believe that students learn in inconsistent surges. Their rate of content absorption is in proportion to their social, emotional, and hormonal situation at any given moment.

I am becoming more and more convinced that middle school students learned something before they got to me, and they'll learn more at a later stage in their lives, but right now, they have more important things on their minds, like what to wear, who's going with whom, why Susan didn't smile today, or why she smiled at someone else. They are distracted by the unpredictable changes associated with unstable families, economic conditions, and so on. The plant or animal cell just can't compete. And after visiting with the teachers at the senior high, I learned that when they introduce that same cell, they start from the beginning, assuming that most 15- to 16-year-olds will not remember too much from middle school anyway.

I used to spend so much time on content. That's what the experts said was right at the time, I guess. . . . That was then, this is now, and I'm learning.

My teaching style has changed. I'm trying to match it to something unknown, unpredictable, inconsistent: a middle school student. If they aren't physically, emotionally, or socially able to learn and apply a bunch of big words mingled with abstract ideas and global concepts, then I must focus on something more concrete, like the skills that a scientist will need. In my classroom, we make observations, measure, keep records, analyze our data, make comparisons, predict based on patterns, and draw conclusions. During a project such as the design of a controlled experiment with bean seeds, my youngsters are expected to use all of the above as they construct meaning from their experiences. They work with their cooperative learning team to make their own observations, taking their own measurements, keeping their own records. They feel more of an ownership and involvement than if I had just told them about when someone else grew beans. (It's also safer to express an opinion, make a suggestion, or verbalize a revelation while working in a small group instead of in front of the whole class.) Now, are they ready to go out into the world as master bean growers? No, even though some relatively thorough content did get slipped in. But they will have practiced some useful scientific skills, constructed some important science concepts, and developed a greater ability to think, along with some critical social skills. They have a greater chance of remembering something they did rather than something they heard about. And who knows if there will even BE bean farms in fifty years?!? Look what happened to the four food groups! I do feel certain however, that the skills of doing science and importance of constructed meaning will endure. People will still have to observe, predict, compare, keep records, and so on; people will have to think and solve problems.

the number of persons in groups; some contained only two, while others consisted of three to five students. Most realized that working with others was a better way to form understandings because ideas and explanations always had to be tested; cases had to be presented and pass the scrutiny of other group members.

When ideas did not fit with existing conceptions, there seemed to be four options.

1. The uneasiness many individuals in a group experienced became a source of motivation as students attempted to create mini-theories to help them include the new experiences into their conceptual structures.

2. When some fit was constructed, students achieved a level of learning that was meaningful to them by regaining their equilibrium and changing previous ideas by adjusting their schema through a process of accommodation; this was regarded as the preferred learning outcome (see Figure 2.6, Exit 2). Jessica realized that a single successful

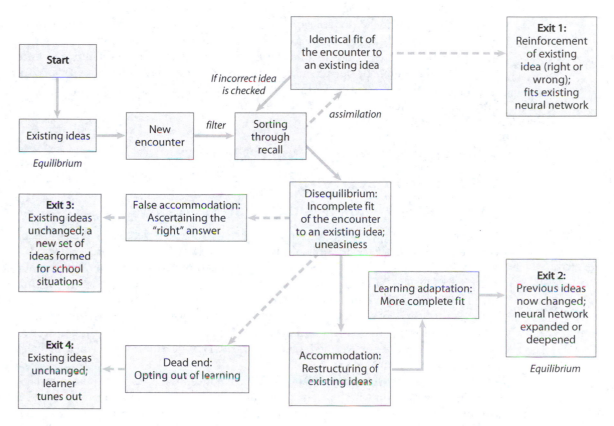

FIGURE 2.6 Science Education Learning Model

Source: Adapted from K. Appleton, "Using Theory to Guide Practice: Teaching Science from a Constructivist Perspective," *School Science and Mathematics,* 93 (5) (1993): 270.

experience was not enough to cause major changes in student thinking. Recalling her son Jonathan's learning about friction, Jessica determined that multiple experiences in a variety of situations were helpful, and she used this notion to plan many opportunities for her students to expand their understanding of science concepts. She discovered that her role was important. At times, she became the source of information and explanation, although she usually functioned as a guide and questioner.

3. Despite Jessica's best efforts, some learners preferred to wait for the answer to be given—by a book, a search on the Internet, other students, or Jessica. These few students seemed to prefer to learn the answer by rote (see Figure 2.6, Exit 3). As unsatisfying as this was to Jessica, she realized that it was a beginning for these youngsters, so she resolved to help them by challenging the students to use the answer in other contexts, much like Jonathan's uncle had encouraged him to do when constructing an understanding of friction.

4. Jessica was most disappointed by the two or three children who opted out of the learning experience (see Figure 2.6, Exit 4). These learners included not only the isolated, surly types who did not consider the science topic interesting or the effort worthwhile; they also included the happy social types who were present in group activities, yet—perhaps because of poor prior experiences in science or repeated failures—chose to avoid further failure by opting out of the learning situation (Appleton, 1993, p. 270). This disconcerting student behavior motivated Jessica to seek teaching guidelines and intervention strategies that would serve all learners.

What Techniques and Roles Support Constructivist Learning?

A Constructivist Learning and Teaching Model

Constructivism strives toward a deeper understanding and is served by the desire for children to experience science holistically, as described in Chapter 1. Frontal teaching—telling and showing students all kinds of things—is minimized. According to Eleanor Duckworth (1989), all people ever have is their own understanding, and you cannot make them believe anything unless they construct it for themselves. Students can be encouraged to learn by reinventing the wheel for themselves—not a particularly time-efficient approach, but it *is* effective: retention is greater and understanding is deeper. The learner does the discovering by forming mental connections; the teacher mediates the learning environment.

There is a downside, though. Not all student conceptual constructions are correct, and simply voting on what is right does not make it so. At times, a teacher may feel compelled to step in and correct the record. This can be fine, but beware of too much telling. Instead, try an approach like the one shown in Figure 2.7. A learning cycle uses constructivist techniques and helps learners achieve deeper understanding through metacognitive strategies (Krueger & Sutton, 2001). Provide an opportunity for children to explore and be directly involved in manipulating objects; ask questions and encour-

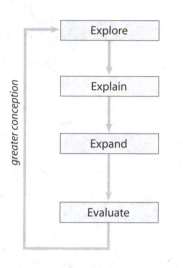

TEACHER'S ACTIVITY

Provide opportunities for students to explore through all appropriate senses and to be fully involved through engaged attention. Encourage group cooperation during investigations; encourage questions.

Interact with children to discover their ideas. Question to cause them to reflect. Help them use ideas formed from exploration to "construct" concepts and meaning sensible to them.

Help children develop their ideas further through additional physical and mental activity. Help them refine their ideas and expand their repertoire of science process skills. Encourage communication through group cooperation and broaden experience of nature and technology.

Evaluate conception by examining changes in children's ideas and by their mastery of science process skills. Use hands-on assessment, pictorial problem-solving, and reflective questioning. Encourage children's interest in the ideas and reasoning of others. Frequent evaluation improves each of the prior steps.

FIGURE 2.7   A Constructivist Learning and Teaching Model

age children to ask useful and productive questions themselves. Help children to construct best explanations from their direct experiences by finding out their ideas and encouraging them to reflect on similarities and differences, to construct connections among and between their ideas. Encourage children to expand on their ideas by using them in other settings, such as the natural world and technology, and to develop process skills to enhance their thinking. Try to evaluate children's thinking by assessing any change in their ideas and process skills. Also encourage children to evaluate ideas by helping them to become interested in the explanations of others.

Constructivist Teaching Roles

Constructivism has become a popular catchword in education. Teachers may mistakenly believe they are already using constructivism. While hands-on science, mathematics manipulatives, and process writing share some common intentions with constructivism, applying constructivist research is much more difficult. The constructivist teacher must fill many roles but largely functions as a facilitator of knowledge construction. Young children can be encouraged to construct their own understanding if you perform these roles (Chaillé & Britain, 1991, p. 54):

+ *Presenter*—not a lecturer but one who demonstrates, models, and presents activities to groups of children and options to individuals so that direct pupil experiences are encouraged in an ongoing fashion.
+ *Observer*—one who works in formal and informal ways to identify children's ideas, to interact appropriately, and to provide learning options.

(text continues on page 58)

Bubbles

Inquiry Question: How can we determine which type of detergent produces the largest bubbles?

Concept to Be Invented: *Variables* are things that can affect the outcome of an experiment. All variables that can affect the outcome must be identified and controlled so that the research question is truly answered without unintended interference.

National Science Education Standards: 5–8 Science as Inquiry—Students should develop abilities necessary to do scientific inquiry by designing and conducting a scientific investigation, using appropriate tools and techniques to gather, analyze, and interpret data, and develop descriptions, explanations, predictions, and models using evidence.

Scientific Attitudes to Nurture: Curiosity, open-mindedness, cooperation, avoidance of broad generalizations, willingness to withhold judgment until all evidence of information is examined.

Materials Needed: 3 different brands of detergent, glycerin, drinking straws

Safety Precautions: Wear goggles to avoid chemical eye splash.

Exploration *Which process skills will be used?*

Predicting, measuring, inferring

Offer a scenario that asks the class to determine which type of detergent produces the largest bubbles for a planned contest. Will it be the more expensive brand? Or, will an inexpensive brand do just as well? Pose the inquiry question. Ask the student groups to design their own experiment following general instructions. Introduce students to the materials and the requirements of an activity sheet that is prepared to record the measures of the diameters of at least four trials of at least three different brands of detergent. Measure the diameters of the soap rings left on the table surface after the bubbles are blown as large as possible and pop. Avoid telling the students the identities of the detergents until after the experiment. Bubbles can be made using 25 ml of detergent, 500 ml of water and 7 drops of glycerin. Take care not to structure the investigation, but encourage students to decide for themselves how to prepare the table surface, use the straws, determine duties of group members, etc. Construct a class data table using each group's record of the average diameters for each bubble solution.

Bubble solution

Explanation

Compile the class's data into a table and investigate, taking care to examine the vertical columns for the range of measures and the horizontal rows for agreement or disagreement about the rank of bubble solutions by size. Identify the detergents used and the cost. Discuss questions such as: "Is there a difference in the size of bubbles? Does cost affect the difference in bubble size? What kinds of factors may have influenced the results of the experiments? Do you believe this is a reliable test? Why? Use the students' answers to lead to the lesson's concept: *Variables are things that can affect the outcome of an experiment.* Deepen students' understandings about the importance of variables and the meaning of the concept of *variables* through the *Expansion* phase.

Expansion   *Which process skills will be used?*

Identifying variables, controlling variables, experimenting, investigating

Science in Personal and Social Perspectives

+ If left uncontrolled, what are some examples of variables that may cause us to get sick or become injured?
+ Who needs to know about variables and use them in their daily lives? What are some examples of careers that use variables?

Science and Technology

+ What are some examples of natural variables and examples that are mostly attributed to humans?
+ What are some examples of technology that identify or control variables?

Science as Inquiry

1. Discuss with classmates the different variables that may have affected the outcome of our investigation. Agree how to limit the influence of at least three variables, redesign the experiment, repeat, and report results. How do the size of the bubbles now compare with those of classmates?
2. Select one of the following research questions: (a) What detergent produces the most cost-affordable bubbles? (b) What formula additives produce the longest lasting bubble? Write a description about how to design an experiment to answer the research question. Take care to identify all variables and provide a description about how to control them in order to provide the most accurate answer to the research question.
3. For the upcoming school science fair, compose a research question that will compare experimentally two or more things. Identify all variables that may affect the outcome of the experiment and describe a research design that could produce an accurate answer to the question.

History and Nature of Science

Name three scientists who have made important discoveries. At least one scientist must be a female or person of color. Research their discoveries. What are some examples of variables that they encountered? Report on how they identified and controlled variables. How might modern technology have made their discoveries easier or more accurate?

Evaluation

Upon completing the activities, the student will be able to:

✦ describe what a variable is and why it is important;

✦ identify at least three affecting variables and how to control them or respond to them;

✦ plan a scientific investigation, conduct it, report the results, and describe in the report what steps assured accurate and repeatable results;

✦ exchange a scientific report with a classmate, examine the classmate's report, review it for proper identification and control of variables, and report a summary of the review.

✦ *Question asker and problem poser*—one who stimulates idea formation, idea testing, and concept construction by asking questions and posing problems that arise from observation.

✦ *Environment organizer*—one who organizes carefully and clearly what children are to do, while allowing sufficient freedom for true exploration; one who organizes from the child's perspective.

✦ *Public relations coordinator*—one who encourages cooperation, development of human relations, and patience with diversity within the class, and who defends this practice and educates others outside the class about the benefits for children of this approach.

✦ *Documenter of learning*—one who satisfies the accountability expectations and gauges the impact of these practices on each learner in terms of knowledge construction and science skill development.

✦ *Theory builder*—one who helps children to form connections between and among their ideas and to construct meaningful patterns that represent their constructed knowledge.

Intermediate and middle school children can benefit from these same roles, particularly if cognition is elevated to a stimulating and challenging level that is developmentally appropriate.

How Jessica Constructs Knowledge

Throughout this chapter we have seen how Jessica wrestled with her own learning as she attempted to reconceptualize learning and teaching. When this happens to a professional or even a student, there are often several recurring actions that are important to recognize. First, Jessica was dissatisfied with her teaching and what children were learning. This dissatisfaction perturbed her and motivated her to seek change. Shaw and Etchberger (1993) claim that change cannot occur without some *perturbation.* Jessica's perturbation stimulated considerable thought about how children learn and how she could teach more effectively. Students too must become perturbed in order to stimulate learning.

Perturbation often encourages *commitment*—a personal decision to make a change. Commitment and progress toward change often cause additional perturbations. If you commit to a course of constructivism in your science classroom, you are likely to encounter many such perturbations that disrupt your "mental state of equilibrium" (Shaw & Etchberger, 1993, p. 264). When this happens, say Shaw and Jakubowski (1991), there are three likely pathways for you to deal with when experiencing this disequilibrium: (1) block the perturbation and reduce the opportunity for meaningful change; (2) rationalize excuses for not dealing with the perturbation; or (3) form an active plan for making a change. To which pathway are you likely to commit?

A *vision* may help to keep one's commitments and steer the course toward meaningful change. This vision should be a clear, personal view of what the teaching and learning in your classroom should look like. You should be able to describe clearly to parents, supervisors, and visitors what you are trying to accomplish and the reasons for your choices. Figure 2.8 on page 62 summarizes the differences between traditional and constructivist classrooms.

Reflection helps to evaluate and improve one's vision, strengthen commitment, and construct options to overcome perturbations. Thinking reflectively means to give serious and frequent consideration to the factors associated with one's vision. The following questions illustrate a reflective process and can help bring congruence to your desires, beliefs, and teaching practices: "What do students know about this topic? How are students thinking about what I am presenting to them? How do they come to think this way? How can they learn to value new ways of thinking about things? How can I help them to grasp scientific ideas? How do learners feel uncomfortable with science?" (Shapiro, 1994, p. xv).

For successful constructivist teaching and learning to occur, the teacher must become perturbed, commit to change, envision the type of change preferred, plan for change, garner the support for pursuing the vision, and reflect consistently about the progress and perturbations encountered along the path toward change. Change is a slow and deliberate process; for students, constructivist learning requires patience, persistence, and respect for another's thinking (Shaw & Etchberger, 1993).

What Is Constructivism?

Video Summary

Learners' brains function in ways that make meaning. Constructivist classrooms encourage learners to make meaning from direct and meaningful experiences. Constructivist classrooms differ from traditional classrooms in appearance, intent and impact. The constructivist teacher emphasizes the development of thinking skills and development of conceptual understanding. The teacher engages learners with interesting challenges, interacts responsively during hands-on explorations and relies extensively on uses of manipulatives and primary sources of information. Group work is common and individuals compare and combine ideas to form explanations that describe their thinking about causes and effects. The teacher uses questions skillfully to seek students' points of view and to understand their present conceptions. Connections are made with prior lessons. Evaluation takes the form of both ongoing informal assessment during activity and summative measures focusing on student outcomes.

Tips for Viewing, Objectives, or What to Watch for

Keep in mind the following as you watch these videos:

+ Refer to "What Research Says," which provides a summary of principles that are compatible with how our brains function.

+ There are different interpretations about what constructivism is and how it may be used.

+ Refer to Figure 2.8.

Questions for Exploration

1. How do the video images compare to the descriptions of traditional and constructivist classrooms described in Figure 2.8?

2. How would you describe the behavior and relationship between the teacher and the students?

3. What relationships do you notice among the students? Do these relationships seem productive? Why?

4. What else might you expect to see in a classroom that would fit your image of a constructivist inquiry classroom?

Activity for Application

What is it about the constructivist learning model (shown in Figure 2.7) that differs from teaching and learning methods that you typically see in school classrooms? If you were using this model, what would you especially emphasize to ensure that learners were able to "make meaning" and what would you do to assure that their understandings were correct? How else might you teach a science lesson to emphasize constructivism and natural learning while including science attitudes, processes, and knowledge (Chapter 1)?

TRADITIONAL CLASSROOMS	CONSTRUCTIVIST CLASSROOMS
Curriculum	
• Presented part to whole; emphasis on basic skills	• Presented whole to part; emphasis on big concepts and thinking skills
• Fixed curriculum	• Responsive to student questions and interest
• Relies heavily on textbooks and workbooks	• Relies heavily on primary sources of data and manipulative materials
Role of students	
• "Blank slates" onto which information is etched by the teacher	• Thinkers with emerging theories about the world
• Work alone	• Work in groups
Role of teacher	
• Generally behaves in a didactic manner; disseminates information to students	• Generally behaves in an interactive manner; mediates the environment for students
• Seeks the correct anwer to validate student learning	• Seeks the students' point of view in order to understand students' present conceptions for use in subsequent lessons
Assessment	
• Viewed as separate from teaching: occurs almost entirely through testing	• Interwoven with teaching; occurs through teacher observations of students at work and through student exhibitions and portfolios

FIGURE 2.8 Traditional Versus Constructivist Classrooms

Source: D. C. Cantrell and P. A. Barron (Eds.). *Integrating Environmental Education and Science* (Newark, OH: Environmental Education Council of Ohio, 1994): 148.

Chapter Summary

This chapter is different from what you might find in textbooks on teaching science. We assume you have completed a course in psychology or educational psychology, maybe even a course in child development. Therefore, rather than revisit some theories you may have studied, we have recounted the emergent findings from brain research and the fundamental ideas behind the dominant belief about learning science from the perspective of a practicing teacher. How can we apply this dominant perspective on learning and teach science better?

No perspective on learning is complete without considering the potential of neural networks that arise through experiences and represent the ideas children bring to the classroom. These ideas represent preconceptions—conceptual understanding in the early stages of development—and misconceptions—conceptual understandings that do not agree with the concepts of the scientific community. These ideas are personal, may be contradictory when examined under a variety of circumstances, and are stubbornly rooted in children's minds. That their ideas may be resistant to change poses a big challenge for teachers.

Children's learning benefits from enriching experiences that helps to fulfill needs and must be considered and assimilated into a perspective on learning. As children develop over time, their needs change, and their exact cognitive capabilities are dynamic rather than static.

Experience is the one factor that unites the dominant perspectives on how children learn science. But not all experiences are equivalent, and experience alone is insufficient. Constructivists advocate several approaches for stimulating mental action and learning in conjunction with experience. These approaches stimulate inquiry, which is the foundation of science.

Constructivism is the contemporary concept we use to think about a child's learning. This perspective focuses on the child and what the child does during learning. It holds that knowledge cannot exist outside the mind of a learner, it cannot be directly transferred, and it must be each learner's construction of reality. The teaching recommendations offered should help you construct appropriate roles for yourself. If you follow these recommendations, you will find yourself covering less and guiding more, and your students will learn more in the deepest sense of the word. The chapter ends with discussion of the relationship of dissatisfaction, commitment, vision, and reflection as a process for becoming the type of science teacher you wish to be. We challenge you to envision the type of learning you wish for children and to construct a classroom that supports this vision.

Discussion Questions

1. In what ways do children benefit from learning through experience? What types of materials or problems are developmentally appropriate for children in the primary grades? For the intermediate grades? For middle school youth? What similarities and differences do you detect when you compare the materials and problems for each group?

2. As may be revealed by their prior ideas, how might children's science misconceptions affect how you teach? What can you do to learn about these prior ideas and to identify misconceptions? How do you think you can help children correct misconceptions?

Build a Portfolio or E-Folio

1. Select a few science concepts from your state's standards or from the *National Science Education Standards* (see the Appendix). Interview several children, perhaps from different age groups, to determine their ideas about the concepts. What are their misconceptions? What similarities or differences do you detect across the age groups? How do you think you can correct these misconceptions? What perspectives on learning would help with this task? You might try using Suchman's inquiry method (Chapter 6) and science discrepant events to encourage children to reveal their understanding.

2. Prepare a lesson designed to teach a particular science concept. What teaching and learning recommendations do you plan to use to help your learners be successful? Videotape your lesson as you teach it. Analyze the tape. How consistent were you in using the recommendations you selected? What do you plan to do to become the type of science teacher you prefer? What are your specific goals and action plan for accomplishing your goals?

Inquiry for All Children

*J*ulie B., a recent graduate from a liberal arts, teacher-preparation program, exuded confidence and passion for her first teaching position. Prior to the school year she decorated her classroom with colorful and interesting displays. Her first primary class was a dream come true after four and one-half years of preservice teacher preparation and a semester of substitute teaching.

The children's names and a review of records suggested she would have an enriched class. Julie's meeting with parents and children on the first day proved her hypothesis: Several ethnic groups and races were representative of the school's diverse community. Some spoke English as a second language, and a number of children came with Individualized Education Plans (IEPs) to help them overcome learning disabilities. The school was committed to inclusion. A few children's records suggested potential for giftedness.

The excitement of the new school year and the novelty of having a new teacher subsided after the first week. Toward the end of the first month Julie noted tensions among the children that she suspected were related to differences in culture, language, gender, and social class, and the children's self-perceived shortcomings in academic ability.

The autumn outdoor science projects did not progress as smoothly as Julie had planned; some children remarked that science was too difficult for them, and some of the boys stated with derision that girls couldn't do science. The children who had learning disabilities especially concerned her. Julie had been taught and passionately believed that all children could learn. She shared her concern with a veteran teacher: "How can I teach all children when the class is so diverse?" Many children exhibited low self-perception, language was a barrier for some, and those who had gifted talents were impatient and constantly asked questions that seemed to take her plans off track. She had also concluded that three students probably ought to be placed in a special class. Julie asked the advice of Mrs. Rice, an experienced colleague and a resource teacher. Mrs. Rice offered several practical suggestions. She gave further encouragement by sharing a story from her first years of teaching:

It had been at least seven years since my school had a science fair. Late in the fall I asked my principal if I could organize and sponsor a science fair for my class and the other students in grades four through six. My main concern was to get as many students as possible to follow a project through to completion so they could experience the reward of displaying their work. The principal immediately gave her permission and support.

My sixteen boys and one girl, aged eleven to thirteen, had reading abilities ranging from beginning first grade to high third grade. Their math skills were somewhat higher, and handwriting and spelling varied but were generally low.

According to intelligence test scores, these students had at least average potential, but they had not achieved at the same rate as most of their peers. They were placed in my class in order to receive special and individualized instruction.

The behavior and attitudes of children with learning disabilities have been described as impulsive, distractible, frustrated, stubborn, disruptive, defiant, obstinate, and extremely disorganized. One word I never used to characterize my students, though, was "unmotivated." Of course their motivation varied according to the activity at hand, but when their interest was roused, they really got into gear. Fortunately, my explanation of a science fair induced every member of the class to enter the project.

During the three months the school was involved in the science fair, I noticed some important changes in my own students and in other students and the faculty.

Learning-disabled children have difficulty getting along with one another in group situations. They are easily frustrated and tend to argue and become angry. Much to my surprise, however, this did not occur when my students worked on their science fair projects. I must stress the significance of this change in behavior. Naturally, it improved the quality of their work for the science fair, but it also demonstrated to me—and to them—that they could control themselves and cooperate to solve difficult problems.

While my students' perceptions of what they could do were changing, the attitudes of other students toward my class were also shifting. At the beginning, most of the other students in the school had little information about learning-disabled children. They only knew that my students were somehow different, and they usually called ours the "dummy class." I, of course, was the "dummies' teacher." But during preparations for the science fair, the perceptions of some of these other students began to change. They found it difficult to understand how a "dummy teacher" could run a science fair and why she'd want to. The fact that I seemed to be doing a good job created a halo effect that was important: As my image began to improve among students throughout the school, so did the image of my students. For the first time, members of my class began to develop friendships with other students.

Many teachers were as uninformed as their students about the limitations and the capabilities of learning-disabled children. These colleagues often viewed students in my class simply as behavior problems. This misapprehension was not necessarily the fault of the teachers, since many of them finished college before courses in special education and learning disabilities had become part of the curriculum.

I initiated our science fair with one goal—to have my students complete and display science projects. However, as preparations for the fair progressed, it became clear that my students were learning more than I had originally imagined possible. I was curious about their perceptions of what they were accomplishing, so I asked them.

My students did not doubt that they'd learned some valuable lessons by participating in the science fair and neither did I. In fact, it was clear that several important academic and personal goals could be accomplished by involving learning-disabled children in a science fair.

The school science fair was an extremely satisfying experience. Of the nine winners chosen by outside judges, four were from my learning-disabled class. And while getting prizes was exciting, equally important for my students were the intangible rewards of embarking on a joint enterprise with others, and discovering within themselves capabilities of which they had not been aware. (Rice, 1983, pp. 15–16)

Introduction

Have you ever heard someone reason: "If you can't walk, talk, or hear, or if you look or sound different, you must be intellectually and socially inferior"? Most physical differences have no connection to one's intellect or mental capability. The biases of our hypothetical conversationalist are based on two important factors: stereotypes and a lack of information. Stereotypical thinking caused the learners without disabilities in Ms. Rice's school to refer to her students as "dummies." An uninformed teacher can stifle the intellect by holding low expectations for children with learning disabilities. Without realizing just how unfairly their expectations may affect children, teachers may actually reinforce the wider perception that learners who have disabilities or are different in some other way are dummies, and this type of teacher behavior may tend to reinforce the prejudices held by others. Julie's desire to reach for help was wise. The challenges for teachers in knowing the right things to do increase as classrooms become more diverse.

Children with learning disabilities are only one example of students who have special needs. Each child is a special case and deserves special attention and encouragement. You will be in a better position to teach, to strike down unfair stereotypes, and to serve the needs of *all* learners if you become informed about the special needs many school children have. This will be a great service for all of your students and will especially benefit those who need special assistance.

This chapter is about teaching science to serve *all* children's needs. Technically, of course, all students are culturally different; each family is unique and has its own identity. The multicultural focus of this chapter explores the special needs of culturally diverse populations (groups of students with home environments very different from society's mainstream in terms of economics, ethnicity, religion, race, and/or language) and learners who have distinct disabilities (children with differences in vision, hearing, speech, emotions, giftedness, and so on). In both instances, the science teaching techniques we recommend to help the few students in your class who may have special needs will better serve the needs of all learners.

The chapter begins with an investigation of several general factors that impede science learning and provides teaching recommendations beneficial for all children and is built around the question of: "How can you teach science for all children?" After reading the first part of this chapter, you will be able to

1. describe the special needs of children who are members of minority groups, culturally different, and/or multilingual;
2. practice techniques that help meet their special needs;
3. promote gender equality in your classroom;
4. identify the different learning styles;
5. discuss management and teaching practices that encourage all learners.

The second part of this chapter should help you to

1. identify characteristics of the exceptional students who will enrich your classes;
2. practice classroom techniques that help meet these special needs.

The third part of this chapter explores ways to include parents in science teaching.

Science for All

Not all children come to school able to function effectively within a school's culture. Some children lack the skills necessary to cope with the routines or rigors of schooling. These children often feel hostile toward school and toward any authority figure, especially a teacher.

Being different carries liabilities. The price of being different may be exclusion from social groups at school and prejudiced treatment from those who appear not to be different. Cultural differences can contribute to the difficulties and problems of schoolchildren. The principles of cultural diversity and equity can help us meet the needs of all children (Krueger & Sutton, 2001).

Celebrating Diversity

All children are unique and culturally different. Children who are culturally different may include those of non-majority races or children who have special needs. Cultural differences may also include those of race, religion, economic level, ethnic background, the primary language used by the child, and in some instances gender. Hence, teachers must value the contributions and uniqueness of children from all backgrounds and be aware that a country's welfare is ultimately dependent upon the productivity of all its people. All children can learn and be successful in science and our nation must cultivate and harvest the minds of all children and provide the resources to do so (Kahn, 2003). In this spirit, the National Science Teachers Association (2000) urges that

- ✦ schools provide science education programs that nurture all children academically, physically, and develop a positive self-concept;
- ✦ children from all cultures have equal access to quality science education experiences that enhance success and provide the knowledge and opportunities for them to become successful participants in a democratic society;
- ✦ curricular content incorporate the contributions of many cultures to our knowledge of science;
- ✦ science teachers be knowledgeable about and use culturally-related ways of learning and instructional practices;
- ✦ science teachers accept the responsibility to involve culturally diverse children in science, technology and engineering career opportunities; and
- ✦ instructional strategies selected for use with all children recognize and respect the cultural differences students bring.

Although the challenge can be great, preparation in science can lead to higher paying careers, more critical thinkers, and a greater number of future technical workers who can fill vital vacancies and support our nation's economy (Linn, 1994).

Who Makes Up Culturally Diverse Populations? Often an African American child who is poor is envisioned as a typical example of one who is culturally different. This is an inaccurate stereotype of African Americans. Although the example does apply, culturally different children are as likely to come from the hills and mountains of Appalachia, Spanish-speaking communities of the Southwest, French settlements of the northernmost regions of Maine, or Asian communities of the West Coast. Let us not overlook the Native Americans who once were the majority on this land. They, too, are now culturally different from a changed mainstream society. In fact, each of us can become culturally different when we enter a community or region where our identity is not among the majority of the residents.

How Can You Use Cultural Differences to Promote Greater Science Understanding? Science classes can reflect greater cultural diversity if instruction reflects contributions made by people from all over the world. Often our print materials and media leave the impression that science is a recent white European construct. In fact, this impression is very wrong.

All children benefit from learning science.

Over 5,000 years ago in Egypt and Mesopotamia, copper was being extracted from its ores, glass was made, and fabrics were dyed with natural colors. . . . Iron swords are known to have been produced over 3,000 years ago. . . . Distillation was used in Mesopotamia as far back as 1200 B.C. for the production of perfumes. . . . Many of the techniques and much of the terminology of modern chemistry derives from ancient times; for example, *alkali* from the Arabic *al qality*—the roasted ashes; *soda* from Arabic *studa*—a splitting headache. (Williams, 1984, pp. 133–146)

You can promote diversity education in your science class by

✦ *Developing science themes related to conservation and pollution, disease, food and health, and population growth and teach with consideration for humankind as a whole.* Develop an understanding among your students about the interdependence of people and unequal distribution of natural resources.

✦ *Selecting classroom teaching examples that address the contributions and participation of people from a range of backgrounds, cultures, and genders.*

✦ *Considering carefully any issues of race, gender, and human origins by exploring the myths that surround them* (Antonouris, 1989, p. 98).

✦ *Challenging inaccurate statements students make about ethnic minority communities and people.* Statements may refer to different physical features, countries of origin, religion, language, and customs (Antonouris, 1989). For example, we have all heard myths about the strengths and weaknesses of blacks, Asians, women, and so on. As educated adults, we understand that these alleged qualities cannot be applied to a group and that beliefs like these arise from ignorance. We know that human beings are much more alike than they are different. Use science teaching as an opportunity to refute these myths when children repeat them.

How Can You Meet the Needs of Children from Diverse Backgrounds? All children seem to share some characteristics. Here are some tips for meeting the needs of culturally different children:

✦ *Share different activities.* What most of us take for granted may be completely lacking from the childhoods of children who are culturally different, minority, low income, or disabled. For example, herds of domestic animals, menageries of pets, and/or wild animals that roam at will may be as foreign to a city dweller as the piles of wind-tossed convenience packaging, crowds of densely packed people, and smog are to the rancher. Classroom activities, videos, and field trips with planned comparative discussions help to build awareness about and tolerance for differences by adding new experiences. Yet real experiences are a better choice. Activity-based science learning has long proven to help the students who are culturally different reach higher levels of science achievement, develop better process skills, and develop more logical thought processes (Bredderman, 1982).

✦ *Use science demonstrations rather than words.* Few children who are multilingual or multicultural will be patient enough to listen to long instructions or descriptions. Get to the point. Provide simple, direct demonstrations and concrete experiences. Indeed, all children benefit from clarity and directness.

◆ *Introduce science vocabulary.* Rough, blunt street talk or backwoods language of some children can cause quite a culture shock. In the same way, the child with limited English proficiency who speaks haltingly may have difficulty following a normal conversation. Children need a vocabulary suited to the mainstream if they are to become competitive in the workplace. Science offers abundant opportunities for developing vocabulary and effective communication skills.

◆ *Use simple, clear instructions.* Children can become frustrated and misunderstand the purpose of an activity if there are too many choices or if your instructions are too flexible. Some children may live in cultures in which they are not encouraged to make many of their own decisions. Be definite and clear with your instructions.

◆ *Develop genuine relationships.* Be empathetic rather than sympathetic. Looking down on the students' different social or economic standing is demeaning despite your best intentions.

◆ *Show children how to control their own results.* Poverty tends to produce feelings of hopelessness and desperation. Children who are culturally different, in the minority, low-income, or disabled may feel that they have little or no control over their lives and may look for immediate gratification. Fate control is defined as the belief that you can control what happens to you. Many children from culturally different backgrounds believe that what happens to them happens by chance or that their future lies in the hands of others who are more powerful and beyond influence. Science experiments help children to learn that variables can be manipulated to produce different outcomes. Educators have realized for decades that children can apply this understanding about variables to themselves and eventually use their understanding to help shift the locus of fate control to a point where they perceive the power to control their own lives (Rowe, 1974).

How Can You Help Non-English-Speaking Students?

Having a shortcoming in using the dominant spoken language may not indicate a lack of intelligence. It is possible that the non-English-speaking student possesses what Howard Gardner calls "linguistic intelligences," the capacity to use native language to express thinking and to understand other people (Checkley, 1997). Therefore, children can be helped if your efforts are focused upon helping them to use the second language proficiently. The following tips can assist non-English speakers in your classes.

Help Students to Help Themselves. Students will learn to help themselves from these approaches:

◆ *Distribute a vocabulary list and/or copy of the curriculum guide at the beginning of each unit.* This material helps students know exactly what will be expected of them and will give them additional time to master the difficult terms.

◆ *Ask students who are readers of their native language to carry pocket dictionaries (English-to-native language and vice versa).* At times, simple words create communication barriers. Pocket dictionaries can solve the problem and help create the self-sufficient habit of looking up unfamiliar words. English-speaking students can be encouraged to do the same as a way of learning words in another language.

◆ *Invite the students who are uncomfortable with English to ask questions.* This personal invitation, in a nonthreatening environment, will help students to overcome fear of using the new language. The joy of being successful at expressing opinions or asking questions becomes a positive reinforcer.

◆ *Be patient.* Wait-time is particularly important for multilingual speakers, to allow them to form their questions or answers.

◆ *Encourage the children to write their own translations of words in their notes.* As you examine lab notebooks and see translations, you will be aware that the student has looked up the words and probably understands them better.

◆ *Encourage students to read science articles and books in their own languages.* Additional supplemental readings such as those available from *Scholastic* provide brief, popular articles and photographs that encourage additional practice with the language.

I Hear and I Forget. For those times when you feel you must lecture, try the following techniques to help students remember (Kahn, 2003).

◆ *Speak slowly and enunciate clearly.* All students benefit from this because the technical words of science at times seem like a foreign language.

◆ *On the chalkboard or overhead projector, display an outline or definitions, descriptions, or figures to add meaning to your spoken words.*

◆ *Add emphasis to the main ideas.* Underline concepts or highlight the important meanings. Non-English speakers will remember to look them up later, while other students will treat the emphasis as a study cue.

I See and I Remember. A picture really is worth a thousand words. It provides another mode for learning, and it is helpful for memory retention. Try these suggestions:

◆ *Use visual aids as often as possible.* The problem in science education is deciding what to teach and what materials to use, not the availability of interesting, useful materials. Check the school district's resource center or curriculum library or the education resource co-op that serve your school. There is a wealth of films, videos, filmstrips, bulletin board ideas, computer programs, models, posters, and charts. Old, discarded science textbooks or magazines can be salvaged for useful visual aids.

◆ *Nurture animals and plants.* They add excitement and can also make superior visual aids.

◆ *Use artwork.* Add your own artwork and invite talented student artists to contribute to your notes, transparencies, learning activity illustrations, and lab activities. Stick figures with details are fine too.

I Do and I Understand. All three learning approaches—hearing, seeing, and doing—are important, especially when all five senses are stimulated. Combined approaches provide better opportunities for understanding than a single approach. The power of activity learning stimulates improved communication as well as greater levels of science achievement, process skill development, scientific attitudes, and logical thinking than traditional teaching, where teacher talk and student reading dominate (Shymansky, Kyle & Allport, 1982).

Demonstrate—Group Investigate—Individual Investigate Teaching Language Model.
By demonstrating a concept you create interest as well as stimulate curiosity. A demonstration gives students an opportunity to listen and observe before having to produce any language. Student group investigation can help learners comprehend and practice communication skills with peers. Language skills develop naturally as students observe and communicate with others. Independent individual student investigation helps students explore questions that are related to the concept that is already familiar to them. Table 3.1 provides some examples of this teaching and learning model.

✦ *Have students do hands-on, lab-type learning activities often.* The minds-on experiences that accompany hands-on learning can contribute to language and reading development. Some non-English-speaking students may not understand a lecture, discussion, or teacher demonstration, but once they have done it themselves, the experience is easier for them to link with language. Focus on one or two language functions that are particularly appropriate for the planned activities. "Language functions are

TABLE 3.1 Language Development Model

Teacher Demonstration	Group Investigation	Individual Investigation
Concept: **Electrical energy causes motion**.		
Use an inflated balloon to pick up small pieces of paper.	Use an inflated balloon to cause another balloon to move.	Use an inflated balloon to test what objects it will pick up.
Concept: **Rapid motion causes the temperature of objects to rise**.		
Rub a wooden block over sandpaper to show how the temperature of the block goes up.	Bend paper clip rapidly back and forth, and use cheeks to test for temperature change.	Find other objects (e.g., saw, chisel, file) outside the classroom that change temperature after rapid motion, and test them for temperature change.
Concept: **Animals move in different ways; some animals move by stretching**.		
Use earthworms to show how they move by stretching because they have no legs.	Observe earthworm activity when these are placed in a carton of soil.	Find examples of other animals without legs outside the classroom or in pictures. Name and classify them according to how they move.
Concept: **Rapidly moving air causes some objects to rise**.		
Hold a long piece of paper to the bottom lip and blow hard across the top of the paper to show how it moves up.	Blow hard across the top of a balloon, and then try to explain why it rises and what makes airplanes rise into the air.	Use a fan to see what objects you can lift up into the air.

Source: A. K. Fathman, M. E. Quinn, and C. Kessler, *Teaching Science to English Learners,* Grades 4–8 (Washington, DC: National Clearinghouse for Bilingual Education, 1992), p. 13 (ERIC Document Reproduction Service No. ED 349 844).

specific uses of language for accomplishing certain functions. . . . For example, *directing* (giving and following directions) may be emphasized in an activity where the teacher first gives directions on how to build a rocket" (Fathman, Quinn, & Kessler, 1992, p. 16) and then has students work in groups to direct each other in building their own paper rockets. Table 3.2 shows several language functions that are commonly used in science classrooms.

✦ *Coordinate your teaching with the English as a Second Language (ESL) teacher.* Blend the grammar and vocabulary used in both classes so the students have a double exposure to the science vocabulary.

✦ *Link science concepts with the students' background experiences.* Learn what you can about the children's countries of origin and refer to geographical locations, climate conditions, fauna and flora, and so on to link new science concepts with what the students already know. For example, always mention the Rocky Mountains or the Mississippi River. The rest of the class will benefit from the geography enrichment.

✦ *Use appropriate guest speakers and field trips.* These additions will help multilingual students become more accepted and feel at home in their new environment and with science. Include all children in the full range of activities. Invite speakers from the students' countries of origin to help classmates become familiar with people from other cultures.

Try to Reduce Test Anxiety. Children from other countries often attach more importance to testing and achievement than native-born American children might. The mere mention of a test can evoke much anxiety because of its importance in determining children's academic futures, and a test in English can pump anxiety to counterproductive levels. The following suggestions offer some ideas for reducing test anxiety:

✦ *Try puzzles.* Crossword puzzles assist spelling and provide additional cues for correct answers. Students seem to do better when they know how many letters to expect in an answer. A list of words helps, too, for crosswords and fill-in-the-blank questions.

TABLE 3.2 Language Functions

Language functions are specific uses of language for accomplishing certain purposes. Teachers can help students develop an understanding of these functions by building them into their lessons. Verbal ("What to Discuss") and written ("What to Record") exercises can be included in teacher demonstrations and student group and individual investigations.

Directing	Refusing	Describing	Disagreeing
Praising	Requesting	Accepting	Expressing opinions
Advising	Cautioning	Questioning	Defining
Agreeing	Suggesting	Encouraging	

Source: A. K. Fathman, M. E. Quinn, and C. Kessler, *Teaching Science to English Learners,* Grades 4–8 (Washington, DC: National Clearinghouse for Bilingual Education, 1992), p. 13 (ERIC Document Reproduction Service No. ED 349 844).

◆ *Encourage children to draw.* Invite children to draw answers rather than write. This is a good way to communicate ideas as the child gets around the temporary language barriers.

◆ *Encourage students to check their work.* At the end of each test, consider allotting 3 to 5 minutes for students to check answers. Permit them to use books, notes, and class handouts.

◆ *Try bonus points for extra credit.* Offer bonus points for student creations. Science-oriented jokes, riddles, poems, and songs that use the concepts and vocabulary being studied can be a great way to encourage review and creativity. Permitted as homework, creations for extra points can be a good way to promote language study between the child and parents.

Is Gender Equality a Special Need?

Females do not have equal access to nor do they receive equal encouragement to pursue careers in science. This appears to be a cultural problem linked to how females are socialized in the mainstream of society; it is not a women's problem. Often males and females, by age 11, have developed strong sex-stereotyped attitudes concerning socially appropriate behavior and gender roles in society (Chivers, 1986). Although improvements have been made, many people still attribute cultural differences to gender. Cultural gender differences play an important role in career selection.

How Does Culture Affect Females in Science? There are cultural disincentives for women to pursue careers in science, technology, and mathematics. Proportionally fewer women and minorities have been encouraged to develop a sufficient background for scientific careers, and they are underrepresented in these careers, although more women are employed in science careers today than during the prior decade.

Females now receive equal encouragement and access to science.

The current problem of gender inequity has arisen from several factors; some still persist despite the enlightened efforts or many to improve conditions and to encourage more females to pursue science. Consider:

◆ Parents, teachers, school counselors, and peers discourage females from pursuing scientific careers (Elfner, 1988).

◆ Most early childhood elementary teachers are women who lack strong background in science; their lack of confidence can reinforce children's beliefs that women are not supposed to like science (Chivers, 1986; Shepardson & Pizzini, 1992).

◆ A shortage of appropriate female science and engineering role models reinforces the belief that science is a male domain (Jones & Wheatley, 1988; Hammrich, 1997).

How Can You Teach Science for All Children?

by Joan M. Yospin
Grade 5, Franklin Elementary School, Newton, Massachusetts

Science, more than any other subject allows children to connect to their own lives, something essential to involvement, interest, and motivation. Beginning the school year with a study of some aspect of our planet—climate regions, topographical features, oceans, rivers, ponds, or forests—lets children connect their own life to the greater environment. Some have visited mountains, some have been to the city park, but all are aware of local plant and animal life, and can understand where they might expect to find similar life forms. Children are fascinated to learn of their close connection to our planet; that their bodies contain proportionally as much water as Earth is often a new idea, and helps them see that they are special beings, uniquely suited to living in their environment. That life forms are suited to the place where they live is meaningful to all children, regardless of gender, race, or language spoken at home. Most are eager to participate in reflective discussions about their place in the world.

Any of the big "why" questions produce similar interest and involvement: Why is the sky blue? Why are leaves green? Why are the days longer in the summer? Some students may have no idea of the reasons, some may provide partial information, some may have long, involved misconceptions that they share with the class. Discussing and getting some to think about the questions is a goal for my science classroom. Students who do not speak English or are very quiet may be left out of discussions unless they are provided with interpreters or pocket dictionaries (and help to use those dictionaries), so it is important to have frequent discussions, and keep them short.

Exposure to the language and to the vocabulary of science is helpful to non-English speakers; many of my ESL students copy words from the board, and discuss the vocabulary at home with their parents. All students keep an "interactive notebook," or science journal, where they record ideas and vocabulary that are discussed in class. The left side of the page is for the student's own use of symbols, drawings, or words that will help them remember the vocabulary or idea that is written on the right side of the page. Students should come away from a 10-minute discussion with a written record, and with the idea that exchange of ideas and brainstorming are valued as part of scientific inquiry. Not all students will have a chance to participate during each short session, so the teacher must not allow one student or group of students to monopolize the time. Students must understand that everyone's ideas and opinions are welcome, and needed by the group, but that proceeding to the day's hands-on activity limits the time for discussion.

Science is "asking and doing," and focusing on an area of earth science—pond life, for example, or earthworms—allows students to learn more about a particular environment, while developing science process skills. The manner in which a topic is presented and students are asked to approach its study can insure that all students are interested and involved. Science lessons must focus on developing the investigative skills that will be used at any level of scientific inquiry, and that will be valuable tools throughout life. Observing, recording, formulating questions, making predictions, drawing inferences, and classifying are process skills that must be practiced and developed regardless of the topic; the topic is the frame inside of which the skills are practiced.

A trip to a pond lets children observe that environment; making a sketch and detailed drawings of

✦ Young males report more positive attitudes toward science and young females less positive attitudes; females report less confidence and more fear of success in careers like engineering; females report that physics courses are too difficult (Jones & Wheatley, 1988; Kahle & Rennie, 1993; Hammrich, 1997).

plants, insects, or the surface of the pond are ways to gather and record data. If there is no pond or puddle to observe, the teacher can provide pond water and examples of plant life for a "classroom pond" in an aquarium. Field guides can be used to identify plants, either at the pond or back in the classroom. Students who are gifted at drawing and those who have made detailed observations use those strengths to advantage. Students who do not speak English can excel at detailed drawings, and share their work with others who have the skills to use a field guide. In this way, students learn to draw on individual strengths and work cooperatively with others.

Working together is not only acceptable in science learning, it is essential. When microscopes or other science materials must be shared, students need to take turns, express their findings verbally, and help one another. Assigning roles in a group helps students understand the tasks that must be done, and gives them an opportunity to gain skill in different roles. The recorder does the drawings, or makes the tally marks, for the group; the equipment manager gathers the materials for the group; the messenger asks questions, or shares information with other groups. Next time, each student will be assigned a different job. Students who have strong skills in one or another area have a chance to model those skills for others, and practice in areas where their skills are weaker. Working cooperatively is a life skill, valued in the workplace as well as in the family and classroom. Physically handicapped, severely learning disabled, and non-English speaking students may not be able to perform their job without assistance, but assistance is at their side, provided by other members of the group as needed.

Working in pairs is another technique to ensure that all students develop needed skills, and varying the partnerships keeps students interested. Girls are often more interested in keeping peace with a part

ner, or getting to know someone new, than finishing an assigned task. Boys may not have strong relational skills, and may be more task oriented. Same-sex partnerships can give girls the opportunity to get into a task, where a male partner might upstage them. Girls who are used to taking a backseat may be thrilled to have the job "all to themselves," or they may need encouragement to get started. Boys paired with boys have to listen to each other, and work together to accomplish a task. It is important to create mixed gender partnerships, too, because that is what one finds in the "real world"—men and women working together as equals.

One of my most successful partner activities has been a Mystery Skulls observation lesson, done during our study of the human body, with our first-grade buddies. Together, as cross-age pairs, the students handle and make observations about several animal skulls, draw a skull, and discuss what kind of animal they think it is. Fifth graders are full of pride as they ask their young buddies questions about placement of the eye sockets, or call attention to the animal's teeth. They are making inferences about what the animal eats, whether it is a predator, and practicing questioning skills. Being a teacher is satisfying for us; it is an equally satisfying feeling for a ten-year-old.

Hands-on activities, partner work, animated discussions, group presentations—these are the methods science teachers use to insure success for all their students. Not every student will be fully engaged by every lesson, but a variety of working arrangements and levels of activity, and opportunities to go beyond assigned work, such as researching an area of interest or point of contention in the library, or on the Internet, will help learners achieve the habits of mind and process skills necessary for success in science study.

✦ Females may not be socialized at home or at school to develop and demonstrate scientific skills and may not be encouraged to develop practical ability, independence, and self-confidence. Several studies reveal that skills and characteristics associated with scientists are those often attributed to masculine character: high intellectual ability, persistence at work, extreme independence, and apartness from others. Females may be hesitant to pursue science because they fear that they will be considered unfeminine (Jones & Wheatley, 1988; Shepardson & Pizzini, 1992; Hammrich, 1997). Even the toys typically given to boys require more assembly and manipulation than the toys given to girls.

✦ When women have problems, they tend to blame themselves for the problems or the inability to solve them, whereas when men have difficulties, they tend to place the blame outside themselves. These differences can tend to develop female feelings of learned helplessness and may cause females to believe that they are not intellectually capable (Jones & Wheatley, 1988).

✦ Teachers reflect the values and expectations thrust upon them by the dominant society and can unintentionally perpetuate sex stereotypes in science. In addition, sex bias can be observed in the practices of teachers and the assignments of science teachers. Female science teachers usually are assigned to introductory science classes and biology, whereas males more often are high school department chairmen and are assigned to teach such advanced science classes as chemistry and physics (Jones & Wheatley, 1988; Kahle & Rennie, 1993).

How Do Teachers Contribute to Gender Problems in Science? Although the role of teachers perpetuating sex-role stereotypes has not been fully explored, the literature indicates that teachers are not consciously and intentionally sex stereotyping students. Many teachers do try to treat males and females fairly and equally. Often teachers say that they want all children to develop to their full potential. However, parents, school counselors, other teachers, social workers, books, and television have taught teachers (even you!) that certain behaviors are appropriate for females and others are appropriate for males (Sadker, Sadker, & Thomas, 1981; Shepardson & Pizzini, 1992; Hammrich, 1997; Pollina, 1995; Shakeshaft, 1995). Bias by gender will begin to change only when you are able to recognize the subtle messages that steer males and females toward particular behaviors and career choices.

Considerable evidence indicates that teachers' expectations affect students' performances and that elementary teachers often perceive males to have higher scientific ability than females. This perception usually sends a negative message to females, influences the self-perceptions of females, and determines the tasks and responsibilities that teachers assign to students during scientific activities (Shepardson & Pizzini, 1992). More likely, females are given passive roles to perform during group activities (Baker, 1988; Kahle, 1990; Shakeshaft, 1995), which reinforce teachers' perceptions that females are less interested and less capable in science (Shepardson & Pizzini, 1992). Cooper's model (1979) is based on this evidence and explains how sex differences in achievement may stem from differences in teacher expectations (see Figure 3.1). The model, which consists of the following steps, can be useful for overcoming gender stereotypes:

Step 1. Form different expectations for students.

Regardless of gender, hold high but realistic expectations for all students.

Step 2. Believe that females are capable in science.

Do not assign class roles or jobs based on beliefs that females are better note takers and writers and males are better handlers of equipment.

FIGURE 3.1   Overcoming
Gender Stereotypes

```
┌─────────────────────────────────┐
│          Expectation:           │
│   Expect all students to do well,│
│         despite gender.          │
└─────────────────────────────────┘

┌──────────────────────┐         ┌──────────────────────┐
│    Self-motivation:   │         │      Perception:      │
│ Motivate females toward higher  │  Perceive no difference in │
│ levels through positive and     │  capability of students,   │
│ successful experiences.         │  irrespective of gender.   │
└──────────────────────┘         └──────────────────────┘

┌──────────────────────┐         ┌──────────────────────┐
│Influence through attention:│    │       Feedback:       │
│ Boost females' self-esteem and  │ Encourage females to take the │
│ increase their confidence about │ lead, manipulate equipment,   │
│ their capabilities in science.  │ and make decisions.           │
└──────────────────────┘         └──────────────────────┘
```

Step 3. Encourage females to take the lead in activities, to make lab decisions, to take measurements and handle equipment.

Do the same for males, but without leading them to believe they are better at it than females.

Step 4. Strive for equal amounts and types of nurturant contact with females and males.

Several studies in preschool and elementary classrooms indicate that males often receive more attention from teachers and more feedback about their performance (Jones & Wheatley, 1988; Shepardson & Pizzini, 1992). Added attention can bolster student beliefs about the importance of their effort and encourage them to work harder.

Step 5. Provide opportunities for success.

As children master classroom tasks, they become more motivated to strive for even higher quality. Females will undertake and excel at physical science study instead of achieving dramatically less than males do by the seventh grade.

What Can You Do to Overcome Gender Inequality in Science? The earlier a teacher can address gender bias, the better chances of having an impact. From early childhood, males are often treated as if they are expected to be more independent, creative, and manipulative. These early experiences may affect their development of spatial and verbal abilities (Levine & Ornstein, 1983). Males often have more opportunities to experience science-oriented activities than females, although females have the interest to become more involved in science, if given the opportunity (Kahle & Lakes, 1983; Kahle

& Rennie, 1993; Shakeshaft, 1995). To help promote gender equality in your science class include the following:

✦ *Strengthen your science preparation.* Particularly if you are a female, strive to strengthen your experience with science. Project the importance of science for all students; do not suggest that science is risky for women. Your attitude toward the subject will have a powerful effect on all the children.

✦ *Strive to become aware of your own subtle biases and different expectations for students.* Examine how you assign classroom tasks and the daily life examples you use of science at work for evidence of subtle gender bias.

✦ *Experiment with single-sex class groups.* Until you can create and maintain a non-sexist learning environment, females may receive less-biased treatment if they are not paired with males for small-group activities. Females in mixed groups have been found to spend more time than males watching and listening, whereas in same-sex groups females spend the same amount of time as males in same-sex groups on hands-on science processes and experimental tasks (Rennie & Parker, 1986; Shepardson & Pizzini, 1992; Rop, 1998).

✦ *Expect the same from females as from males.* Examine your reinforcement for equality, fairness in discipline, and encouragement of nonverbal behavior toward females, especially during science class. Ensure that females participate fully in all science activities.

✦ *Be aware of the difficulties some females may experience when using equipment unfamiliar to them.* Logical-mathematical, spatial, and bodily kinesthetic intelligences (Gardner, 1983) are essential in science; however, they are not confined to one gender. Rather, differences in social expectations often lead parents to give different types of toys to boys and girls and encourage different types of social interactions through games and sports. Young males are often encouraged to manipulate objects that are very similar to the tools and equipment of science. Young females may not have been encouraged by their parents to use a variety of tools and could have some initial difficulty with science equipment. A little extra time and encouragement early on will help females build their confidence so they can cope easily (Pollina, 1995) and develop important skills.

✦ *Hands-on learning is a great equalizer.* Science process-oriented learning tasks help females to acquire manipulative experiences that put them on par with males, making access to science learning more equal (Humrich, 1988; Shepardson & Pizzini, 1992).

✦ *Treat science as gender-free.* Do not always refer to scientists as males; lift up female scientists as role models.

✦ *Invite female science role models.* Males will be well served too, because they will see new opportunities for females.

✦ *Help female students develop personal characteristics that are associated with success in science.* Encourage them to break away from any submissive behavior patterns and encourage them to become more independent and self-reliant. Also encourage females to explore new topics and materials and to test out their new ideas and interests (Kahle & Rennie, 1993; Shepardson & Pizzini, 1992).

✦ *Screen teaching materials.* Examine all print materials and media for gender bias. Posters, textbooks, filmstrips, and other media should have equal representations of males and females.

Anna Pollina (1995) offers specific actions in Table 3.3 to help you bring gender balance to your science lessons.

TABLE 3.3   Bringing Gender Balance to Your Science Lessons

Despite change efforts for more than a decade, females are greatly underrepresented in fields such as physical sciences, engineering, and technology. Past efforts that have attempted to increase female involvement in the sciences ranged from awareness programs in elementary schools to direct intervention at the collegiate level. Often the change efforts attempted to "masculinize" the females—to help them participate in the sciences by becoming more aggressive, more analytical, emotionally tougher, and more competitive. These efforts yielded spurious results; decreases in female self-esteem were recorded. Anna Pollina reports ten recent successful and proven strategies, based on research, that celebrate the characteristics that many females bring to science, which are vital to science and science education.

1. *Connect science and technology to the real world.* Connecting any subject to the lives of real people and the good of the world is a powerful hook for females.

2. *Choose metaphors carefully, and have students develop their own.* In the past we have asked females to "tackle" problems, used "batting averages" to illustrate points, and have used the "paths of rockets" to demonstrate principles of physics. Use images of science that are more comfortable for females. This is more than political correctness—it is essential.

3. *Foster an atmosphere of collaboration.* Turn taking in small groups of circled students is not collaboration. Small groups work for females if all group members are taught to listen, be respectful, be noncompetitive, and are held responsible for one another's learning.

4. *Encourage females to act as experts.* Females begin to see themselves as scientists when the group is responsible for verifying its own logic, and when the students are responsible for critiquing their own work as well as the work of their peers.

5. *Give females the opportunity to be in control of technology.* Expect females to share in the uses of technology, to demonstrate its uses to others, to complete basic repairs, and to deal with simple emergencies.

6. *Portray technology as a way to solve problems.* Females most often use technology as a tool rather than as a toy. One way to help them see that technology is relevant to their lives is to emphasize the networking and communications capabilities. Pairing females can help to create a comfortable, supportive way to use the technology.

7. *Capitalize on females' verbal strengths.* Encourage all students to express the logic for their choices and solutions in spoken, written, or picture form. Proofs should be well-constructed, complete arguments.

8. *Experiment with testing and evaluation.* Embedded assessments work well for females. These are alternatives to right/wrong choices and make use of females' abilities to synthesize material, make connections, and use their practical intelligence. Some examples could be working in groups to perform experiments, identify patterns, hypothesize outcomes.

9. *Give frequent feedback, and keep expectations high.* Females may tend to need more encouragement than males in science. You can do this by giving frequent feedback such as homework checks, quizzes, and comments that reinforce the students' beliefs in their control over the material.

10. *Experiment with note-taking techniques.* Females are dutiful learners who can become so absorbed in the task of note taking that they miss opportunities to become involved in important discussions. Try "no-note-taking-allowed" times, distribute written summaries, or have diagrams and figures on file for learners to access when they are needed.

Source: A. Pollina, "Gender Balance: Lessons from Girls in Science and Mathematics," *Educational Leadership 53*, 1 (1995): 30–33.

Similarities in Learning

Children from other cultures or who are not English speakers benefit from specific management and teaching techniques. Indeed, most children can benefit from the suggestions recommended for special groups of learners. Children benefit when they are taught with the learning styles they prefer (Krueger & Sutton, 2001).

Multiple Intelligences and Learning Styles. Multiple Intelligences (MI) is a popular psychological and educational concept that embodies an effort to understand how cultures and disciplines shape human potential by studying how individual learners respond to different types of content and solve problems or construct something that is valued (Checkley, 1997). Eight intelligences are recognized: linguistic, logical-mathematics, spatial, bodily kinesthetic, musical, interpersonal, intrapersonal, and naturalist. Each intelligence has a particular representation in the brain and each individual may be particularly good or impaired in one or more of these intelligences (Gardner in Checkley, 1997). Multiple Intelligences is focused on content or products of learning (Silver et al., 1997), whereas learning styles focus upon the processes of learning—the ways learners think and feel as they solve problems, interact, and create products that represent learning (Silver et al., 1997).

The concept of learning styles arises from the general acceptance that we all learn in a variety of ways (processes), that those ways can be identified, and that teachers can teach in ways that capitalize on student preferences. If they begin from a position of strength (preferred learning style), learners can be exposed to other ways of learning and expand their repertoires as they overcome weaknesses.

Teaching to accommodate different learning styles helps teachers reach each individual. Students who need special assistance receive instruction through their preferred learning style during the intervention process. Children learn about how they learn and are encouraged to use their strengths. All benefit from the variety of approaches. Teachers also plan instruction carefully to make certain that all children have an opportunity to learn through their own preferred styles.

Children perceive in different ways and prefer various learning environments.

Types of Styles. Learning styles are often classified by function. As learners, we have different modes of perception, we prefer various environments, we are motivated by different things, we express ourselves uniquely, we think differently, and we prefer various levels of mobility as we learn. True individualization is a challenge. At least nine learning styles can be identified by function (Dunn & Dunn, 1975) and are considered widely representative of children's preferences for processing information:

1. *Visual*—prefer to perceive by reading and seeing words, numbers, charts, models, and objects.
2. *Auditory*—prefer to perceive meaning by hearing and listening.
3. *Bodily kinesthetic*—prefer tactile, hands-on involvement.
4. *Individual learners*—prefer to work alone. This type of student may be more confident in his or her own opinion than in the ideas of others.
5. *Group learners*—prefer to learn with at least one other child.
6. *Oral expressive*—can easily speak or explain their ideas and opinions. They may know more than they can reveal on a written test.
7. *Written expressive*—write fluent essays or good answers on tests. Their thoughts are organized better on paper than they are presented orally.
8. *Sequential*—have the ability to arrange thoughts and ideas in a linear, organized fashion.
9. *Global*—have the ability to be spontaneous, flexible thinkers. These learners may be quiet and intuitive and order their thoughts randomly, preferring to do things their own way.

All learners do not fit exclusively into one style and an outstanding performance using one or more of these styles may indicate a strong, specialized intelligence. Many children may share strong preferences among several styles. All students can be served better when learning opportunities are provided in multisensory, multiexpressive, and multienvironmental modes. The following suggestions can help a wide variety of learners, particularly those who have special needs.

✦ *Establish classroom and study routines.* Many children are unable to organize unaided, and traditional school learning cannot occur until organization is established. You can provide a helpful model for children if you are well organized and consistent in your classroom. Children will then know what to do and how to do it.

✦ *Limit choices.* Democratic learning and cooperative learning encourage choices, but this approach may not help children who get confused easily. Asking "Would you like to . . ." implies choice. As an example, if your intention is to have a child put science equipment back on the storage shelf or follow a specific instruction, it is better for the child if your instructions are explicit and/or provide limited choices.

✦ *Make certain the children are attending to what is going on.* Asking students to repeat instructions or information, requesting a response to a specific question, requiring that a child complete a specific motor task, and maintaining eye contact are some ways to determine the extent to which a child may be attending. Focus on each child often.

✦ *Give clues to help remembering.* Use mnemonic devices, rhymes, auditory associations, linking associations, and visual clues to help the child remember. Help the children construct personal memory devices.

✦ *Sequence instruction carefully.* Concept mapping and task analysis can help you to find the most logical sequence of any task. The four Ws help to begin a task analysis: *what* to teach, *where* to begin, *when* the objective has been met, and *what* to teach next. Figure 3.2 provides a more detailed model for analyzing and determining the sequence for science concepts.

FIGURE 3.2 Concept Analysis Model for Teaching Children Who Have Special Needs

Source: Adapted from "Concept Analysis: A Model for Teaching Basic Science Concepts to Intellectually Handicapped Students" by Jack T. Cole, Margie K. Kitano, and Lewis M. Brown in Marshall E. Corrick, Jr. (Ed.), *Teaching Handicapped Students* (Washington, DC: NEA, 1981), p. 52. Reprinted with permission.

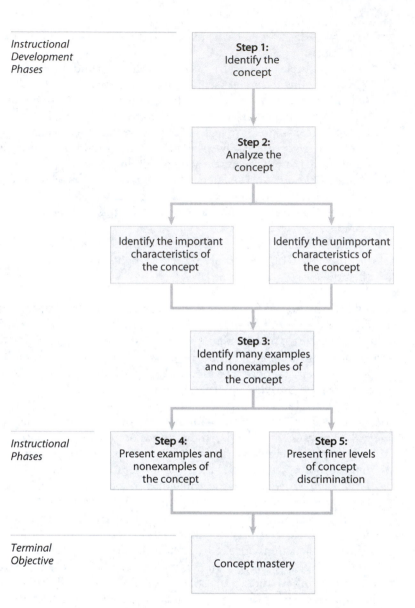

Instructional Development Phases

Step 1: Identify the concept

Step 2: Analyze the concept

Identify the important characteristics of the concept

Identify the unimportant characteristics of the concept

Step 3: Identify many examples and nonexamples of the concept

Instructional Phases

Step 4: Present examples and nonexamples of the concept

Step 5: Present finer levels of concept discrimination

Terminal Objective

Concept mastery

✦ *Separate teaching and testing.* Use worksheet assignments as a type of reinforcement activity, and not as a test. Provide instructional assistance to encourage learning and to help lower the failure rate. An example at the top of a worksheet or a list of guiding questions can transform the assignment from a test into a learning task. Also provide models, cues, verbal and written prompts, and correct answers as feedback.

✦ *Be specific with criticism and praise.* Tell the child exactly why a response is correct or wrong. When part of an answer is correct, tell the child; also identify what is not correct.

✦ *Provide time clues.* Some children may have difficulty remembering time sequences, estimating time intervals, and determining the amount of time needed to complete tasks. By routinely displaying schedules in prominent places and referring to time in the classroom, you can help students learn to structure their school work.

✦ *Confer with special education teachers, second-language teachers, and gifted and talented coordinators.* Continuity of content and consistency of management and routines help many children. Coordinate your classroom activities with those of other classes the child attends.

✦ *Show empathy, encouragement, sensitivity, and understanding for each child's attempts to learn, to remember, and to conform to your routines.* Point out the child's abilities and respect the child as a human being.

✦ *Provide kinesthetic experiences, practical hands-on learning activities with concrete, relevant materials.* Children who are experience-deficient will benefit, as will children who prefer this type of learning. Hands-on experiences stimulate minds-on learning.

✦ *Identify desired behaviors, set clear expectations, and reduce distractions.*

✦ *Simplify.* Break each task down into its simplest steps; assist the students with step-by-step instructions.

✦ *Give frequent feedback.* Small improvements deserve praise, and precise direction helps children continue to improve.

✦ *Use the preferred learning mode.* If the child has a dominant mode of learning (visual, tactile, auditory), use it. Regard the preference as a strength and try to build success on it. Then use this preference to help build self-esteem on successes before tackling learning weaknesses.

Science for Exceptional Children

Public Law 94–142 of 1975 (Education for All Handicapped Children Act) was part of a federal law (Individuals with Disabilities Education Act, IDEA) that helped to ensure a place for students with disabilities in American public schools. This law was amended in 1990 and again in 1997. IDEA ensures that all children with disabilities have the right to a free, appropriate public education. The law includes specific categories of disability: deafness, hearing disability, mental retardation, orthopedic impairment, other health impairment, serious emotional disturbance, specific learning disability, speech impairment, and visual impairment.

The "least restrictive environment" is encouraged so that students with disabilities are educated in regular classrooms where appropriate. Placement decisions are based on extensive assessment, parental consent, and decision making among school personnel that must follow due process of law.

The presence of students with disabilities in regular classrooms does not mean that the curriculum must be the same for all children. Federal law states that the schooling of children with disabilities must be differentiated according to their special needs and provided with necessary support. This may require a degree of individualized education not usually found in typical classrooms. The Individualized Education Program (IEP) prescribes goals for the school year based on present performance levels, specific educational services the school must provide, the extent to which the student participates in the regular classroom, and schedules and procedures for evaluation. Indeed, many educators believe the intent of the IEP benefits all children. Table 3.4 provides a brief description of adaptations that help students who have special needs.

Teaching Children Who Have Learning Disabilities

A child with a learning disability has the intellectual potential to succeed in school. But for some reason, the child's academic achievements are significantly below the expected level of performance in a specific subject, such as reading or mathematics. Krueger and Sutton (2001) suggest that restricted access to science causes this difference. Understanding learner needs and modifying lessons can help children succeed.

A child can be identified as having a learning disability if a school evaluation team finds a severe discrepancy between the child's achievement and intellectual ability in one or more of these areas: oral expression, listening comprehension, written expression, basic reading skill, reading comprehension, and mathematics calculation (Hallahan & Kauffman, 2000). The child may perform at or above the expected level in some school subjects but poorly in others. When this happens it is especially frustrating for the child and makes identification of the disability difficult. The child may develop failure-avoidance techniques that surface as behavior problems to draw attention away from areas of academic failure.

Over 10 percent of U.S. students have a disability who are served by an IEP (Krueger & Sutton, 2001), and at least 5 percent of school-age children have learning disabilities (Hallahan & Kauffman, 2000). The number of school children who have a learning disability has increased over time, in part because of greater sensitivity in assessment and diagnosis, teacher alertness for possible learning disabilities, and increases in poverty. For example, the number of children who live in poverty has increased from 15 to 19 percent since the 1970s (U.S. Department of Education, 1977; Hallahan & Kauffman, 2000). Nationwide, nearly 30 percent of the students who receive special education services attend regular classrooms (Hallahan & Kauffman, 2000).

Learning disabilities are not diseases. There is no single learning disability. Disabilities include dysgraphia, disorders in written language; dyscalculia, disorders in arithmetic; dyslexia, disorders in receptive and expressive language and reading; and difficulties in perception of spatial relations and organization. Some famous people who have had learning disabilities include Thomas Edison, Albert Einstein, Winston Churchill, Cher, and Tom Cruise.

Exceptional children learn science with the proper type of support and encouragement.

TABLE 3.4 Teaching Children Who Have Special Needs

Special Need	Environmental Adaptation	Materials Adaptation	Teaching Adaptation	Assessment Adaptation
Cultural	Carefully select visuals and non-print materials for cultural inclusion. Represent plural culture. Maintain clear classroom organization. Establish empathic relationships.	Use culturally representative materials. Avoid cultural stereotypes. Use broad themes to include all cultures.	Set explicit expectations, and give explicit instructions. Use divergent questions to encourage pluralism and inclusion. Challenge inaccurate statements. Include careful consideration of issues. Use experience-rich methods.	Provide and accept diverse contexts for assessment activities.
Non-English-speaking	Be patient. Use visual aids to help communicate. Provide direct experience. Encourage high levels of activity.	Maintain a conceptual focus. Enrich vocabulary development.	Be verbally clear. Maintain written clarity; use outlines. Emphasize concepts. Link concepts to experiences. Use guest speakers and field trips. Reduce test anxiety.	Encourage the use of pocket translators and dictionaries. Use pictorial assessment devices, puzzles, and performance tasks.
Gender	Nurture independence and self-confidence. Use hands-on learning activities. Use female role models in the sciences.	Identify and eliminate gender bias in materials. Use a wide variety of manipulatives.	Experiment with heterogeneous and single-sex grouping. Use cooperative learning techniques. Maintain high but realistic expectations for all. Provide frequent progress feedback.	None
Learning style preferences	Include all styles.	Select a balance of visual, auditory, kinesthetic, oral, and written materials.	Provide activities to match preference for individual, group, sequential, visual, verbal, auditory, and global learners.	Assess concepts through verbal, written, kinesthetic, individual, and group opportunities.

(continued)

TABLE 3.4 Teaching Children Who Have Special Needs (continued)

Special Need	Environmental Adaptation	Materials Adaptation	Teaching Adaptation	Assessment Adaptation
Learning disability	Show empathy. Seat away from distractions during introduction and when giving instructions. Focus attention by putting with well-behaved student for activity	Use concrete manipulatives. Screen out irrelevant materials and distractions.	Show clear expectations. Simplify; give cues and specific praise. Use dominant learning mode and multisensory activities. Use concept analysis.	Provide specific criticism and praise. Try oral tests. Modify reading and writing exercises if needed.
Cognitive visability	Limit visual and verbal distractions.	Select appropriate reading level. Use concrete, relevant manipulatives.	Use concept analysis. Simplify. Praise. Use repetition. Maintain eye contact. Engage in physical activity. Give feedback, use cues, cooperative learning. Use examples and non-examples. Use brief periods of direct instruction.	Verbal tests. Provide assistance with written tests. Provide small-step progress checks.
Visual	Provide clear, predictable traffic pathways. Maintain organized, predictable locations for materials and storage. Provide good lighting. Seat student near activity. Sighted student tutor can assist.	Use voice tapes and audiotapes. Print materials should be large, clear, and uncluttered with numerous colors and geometric designs. Adapt materials to special equipment students may have to use.	Emphasize uses of other senses. Taped instructions or science information can be provided. Pair with sighted students.	More verbal assessment. Assist with written assessment. Assist with physical manipulation of objects during performance assessment.

Special Need	Environmental Adaptation	Materials Adaptation	Teaching Adaptation	Assessment Adaptation
Hearing	Seat so vision is not obstructed. Seat away from distracting background noises.	Modify for making observations through other senses. Use captioned films and videos. Use printed text to accompany audiotapes. Model or illustrate spoken instructions.	Face the child when speaking. Speak distinctly; do not shout. Use written outlines.	Avoid spoken forms of assessment.
Orthopedic	Identify and remove physical barriers. Provide adequate space for movement. Seat near exits for safety. Check tables and desks for proper height.	Identify devices that assist handling of objects, such as spring-loaded tongs, accountant's pencil grips, test tube racks.	Encourage physical manipulation of objects. Pair with nonimpaired student peer. Provide student training time with equipment prior to use.	Provide assistance with writing and manipulation of materials.
Behavior	Seat away from distractions. Provide well-lighted quiet space for study.	Train in use prior to providing special equipment.	Use brief activities. Give praise and cues. Reinforce desired behaviors. Obtain attention and establish eye contact prior to discussion or giving instructions.	None
Gifted	None	Advanced reading materials. Greater application of technology.	Emphasize problem solving. Accelerate pace. Arrange mentorships. Emphasize processes, mathematics, and uses of technology.	Increase expectations for analysis, application, and hypotheses. Use open-ended assessment devices.

How Can You Help a Child with Learning Disabilities? Structure is the most important concept when teaching children with learning disabilities. These children have perceptual and cognitive difficulties that may make it impossible for children to mask out unnecessary stimuli such as sights and sounds in the background of the classroom. Ways to promote structure include class and study routines, limited choices, focused attention, memory clues, sequenced instruction, clear distinctions between instruction and testing, specific criticism and praise, time clues, conferences with special education teachers, and empathy and encouragement (Coble, Levey, & Matthies, 1985).

Learning disabilities can be difficult to diagnose and teachers can be left alone to respond to a child's off-task or aggressive behavior, resulting from learning frustrations. A school's community may have resources that can help to mitigate some of these frustrations, help children seek topics of interest and demonstrate their special talents. For example, the World Forestry Foundation, based in Portland, Oregon, sponsors the Forestry Discovery Center in real and virtual settings. The center focuses on forestry concepts of the Pacific Northwest that are widely generalized to most temperate forests. Tours and education programs are available for teachers and children focusing on urban and forest trees and tropical rain forests. All learning opportunities and educational kits are correlated to national and state science standards (www.worldforestry.org).

On the East Coast in Port Clyde, Maine, the Herring Gut Learning Center (hglc@gwi.net) strives to educate local youth about aqua- and mari-culture in a North Atlantic community. HGLC offers summer and school-year programming, correlated to state science standards and unique to its locale, to "fill in the blanks" of school science programs. Led by marine science specialists, preschool through high-school youth are treated to interesting field-based programs, such as marshes and mudflats, rocky-shore geology, tidal pools, and island life. Older youth use the alternative science education programs to overcome learning differences and behavioral difficulties, while progressing with mathematics and reading. Life skills are developed, school attendance improved, and drop-out rates reduced, as a potential new generation of fishermen and lobstermen and women discover marine science careers.

Each program, in a different setting, illustrates a real-world example of unique community-based resources available to teachers and schools for helping youth with the learning difficulties experienced in typical school settings. Whether you are based in a densely populated urban center or the rural heartland, consider contacting the local chamber of commerce or educational resource center to discover the unique opportunities available to help the children of your community.

Teaching Children Who Have Cognitive Disabilities

Some children in your classes will have cognitive disabilities, also referred to as learners with *mental retardation*. There are different categories of cognitive disabilities, and each has a range of different functions. The American Association of Mental Deficiency describes children who have cognitive disability as having subaverage intelligence and being deficient in behavior and responsibility for their age-related cultural group. These limitations affect academic and motor skills. Children with cognitive disabilities are capable of learning some academics, acquiring social skills, and developing occupational skills.

Children with a mild cognitive disability requiring intermittent support may be included in a general education science classroom. *Educable mentally retarded* (EMR) has been a term used to describe this level of intelligence and applies to about 11 percent of special needs children in U.S. public schools (Cheney & Roy, 1999).

How Can You Teach Children Who Have Cognitive Disabilities? By acquiring as much information as you can about a child, you will be able to emphasize strengths while teaching to overcome weaknesses. School-support services and special-education personnel can make situation-specific suggestions to assist any particular child. The recommendations in Table 3.4 on pages 87–89 can help enhance a child's academic skills. Concept analysis as shown in Figure 3.2 on page 84 is a time-tested strategy for teaching science to children who have cognitive or learning disabilities as well as children who are not disabled.

Teaching Children Who Have Physical Disabilities

Physical disabilities include visual, hearing, and orthopedic impairments. Conservative estimates suggest that less than 0.5 percent of school children may have a physical disability and about half of those have multiple disabilities, one-fourth have a chronic health problem and one-fourth have an orthopedic impairment without other serious complications (Hallahan & Kauffman, 2000).

What Barriers Do Children with Physical Disabilities Face? Children with physical disabilities carry burdens that often limit their access to science education. Most of these burdens arise from the barriers the children encounter, such as

- ✦ parents and school advisers who perceive children with physical disabilities through stereotypes and low expectations,
- ✦ classroom structures that limit accessibility and exposure to tactile, manipulative experiences, critical to basic science learning,
- ✦ science programs that have not been modified or adapted to meet the needs of children with physical impairments,
- ✦ teachers who may harbor fearful or negative attitudes or who may treat the children in an overly protective or cautious manner.

Why Is Science Important for Children Who Are Physically Disabled? Science instruction should begin at an early age and continue throughout schooling for children who are physically disabled. As early as 1983, the National Science Board Commission on Precollege Education in Mathematics, Science, and Technology offered three reasons for early and sustained education in science:

1. Science emphasizes hands-on experience and exploration of the environment. It can help to fill some experiential gaps that may have evolved because of extensive hospital stays and/or overprotectiveness of schools or parents. Science can help to develop the individual's independence and overall positive self-image.

2. Recent scientific and technological advances have provided tools such as computers, talking calculators, control systems, versabraille hook-ups to computers, and special

telephone systems. These advances can help to mitigate the limitations imposed by a physical disability and can enable the individuals to become independent, contributing members of society. Science instruction that emphasizes making observations, collecting and organizing information, and making conclusions can help develop the individual's mental and manipulative readiness for using new technology.

3. Job opportunities will require knowledge and understanding of technological devices. Computers will continue to be an important part of many jobs. Advances in technology have helped children with physical disabilities learn and have provided new employment opportunities. Children with physical disabilities will need the background, training, and self-confidence to seek these opportunities.

Visual Impairments. Children who are *educationally blind* and *partially sighted* are increasingly benefiting from regular education experiences. They must learn from voice, audiotapes, braille, and other devices designed for the visually impaired. Children who are partially sighted may require printed materials larger than standard school print size. Magnifying devices can be used to enlarge standard print.

Children with severe vision problems are identified at an early age. However, less severe problems often go undetected for years. Regular classroom teachers may be the first to notice sight problems. Some behaviors that may indicate vision loss include squinting at the chalkboard, holding a book closer or farther away than most other children, blinking or otherwise distorting the eyes, holding the head at an odd angle, and unusual sensitivity to light. Refer all children who demonstrate any of these behaviors to the school official who can arrange a vision screening. Parents and children appreciate early notification.

Teaching Children with Visual Limits. An audio-tactile teaching approach may help children who have visual limits. Lessons can be audiotaped for later playback, written assignments and tests can be tape-recorded, and a personal recorder with headphones can be used by children who are educationally blind without disturbing the rest of the class. (Be certain to provide verbal or tape-recorded feedback about answers too.) Magnified print materials and visual aids with high contrast can help children who are partially sighted.

Science process skills (Chapter 1) can provide helpful tactile experiences for the student with a visual impairment. Tactile experiences are more helpful than passive participation. Ideas include:

- modeling various birds and habitats with clay
- illustrating the carbon cycle of a forest with papier-maché
- constructing leaf print books from old newspapers
- designing constellations by constructing paper stars
- illustrating the food chain by using natural objects
- designing cloud formations from cotton balls
- building bridges and other structures using drinking straws
- building a replica of a coral reef
- illustrating an electromagnetic wave by using iron filings and magnets
- constructing replicas of prehistoric tools

Instruction that stimulates the greatest range of senses (multimodal instruction) is vital for children with physical impairments. Commercial materials exist and may be modified to assist the student who is visually impaired. Programs such as the Elementary Science Study and Science: A Process Approach II have been used with over 3 million students. Teacher supplements are available with suggestions for modifications for students with disabilities. Adapting Science Materials for the Blind (ASMB) was developed from two Science Curriculum Improvement Study units for use with visually impaired children in mainstreamed classrooms. Science Activities for the Visually Impaired (SAVI) have been designed especially for middle-level children.

Pair children with visual disabilities with sighted children. Several researchers have found that this approach enables the child with a visual impairment to achieve on par with their nondisabled peers. The sighted member of a team can translate the class experiences to the child with a visual disability, who can obtain an understanding through other senses. Together both can report the results of an experiment or activity.

Hearing Disabilities. *Deaf* and *hard of hearing* are two types of hearing impairments. Regular classroom teachers occasionally work with children who have profound hearing losses, but more often have students with some lesser degree of hearing loss. Common types of hearing impairments concern volume and pitch. Another type is intelligibility—the volume of a sound may be adequate, but it is garbled. Hearing aids, lipreading, expressions, and gestures help the child with a hearing disability succeed in the regular classroom.

Deafness is often identified early in childhood, but mild hearing losses frequently go undetected. The following behaviors may signal a hearing impairment that should be referred to school personnel for screening: odd positioning of the head while listening, inattention during discussions, often asking the speaker to repeat, and asking classmates for instructions.

Teaching Children Who Have Hearing Limits. Language development is one of the major problems for children who are hearing impaired. Direct experience with objects is essential if children are to develop language sufficiently, and objects from a child's environment enhance learning of scientific concepts. When we provide rich experiences, children who have hearing impairments can improve

> language performance, observing and listening skills, vocabulary, the learning of science concepts and development of cognitive skills through direct experiential experiences in science. In order for this learning to occur, students must have the opportunity of "doing science" by hands-on, inquiry, real-life experiences through direct physical manipulation of objects that focus attention on patterns of interaction in physical and biological systems. The pairing or coupling of disabled and nondisabled children also seems to be an effective means for students to learn science. (Brown, 1979, p. 89)

Observations students must make can be adapted. For example, auditory observations may be changed to visual observations, as in the case of the sounds made by different sizes of tuning forks. Have the child transfer the sound wave to water or sand and compare what happens as an alternative to hearing. Other techniques teachers can use are similar to those used for multilingual children, including seating the child near the front of the room so vision is not obstructed, looking directly at the child and obtaining his or her attention before speaking, shaving beards or mustaches so lips are visible for the student's lipreading, speaking loudly and distinctly without shouting, pairing students, and using a written outline for activities that require several steps.

Orthopedic Disabilities. Orthopedic impairments are disabilities caused by diseases and deformities of the muscles, joints, and skeletal system. Examples include cerebral palsy, spina bifida, amputations, birth defects, arthritis, and muscular dystrophy. Temporary injuries are not covered by federal law because they can be corrected. A child with an orthopedic impairment may require an appliance such as a wheelchair, walker, crutches, or skeletal braces.

Teaching Children with Orthopedic Disabilities. An orthopedically disabled child generally requires adjustments that are physical rather than educational. Be aware of and attempt to remove physical and psychological barriers in your classroom. Examine the curriculum materials and activities and modify them to include the child with a disability without sacrificing their purpose or science content. Do not underestimate the capabilities of the child. Become familiar with the function and maintenance of any appliance the child uses.

Teaching Learners Who Are Gifted and Talented

Children who are gifted or talented may comprise 3–5 percent of the U.S. school population (Hallahan & Kauffman, 2000) and are not included in the federal law. However, federal legislation does encourage states to develop programs and support research for students who are gifted and talented (Hallahan & Kauffman, 2000). Gifted or talented children do have special needs that are not usually served well by the instruction given to most children. Most teachers have gifted and talented children in their classrooms, and authorities have questioned the wisdom of pulling gifted children out of the regular classroom for special instruction.

Some of the problems experienced by these children parallel disabling conditions described earlier. The definition and processes used to identify children who have special gifts involve similar difficulties that exist for children who have mental retardation or learning disorders. Whereas most may feel a moral obligation to help those who have a disadvantage, the child with a special gift may be presumed to find a way to excel on her or his own (Hallahan & Kauffman, 2000).

However, like children who have disadvantages or who are different, children who are gifted and talented also benefit from a balanced view of humanity and become prepared to work and live in the greater society. Children who are gifted should be considered as individuals who have unique needs and abilities, and their education should attend to those specific needs and abilities.

Who Are Gifted and Talented Learners? Children who are gifted and/or talented show promise of making superior progress in school. These children may demonstrate advanced progress in academic achievement in a school subject or exceptional ability and creativity in the arts. Their special intelligence and talents are observed and may be verified by achievement and IQ tests or superior performance in a subject or artistic area. In addition, gifted children may demonstrate other traits such as sensitivity to the needs of other children, a need for independence, a predisposition for expression, a capacity for social leadership, broad interests in different school areas, apparent natural talents in the arts, and such noticeable behaviors as intensity, persistence, self-assured introversion, or detachment from what they believe are mundane topics.

Children who are gifted and talented have a wide range of characteristics. This range makes it difficult to generalize about all gifted children. Gifted and talented children can represent a tremendous challenge to the science teacher.

Academically gifted children may appear to become easily bored with instruction offered to the rest of the class. If you have not majored in science, you may have some anxiety about having a scientifically gifted child in your class. Fear not. Feeling unprepared in science should not stop you from teaching gifted children. Perhaps your anxiety will be eased if you can keep the issue in perspective. Remember that you are an adult who teaches children, and the experiences of adulthood provide advantages when working with the student who is gifted. Despite all the knowledge a young gifted learner may have, he or she is still an elementary or middle school student, and the student's social, emotional, physical, psychological, and cognitive development is not complete. As an adult, you still have much to offer. All learners enjoy seeing their teacher get excited about their students' work. Having a gifted child in your science class is reason to rejoice and will give you a wonderful opportunity to become a real facilitator and guide rather than a messenger.

Teaching Learners Who Are Gifted and Talented. Children who are gifted in science often are capable of accelerated and more detailed learning. You can enrich their experiences by encouraging them to pursue the subject to a greater depth. You may also accelerate their instruction by drawing on topics from advanced grades or by arranging for the child to work with a mentor (perhaps an older student, another teacher, or a science career professional) on special science topics. It is not uncommon for gifted students to perform two or three years above grade level in the subject or area where they show talent (Hallahan & Kauffman, 2000; Piburn & Enyeart, 1985). Therefore, more flexibility in written assignments and higher expectations for verbal communication are

When encouraged and supported, exceptional children can overcome exceptional challenges.

Teaching Students Who Have Exceptionalities

Who has the wisdom and ability to predict which of our students will succeed and which will not? People who have disabilities are often erroneously thought to be mentally deficient, but the prevailing social attitude has slowly changed. Thanks to federal laws, inclusion, and local school efforts to service better the special needs of children are greater than at any time in the history of schooling. All children are given more encouragement and are provided with more opportunities to achieve their full potential.

After decades of turning away students with disabilities, universities learned to accept them for scientific career training and removed physical and psychological barriers. A three-year survey by the American Association for the Advancement of Science reported a resource group of more than 700 scientists with disabilities. People with disabilities *can* do science. But our schools still must do more. Robert Menchel, a senior physicist for the Xerox Corporation who has been deaf since the age of 7, has visited many schools. He says:

> The lack of development of a basic science curriculum from kindergarten to the twelfth grade is a national disgrace and one that puts the deaf child

at a disadvantage in comparison to the nonhandicapped child. Furthermore, these students are still being pushed into stereotyped job roles and dead-end jobs. For the female students it is even worse.

Robert Hoffman, a researcher who has cerebral palsy, speaks about the effects of isolation due to a disability:

> When one is born with a disability severe enough so society shoves him into a special program (which nonhandicapped people develop), one becomes separated from "normal" persons. All through his school years, he learns from other disabled students, and the teachers design studies to fit the limitations of his physical disability.

John Gavin, a research scientist with a physical impairment, cautions those who have no apparent disability:

> One of the least desirable traits of the human condition is our propensity to avoid those among us who are afflicted with overt physical disabilities. While this may be an inherent psychological carryover from those days of survival of the fittest, it is more likely we do not wish to have a reminder

necessary. Try having gifted learners engage in more speculation about scientific events, hypothesize, and develop arguments and counterarguments that pertain to scientific/social issues. Have gifted learners demonstrate the application of science as well as the relationships between science and material learned in other subjects. The following teaching strategies are often appropriate for gifted learners.

◆ *Develop open-ended learning activities.* Children who have learning and intellectual disabilities benefit from narrowly focused, sequential activities. Children who are gifted should be challenged to develop their intellectual reasoning through open-ended activities that have many possible outcomes. These activities avoid step-by-step recipe procedures and do not have predetermined results. Several of the cooperative inquiry teaching methods and the tools of questioning in Chapter 7 are useful when working with gifted learners.

◆ *Use gifted students as classroom leaders.* These children may become reliable informal teachers of their peers who can greatly enhance the classroom atmosphere. Chil-

that we are potentially and continually eligible to join them.

Teachers become the key. A caring teacher with a positive can-do attitude is consistently ranked highly by children with disabilities. Teachers who care seem to expect that their students can learn at a high level. These teachers try to see that all children fulfill the high expectations held for them.

Language development is one of the major problems of children with hearing impairments. Researchers report that direct experience with objects is essential and that utilization of objects from a child's environment enhances his or her learning of concepts.

The most significant changes needed for teaching children who have visual impairments are related to the adaptation of educational materials and equipment to take advantage of each child's residual vision.

Children who are orthopedically disabled are a heterogeneous group, and it is difficult to prescribe general methods and adaptations that will serve each child well. However, pairing a child with an orthopedic impairment with a child with no disabilities helps both. The child who is impaired still needs direct physical experience with the science phenomena to the greatest extent possible. For example,

> a magnet can be taped to the arm or leg. Another student can bring objects in contact with the magnets. The child should be able to feel and see which objects interact with the magnet and which do not. In this way, the child [with a disability] is involved in the decision making and discovery that is the major emphasis of [the] lesson.

Dean Brown's ground-breaking research showed that children with physical disabilities learned to understand science concepts and that they developed higher levels of reasoning skills if given the opportunity. Children with disabilities need direct, experiential, sensory experiences in science. Many researchers have repeatedly expressed the need for doing science through hands-on, inquiry-based, real-life experiences.

Source: Adapted from the literature review by Dean R. Brown, "Helping Handicapped Youngsters Learn by 'Doing,' " in Mary Budd Rowe (Ed.), *What Research Says to the Science Teacher,* Washington, DC: National Science Teachers Association (1979), 2: 80–100 and D. P. Hallahan and J. M. Kauffman, *Exceptional Learners,* Boston: Allyn & Bacon, 2000.

dren who are gifted can also be used as resource persons, researchers, science assistants, and community ambassadors for exciting school programs.

✦ *Use technology, science processes, and mathematics.* Scientific observation can be enhanced through mathematics. Encourage gifted children to use higher forms of mathematics and statistics as often as possible. Engage them in more precise measures and more extensive uses of science process skills. Technology will challenge gifted students to expand research capabilities as well as quantify and communicate their scientific findings.

✦ *Reinforce and reward superior efforts.* Some school programs for gifted and talented children use pull-out approaches: learners are placed in special programs or given accelerated instruction. Inclusion can also benefit children who are gifted. Adaptations of science content and changes in instruction with more options for the gifted learners can provide suitable instruction in the regular classroom. Science content adaptations could include emphasizing higher levels of thinking, abstraction, and independent thinking. The challenge is fundamentally the same as with any other child: Help the child learn how to learn. Reinforcement and rewards for effort and work well done

(text continues on page 100)

4-E Feature Lesson

Magnets

Inquiry Question: What is a magnet and what does it do?

Concept to Be Invented: Magnets attract (pull) and repel (push) each other and certain kinds of metals.

National Science Education Standards: K–4 Physical Science—Light, heat, electricity, and magnetism concepts. Magnets attract and repel each other and certain kinds of metals.

Science Attitudes to Nurture: Open-mindedness, curiosity, perseverance, positive approach to failure, cooperating with others

Materials Needed: Bar magnets—masking tape on the ends for Exploration, and a variety of additional magnet shapes (such as a horseshoe, disk, button, rod, and so on); an assortment of materials from the classroom including steel and iron objects, non-metal objects, and metallic objects, such as coins, aluminum cans, tinfoil, brass

Safety Precautions: Refrain from using iron filings. If iron filings are used, insist that students wear goggles to avoid filings getting lodged in their eyes. Adaptation for a student with visual impairment: Glue or tape a small object, such as a button, on one end of the bar magnets. The tactile relief will assist in identifying "same" ends of a magnet.

Exploration *Which process skills will be used?*

Observing, classifying, communicating, inferring

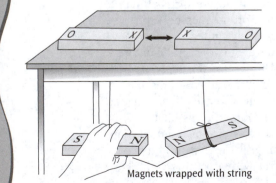

Magnets wrapped with string

Suspend 2 bar magnets from a thread from a small table and demonstrate how one magnet can make another spin or swing or change position. Ask: Why do magnets seem to push or pull at each other? Do you suppose they always do this? Encourage children to investigate the behavior of 2 bar magnets by pushing and pulling them toward each other on a flat, non-metal table. Cover N and S on the magnets with masking tape. Ask the children to use a crayon or marker to place an X on the ends that pull together and an O on the opposite ends. They will eventually notice that the

X's attract each other and the same with the O's. Avoid dropping the bar magnets; they will tend to lose their strength, but the magnetic forces can be strengthened if you have a magnetizer available from a science supply catalog.

Explanation

Compose and use questions that cause the children to describe their experiences, such as: Which ends of the magnets seemed to pull together? Which ends seemed to push away? What kind of pattern did you notice? Remove the masking tape from the ends of the magnets and notice the N and S stamped on the bars. Ask the children to fill in the sentences that represent the concept, such as: "Magnets _____ away from each other when the ends are not the same." "Magnets _____ together when the ends are the same." Develop vocabulary, if appropriate, for students by using "attract" and "repel" or "pull" and "push."

Expansion *Which skills will be used?*

Classifying, communicating, inferring

Continue to use the language of "pull" or "attract" and "push" or "repel" as children investigate the behavior of different types of magnets. Ask them: Can you find a way to use the disk magnets and make them roll away from or toward another disk magnet? Encourage the children to use a variety of magnets to examine the behavior of common metallic and nonmetallic objects from the classroom. Challenge them to group the objects and explain their reasons and to communicate their findings by making a chart to illustrate the types of objects that a magnet attracts. Discuss with the children where magnets exist in their homes and what these magnets do.

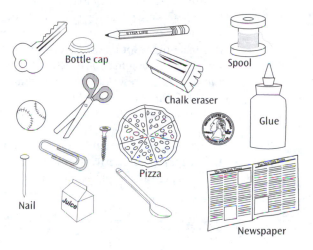

Bottle cap
Spool
Chalk eraser
Glue
Pizza
Nail
Juice
Newspaper

Evaluation

Upon completing the activity, the student will be able to:

+ identify like and unlike poles and label appropriately;
+ use the concept of push and pull or attract and repel appropriately to describe the behavior of magnets;
+ predict and test objects that may be attracted to a magnet;
+ classify objects as attracted or not attracted to a magnet.

(continued)

Magnet 1   Magnet 2

S   N   N   S

This picture shows a hand pushing Magnet 1 toward Magnet 2. The magnets are on a flat table. What do you think will happen to Magnet 2? _____

_____

_____

Why do you think this will happen? _____

_____

_____

are usually all that is necessary to help gifted children keep their high level of motivation for learning. Some suggestions for reinforcing and rewarding superior effort include public recognition for effort, extra credit or waiver of standard assignments, positive teacher comments, extra leadership opportunities and/or classroom responsibilities, and encouraging students to do real research projects.

✦ *Provide extra- or cocurricular learning opportunities.* Your classroom will have limited teaching resources, and your time will also have limits. Out-of-class or out-of-school learning options may also help the gifted student continue to learn science. Use community library resources or make arrangements for the child to do special work at a community college or nearby university. Develop and utilize community resource personnel: Construct a network of science-related resource people and arrange mentor-intern relationships. Start a science club for students with special interests. Begin an after-school science lab—encourage the learners to design and pursue experiments. Student teachers or field experience interns from a nearby university may be able to assist with the science lab instruction and programming.

How Can Parents Help Meet Children's Special Needs?

More parents are realizing the importance of science and involving parents helps to increase children's success by

- ✦ encouraging greater achievement in school
- ✦ increasing parent-family participation in school activities
- ✦ supporting positive changes in school climate
- ✦ improving student attendance
- ✦ decreasing the school dropout rates
- ✦ decreasing substance abuse, violence and antisocial behavior
- ✦ increasing the collective efforts among school personnel, parents and families toward greater productive partnerships. (Krueger & Sutton, 2001, p. 92)

Science skills develop over time, and development builds on older skills. "If you don't use it, you'll lose it" applies here. The science foundation begun during childhood will increase each individual's potential for later success. Also, science depends on mathematics. Students should be encouraged to study mathematics every school year.

All students learn science through hands-on, minds-on experiences. Children should be encouraged to handle physical objects, make measurements and direct comparisons, and ask frequent questions about what they observe and experience.

Science is found in all aspects of life and is important to children's successful futures.

How Can Parents Help Their Children Study and Prepare for Science?

Parents are invaluable when it comes to educating children. They are closest to the special needs their children may have. Parents can help their children succeed in science by following these suggestions:

✦ *Stimulate interest in and foster feelings for science.* Parents can help their children realize that science can be fun and help them experience success, with its feelings of excitement, discovery, and mastery.

✦ *Include science in the child's everyday experiences.* Children can be asked to count and form sets of utensils at dinner time and can help to measure ingredients. Include them also in repairing broken appliances or building a model airplane.

✦ *Establish a regular study time and provide a designated space for study away from distractions.* Work with the teachers to develop effective ways to communicate with children who have vision and hearing disabilities. Equipment modifications can be developed for children who have physical disabilities, and these can be shared with the school.

✦ *Check with children every day to make sure homework and special projects are completed.* Parents should ask to see completed homework and any tests or projects that have been graded or returned.

✦ *Offer to read assignment questions.* Even if the parents do not know the answers, a stronger academic bond will be formed between parent and child. The child will benefit from an interested adult role model, forming the impression that school, homework, and effort are important.

✦ *Ask whether children have any difficulties with science or mathematics.* Parents should talk with their children often about any difficulties and then follow up if there appear to be continuing problems.

✦ *Use a homework hotline if the school has one.* This may be school-based or supported by individual teachers during designated hours.

Inquiry for All Children

Video Summary

It is important that teachers of science serve all children. Each student is a combination of unique characteristics from a diverse background. Some children need help in developing the necessary skills to cope with the rigors of school and in turn have difficulty "fitting in" to social groups within the school. The development of concept mapping skills by the teacher and student can greatly enhance learning and provide the needed support for science understanding while offering the student with an opportunity to excel.

Tips for Viewing, Objectives, or What to Watch for

As you watch the video, make note of the following:

◆ What characteristics of concept mapping did the teacher identify as beneficial when working with hearing-impaired students?

◆ What other instructional strategies might a teacher use to improve science understanding with special needs students?

◆ After reading the chapter and viewing the video, how has your thinking changed concerning students with special needs?

Questions for Exploration

1. How does equitable access to quality science education experiences promote the development of successful participants in a democratic society?

2. How might cultural influences deter women and minorities in developing the needed skills for a career in science?

3. What experiences have you had in a culturally diverse setting? How did these experiences contribute to a better understanding of the diverse needs of students?

Activity for Application

This video included a brief discussion concerning the diversity of students. Observe a science lesson in the grade level you intend to teach. Develop a chart from the information provided in the video and chapter that can be used as an observational checklist for examining issues of diversity. During the observation period, use the checklist to identify how the classroom teacher promotes equitable science experiences for all students. Share this information with your classmates and teacher. Describe how you as a teacher might create an atmosphere in your classroom conducive to equitable access to science experiences. How do you envision your own classroom changing to meet the needs of all learners?

What Are Some Extra Science Activities Parents Can Do to Help Their Children?

Some teachers, even entire schools, arrange home-based science activities to supplement school instruction. Parents become enthusiastic and develop a stronger bond with the school. They often say, "Let's have parent involvement programs more often." "It helps me keep in touch with my child." "The activities didn't take too much time, so it was simple to include them into our busy evening schedule." "I think it's great to get the parents involved. Each activity we did benefited our older child and our younger child who is not even in school!" (Williams-Norton, Reisdorf, & Spees, 1990, pp. 13–15). Meaningful activities can be found for young children in magazines such as *Click* and *Dragonfly* and in Nancy Paula's *Helping Your Young Child Learn Science* (1992, U.S. Department of Education).

The rich variety of science teaching resources makes it easy to suggest home study extensions. Giving parents options helps them overcome limits of time and materials. When making suggestions to parents, keep these criteria in mind (Williams-Norton, Reisdorf, & Spees, 1990, p. 14):

◆ *The activities should be at grade level and developmentally appropriate for the child.* Select options with the special needs of the children in mind.

◆ *Activities should require materials that are available at home.* No parent will welcome traveling to gather together materials, and many cannot afford the expense.

◆ *The activities should supplement what is taught in school, not duplicate it.* Do not expect parental teaching to be a substitute for your own responsibility.

◆ *Provide complete and accurate instructions including instructions for safety.* Try the activities yourself before sending them home. Can a child do the activity with minimal adult guidance?

◆ *Select activities that emphasize simple and accurate concepts.* Cross-check the concepts of the activity with those of your textbook or science program. Are they consistent? If they are different, modify them or select another activity. Choose activities that emphasize a main science idea, and encourage the parents to continue emphasizing this main idea.

◆ *The activities should be fun.* Parents and children will enjoy a special time together when the activity is fun. Encourage parents to share the joys and mysteries of science with their children. Positive attitudes toward science from parents will benefit school science.

◆ *Develop the concepts of sink or float and density* by floating common objects such as straws and plastic buttons in plain water and in salt water. Because the density of salt water is greater, objects that sink in plain water often float in salt water. Try adding different amounts of salt to water to explore the effects of salt concentration on density and floating.

◆ *Explore primary and secondary colors.* Following the directions on food coloring packages, prepare different colors and arrange them in glass jars. Dye macaroni or paper to represent the colors of a rainbow. Combine the three primary colors to produce every color.

◆ *Demonstrate magnetism* by having children compare the effects of magnets on different objects in the kitchen. Let the children predict which objects will and will not be attracted to the magnets.

◆ *Use building blocks to develop the concepts of set and order.* Lay a foundation of three blocks; then place two blocks on the next layer and one on the top layer. Ask the children to count the blocks and to estimate how many blocks would be necessary to build towers six and ten blocks high.

Chapter Summary

A single science teaching method by itself is insufficient. Each hands-on science lesson must be accompanied by adaptations to suit the needs of each special student.

There is no single method or science program that can be used to teach all children. One single factor does benefit *all* children: hands-on science—where all children have abundant opportunities to benefit from multisensory stimulation in cooperative settings. This approach has the potential to become the great equalizer. Children who are culturally different may acquire missing experiences through hands-on science. Non-English-speaking children can use science to learn and develop language skills. Young females can overcome skill deficits, gender stereotypes, and career limitations through hands-on, minds-on science. Exceptional children are given new opportunities because of hands-on science and its ability to include all children in minds-on experiences. Gifted and talented children also benefit as they are introduced to new experiences and are motivated to process these experiences at an advanced intellectual level.

Parents play a vital role with students who have special needs. Teachers should inform parents about the importance of science and offer activities to strengthen the school-home learning connection.

Discussion Questions

1. Cultural differences can have a positive impact on the social climate of a classroom. What are some ways you can encourage the expression of differences and make a positive impact on all children?

2. Take the picture of a scientist you drew in Chapter 1, and draw another one now. How do the pictures compare? What features are similar? How many of these same features do you observe: male, middle aged, bald, glasses, facial hair, lab coat with pocket protector, test tubes? How can these features reflect bias, attitudes, stereotypes, and values? Where did the impressions portrayed in the pictures come from? What types of multicultural education concepts are reflected in the picture? How can social context and media influence impressions? How are the impressions you have of science and scientists likely to influence young children?

3. Blindfold yourself or attend a class while wearing earplugs. How is your ability to function impaired? What long-term cumulative effects could result from your temporary disability if it were to become permanent? How could these effects influence your ability to function in a regular classroom?

4. Brainstorm ideas suitable for teaching science to gifted students. What differences are found on your list according to grade level? How would you work with a youngster who is gifted and who also has a cultural or language difference and/or a disability?

5. Brainstorm ideas related to classroom organization. How can a typical self-contained room be converted to better suit the needs of special students? Look especially for barriers that might limit the inclusion of children who have physical disabilities. What complications might a teacher encounter? What are some ways to overcome these complications?

Build a Portfolio or E-Folio

1. Interview a teacher whose students are culturally different from himself or herself. Inquire about how the science program or instruction has been modified to recognize and use cultural differences in a positive way. What effects have the teacher's efforts had on all of the children?

2. Peruse several science textbooks from different publishers. Report observations about possible gender bias, omitted discussion of cultural differences, and potential for adaptation for non-English-speaking, disabled, and/or gifted children. What suggestions are provided in the teacher's guide?

3. Choose any lesson from a science textbook or hands-on program. Demonstrate how you would adapt it to provide special instruction for female students or children with learning disabilities, intellectual disabilities, impaired vision, hearing loss, or orthopedic impairment.

Directions: Answer each question with a yes or no. If a question does not specifically or completely pertain to you, try to offer a yes or no response based on what you know and think you would do. If possible, respond to each item as a member of a multicultural, gender, and exceptional representative team including parents, learners, administrators, and other teachers. If uncertain, try to collect the necessary information in order to substantiate your answers.

The General Science Education Program Survey

Does the school's science instruction and curriculum:

_____ 1. Use hands-on activities on a regular basis?

_____ 2. Include grouping and cooperative learning activities routinely?

_____ 3. Emphasize content and the processes of problem solving equally?

_____ 4. Encourage learners to talk about their science learning?

_____ 5. Relate written class materials to science in the everyday lives of a culturally diverse society?

_____ 6. Include information on a regular basis about careers using science?

_____ 7. Include role models who represent both genders and persons of different racial, cultural, linguistic, and exceptional (disabled and gifted) groups for students to interact with on a regular basis?

_____ 8. Provide access for all students to technology and ensure equal experiences with it?

_____ 9. Integrate science content and processes with other core subjects, such as language arts, social studies, and mathematics?

_____ 10. Strive to develop and encourage positive attitudes toward science for all teachers, administrators, parents, and students?

_____ 11. Develop partnerships with science and industry that include participants who represent both genders and people of different racial, cultural, linguistic, and exceptional (disabled and gifted) groups?

_____ 12. Assess what students know and can do in science with performance-based criteria that emphasize the open-ended nature of science and the importance of using language for description and questioning?

_____ 13. Ensure that all counselors, teaching staff, and parents are aware of strategies that encourage equitable participation of female, minority, and exceptional students in science?

_____ 14. Monitor all teaching materials for equal representation of both genders and people of different racial, cultural, linguistic, and exceptional groups in the science community?

4. Sketch the floor plan of an elementary class-room. Examine the floor plan carefully and make changes to show adaptations that would assist children with orthopedic disability.

5. Use the concept analysis model presented in this chapter (Figure 3.2) to make changes in a science lesson plan. How would you use the model to instruct children who are learning disabled or intellectually disabled? How could the model be used with all children? What are the possible benefits and limits?

6. Complete the survey on pages 106–107 "How Equitable Is Your Science Program and Your Teaching?" What do you conclude about your willingness or ability to provide equitable science teaching and learning?

Science in Pre-K Through Upper Elementary

_____ 15. Provide professional development for all teachers to update and improve their science teaching skills?

_____ 16. Support and train teachers who are uncomfortable teaching science?

_____ 17. Emphasize accountability for teaching science on a regular basis in all classrooms?

_____ 18. Encourage and facilitate out-of-school learning experiences at all levels and for all skills groups?

_____ 19. Monitor extracurricular activities for equitable representation of students of both genders and of different racial, cultural, linguistic, and exceptional groups?

_____ 20. Establish guidelines for science fair projects that deemphasize the "wow" effect of experiments and encourage children to formulate their own questions and explore science in their own natural environments?

_____ 21. Publicly acknowledge strong commitment to science as an integral part of the school curriculum rather than as enrichment or an option?

_____ 22. Provide assistance for teachers in obtaining the necessary materials and equipment for teaching science with an experiential emphasis?

_____ 23. Form partnerships with parents to define their roles in supporting science education for their children?

_____ 24. Deemphasize the textbook approach to science in favor of an experience-based approach?

_____ 25. Include outreach efforts to parents who are representative of the entire student population on decisions regarding science activities and explorations with children?

Scoring

If you have scored as an individual, then credit one point for each question you answered yes.

- **20–25 points:** Congratulations! Share what you do with other schools and take a look at what is happening at the secondary level in your district.

- **10–19 points:** Good start, keep working at it! You have the elements of a good beginning. Check to see if your negative responses form any pattern. What is working for the school at this grade level? What is missing? Share the checklist with others and discuss a plan of action for improving.

- **0–9 points:** It's never too late. Examine your positive responses and try to build on your successes. What has made it possible for these to be incorporated in science education in your school? Then, examine the questions where you provided a negative response. Try to identify barriers and speculate about potential solutions to help your school to elevate its science program to a more equitable level for all students.

Source: Adapted from the work of Martha A. Adler: How Equitable Is Your Science Education Program? The Checklist. (_Dwight D. Eisenhower Mathematics and Science Education, 4, 1,_ 1994): 6–8.

Planning Inquiry Lessons

*I*t was spring and Jennifer was near the end of her first year of teaching fourth grade, a position that she had won over forty-two applicants. Jennifer did not believe that she was better prepared for the position than the other applicants, especially since some had several years of teaching experience. Midway through her first semester, Jennifer learned that she had impressed Mr. Emerson, the principal, and the teaching staff with her views on teaching and that the science demonstration lesson that she taught was perceived by the staff as being on the cutting edge of meeting her state's standards which were stimulated by the National Science Education Standards. Mr. Emerson and her fourth-grade teaching team of three other teachers had high expectations for Jennifer. The fact that she was a first-year teacher did not tempt them to make excuses for her; the school's staff had its focus on providing what was best for the students in order to meet state achievement test standards.

Jennifer did not disappoint anyone. She proved her value among her teammates, and her humble, self-effacing ways made her a joy to collaborate with. Jennifer read widely, eagerly collected teaching ideas, and was genuinely grateful for suggestions. She was flattered when other teachers indicated interest in her science lessons and how those lessons could interface with some of the topics taught by her teammates who specialized in one subject, which was taught to all fourth-grade students who rotated through the mod. Jennifer thought her teammates were only being kind, but they recognized considerable skill and potential for teacher leadership and recommended that Mr. Emerson appoint her to the Professional Development Council (PDC).

Jennifer accepted the appointment to the school PDC, although she thought the appointment should be given to someone with more experience. Science was the topic for next year's PDC agenda. The school had recently revised its curriculum to fulfill the state and National Science Education Standards. Curriculum decisions for the school district were made by the school board using site-based management. The state recommended a general curriculum model and materials that schools might use but let the schools determine how best to devise and implement the curriculum. The standards made it difficult to select a single textbook and still be able to prepare students well for the statewide mandatory achievement test given to all grades each year. The test was designed to measure progress toward fulfilling the standards. The PDC was concerned with the teachers' needs that were identified on a survey they had taken. The survey spoke of high frustration levels and a desire for extensive inservice training for teaching toward the standards.

Coincidentally, the school's student achievement test scores were received the same day as Jennifer's first meeting with the council. Teacher comparisons were discouraged but were unavoidable. Jennifer's students were the only ones who scored above the norm. Was this a fluke, or did this first-year teacher do something different to encourage higher student performance?

Jennifer felt somewhat defensive at first but soon realized that her colleagues' questions were professional and were asked in the spirit of schoolwide collaboration. Did she feel overwhelmed by the standards? What science concepts did she teach, and how did she decide when and how to teach them? Was there an order that worked best? How did she bring some balance from the science disciplines into her lessons? What did she do with the four new dimensions of science: science as inquiry, science and technology, science in personal and social perspectives, and history and nature of science? How could she possibly fit them into science lessons?

Jennifer described the frustrated feelings she too experienced at first. The standards advocated covering fewer concepts but expected teachers and students to go to a greater depth in science than had ever been attempted. Jennifer explained that desperation motivated her to think back to her experiences during teacher preparation. She had found a way to connect certain experiences and use them as tools for dealing with the expectations set by the standards.

Jennifer described a tool called *concept mapping* that helped her to sort and organize the science content concepts into story lines regarding specific themes. One teacher thought that the concept mapping technique seemed like brainstorming and webbing used in language arts, but Jennifer demonstrated that mapping was much more than that and explained how the techniques helped her to find a focus for individual lessons. Jennifer designed each of her lessons for a single concept but planned comprehensively to help students construct their understanding of the concept and to connect it with other concepts from other lessons. Over time, students seemed to be able to make many connections to what they learned. Students even learned to make their own concept maps to illustrate their understanding. Jennifer used these maps to conduct formative evaluations of her teaching and her students' learning.

Jennifer also described a *learning cycle model* that she used to foster a culture of inquiry and to plan the sequence of student activities, in order to ensure that the concept was built from direct student activity and then expanded in order to connect with the new content outcomes given by the science standards.

She shared some of her lesson plans with the other PDC members. Some members asked her to explain what she meant by *explore, explain, expand,* and *evaluate.* They were curious why Jennifer had students do activities first without explaining the point of the lesson and why she did not always test students at the end of her lessons, although the "evaluate" part of her planning model seemed to indicate that she would assess student learning at the end of each lesson.

Her lesson plans contained several activities that were related to each other, in a sequence over several days, sometimes requiring that almost a whole day be devoted to science. Of course, these special occasions were supported by Jennifer's teammates and at times they helped her teach science to all of the 100 fourth graders whom they shared. The PDC concluded that the ideas that Jennifer learned and used might help other teachers, and they decided to plan next year's professional development agenda around concept mapping, learning cycle planning, inquiry, teaching techniques, and authentic embedded assessment. Jennifer was consulted often about how to do this and to suggest where the PDC might find assistance.

Introduction

You say that this scenario is too far-fetched? Rest assured, it is not. We find that many new teacher graduates experience situations very much like this one. They have skills that are different—in some ways more sophisticated—than more experienced teacher professionals have and that make them in demand when schools and teachers find themselves facing the challenges afforded by change and meeting the pressures of public accountability.

Rising expectations for students and teachers require new ways of thinking and teaching, guided by state and national standards, which can be addressed through purposeful planning. One new challenge is to convert typical planning processes into an approach that helps learners to "make meaning" from the inquiring experiences that they acquire. How can you plan interesting, high impact lessons, and what is a potent tool that you can use to help make decisions about what and how to teach? In this chapter, we

1. examine National Science Education Standards for content to identify the concepts to be taught,
2. explore the use of concept mapping as a planning and assessment tool, and
3. investigate a constructivist inquiry-based learning cycle for planning lessons that specifically addresses the NSE standards for content in a direct and effective manner.

Using the National Science Education Standards for Content and Promoting Science Inquiry

"What do I expect students to understand and want them to be able to do?" is a fundamental question that all teachers ponder. This is an outcomes-based question whose answer is the heart of lesson planning. The question is consistent with the inquiry intentions of the National Science Education Standards and the science standards of most states. If our desire is to embrace and use those standards, then we subscribe to a goal of helping children to become scientifically literate. This means that the lessons that we select or plan will involve learners in numerous processes of inquiry and the development of essential thinking and problem-solving skills. The experiences that we plan and provide for children will help develop and nurture scientific attitudes, which will motivate intellectual inquiry and result in an understanding of scientific concepts. Processes, attitudes and concepts (commonly called the knowledge of science) are emphasized in our lessons.

The National Science Education Standards outline important concepts for grade level clusters, and is a place to begin to make decisions about what you may wish learners to understand and be able to do. Table 4.1 provides an excerpt taken from the National Science Education Standards for content for K–4 Physical Science. The rest of the related standards are provided in the Appendix.

Examine your state documents, or the National Science Education Standards. You will notice that these documents do not precisely describe everything that you may be expected to teach or how you should teach. Try sketching the relationships among the concepts, as in Figure 4.1, as a tool to understand expectations, and for translating stan-

---

TABLE 4.1 K–4 Physical Science Standards: Standard B

All students should develop an understanding of:

- Properties of objects and materials*
- Position and motion of objects*
- Light, heat electricity, and magnetism*

Properties of objects and materials concepts:

- Objects have many observable properties, including size, weight, shape, color, temperature, and the ability to react with other substances. These properties can be measured using tools such as rulers, balances, and thermometers.

- Objects are made of one or more materials, such as paper, wood, and metal. Objects can be described by the properties of the materials from which they are made, and these properties can be used to separate or sort a group of objects or materials.
- Materials have different states—solid, liquid, and gas. Some common materials such as water can be changed from one state to another by heating or cooling.

---

*See Appendix.

Source: NRC. Science content standards. *National Science Education Standards* (Washington, D.C.: National Academy Press, 1996): 123.

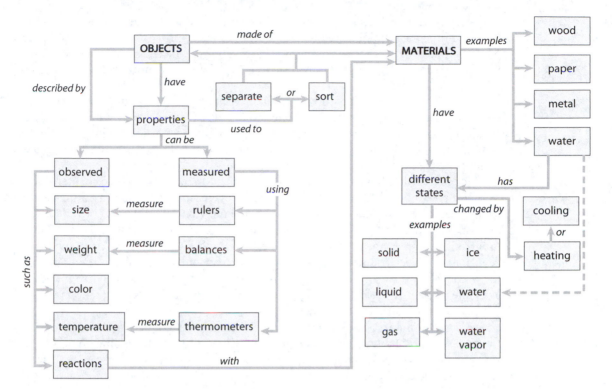

FIGURE 4.1   K–4 Properties of Objects and Materials

dards and outcomes-based documents into a general plan of topics, concepts, and sequences. This tool is called a concept map.

Concept Mapping

"Outcomes are high quality, culminating demonstrations of significant learning in context" (Spady, 1994, p. 18). William Spady reminds us that *demonstration* is the operative word. Outcomes identify in general terms the end product that we expect students to develop or achieve. The National Science Education Standards, and other reform movements (such as Project 2061's Benchmarks), identify the essential contexts and the types of high-quality end products that we should expect from scientifically literate students. Sometimes these end products—outcomes—are described for a particular grade level, but most often they are listed for a cluster of school grades. The grade-level placement, order, fit, and process of the steps required for successful demonstration of these end products are not defined. This planning chore is the duty of the curriculum developers or, more likely, each teacher. Several of the questions asked of Jennifer in our chapter scenario reflect the anxiety and uncertainty that this chore can cause for teachers.

As shown in the scenario as well as in Chapter 3, concept maps are essential tools for planning and teaching, and they can help students improve concept constructions, while helping to avoid misconceptions (Haney, 1998). Concept mapping is becoming widely used as constructivist-inquiry learning models become more accepted in science education.

Concept mapping helps students fulfill high-quality and meaningful learning outcomes in science. Maps provide concrete visual aids to help organize information before it is learned. Students can make their own maps while they learn, and examine the changes in their thinking as they construct their understanding. Maps can also be made as a type of assessment at the conclusion of lessons.

Science textbooks are beginning to use concept maps to introduce chapter materials and are among their end-of-chapter activities. Teachers who have used them have found that they provide a logical basis for deciding what main ideas to include in (or delete from) their lesson plans and science teaching. Concept maps can be developed for an entire course, one or more units, or even a single lesson. We have developed concept maps for each chapter of this book. These maps introduce you to the dominant ideas and illustrate the relationships among the chapter's concepts. These maps are available in the instructor's manual and are provided on the book's companion website. Please ask your instructor for copies.

A concept map is a tool that illustrates the conceptual connections understood by the map's creator. Each person may construct a different map, depending on how he or she understands the subject of the map. Never try to memorize a concept map. Instead, study it for the conceptual story that it tells, paying attention to the main ideas and the relationships among them.

Necessary Definitions

Some definitions must be provided before we can proceed. The fundamental purpose of education is to help students find new meaning in what they learn and to make meaning from what they do. We refer to this as *meaningful learning*. Meaningful learning implies that as a result of instruction, individuals are able to relate new material to previously acquired learning. This means that learners see new knowledge in the light of what they already know and understand; hence they find new meaning. Knowledge continually grows, but in a fashion that encourages connections with what learners already know. If these connections are missing, learners may regard the ideas they are taught as useless abstractions that only need to be memorized for a test. David Ausubel (1968) contrasts meaningful learning with rote learning, which is the result of many disjointed lessons.

Concept maps use three types of knowledge: facts, concepts, and generalizations.

Facts. A *fact* is a singular occurrence that happens in the past or present and that has no predictive value for the future. Thus, the information that you are now reading in this book at a specific time of day is a fact, just as a statement about what you ate for lunch or dinner yesterday is a fact. These facts may be completely isolated events that give no indications about your study or eating habits. On the other hand, if you regularly read your science methods book at the same time, or if you consistently eat salad for lunch and chicken or fish for dinner, then these seemingly isolated facts have much in common with your similar actions at other times.

Concepts.   Common attributes among facts can be described and facts that form related clusters of ideas can be named. The name given represents a *concept*. Interestingly, your behavior today or yesterday can be described by a single word or brief phrase. Words such as magnet, pole, attract, repel are examples of concepts based on an accumulation of facts. The definitions of these concepts may include descriptions, such as "You read your textbook before and after the science methods class," or "You try to eat foods that are low in calories, fat, and cholesterol." A concept covers a broader set of events than a singular occurrence that might happen at random. Therefore, concepts by their nature are abstract. Other examples of concepts are computer, animal, mineral, vegetable, food chain, solution, conservation, and buoyancy. All examples require that we know the definition to understand their meaning. In fact, most words in the dictionary represent concepts. All learners, especially young children, need to experience many examples of singular occurrences or facts before they can develop the abstract understanding necessary for conceptualization. But once they learn the concept, they do not need to learn isolated facts that are subsumed in it. They can reconstruct these facts when they need them.

Generalizations.   *Generalizations* are broad patterns between two or more concepts that have predictive value. Generalizations are rules or principles that contain more than one concept and that have predictive value. Thus, a statement such as "like poles in magnets repel each other and opposite poles attract" is a generalization, and it can predict what would happen if two magnets were brought next to each other. Learners must know the concepts of *magnets, poles, attraction,* and *repel* before they can fully understand the meaning of the generalization.

What Are Concept Maps?

Concepts are abstract ideas. Concept maps are also concrete graphic illustrations that indicate how a single concept is related to other concepts in the same category (see Figure 4.2). As you begin to learn about concept maps, you may prefer to think of them as sophisticated planning webs that reveal what concepts children must learn and how the concepts must be related. Curricula are primarily designed to teach concepts that students do not already know. Therefore, teaching and learning will be greatly enhanced if we know which concepts should be included and which need to be excluded from instructional programs.

Concept maps show relationships among different smaller and larger concepts. By looking at a concept map and considering the level of the children's abilities and other instructional factors, you can make a decision about the scope of the concepts you need to cover in an instructional program. Joseph Novak states that

> a good curriculum design requires an analysis first of the concepts in a field of knowledge and, second, consideration of some relationships between these concepts that can serve to illustrate which concepts are most general and superordinate and which are more specific and subordinate. (Novak, 1979, p. 86)

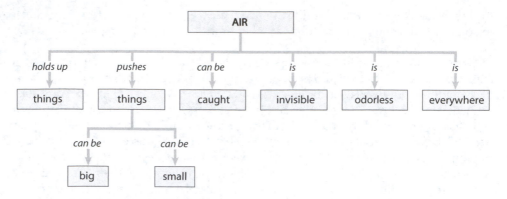

FIGURE 4.2 Concept Map for Air

Source: This figure represents concepts found in the first-grade text (Addison-Wesley, publisher) described by John R. Staver and Mary Bay in "Analysis of the Conceptual Structure and Reasoning Demands of Elementary Science Texts at the Primary (K–3) Level," *Journal of Research in Science Teaching* 26, no. 4 (1989): 334. Reprinted by permission of John Wiley & Sons, Inc. Copyright © 1989 by John Wiley & Sons, Inc.

A concept map's visual illustration of main ideas is the primary advantage it provides over other ways of planning instruction. A concept map shows hierarchical relationships: how various subordinate concepts are related to the superordinate concepts. A relationship can descend several levels deep in the hierarchy of concepts. The relationship between superordinate and subordinate concepts is shown in Figure 4.3.

A concept map is different in several ways from the outline or table of contents generally found at the beginning of a book. First, outlines do not show any definite relationships between concepts; they simply show how the material is organized. Concept maps, on the other hand, show a definite relationship between big ideas and small ideas, thus clarifying the difference between details or specifics and the big idea or superordinate concept. This can be helpful when a teacher must decide how much emphasis to give to specific facts as compared to concepts in a lesson.

The second difference is that concept maps provide visual imagery that can help students recall information and see relationships between concepts. Outlines do not provide such imagery. Outlines do serve a useful function: They indicate a sequence of different steps. Concept maps, on the other hand, show hierarchies of ideas that suggest psychologically valid sequences. These hierarchies may not match the linear sequence, or outline, that a teacher has decided to use for a presentation.

Third, concept maps can show interrelationships between ideas, or *cross-links*. These help to "tie it all together," as students often remark.

Why Develop Concept Maps?

Concept maps help teachers understand the various concepts that are embedded in the larger topic they are to teach. This understanding improves teacher planning and instruction (Starr & Krajcik, 1990). Since the science knowledge domain is vast, and most

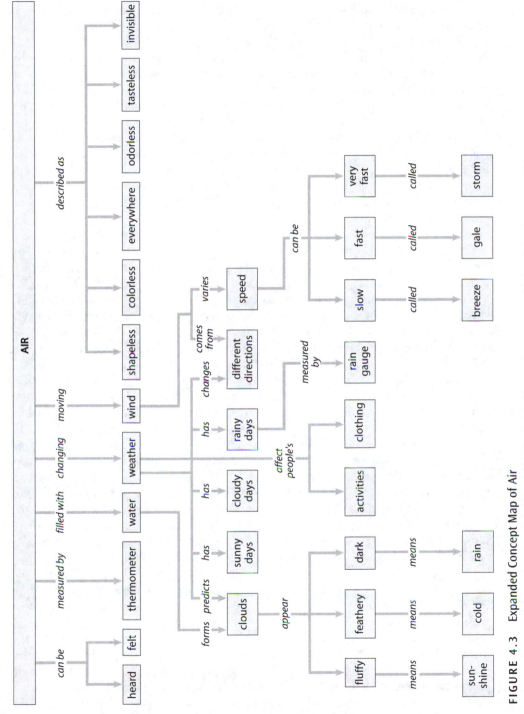

FIGURE 4.3 Expanded Concept Map of Air

Source: The figure shows the relationship of several levels of subordinate concepts as provided by John R. Staver and Mary Bay, in "Analysis of the Conceptual Structure and Reasoning Demands of Elementary Science Texts at the Primary (K–3) Level," *Journal of Research in Science Teaching* 26, no. 4 (1989): 339. The researchers examined the contents of the Merrill first-grade science text. Reprinted by permission of John Wiley & Sons, Inc. Copyright © 1989 by John Wiley & Sons, Inc.

of us have acquired it in pieces at different stages, we are not likely to see the important connections between the separate ideas we teach. As an exercise, mapping provides an opportunity to express our understanding about various concepts and to show relationships with other similar and dissimilar concepts. Ultimately, the larger topic or unit (superordinate concept) is hierarchically arranged. This arrangement shows facts at the bottom and subordinate concepts arranged in relationships with each other in the body of the map (see, for example, the details of Figures 4.2 and 4.3). Our experience with hundreds of teachers and students has convinced us that they gain new insight from developing concept maps when they structure what they know around a superordinate concept. This observation is also supported by Novak and Gowin (1986): "Students and teachers often remark that they recognize new relationships among concepts that they did not before" (p. 17). As well, concept maps help learners encode information into meaningful networks that enhance long-term memory (Eggen & Kauchak, 1992) and help reduce students' anxiety while improving achievement and enhancing self-worth (Jegede et al., 1990).

Concept mapping is one of the most crucial steps to take while deciding what to include in a curriculum, unit, or lesson plan. Clear mapping may help to avoid student-formed misconceptions (Czerniak & Haney, 1998). Without concept maps, teachers choose to teach what they can remember or what they prefer. The topics they select in this manner may be appropriate at times, especially for teachers who have had previous successful experiences with the material, but this process opens a major psychological flaw in the process of curriculum development and lesson planning. The concepts or topics chosen may be so disconnected from each other that learners are baffled and see no connections. Learners may also fail to receive new meaning because they cannot link the new material with what they have previously learned. As a result, learners may resort to memorizing isolated facts, treating the experiences and ideas with less thought than we prefer. This mental inaction would defeat the modern science goal of developing new habits of the mind.

Although some material must be memorized, sustained memorization has questionable value in science. Taking the time to identify concepts yields clear science topics and helps to determine which topics are worth learning. Mapping concepts suggests specific objectives that teachers must establish for pupils. Concept maps can help you see the logic of the relationships among specific concepts. Once you see this logic, you can decide how much depth or breadth to include in lessons so that students will see the same conceptual relationships. These decisions consist of choosing the proper activities and learning aids, as well as selecting the appropriate type of pupil evaluation.

You can also use concept maps to organize the flow of the classroom lessons. We have used concept maps as advance organizers to focus students' attention and guide them along to seeing a bigger picture and for use as a mental scaffolding for organizing their thoughts and discoveries. You can use concept maps as road maps to indicate the direction in which instruction is to proceed in your classroom—up, down, and across the map. Students can be shown concept maps several times during instruction so that they can see what has been covered and how it fits with the rest. Creative primary teachers have used concept maps as a reading and meta-cognitive tool by posting sight words that represent the science idea of the day on a large bulletin board, then discussing cumulative meanings with children and inviting them to suggest organizational relationships between and among the words. Over time, the class of young learners cooperatively constructed a class concept map that illustrated their emergent and changing conceptions.

Another way you can use concept maps is for student evaluations. For example, display large pieces of newsprint in a conspicuous place and use them daily to show the science ideas students have learned and how these ideas interrelate. This daily effort is an example of formative evaluation. You could ask primary grades children to "fill in the blanks" of a constructed map using a familiar word bank, or intermediate and middle school children to develop their own maps at the end of instruction to reflect what they understand, a process called *summative evaluation*.

Steps for Developing a Concept Map

A concept map can be developed for the entire course for a year or semester, or for a single unit, or even for a single lesson. Figure 4.4 shows the relationship of concepts in a concept map. The following steps work for all concept maps:

1. List on paper all of the concepts (names of topics) that pertain to a general area you will teach. Only the names are needed at this stage. No descriptions are necessary. For example, let us say you have examined your next science chapter or module and have listed the following topics: air, weather, clouds, storms, and effects of weather.

2. Note any specific facts (examples) that are either essential for students to learn or that you find especially interesting. The facts and examples you list might include air moves, measurements are used to track air movement, moving air causes weather, weather can be helpful or harmful, and weather helps us decide what clothes to wear.

3. From the list of concepts, choose what you find as an overarching concept (superordinate), and place it at the top of the paper. (You may want to use a large sheet of newsprint or other suitable drawing paper.) You decide that the overarching concept is *weather*. It seems that all other ideas relate to it. Satisfied, you now line up the other concepts by going to Step 4.

4. Arrange the first level of subordinate concepts underneath the superordinate concept. Generally, this stage requires the use of propositions or linking words like *provides, types, contains, can be,* and so on to develop the appropriate connections between subordinate concepts. Refer to the second line of boxes in Figure 4.4. (The first level of subordinate concepts is known by another term, *coordinate concepts,* because they link or coordinate the superordinate concept and the subordinate concepts found lower in the hierarchy. Each coordinate concept is related to the same superordinate concept, but it is distinctly different from other concepts arranged at that level of the hierarchy.)

5. After the first level of coordinate concepts has been identified, start arranging other subordinate concepts that are directly related to the level above. Similarly, you can develop further hierarchies by going down several levels. You will find that specific facts will be examples of certain individual subordinate concepts that will most likely be at

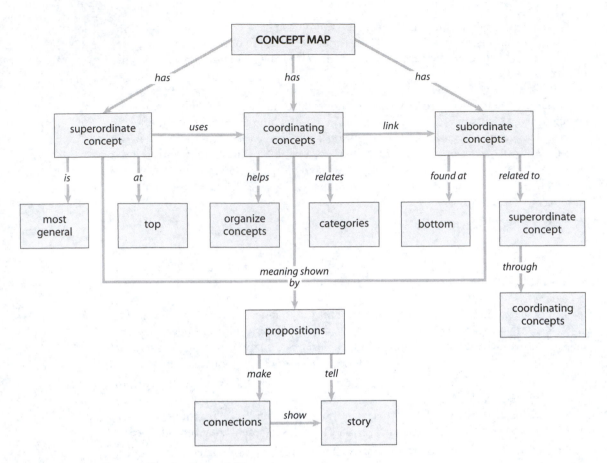

FIGURE 4.4 Concept Map for Concept Maps

the bottom of the hierarchy. See, for example, in Figure 4.3 that *clouds* is a subordinate concept connected to coordinate concepts of *water* and *weather,* and the concepts *fluffy, feathery,* and *dark* are connected to *clouds* to show other subordinate concepts in the hierarchy; each concept relates back to the superordinate concept, *air.*

6. Draw lines to show relationships among the subordinate, coordinate, and superordinate concepts. The entire hierarchy should resemble a pyramid. Write linking words (propositions) on the lines to show relationships among concepts. These relationships form principles. Refer to Figure 4.4 and notice the connecting lines with propositions—for example, *has, uses,* and *through.*

7. After the entire map has been developed, mark or circle certain subordinate concepts that are particularly appealing for your students or are at the appropriate difficulty level. These would generally constitute your course or unit for the given time period.

There are three more important points. First, try to minimize jumping around the entire map; try not to select topics without a strong rationale. The strongest reason for a choice of topic is to build on the knowledge the children have already acquired. During the appropriate phases of your instruction (called *concept invention* and *expansion*, which are explained later in this chapter), you need to help children link the new concept with previous learning.

Second, balance the number of specific details you teach in terms of how well they contribute to overall conceptual development. Remember, the factual information sits at the bottom of the map, and your purpose is to have children understand what rests at higher levels of the map. Teaching factual information alone does not help children to develop concepts at a higher level unless you make specific attempts to move up the hierarchical ladder.

Third, use Figure 4.5 to self-evaluate your concept map. The criteria of the rubric will help you to move from a novice level of mapmaking toward a level of mastery and integration of conceptual understanding of science into your graphic portrayal of abstract ideas.

4 Integrating

- Map has frequent branching.
- Cross links are frequent and logical.
- Linking words are present and appropriate.
- Concepts are logically presented and show various levels.

- All concepts are included on the map and others are added to support related concepts.
- Examples are abundant and relevant.

3 Mastering

- Map has frequent branching.
- Cross links are present and logical.
- Linking words are usually present but not always appropriate.

- Most concepts are logically presented and show various levels.
- Most concepts are included on the map.
- Examples are present and relevant.

2 Developing

- Map has some branching.
- Cross links are few and not necessarily logical.
- Linking words are used sparingly and are not always appropriate.

- Concepts are not logically presented and/or lack various levels.
- Several concepts are not included on the map.
- Examples are sparse.

1 Novice

- Map is rather linear.
- Cross links are not evident and/or are not logical.
- Linking words are not evident and/or are inappropriate.

- Concepts are not logically presented and/or lack various levels.
- Large gaps exist in concept representation.
- Examples are not evident or are irrelevant.

FIGURE 4.5 Holistic Scoring Rubric for Concept Maps

Source: Haney, J. (1998) Concept mapping in the science classroom: Linking theory to practice. *The Agora*, Vol. VIII, September, p. 6.

Video Explorations — Planning Inquiry Lessons

Video Summary

This video describes the nature of concepts and the processes for mapping conceptual understanding. Preservice teachers are taught to make a concept map through a card-sorting exercise, which may be modified and used in university or school classrooms. Concept maps have many uses,

con • cept (kŏn′ sĕpt′) *n.* 1. A general idea or understanding, esp. one derived from specific instances or occurrences. 2. A thought or notion. [LLat. *conceptus* < p.part of *concipere,* to conceive.]

which are described in the video, but ultimately "tell a story" about what is known and understood. Maps provide useful tools for planning curriculum and lessons. Concept maps have common components, but maps can be drawn in different ways to illustrate what their creators understand. Group-constructed concept maps often undergo a period of negotiation as group members individually share viewpoints to arrive at collective constructed understanding. Concept maps may be used to help children who have learning disabilities, as described by on-camera teacher testimony.

Tips for Viewing, Objectives, or What to Watch for

Keep in mind the following as you watch this video:

   ✦ The classroom scenes were unrehearsed; what you see is authentic learning.

fact (făkt) *n.* 1. Something done. 2. Something presented as objectively real. 3. Something that has been objectively verified. 4. a. Something having real, demonstrable existence. b. The quality of being real or actual. 5. Something that has been done or performed.

   ✦ The students in this video read chapter material in a school science text; their concept map's structure changed as they worked together to share understanding about the school science text material.

   ✦ The concept map graphic featured in this video is also provided in the textbook as Figure 4.4 on page 120.

   ✦ Teacher and student testimony about learning and using concept maps is authentic and unrehearsed.

   ✦ This video lasts 15 minutes.

Questions for Exploration

1. What are the various ways that concept maps can be used? How do you think mapping might be modified for younger learners?

2. What benefits could concept maps provide for users?

3. Think back to Chapter 2. How do the processes of making and using concept maps seem to be compatible with how children learn?

4. Think back to Chapter 3. What types of benefits do you think concept maps could provide for learners who have special needs?

5. If you had mapped the relationships among science materials and then planned a series of lessons, how do you think you might "think" differently or teach differently while leading lessons for learners?

Activity for Application

Consider the processes seen in this video that were used to make a concept map and try them for yourself. Select some science material to be taught, perhaps a couple of related chapters. Indentify and list all of the concepts. Prepare 3 × 5 cards or post-it notes and sort them into a map; be certain to select a super-ordinate concept (the big idea to be placed in

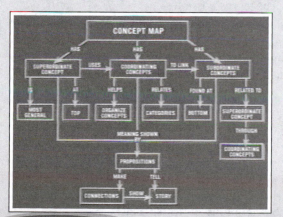

the box at the top of your map). Use lines and arrows to reveal relationships and make those clear by using propositions. Read your map. What story of understanding is shown? What uncertainties about the science concepts do you have and what will you do to improve your understanding? How will you use your map to plan lessons? When you teach, what will you do to help learners form understandings about the relationships among science concepts?

Planning Constructive Inquiry Science Lessons

Reform efforts, such as the National Science Education Standards, direct our attention toward teaching to the goal of scientific literacy. Standards identify numerous outcomes that we attempt to help students achieve. Embedded in the outcomes are dozens of essential science concepts, skills, values, and cross-disciplinary science knowledge that students are expected to demonstrate. Constructivist learning theory and inquiry research caution us against attempting the futile effort of frontal teaching. How can we address the new expectations held aloft for science teachers and students?

Selecting Performance Outcomes and Developing Curriculum

Concept maps (see Figure 4.6) illustrate clusters of concepts that share relationships with other science concepts. These relationships make it possible to identify a unifying theme that can help us construct units of science experiences for learners. The standards' outcomes help to provide parameters that are useful for selecting learning outcomes and developing a curriculum that encourages full, active participation and student conceptual constructions. See the Appendix for a list of outcomes for grades K–4 and 5–8. The standards, outcomes, and concept maps are tools for making prudent selections to avoid the "fill-up-the-empty-time" approach. Used appropriately, mapping and planning can help to make wise choices so lessons have clear expectations, abundant opportunities for students to construct understanding through inquiry, and expanded contact with science in many contexts. Some general planning principles can help us help students develop their thinking skills and learn meaningful science:

1. *Provide a variety of activities for learning.* Activities that provide children opportunities to experience and manipulate real objects are essential. Emphasize direct physical and mental involvement for children in primary and intermediate grades. All children must be given opportunities to explain what they experience and to communicate this to others in written and spoken language. All learning activities should be expanded to address as many of the goal clusters as possible.

2. *Introduce concepts and specialized vocabulary after children have gained first-hand experiences with the object or concept.* As a general rule, teachers should talk less and involve students more. One way of doing this is to tell less and ask more. Questions are devices for encouraging children to use their minds. Chapter 7 is devoted to the uses of questions.

3. *Interact with children and have them interact with each other.* Questions stimulate interaction, and interaction encourages thinking. Ask children to describe what they have done or observed. Encourage children to ask each other questions about their experiences and to ask *why* questions.

4. *Focus learning experiences so that children are encouraged to discover concepts.* Focusing on concepts, the main ideas behind learning, helps children learn connections more easily and removes the learning barrier of disconnected facts.

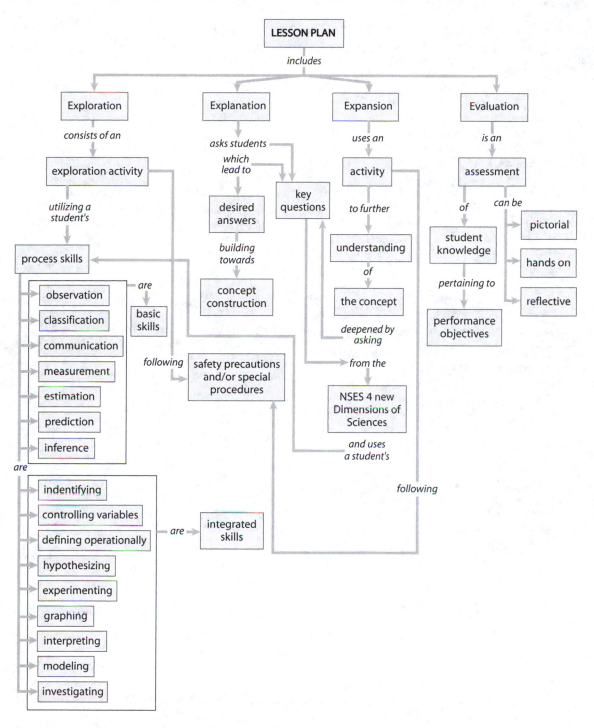

FIGURE 4.6 Concept Map of Inquiry Lesson Plan

Standards-Based Science Lesson Planning

Why spend time planning detailed science lessons when there could be simpler and less time consuming ways to plan? The big picture for thoughtful teacher science lesson planning comes from the Glenn Commission Report, *Before It's Too Late*. The report challenges us to keep in mind four reasons to focus carefully on planning effective, standards-based lessons so that learners can become proficient in science include: (1) a rapidly changing workplace within a global economy demands a strong understanding of science, (2) everyday decision making requires scientific and technical competency among all citizens, (3) national security is dependent upon science and technology, and (4) science shapes and defines human history and culture. Collectively, these reasons comprise a compelling goal of pursuing scientific literacy for *all* students, which requires that primary- and middle-school science lessons:

- help learners understand the important and fundamental ideas of science,
- stimulate active learning through inquiry-based, question-driven lessons,
- motivate learner-constructed connections across the scientific disciplines,
- orient all learners about potential future careers, and

- use learning strategies and mental tools that help students with personal decisions related to issues in science.

Successful science lessons are planned to provide all students with opportunities to learn, meaning that student-centered, real-world contexts and uses of inquiry processes afford each learner an opportunity to use preferred styles of learning for building confidence and self-esteem about successful performance, and sufficient challenge for developing additional skills that reside outside their comfort zones. Lessons must be well balanced in opportunities to learn. Individual tasks should be complemented with group investigations and cooperation; an array of skills must be developed to stimulate mental, physical, social, and emotional dexterity. While planning for learning, teachers strengthen students' achievements if they plan to teach around the cycle: balancing the challenges and instructional methods so all children are met partly in their preferred style, but also gain confidence in learning with less preferred modes. Planning for a learning cycle can help ensure that teachers sufficiently challenge, motivate, and support all of their learners, and avoid the limitations of unidimensional teaching.

Source: National Commission on Mathematics and Science Teaching for the 21st Century, *Before It's Too Late: A Report to the Nation from the National Commission on Mathematics and Science Teaching for the 21st Century.* Washington, DC: U.S. Department of Education. A. Krueger and J. Sutton (Eds.). *EDThoughts: What We Know About Science Teaching and Learning* (Aurora, CO: Mid-continent research for education and learning, 2001).

Planning the Lesson—4–Es

Effective science lessons have a central focus and clear expectations for student performance. The *lesson concept*—the main science idea—is the central focus, and is the heart of the 4–E inquiry lesson plan—select or develop it first. Your planning in other education courses may have taught you how to write objectives. Lesson objectives help define the expected types and levels of performance, or what and how the students are to demonstrate that they understand the concept and can apply their understanding to useful matters. Objectives are important for helping to evaluate what learners know and can do. Conceptual understanding, to have lasting value, must be applied to the student's world. This application expands the depth of learning and helps fulfill the new dimensions of science outcomes: experiencing science as inquiry, understanding the interrelationships of science and technology, using personal and social perspectives to understand science, and comprehending the nature of science throughout its history. Table 4.2 lists these expected outcomes.

The planning model presented here uses a conceptual focus, helps learners to construct meaning, encourages students to expand understanding of that fundamental meaning, and evaluates student performance in authentic ways. Called a *learning cycle* (see Figure 4.7, page 131), this series of planning and teaching steps helps teachers to encourage learners to construct meaning from direct experiences, then expand that understanding through direct treatment of the new dimensions of science. The lesson planning model in this chapter closely follows the

Effective science lessons stimulate learners' minds, shape attitudes, and provide learning opportunities for physical manipulation of learning materials.

original format of the Science Curriculum Improvement Study, which major research studies credit with the greatest student achievement gains and significant improvements in student science attitudes and inquiry skills, when compared to similar experimental

(*text continues on page 130*)

TABLE 4.2 Four New Dimensions of Science Content Standards and Outcomes

Dimension 1. Science as Inquiry Standard

The students will

1.1 Develop abilities necessary to do scientific inquiry.
- Ask questions about objects, organisms, and events in their natural environment.
- Plan and conduct simple science investigations.
- Use simple science equipment and other appropriate tools that extend their senses in order to gather, analyze, and interpret data.
- Use data to construct descriptions, explanations, predictions, and models.
- Identify relationships between evidence and explanations.
- Communicate, critique, and analyze the work of other students and recognize and analyze alternative explanations and predictions.

1.2 Understand about scientific inquiry.
- Ask and answer questions and compare answers to what scientists already know about the world.
- Select the kind of investigation that fits the questions they are trying to answer.
- Realize the instruments provide more information than a scientist can obtain only by using his or her senses, and enhance the accuracy of that information.
- Develop explanations that are based on observation, evidence, and scientific concepts.

(continued)

TABLE 4.2 (continued)

- Describe investigations in ways that make it possible for others to repeat the same investigation.
- Review and ask questions about the results of others' work and realize that science advances through legitimate skepticism.

Dimension 2. Science and Technology Standard

The students will

2.1 Develop an ability to distinguish between natural objects and objects made by humans.
- Realize that some objects occur in nature and that other objects have been designed by people to solve human problems.
- Categorize objects into two groups, natural and designed.

2.2 Develop an ability to understand and produce a technological design.
- Identify an age-appropriate problem for technological design, propose a solution, and design it, perhaps by collaborating with others.
- Evaluate a product or design and communicate the results to others by describing the process of technological design.

2.3 Understand about science and technology.
- Realize that science and technological design often have similarities and differences that make it necessary for scientists and engineers to work together, often in teams with other professionals, in order to solve problems.
- Understand that science and technology provide opportunities to women and men of all ages, groups, backgrounds, races, religions, and abilities to do various scientific and technological work and that a person's appearance, gender, race, or national origin should not influence acceptance or rejection of his or her contributions to science or technology.
- Understand that tools help scientists to make better observations, measurements, and equipment for investigations and that science helps drive technology.
- Understand that people have always had questions about the natural world and that scientists have invented tools and techniques to help answer those questions.
- Understand that technological designs have constraints and that the technological solutions may have intended benefits and unintended consequences, some of which may not be predictable.

Dimension 3. Science in Personal and Social Perspectives Standard

The students will

3.1 Develop an understanding of personal health.
- Understand that safety and security are basic needs of humans.
- Demonstrate responsibility for their own health through regular exercise routines.
- Understand that good nutrition is essential to health, develop nutritious eating habits, and recognize that nutritional needs vary with age, sex, weight, activity, and body functions.
- Recognize and avoid substances that can damage the human body, including environmental hazards (e.g., lead, radon), and recognize that prescription drugs can be beneficial if taken as directed.

TABLE 4.2   (continued)

- Recognize the potential for accidents, identify safety hazards, and take precautions for safe living.
- Understand that the sex drive is a natural human instinct; the consequences of new life and disease must be understood.

3.2   Identify characteristics and describe changes in populations.
- Understand that human populations include groups of persons who live in a particular location.
- Understand that density refers to the number of individuals of a population who can live in a particular amount of space.
- Realize that the size of a human and animal population can increase or decrease and that populations will increase unless factors such as disease, insufficient food, or disasters limit it. Overpopulation increases the consumption of resources.

3.3   Identify types of resources.
- Understand resources are materials we get from the living and nonliving environment to meet the needs of a population.
- Identify examples of resources such as air, water, soil, food, fuel, building materials, and the nonmaterial such as quiet places, beauty, security, and safety.
- Understand that the supply of resources is limited but that recycling and reduced use can extend the length of time that resources are available; overconsumption and overpopulation deplete resources.

3.4   Identify environments and changes.
- Understand that the concept of environment includes the space, conditions, and factors that affect an individual's or an entire population's quality of life and ability to survive.
- Realize that environmental changes can be caused by natural or human causes and that some changes are good, some bad, others neither good nor bad.
- Understand that internal and external changes in the earth's system cause natural hazards and destruction of life.
- Understand that pollution is a change in the environment that can influence health and survival or limit the activities of organisms, including humans; pollution can be caused by natural occurrences and human activity.
- Comprehend that some environmental changes occur slowly and others rapidly and describe examples of each (e.g., weather, climate, erosion, movements of large geologic masses).

3.5   Recognize the benefits and challenges of science and technology.
- Understand that inventions and problem solutions can affect other people in helpful and harmful ways.
- Recognize that science influences society through its knowledge and worldview and that technology influences society through its products and processes.
- Identify risks and analyze the potential benefits and consequences and understand that risks and benefits relate directly to personal and social decisions.
- Describe how science and technology have improved transportation, health, sanitation, and communication and realize that the benefits of science and technology are not always available to all people.

(continued)

TABLE 4.2 (continued)

- Understand that science and technology have advanced through the contributions of many different people, different cultures, and at different times throughout history.
- Realize that scientists and engineers have codes of ethics that require humans who are part of their research to be fully informed about the risks and benefits associated with the research.
- Understand that science cannot answer all questions and that technology cannot solve all human problems or meet all human needs.

Dimension 4. History and Nature of Science Standard

The students will

4.1 Understand that science is a human endeavor.
- Realize that science and technology have been used for a long time.
- Understand that women and men have made important contributions to science and technology throughout history.
- Understand that there is still much to learn about science.
- Understand that doing science requires persons of different abilities and talents.

4.2 Understand the nature of science.
- Realize that scientists use consistent procedures to test explanations and to form ideas.
- Understand that scientists do not always agree, particularly when active research is pursued in new experimental areas, but that science ideas are supported by considerable observation and confirmation, even though the nature of science is tentative.
- Understand that scientists expect their ideas and research to be evaluated by other scientists and that while scientists may disagree over conclusions, they agree that skepticism, questioning, and open communication are essential to progress in science.

4.3 Understand the importance of history to science.
- Realize that studying the lives and times of important scientists provides further understanding about the nature of scientific inquiry and the relationships between science and society.
- Realize that the history of science reveals that the scientists and engineers of high achievement are considered to be among the most valued contributors of any culture.
- Trace the history of science to understand how difficult it was for innovators to break through the dominant scientific preconceptions of their times and to reach conclusions that seem obvious today.

Source: Adapted from National Research Council, National *Science Education Standards* (Washington, DC: National Academy Press, 1996), pp. 121–171.

science programs and traditional science curricula (Shymansky et al., 1982; Bredderman, 1982).

Our planning model has been modified to stimulate a full range of student inquiry, reflect constructivist learning expectations, support inquiry, and emphasize appropriate student evaluation. This approach is simple and thorough, and has considerable potential to effect improvements in students' learning. The planning model also becomes the teaching method. A detailed description of the teaching method is described in Chapter 6. The elements of planning are given here.

The four phases of the science planning and learning cycle provide most of the structure for planning an effective science lesson. Once you identify the concept that is to be learned, you can structure the learning activity to take advantage of the learning cycle. Then you can add descriptions of the proper ways to evaluate what the children learn. Consider these questions in order to see the big picture as you begin your lesson planning:

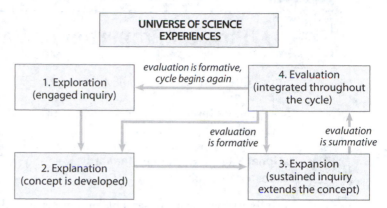

FIGURE 4.7   The Planning and Learning Cycle

+ How can I identify and get to "the point"?
+ How can I faithfully model what science is and help the children experience holistic science?
+ How can I address specific standards?
+ How can I promote science safely?
+ How can I teach effectively and in a manner that fits children's learning?
+ How can I evaluate authentically what children know and can do?
+ How can I pull the answers to all of these questions into a single plan that also becomes my method for teaching?

The *4–E approach* is recommended: exploration, explanation, expansion, and evaluation. The following questions should help you plan for each step of the learning cycle as you write the lesson plan. The parenthetical remarks suggest the aspects of science and teaching strategies that may be used. A sample science learning cycle lesson plan is shown in the 4–E Feature Lesson on page 132.

Step 1. Planning for student exploration

Children must have concrete materials and experiences if they are to learn concrete concepts. Abstract concepts are largely inappropriate for most pupils, even with concrete materials. The learners must become engaged in the context of the inquiry and be stimulated by the teacher and objects in order to undertake free and guided inquiry. Use these guiding questions:

+ What do I want the children to learn? (concept, attitudes, processes)
+ What main concept will be explored? (science products)
+ What must I do to engage the learner's thinking and involve them in inquiry processes?
+ What activities must the children do to find and to construct the needed data? (processes, information, answers to questions)

(text continues on page 135)

Physical Properties of Matter

GRADE LEVEL: K–4

DISCIPLINE: Physical Science

Inquiry Question: How can objects be described?

Concept to Be Invented: Objects have many observable properties, such as size, weight, color, shape, behavior.

National Science Education Standards: K–4 Physical Science—Properties of objects and materials

+ Objects have many observable properties, including size, weight, shape, color, temperature, and the ability to react with other substances. These properties can be measured using tools, such as rulers, balances, and thermometers.
+ Objects are made of one or more materials, such as paper, wood, and metal. Objects can be described by the properties of the materials from which they are made, and these properties can be used to separate or sort a group of objects or materials.

Science Attitudes to Nurture: Curiosity, cooperating with others, tolerating other opinions, explanations, or points of view

Materials Needed

Enough hard boiled, white eggs for half the class. Place the cooked eggs and an equal number of raw (uncooked) eggs, randomly, in a bowl. Allow each student to pick an egg out of the bowl.

1 can of broth or canned liquid, 1 can of dog food, paper towels, clear container or bowl, 3 or 4 different brands of chocolate chip cookies, 1 ruler, 5 to 10 toothpicks, paper for recording data

Safety Precautions: Encourage students to use senses, except taste. Remind students to wash their hands after the Exploration activity, especially before they begin the Expansion activity.

Exploration *Which process skills will be used?*

Observing, manipulating materials, collecting and recording data, communicating

Enter the classroom carrying the bowl of eggs. Act as if you are greatly troubled. Explain to the students that you boiled some eggs last night for dinner and placed them in the refrigerator. When you went to the refrigerator this morning, you found that someone had taken the cooked eggs and combined them with the raw eggs in the bowl. Now you have to determine which are cooked and which are raw without breaking any of them. Ask the students if they can help you solve your problem.

Ask each student to choose an egg from the bowl and to make as many observations about their egg as possible without breaking the egg open. Remind them not to break the egg. Allow sufficient time for students to collect their data and record their observations. For very young students, ask them to draw their observations. Once they have made their observations, move to the concept invention phase of this lesson.

Explanation

As students make their observations, encourage students who appear to be stumped to think of ways to make observations. Ask questions such as: When I make an observation, am I using only my eyes? What other things can I use to make an observation? Encourage the students to think about ways they can manipulate the egg without dropping or breaking it. Remind the students to record the information they are discovering. Guide students to word the concept: Objects have many observable properties, such as size, weight, color, shape, behavior.

Solicit the students' observations. Make a list on the board. Once you have an observation from each student, go back to the original question: Which of these observations will help me solve my problem? Ask a student to restate the problem: Which eggs are raw and which are cooked?

Through the process of elimination, the students will find that some physical properties are more distinguishing than others. For instance, observing that the egg is white is not going to solve the problem, since all of the eggs the students have are white. However, observations such as: "It sounds as if something is moving inside when I shake my egg," or "My egg will spin or stand on end," are observations that will help solve the problem. Ask the students: Is one distinguishing characteristic enough to decide if any egg is cooked or raw? If some students think so, then ask them to make their prediction about whether their egg is cooked or raw based on that one distinguishing characteristic. Let one student crack an egg only to find that the prediction was incorrect. (Make sure that the student chosen to bring out the idea that one characteristic is not enough has in fact made a wrong decision.)

As you progress through the list of student observations, keep referring back to the original problem. As you narrow down their observations to those that help solve the problem, you may find that the students eventually come to an observation that stumps them: Some eggs spin easily and others sort of wobble but don't spin well. The students aren't sure if the raw or cooked eggs spin easily. At this point the teacher should bring out the cans of broth and dog food. (Two cans of each are helpful.) Open the can of broth and pour it into a clear container. Ask the students what state of matter the broth is in. Have a student volunteer to spin the unopened can of broth and ask if it is easy or hard to get the can to spin.

(continued)

Now open a can of dog food and empty it into a clear container. Ask the students what state of matter the dog food is in. Have a student volunteer to spin the unopened can of dog food and ask the student if it is easy or hard to get the can to spin.

Expansion   *Which process skills will be used?*

Designing an experiment, observing, measuring, predicting, hypothesizing, recording data

This expansion activity is more appropriate for students in grades 3–6. For K–2 students, you may want to lead a guided discovery activity using the following ideas:

Remind the students about the concept they have learned about observable physical properties from the Exploration activity. Physical properties of matter help distinguish one kind of matter from another. Ask the students to design an experiment using just physical properties to determine what the best brand of chocolate chip cookie is. Allow sufficient class time for groups of students to brainstorm ways in which they could use only physical properties to determine the best brand of chocolate cookie. Ask the students to submit a copy of their planned experiment and a materials list so that they can perform their experiment in the next class meeting. Suggested materials are included in the materials list at the beginning of the lesson. Be sure to read over the designed experiments to be sure that they are using only physical properties and also that appropriate safety standards are maintained.

On the second day, allow the students to act on appropriately planned lessons. On the third day, ask the different student groups to share the methods they used for determining the best cookie and the results of their experiment. Once all of the groups have had a chance to share their results, and especially if the results were different, ask the students if it is necessary to set some criteria for determining which cookie is best. The students should conclude that the term *best* is arbitrary—the members of the group must decide criteria for judging an object the *best*.

As a final discussion question, ask the students why you asked them to design their experiment around physical properties. Why could they not taste the cookie to determine the best?

Science in Personal and Social Perspectives

+ If you had to describe your best friend to another student, how would you do that? Would a description, such as: "He or she is really nice and cute," be enough? Why or why not?
+ If you were talking with a group of people about the best movie you ever saw, do you think everyone in the group would agree with you? Why or why not?

Science and Technology

+ How does the mineral industry determine which mineral is which?
+ Why has the auto industry gone from metal bumpers to plastic bumpers? What do properties of matter have to do with that decision?

Science as Inquiry

◆ Students engage in manipulative skills during the activities.

◆ How can you accurately describe an object?

◆ How can you tell the difference between a raw and cooked egg without cracking the egg open?

History and Nature of Science

◆ Pretend you want a new sidewalk in front of your house. You need to hire a cement contractor to do the work. One contractor you interviewed said it didn't matter what kind of material he or she used to pour your sidewalk. Does this person know much about distinguishing physical properties of matter? Would you be willing to hire that contractor? Why or why not?

◆ Who do you think should be aware of the many different physical properties of matter for their work? What kinds of skills are needed for that profession? Have the necessary skills changed in the past twenty years?

Evaluation

Upon completing the activities, the students will be able to:

◆ determine, when given an egg, whether it is cooked or raw;

◆ design an experiment to determine the best brand of paper towels;

◆ list the physical properties of three or four different things (the teacher can choose any number of items: a rock, flower, penny, button, or anything else).

◆ How will I stimulate the learners to remain engaged in the processes of inquiry?

◆ What kinds of records should the children keep? (process skills)

◆ What kinds of instructions and encouragement will the children need? (attitudes)

Begin the lesson by directing the children's activities and suggesting what kinds of records they should keep. *Do not tell or explain the concept.* State the instructions succinctly. Plan this step carefully so that it is student centered and student activity based.

Step 2. Planning for explanation

The main purpose of this phase is to reach mental equilibrium through accommodation, as described by Jean Piaget (see Chapter 2). Equilibrium is reached when learners' thinking is guided, meaning is made from direct experiences, and a new concept is formed and/or linked to previously understood related concepts. Here students must focus on their primary findings from exploration, and the teacher must help them by introducing proper language or concept labels. This step was originally called *concept invention*. The teacher's task is to lead students through a discussion so that students can discover the concept by inventing it for themselves. The teacher's technique is to question skillfully so that students use the experiences of their explorations to construct scientific meaning. The teacher acts as a facilitator and introduces any special vocabulary that must accompany the concept. Plan this step carefully so that it does not become completely teacher centered; your lectures must be minimal. Use these questions as you plan for this part of your lesson:

✦ What kinds of information or findings are students expected to provide? (products, process skills)
✦ How will the students' observations and records from the exploration phase be reviewed and summarized? (teacher questioning, pupil discussion, graphing, board work)
✦ How can I use the students' findings and refrain from telling them what they should have found, even if they are incorrect or incomplete? (teacher questioning, guided construction, attitudes)
✦ What are the proper concept labels or terms that must be attached to the concept? (products)
✦ How can I use a sentence starter to involve the students in explaining what the concept means?
✦ What reasons can I give the students if they ask me why the concept is important? (teacher exposition, lesson expansion)

The last question automatically leads to the next phase: Expansion.

Step 3. Planning for expansion

The purpose of this phase is to sustain the inquiry by helping students organize their thinking and by applying what they have just learned to other ideas or experiences that relate to the lesson's concept and to help the students to expand their ideas. It is very important to use the language of the concept during the expansion-of-the-idea phase. Plan this phase for continued student involvement and to limit misconceptions by refining the concept. Consider using these questions:

✦ What previous experiences have the children had that are related to the concept? How can I connect the concept to these experiences? (new activities, questioning)
✦ What are some examples of how the concept and the activities encourage the students' science inquiry skills? (learning activities, questioning)
✦ What activities and key questions can be used to illustrate the interrelationship of science and technology and the contributions of each to society and the quality (or problems) of life? (discussion, readings, uses of multimedia, class projects)
✦ In what ways has science benefited the students personally? (class projects, reflective questioning)
✦ How has science affected the children and influenced our society, policies, and laws? (linkages with social studies, current events)
✦ What have been the dominant ideas of science throughout recorded history, and how have those ideas and the nature of science changed over time?

Teachers on Science Teaching

How Can You Create Learning Opportunities?

by Mike Roberts

Grade 1, Hollister School District, Hollister, California

When I was a student teacher, my master teacher made available to me a space in which to save some of the materials I used in her second-grade classroom. I saved all the odds and ends and eventually this collection included many objects that were useful for creating science activities.

One day a boy brought an old fifth-grade science textbook to school. He had found many activities in it that he desperately wanted to do. I told him to select one we could do with the things we had on hand. He selected a wind speed indicator made from a paper plate, paper cups, a pin, tape, and a pencil—all readily available from the box of extra materials. We constructed it, and he made many more with his friends.

There were several lessons here for me. First, children have a very good idea of what they want to learn about. Second, they can figure out how to create something from the available material. Third and most important, it is very important to keep a significant amount of stuff around for children to use.

Since then, I have tried to ensure that somewhere in the room there are materials that students can use in their own fashion. I collect everyday materials because science is a curricular area that requires that students investigate their everyday world and inquire about its workings. That's all well and good, but there are also practical questions. How does a teacher plan for something like this? How does a teacher set up a classroom for this kind of activity? What are the rest of the students doing while several are messing about with a box of interesting materials? How do we meet students' needs?

Here are some of the ways I dealt with these issues, and I am sure other teachers are inventing different ways also. First, collect things that you suspect may be useful: paper tubes, plates, cups, string, wire, batteries, lights, switches—the list goes on and on. These things are supposed to be in your science kits, but in my experience they have been used up and not replaced. If you do have a pristine kit, then you will be expected to replace what is used. I found it best to collect my own. I don't spend a lot of money. Most of this can be salvaged from the refuse of daily life.

Second, I arrange my school day to accommodate a free time for activities that give the students a chance to use materials with my supervision. I try to encourage, question, and challenge. I try not to direct. I know everyone won't choose every activity every day. The material at hand will allow the students to negotiate and discuss the use of whatever is available.

The goal of our educational system is to engage young minds in activities that lead them to experiment. As they become more aware of their world, they are encouraged to explore and then use their new knowledge to construct a more complete understanding. More understanding means more use of the knowledge and more questions.

I haven't written a lesson plan here, but I've described a plan for creating learning opportunities. This is how I as a teacher present the materials in the room and how I build in opportunities for students to explore them. This way they learn to question each other and me and to experiment and thereby construct a better understanding of their world.

(linkages with social studies, documentaries, class projects, discussion, biographies)

✦ What new experiences do the children need in order to expand on the concept? (processes, attitudes, activities)

✦ What is the next concept related to the present one? How can I encourage exploration of the next concept? (products, processes)

Step 4. Planning for evaluation

The purpose of this phase is to go beyond standard forms of testing. Learning must occur in small increments before larger leaps of insight are possible. Your evaluation of students can be planned in terms of standards-based outcomes and pupil performances, and illustrate what learners know and can do, relevant to your lesson's concept. Several types of records are necessary to form a holistic evaluation of the students' learning and to encourage conceptual understanding as well as process skill development. Evaluation can occur at any point in the lesson. Consistent evaluation can help to reveal misconceptions before they become deeply rooted. Chapter 5 delves more deeply into ways to assess learning. For purposes of completing your plan, ask yourself:

- ✦ What key questions should I ask to encourage purposeful exploration that promotes inquiry? (processes, attitudes)
- ✦ What questions can I ask to help students think about their data in an effort to construct realistic concepts? (processes)
- ✦ What questions will expand conception and achieve selected science standards and outcomes? (processes, products)
- ✦ What behavior (mental, physical, attitudinal) can I expect from the students? (attitudes, processes)
- ✦ What hands-on assessments can the students do to demonstrate the basic skills of observation, classification, communication, measurement, prediction, and inference? (processes)
- ✦ What assessments can students do to demonstrate the integrated skills of identifying and controlling variables, defining operationally, forming hypotheses, experimenting, interpreting data, and forming models?
- ✦ What pictorial assessments can students do to demonstrate how well they can think through problems that require both knowledge and the integration of ideas? (products)
- ✦ What reflective question assessments will indicate how well the students recall and use what has been learned? (products)

Chapter Summary

The National Science Education Standards ushered a new era of exciting learning opportunities for students and new instructional challenges for teachers. Constructivist teaching and inquiry-based learning requires careful planning that places conceptual focus, acts of created understanding, essential experiences, and authentic assessment in a carefully balanced dynamic system. In this chapter we use a 4–E learning cycle to illustrate a planning model that will help you meet the new challenges.

Concept mapping is a tool that helps teachers identify essential concepts and the relationships among concepts. The tool is helpful for making fundamental planning decisions in order to fulfill the outcomes of the content standards. Concept mapping is also a useful evaluation tool.

The 4–E learning cycle provides a dynamic planning system that balances student-centered exploration with teacher-guided conceptual construction. Expansion nurtures understanding as the new dimensions of science learning are fulfilled. Evaluation is continual and is fit to the task.

Discussion Questions

1. Contemporary movements in education usually embrace the preference for students to demonstrate learning outcomes focused upon concepts and skills. Performance or behavioral objectives may be used for this purpose. What advantages or disadvantages do you see with this type of objective?

2. In what ways will the concepts from the Appendix and the outcomes from Table 4.2 help you decide what children should know and be able to do?

Build a Portfolio or E-Folio

1. Examine a textbook, science module, or teacher's manual for any grade level. Construct a concept map for the material you select. State your opinion about how the printed materials' organization makes connections between associated concepts.

2. Prepare several plans for science teaching. First, map the concepts you wish to teach, and then use the learning-cycle planning format discussed in this chapter. What new dimensions of science education are you able to address from Table 4.2?

3. Prepare a lesson plan using the 4–E approach. How many learning activities do you have, and where do they fit into the cycle? What science dimensions do you pursue? How do you evaluate students' learning?

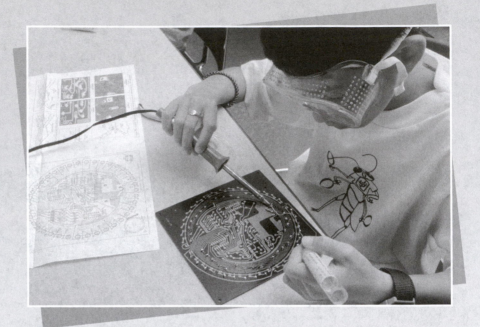

Assessing Student Performance: How Can You Assess Student Learning?

*L*ate one February afternoon as Jim Kestel, a first-year teacher, was completing the lamination of his fifth-grade students' science projects, he was dismayed by the comments he heard in the teachers' workroom. Two fourth-grade teachers were talking about the upcoming state achievement tests. "Well, I think I'm about ready to stop teaching for a while and get these students prepared for the upcoming state tests," stated Kim Carlson, one teacher. "Yeah, I know what you mean," said Kevin Convey, the other teacher. "I've already stopped work on all of my students' science projects just so I can grill them on everything we've learned so far and give them practice taking multiple-choice tests. Most of the other teachers have already started prepping their students for them."

Jim sought the perspective of Joe Pokorny, another fifth-grade teacher. "Is it true that everyone stops *good teaching* just to get their students ready to take the state achievement tests? I always thought as long as I consistently challenged my students and gave assessments that required them to use higher order thinking skills, like analysis, synthesis, and application, regardless of whether I *covered all* of the content, my students would be prepared to take these state exams! Am I wrong?" Joe just looked at Jim in amazement stating, "Oh, you poor, naïve, new teacher!" and walked away, shaking his head and laughing.

Worried that he was doing his students a disservice, Jim went home that evening and called a friend who had been teaching science in a neighboring school district for over ten years. "So, do you think I'm wrong for not stopping teaching like the others to spend time grilling my students on all of the science I've taught them so far this year?" Jim asked his friend, Kathy Jensen, also a fifth-grade teacher. "Well, Jim, that really depends on what you've been doing as far as assessing your students this year. What does a typical 'test' for your science class look like?"

"Well, I've actually used a number of strategies. In the beginning, when I wanted to find out how much they knew about a new topic, I tried pretests, but those soon became overused since the students started feeling as if they had to get a perfect score. Then, I stopped and taught them how to make a concept map when we completed our unit on rocks and minerals. So then, when we began a unit on electricity, I tried the idea of a concept map as a pre- and post-assessment. It was really neat to see how the maps changed from the beginning to the end of the unit."

"Okay. Those were pretty good strategies to find out what they knew to start with. How else did you know if your students were learning the science content?" Kathy asked Jim.

"Well, as you know, I really believe in giving every student as many opportunities as possible to show me what they know and what they can do in science. So for each lesson I created, I followed a learning cycle format, making sure I had assessment built into every phase of the lesson. I identified the process skills the students used during the exploration and expansion phases of the lesson and placed those into a spreadsheet. Throughout the lesson I just kept my computer open to that spreadsheet with the skills listed across the top and the students' names in the first column. When I saw that a student had mastered that skill, I just entered that into the spreadsheet. If I noticed they were having troubles, I jotted a note to myself in the spreadsheet about that student, then tried to work one on one to help them master those skills. Basically, I was assessing the students throughout every phase of my lesson."

"Wow, that sure seems like a lot of work," Kathy noted.

"Not really," said Jim. "Once I set up the initial spreadsheet, it was easy to just copy and paste for each new unit the skills I wanted to address. The hard part was disciplining myself to log in what I observed each day. Sometimes I'd walk around with post-it notes and jot down things I observed on each student, then log in those notes later in the day."

"Okay, so that took care of the science process skills. What about content knowledge, how have you been assessing that?" asked Kathy.

"Well, for each unit, I really try to make sure I address just about every possible learning style by having a performance assessment—some sort of hands-on activity where the students have to apply the science content to a new situation. I also include a picture that they have to interpret, or a picture for them to draw and explain the science concept. Then there's always a reflective question, something that causes them to think about the content in a way not used in class. Hmm . . . maybe I should try to include some multiple-choice questions in there so my students can handle those on the upcoming state proficiency tests."

"Whoa, Jim, don't be so quick to change what I'd call good assessment strategies. It sure sounds as if your students are really learning some science. Even if you don't *cover*

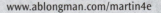

every possible topic they might see on that state exam, it sure sounds as if your students have been challenged to think about what they're learning and how it's applied in other contexts. If you have a chance, go to the state department of education's website or the National Assessment of Educational Progress website. You'll be able to download some of the past years' tests. I think you'll be pleased to find that even though those tests are written in a multiple-choice and extended-response format, the kinds of things they want the students to do are no different than what you've been challenging your students with this year. If you are tempted to add some multiple-choice questions as an assessment, then please make sure they're not just written at the pure memory level. If you keep in mind what you told me earlier—that you're pushing for higher order thinking skills—then be sure to write test questions that require those skills in order to provide a correct response. I think you're on the right track, Jim, for a first year teacher. The best advice I can give you is to ignore what you hear in the teacher's workroom—continue to do what you *know* is good science teaching and you and your students will be successful."

Introduction

Assessing student performance is essential if we really want to know our students have learned and can apply their understanding of the content in a new context. How *can* you assess student learning? Do you want to *test* your students, in the strictest definition of the term— to measure their worth? Or do you want to do, as the term *assessment* connotes—sit with the learner to determine what they know and what they can do with a particular concept? I doubt that the other teachers in the scenario who stopped regular instruction to give students multiple-choice tests that would provide practice in test taking would say they were measuring how *worthy* their students were. Like many teachers caught up in the *fears* that standardized testing brings to the schools, they think they are being *good* teachers by preparing their students to be successful on the exams.

Mr. Kestel's examples of assessment reflect the view that assessment is a means of gathering information about students—what they know and can do. Jim's assessment is authentic. He looks for habits of mind, rather than habits of recall. He uses assessment to monitor how well his students are doing and how he is doing as a teacher. His assessment supports exemplary science teaching. It is consistent with inquiry and constructivist teaching practices. Jim's assessment strategies require students to be active in their learning and in their assessment; and that teachers and parents play a more active role in collecting meaningful data about student performance. The assessing strategies that Jim described more accurately reflect and measure what we value in education.

How can you determine what the learners know and can do? In this chapter we help you to

1. explore the purposes and limits of evaluating learning;
2. investigate the need for alignment of lesson and assessment;
3. compare the benefits of different assessment tools.

Evaluating Student Learning

Children learn more completely when focused on learning outcomes and objectives teachers want them to achieve because planning, teaching, and evaluation go hand in hand. This philosophy of assessment is consistent with the National Science Education Standards for assessment, as identified in Chapter 5 of the document (1996). The five assessment standards state:

Standard A: Assessments must be consistent with the decisions they are designed to inform.

Standard B: Achievement and opportunity to learn science must be assessed.

Standard C: The technical quality of the data collected is well matched to the decisions and actions taken on the basis of their interpretation.

Standard D: Assessment practices must be fair.

Standard E: The inferences made from assessments about student achievement and opportunity to learn must be sound.

Limits and Purposes of Assessments

Typical forms of evaluation, such as standardized tests and teacher-prepared, paper-and-pencil, multiple-choice or true-false tests have severe limits. True, they are easy to use and grade. However, their formats limit what they can evaluate; their almost exclusive focus on facts inhibits inductive reasoning, development of scientific process skills, and affective factors of learning. Indeed, facts are necessary, and children cannot do much science or effectively reason scientifically without a solid factual base. Children may be able to memorize the facts, however, without having any idea about how to apply them. Being able to identify or describe a scientific procedure or apparatus on paper does not mean a child knows when that procedure is appropriate or how to use the apparatus properly.

Consider the following test items posted on the National Center for Educational Statistics website at: http://www.nces.ed.gov/nationsreportcard/. This is the home page for the National Assessment of Educational Progress (NAEP). These questions are actual items found on the 2000 fourth-grade NAEP test given to children across the United States.

1. There is a thunderstorm close to your house. The windows rattle at the same time that you hear the thunder. What causes the windows to rattle?
   a. Sound waves from the thunder
   b. Light from the lightning
   c. Rain from the clouds
   d. The high humidity during the storm
2. [The child is given a picture of six animals; they are a bird, gorilla, cricket, fox, frog, and a fish.] Look at the different kinds of animals in the pictures above. Which three of these animals have a very large number of young every time they reproduce?

3. Sally is swimming in an outdoor pool. She hears thunder. What is the safest thing for Sally to do?
   a. Stay in the water
   b. Stand under a tree
   c. Go into a building
   d. Dry off and stand by the water
   From what you have learned in science, explain why your choice is the safest.

The first item asks for a factual answer that could be memorized. The second item also requires a factual answer, but a student could answer correctly without ever having had science, since everyday experience could prevail. The third item requires a more complex response, and it gives the teacher an opportunity to evaluate the child's reasoning abilities. Number 3 on a standardized assessment shows that we've come a long way from tests consisting of remembered information, rising above the lowest level of Bloom's taxonomy for the cognitive domain: *the knowledge level.* Standardized assessments are moving toward short performance tasks or "enhanced multiple-choice questions . . . made more open-ended by requiring students to explain or justify their responses" (Hart, 1994, p. 46).

Alignment of the Assessment and the Lesson

Exemplary science teaching requires students to be actively engaged in their learning. If they are immersed in a learning environment which gives them ample opportunities to demonstrate their understanding of the science content, their grasp of the science skills, and the formations of essential attitudes for science, then it is inconsistent to fall back on paper-and-pencil, pure knowledge types of tests that require recall of facts, or rote memorization, to determine understanding of what was taught. Authentic assessment strategies are designed to reveal what students can *do* instead of *emphasizing* their weaknesses. Students' benefit when there is flexibility and variety in their learning activities. They also benefit when they are given multiple opportunities to demonstrate what they have learned by participating in those activities. The lesson "Simple Circuits," found in the feature lesson, gives students numerous opportunities to learn the concept of a *circuit* and to practice applying their understanding in various ways. How the student's knowledge is assessed is reflected in the learning outcomes stated in the Evaluation phase of the lesson plan. These outcome statements reflect the kinds of activities the teacher directs the students to do throughout the lesson. Evidence of understanding the concept of a *circuit* is not left for the end of the lesson, where a multiple-choice test would require the students to define the word circuit and the various types of circuits. While quizzes and/or prompts—like homework assignments and questions on key terms can be given—they are *not* the only means of assessing the student's understanding of the concept of a *circuit*. The lesson plan demonstrates that the students are given multiple opportunities to demonstrate their understanding of the concept and that they are able to apply that understanding in a new context. This means of assessment is consistent with exemplary science teaching that reflects constructivist-teaching practices.

(*text continues on page 148*)

Simple Circuits

Inquiry Question: What does it take to make a light bulb light?

Concept to Be Invented: A circuit is a pathway that electricity follows from the power source through the bulb and back to the power source.

National Education Science Standards: K–4 Physical Science—Electricity in circuits can produce light, heat, sound, and magnetic effects. Electrical circuits require a complete loop through which the electrical current can pass.

Science Attitudes to Nurture: Curiosity, open-mindedness, perseverance, positive approach to failure, cooperating

Materials Needed: Dry cells, wires, flashlight bulbs, bulb holders, switches, wire strippers, screw drivers, scissors, aluminum foil, paper clips, paper fasteners, masking tape, small pieces of cardboard

Safety Precautions: Have students use not more than 5 dry cells in the same circuit to limit shock potential and to preserve light bulbs.

Exploration *What process skills will be used?*

Observing, predicting, classifying

Teacher's instructions to students: Using only the 3 pieces of equipment given to you, light the bulb. Once you are successful, find 3 other ways to light the bulb. You can use only the 3 pieces of equipment you have been given. Carefully draw a picture of each method you use to try to light the bulb. Label your drawings *will light* and *will not light*. Be certain to show exactly where your wire is touching and how your bulb is positioned with the battery.

Explanation

Concept: A circuit is a pathway that electricity follows from the power source through the bulb and back to the power source.

Have students draw their pictures on the chalkboard. Use your finger to trace the pathway that electricity from the battery flows through when the bulb light and when it does not light. This path is called a circuit. Using the students' own ideas and words, construct an explanation that a circuit is a pathway that electricity follows from the power source to the bulb and back to the power source. Show the students that contact with the bulb must be made in two specific places. The path must be complete from the battery, through the bulb, and back to the battery for the bulb to light. A key question to ask: In how many places must metal touch the bulb for it to light? The answer is: Two; the side and bottom conductors of the bulb must be included in the circuit.

Expansion *Which process skills will be used?*

Making predictions, classifying, controlling variables

Challenge the students to light more than one bulb, combine batteries for more power, and add equipment, such as a bulb holder, a switch, and more wires. Ask what happens to other bulbs when one is unscrewed. Make a circuit so all bulbs go out when one is unscrewed: a series circuit. Make a circuit so the other bulbs remain lighted when one bulb is unscrewed: a parallel circuit or a separate series circuit; look carefully. Construct a paper clip switch and demonstrate its function.

Science in Personal and Social Perspectives

- ✦ Name some devices you use that require an electrical circuit.
- ✦ What type of circuit is needed?
- ✦ What would your life be like without electricity controlled by circuits?
- ✦ How is electricity "made"? What resources are necessary? How has demand for electricity changed with population growth?

Science and Technology

A set of car headlights is one example of a specific circuit used for safety purposes. When one light burns out or is broken, the others remain lighted.

1. What are other examples in which the type of circuit used is important for safety or convenience?
2. A flashlight uses a simple series circuit and is an example of technology. How has the simple flashlight improved or affected your life? Your community? The world?
3. Use the idea of a circuit to make a flashlight out of these materials: cardboard tube, wire, two D-cell batteries, flashlight bulb, paper clip, two paper fasteners, bottle cap, tape.

Science as Inquiry

Plan, conduct, and explain investigations that illustrate short circuits, open and closed

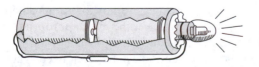

circuits, series and parallel circuits. Identify new concepts in new lessons, such as resistance, cell versus battery, and electromagnetism. Use the concept of open and closed circuit to solve circuit puzzles.

(continued)

History and Nature of Science

+ Thomas Edison experimented thousands of times before he successfully found a material suitable as a filament that could be used to complete the circuit in a light bulb. How would our world be different today if Edison had never succeeded?
+ Who needs to know about circuits? Name careers, and have students identify those careers that they previously did not know about that rely on some knowledge of electrical circuits. Some possibilities include electrician, appliance repair person, architect, city planner, electric power producer, computer engineer, car/truck repair person.
+ How have the expectations changed over time for people in these careers?

Evaluation

Upon completing the activities, the students will be able to:

+ correctly identify all of the circuits as complete or incomplete by marking them *will light* or *will not light;*
+ construct a working switch from cardboard, 2 paper fasteners, a paper clip and 2 wires;
+ construct, demonstrate, and describe the operation of a series circuit and a parallel circuit. Each circuit must include at least 2 bulbs and be controlled by the paper clip switch;
+ accurately draw a diagram and correctly label the parts of the circuit they use to make their flashlights;
+ construct a flashlight that functions properly. (Students must show the teacher that the switch turns the light on and off);
+ cooperate with group partners, volunteers to assist those who request help, and a demonstrate a positive approach when having difficulty with manipulative tasks;
+ describe three ways to use circuits and identify at two different inventions that control the flow of electricity through those circuits;
+ describe at least three safety precautions to avoid accidents with electricity;
+ use inquiry skills to solve correctly four circuit puzzles.

Selecting the Tool for the Task

Evaluation, testing, assessment, performance assessment and *authentic assessment* are terms frequently used by educators interchangeably, but they are not the same. The Evaluation phase of the learning cycle lesson reminds us to select the most appropriate and timely tool for determining what students understand and can do so that modifications can be made to instruction, or appropriate intervention can be given to correct possible misconceptions among students. The evaluation of student understanding and performance should be ongoing and cumulative (formative), rather than only a summative function—that occurs only at the end of units or chapters. Periodic, focused assessments become the tools of evaluation. Some refer to this practice of continual assessment as embedded assessment. "Embedded assessment 'blurs the lines' between teaching and assessment. Many assessment activities become effective teaching activities and many effective teaching activities also are very useful sources of assessment data" (Treagust et al., 2003, p. 37). How this is put into practice is discussed below in Teachers on Science Teaching.

Teachers on Science Teaching

Embedded Assessment

by Mary Walsh Trant
Grade 2, Mark Twain School, Chicago, Illinois

As a teacher of a very diverse group of second graders with varying degrees of English proficiency, I am always looking for new ways to assess their knowledge of science and be sure they can relate what was taught into their everyday experiences. I try to have them see science in their life experiences. I constantly try to reinforce the fact that we are always acting as scientists. For instance, during reading, when I introduce a story, I ask the students what they think the story may be about simply by looking at the title, pictures, and using prior knowledge. The students are encouraged to make predictions. Also, the students are asked to use context clues to help them with new vocabulary words. They make observations, use clues, and infer. The students are asked to explain how this reading lesson was like being a scientist as a way of evaluating their knowledge of the scientific method. After a unit on food chains, I will ask the students to choose one piece of food they had at lunch and create a food chain back to the sun, using a picture graph. After displaying the graphs, they are put in the students' portfolios. I also encourage students to bring in books for me to read to the class, or they may choose to read to the class. They must be able to tell how the story relates to science. For example, one student brought in the story, "If You Give A Mouse a Cookie," and told us that it showed the mouse's habitat. "The

Snowy Day" can relate to evaporation, condensation, heat, etc. You can also pick a book and see if the students can identify the way the story relates to science.

I encourage students to look outside the classroom and bring in things that relate to what they learned in science. They must be able to explain how these things relate to a particular science concept. It is amazing some of the things students bring in, but more amazing is how well they relate to what they learned in science. This transfer of knowledge seems to have deeper and more lasting effects than simply memorizing concepts and spitting back facts on a test. I try to tape the children's presentations whenever possible. They love to watch themselves and really enjoy bringing the tapes home to share with their families.

Each student has a science portfolio. At the beginning of each new unit the children write or create an audiotape of what they would like to know about the topic and what they already know about the topic. At the end of the unit they do a similar activity stating what they learned and what they still want to learn. I design a very simple rubric at the beginning of each unit. We discuss the rubric so the students know what I expect them to learn. As the children bring in books, and complete activities, I use the checklist type rubric as a form of assessment.

Assessment

Video Summary

Assessment can take place at any time during the lesson. The sixth-grade teacher in this video is using her questioning skills during the explanation phase to check for the students' understanding of the term "average." She is making sure that they know how to find an average, as it is central to understanding the key concept behind the activity. Assessment is not limited to a multiple-choice/true-false set of questions at the end of the lesson. It can occur during any phase of the lesson, as the teacher sits with the children observing their

use of various science process skills, or recording their responses to some reflective questions about the content they are exploring. Assessment can also occur through a drawing the students create to explain their understanding of what was studied or through analysis of pictures supplied by the teacher. The literal definition of the term "assessment" is "to sit with." What better way of finding out what science your students learned than to sit down and ask them to tell you what they know and understand.

Tips for Viewing, Objectives, or What to Watch for

As you watch this video, make note of the following:

✦ The kinds of questions used by the teacher,

✦ The atmosphere of the classroom,

✦ The expectations the teacher has of the students.

Questions for Exploration

1. What kinds of questions did the teachers use to promote more student responses?

2. How did the teachers respond to the students once the students answered their questions?

3. Do you think the responses the teachers gave to the students were appropriate?

4. How might the questioning skills of the teacher, including student feedback, contribute to the overall classroom atmosphere and how the students feel about assessment?

Activity for Application

This video provided you with a brief glimpse of informal assessment. What would you do with this class to move from the informal to a more formal assessment? Provide an example of how you could involve the students in creating and scoring a more formalized assessment. Take a lesson you have created and develop a formal assessment for that lesson.

Treagust et al. suggest embedded assessment follows a cycle within a lesson that answers the following questions:

✦ How can I obtain information on students' ideas and reasoning on the topic of instruction?
✦ What does this information tell me about students' understanding and how they make sense of this topic?
✦ What action should I take to help students advance their understanding? (p. 37)

The 4–E Feature lesson on page 146 requires timely and continual teacher assessment of student understanding and skills. Table 5.1 lists several appropriate assessment types that support the expectations for students during each phase of the learning cycle. Most of the effects offered by these assessment types cluster into three types of teacher-designed assessment devices: pictorial assessment, reflective questioning, and hands-on assessment. These approaches were invented by the Full Option Science System (FOSS) of the Lawrence Hall of Science in Berkeley, California, as special techniques to support constructivist teaching and learning through authentic assessment. We used the original version of FOSS as a model for designing authentic assessments for the lesson that is featured in this chapter.

Pictorial Assessment. Pictorial assessment requires students to complete reasoning tasks that differ from traditional fill-in, multiple-choice, and one-answer tasks. The nature of

TABLE 5.1 Types of Appropriate Evaluations for the Learning Cycles

Phase	Purpose of Evaluation	Type of Evaluation
Explore	Determine possible misconceptions.	Questioning and student answers, pictorial assessment
	Document students' uses of process skills.	Process skills checklists
	Encourage exploration.	Record observations, make predictions, ask observation questions
	Improve social skills and interactions.	Teacher observations, checklists
Explain	Clarify concept constructions.	Group discussions, data processing, picture drawing, constructing models, reflective questioning
	Document conceptual change.	Concept mapping, interviews, pictorial assessment
Expand	Document ability to use integrated process skills.	Reflective questioning, hands-on assessment
	Determine students' abilities to transfer learning to new situations.	Inventions, writing activities, presentations
	Stimulate new interests, make connections to previous learning.	Projects and activities that address standards outcomes, portfolios

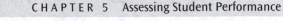

the analysis depends on the types of pictures (or illustrations) used and the context associated with the pictures. Pictorial assessment encourages students to demonstrate their capability to use science process skills appropriately. Some tasks that students may be asked to do could include estimating, predicting, comparing, classifying, identifying properties, determining sequences of events, and designing an experiment.

Pictorial assessment uses pictures to represent familiar objects and events. The assessment device couples well with learning activities and can be completed concurrently. Students are required to apply what they have learned and to communicate what they understand. Often more than one correct answer or solution is possible on an assessment task. Some tasks encourage students to estimate their answers, then do a hands-on task that permits them to check their estimations. Other assessments may ask students to complete a pretest and then use a similar activity as a pictorial assessment posttest, such as those shown in Figure 5.1–5.2. Figure 5.3 (page 156) is another type of pictorial assessment; both complement the learning cycle plan in the feature lesson.

Reflective Questioning. This type of assessment consists of written tasks that expect students to respond to a wide range of intellectual tasks. Use of basic and integrated science process skills may be necessary. For example, students may have to recall essential information, analyze information that is provided, apply what they have learned to new but related circumstances, and integrate information in order to construct answers to unusual situations. Students will find it necessary to read instructions carefully, then follow the directions. Students may list responses, construct illustrations, select the best response from choices given, defend their choices, or write extensive responses that can be evaluated for language arts concepts and skills as well as science.

Reflective questioning assessments require students to reflect on the lesson's content and to use their knowledge in a way that is different from the way it was experienced in the lesson. This type of assessment encourages students to use a variety of approaches to solve a problem. Problems often require more than one step in arriving at a solution, and teachers must be prepared to accept all reasonable and correct answers. We have been delighted to observe students discover creative or unique answers and solutions that we did not have in mind when devising the reflective questioning assessment. Figures 5.4 (page 157) and 5.5 (page 160) illustrate this type of assessment tool; both complement the learning cycle plan in the lesson.

Hands-On Assessment. Hands-on assessment requires what the term implies: Students must manipulate materials from the lesson in order to complete tasks that enable them to demonstrate what they understand. Hands-on assessment permits a teacher to observe how well a student can perform. (*Performance assessment* is another name for this tool.) Students must use their knowledge and skill in a practical way to solve a problem. Students often must use integrated process skills to identify variables, design investigations, gather information, and demonstrate outcomes of their investigations.

Hands-on assessment gives a teacher opportunities to determine how well students use science tools and science thinking. This type of performance assessment directly pursues the science as inquiry and the nature of science dimensions of the National Science Education Standards. Students are encouraged to create their own problems and use their own data in

FIGURE 5.1
Pictorial Assessment
of Simple Circuits

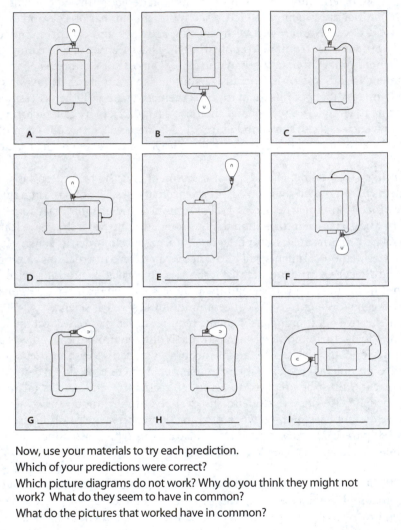

Pretest

Will the bulb light or not? Below each picture, make your prediction by writing either "Yes" or "No."

A _____ B _____ C _____

D _____ E _____ F _____

G _____ H _____ I _____

Now, use your materials to try each prediction.

Which of your predictions were correct?

Which picture diagrams do not work? Why do you think they might not work? What do they seem to have in common?

What do the pictures that worked have in common?

identifying solutions. They are required to think about and analyze science in a practical context—physical science, life science, and earth/space science content standards. Hands-on assessment is easily expanded through the complementary technique of reflective questioning. Figures 5.6 (page 161), 5.7 (page 162), and 5.8 (page 163) illustrate the tools of hands-on assessment and complement the learning cycle plan in the feature lesson.

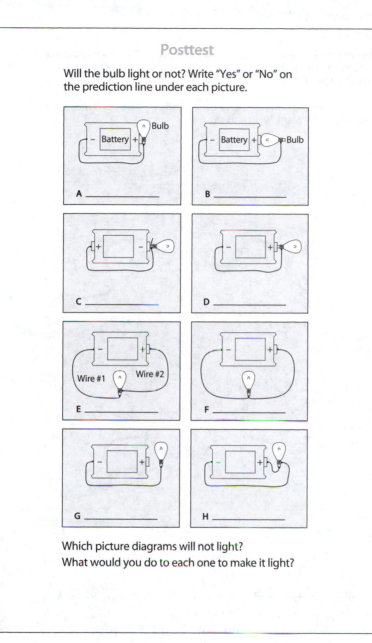

FIGURE 5.2
Pictorial Assessment
of Simple Circuits

Teacher Records and Observations. Tangible records can reveal a lot about what students know and can and cannot do. Useful records can include the successes and difficulties a child has with homework assignments and notations about the quality of a completed science project, written report, class notes, activity data sheets, and so on. Your teacher records are important because they can reveal the interplay among

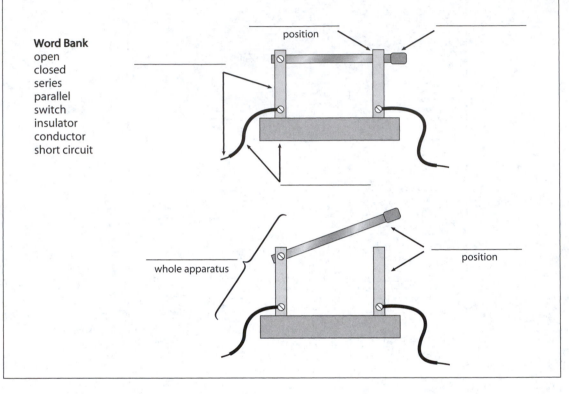

Please examine the pictures carefully. These objects were used in class and contain some parts that relate to concepts that we studied in earlier classes: *insulation* and *conduction*. Other parts and functions represent concepts that we are now studying.

Use the word bank to identify the parts shown by the arrows. Words may be used more than once, or not at all. Write your answers on the blank line by each arrow.

Word Bank
open
closed
series
parallel
switch
insulator
conductor
short circuit

position

whole apparatus

position

FIGURE 5.3   Pictorial Assessment

memorizing, understanding, and using scientific concepts. Emphasis on practical application encourages hands-on, minds-on interaction and helps to address the various dimensions of the science program. Figure 5.9 (page 164) shows a record-keeping system a teacher might use to complement the sample lesson plan on basic electricity. This type of record keeping is useful because it helps to focus a teacher's observations of a child on the concepts and processes to be learned. Figure 5.10 (page 164) shows a generic form suitable for an entire class. It may be used as a check-list to keep track of who has and has not demonstrated mastery of the concepts or preferred science skills. This format can be used to record student progress on the pictorial, reflective questioning, and hands-on assessment techniques.

Pictures A, B, C, and D show batteries, bulbs, wires, and sockets. These pictures represent some of the circuits that we constructed in class. Examine each carefully and answer the questions below the pictures.

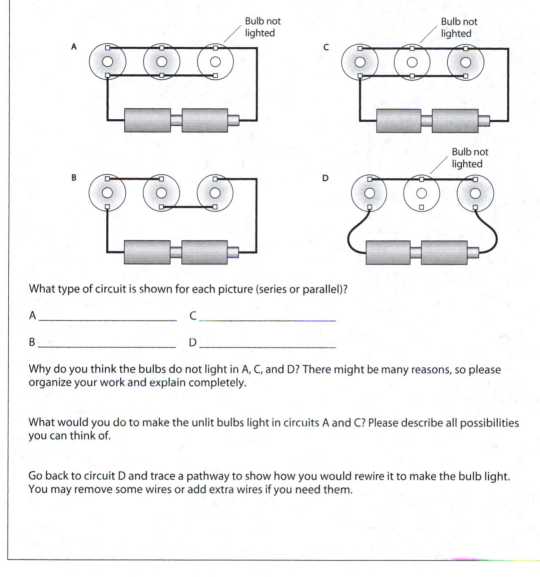

What type of circuit is shown for each picture (series or parallel)?

A _____   C _____

B _____   D _____

Why do you think the bulbs do not light in A, C, and D? There might be many reasons, so please organize your work and explain completely.

What would you do to make the unlit bulbs light in circuits A and C? Please describe all possibilities you can think of.

Go back to circuit D and trace a pathway to show how you would rewire it to make the bulb light. You may remove some wires or add extra wires if you need them.

FIGURE 5.4   Reflective Questioning Assessment of Simple Circuits

Rubrics. Not all student performances can be classified with simple systems, numbers, or letter grades. The sheer volume of a teacher's workload can limit the types of written or verbal comments offered to students. Therefore, many teachers use rubrics to assess

(*text continues on page 160*)

Assessment: What to Emphasize?

Recent research and publication of the National Science Education Standards (National Research Council, 1996) illustrate the need for envisioning systemic changes in the activities and methods used to assess science learning. For example, the assessment standards of the National Science Education Standards (p. 100) urge teachers to place

Less Emphasis on	More Emphasis on
Assessing what is easily measured	Assessing what is most highly valued
Assessing discrete knowledge	Assessing rich, well-structured knowledge
Assessing scientific knowledge	Assessing scientific understanding and reasoning
Assessing to learn what students do not know	Assessing to learn what students do understand
Assessing only achievement	Assessing achievement and opportunity to learn
End of term assessments by teachers	Students engaged in ongoing assessment of their work and that of others
Development of external assessments by measurement experts alone	Teachers involved in the development of external assessments

In the spirit of changing emphasis, fourth-grade teachers in a Concord, New Hampshire school district took on the task of annually assessing their students' ability to "think and behave like scientists." After an extensive review of the literature the teacher teams took on the task of developing performance-based assessments for science. Data were collected and analyzed on the success of their instrument. The concerns their peers shared about this type of assessment were as follows:

- Let teachers correct their own tests (others suggested a paid committee of teachers to score student responses from across the district).
- More anchor papers (examples of responses at each of the four levels) are needed to help with scoring.
- Too much emphasis on grammar and spelling.
- Need a student-friendly rubric.
- Spread the tasks out over the year in order to determine growth.
- It takes a lot of time to do one task.
- It is difficult to conduct the driving test in the confines of the classroom.

Indeed, performance-based assessment administered as a standardized assessment tool is not without its problems. Providing the tests is only half the battle. Working on the mindsets to accept this form of testing will take a lot longer. As the authors of this study conclude, "Most paper-and-pencil assessments provide adequate insight into students' ability and can help effectively guide instruction. A well-designed, performance-based assessment propels a science program beyond this level of adequacy and guarantees that teachers are making curricular decisions based upon a more complete picture. After all, if science literacy is going to be measured in terms of what students know and are able to do, then the tests we give them better allow students to *do* something."[1]

The federal *No Child Left Behind* legislation of 2002 expects school districts to have strategies in place so that *all* children will succeed. The National Science Education Standards' shifting emphasis for assessment suggest that the learner plays a more active role in assessment. Providing authentic assessment for *all* students does not mean excluding those with learning disabilities. In his research on inclusive classrooms, Konstantinos Alexakos, a high school physics teacher from New York City, offers several suggestions on how *all* students can participate in authentic assessment; from prerecording the test questions for auditory learners to having a student aide read the questions. Alexakos suggests that, "Assistive technology, such as computers equipped with touch-sensitive screens or speech synthesizers and voice recognition software, should be employed when appropriate. Such technology can decrease the feelings of separation and isolation of learners with disabilities, reducing their frustration, and increasing their self-esteem."

Alexakos's research suggests that the evaluation of what students should know and be able to do, in an inclusive classroom, does not have to rest solely on individual performance. In fact, the rubrics he created to assess the students' ability in a lab situation stressed that value he placed on teaming. A sample lab evaluation sheet developed by Alexakos follows:

Sample lab work evaluation sheet

A. Written team report (28 points)

____ of 4 points   Need for such experiment

____ of 4 points   Safety precautions

____ of 5 points   Collection of data

____ of 5 points   Calculations

____ of 5 points   Analysis

____ of 5 points   Neatness

B. Team work (24 points)

____ of 8 points   Safety

____ of 8 points   Collaboration

____ of 8 points   Individual participation

C. Verbal assessment(24 points)

____ of 12 points   Team comprehension

____ of 12 points   Individual comprehension

D. Individual written report (24 points)

____ of 12 points   Essay evaluating the particular experiment and outcome

____ of 12 points   Suggestions and criticisms concerning the experiment

Total: ____ of 100 points

Comments:

Note: Specifics of rubrics should be discussed before being made final
so students can express their concerns and suggest changes.

Source: Adapted from Konstantinos Alexakos, "Inclusive Classrooms." *Science and Children* (March, 2001): 40–43.

---

[1]Chris Demers, *Op. Cit.*, p. 60.

Source: Adapted from Chris Demers, "Beyond Paper and Pencil Assessments," *Science and Children* (October 2000): 24–29, 60.

Imagine that a storm has passed, it is nighttime, and you are walking down the street with a flashlight. The street lights are not working and many houses are dark, but you do notice light coming from some houses. You see a loose electrical wire with one end on the ground and the other end attached to a utility pole. What are three safe things you might do?

1. _____

2. _____

3. _____

What are three electrical devices that you use regularly? List them below and identify the types of circuits that they have (series, parallel, or both). Also for each, list inventions that control the flow of electricity to or within the device. You must identify at least two different inventions overall.

Electrical devices	Type of circuit used	Invention that controls
_____	_____	_____
_____	_____	_____
_____	_____	_____

Imagine that our community has a power failure for one week. Life must go on, including school! What things would change in your daily routine in which you usually use electricity, but now cannot? Describe your day without electricity, beginning with your morning wake-up and preparation for school, time spent getting to and from school, and your evening until you go to sleep.

_____

_____

_____

_____

FIGURE 5.5 Reflective Questioning Assessment of Safety, Circuits, and Electrical Uses

the quality of student work. *Rubrics* are devices, such as checklists, scales, or descriptions, that identify the criteria used to evaluate a student's work. Paul Smith (1995), a middle-school science teacher, recommends using rubrics that have been created by the students for students, with teacher guidance. Since students are part of the design process, they clearly understand the expectations and use this understanding to improve their work. The creation of the rubrics also affords additional teaching opportunities.

For written work, Smith (1995) asks students to consider two questions: "What information should go into the written response?" and "How should the information be

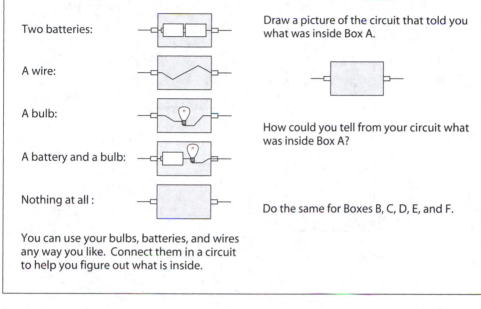

Find out what is in the six mystery boxes A, B, C, D, E, and F. They have five different things inside, shown below. Two of the boxes will have the same thing. All of the others will have something different inside.

Two batteries:

A wire:

A bulb:

A battery and a bulb:

Nothing at all :

You can use your bulbs, batteries, and wires any way you like. Connect them in a circuit to help you figure out what is inside.

When you find out what is in a box, fill in the spaces on the following pages.

Box A: Has _____ inside.

Draw a picture of the circuit that told you what was inside Box A.

How could you tell from your circuit what was inside Box A?

Do the same for Boxes B, C, D, E, and F.

FIGURE 5.6   Hands-On Assessment: Electricity Mystery Boxes

Source: R. J. Shavelson and G. P. Baxter, "What We've Learned about Assessing Hands-on Science," *Educational Leadership* (May 1992): 20–25. Reprinted by permission of the Association for Supervision and Curriculum Development. Copyright © 1992 by ASCD. All rights reserved.

presented?" He uses a peer and parental review system that encourages students to prepare and improve written drafts. Parents and caregivers appreciate the rubrics because the rubrics help them to improve guidance offered while helping with homework. Smith claims that students are able to make better sense of what they learn and that student satisfaction is very high with this participatory approach.

Rubrics can help a teacher encourage students to give better responses to reflective questioning assessments. The rubric shown in Figure 5.11 (page 165) has been generalized for use with reflective questioning assessments. It illustrates Smith's recommendations. Figure 5.12 (page 166) provides a general rubric that you may use for a variety of science tasks.

Systematic Observation.   The types of records shown in Figures 5.13 and 5.14 (page 168) require systematic teacher observation. Systematic observation is another source of information that is helpful to meaningful evaluation. Teachers always make observations,

FIGURE 5.7 Hands-On Assessment: Electric Circuit Boards

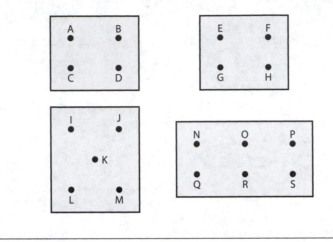

Below are the pictures of four circuit boards you will find in your science center. Design a simple circuit tester from a battery, bulb, socket, and wires. Test the four boards to determine which points (A, B, C, and so on) are wired into the same circuit. Draw lines on the circuit picture showing where you believe the wires make a connection between the points. Show your teacher your work, and then open the circuit folder and check the results. Were you correct?

but systematic observation goes beyond being aware that Emily is interested in birds, Joel asks questions all the time, and David creates messes. Systematic observation is illustrated in this example:

> A teacher divides the class into working groups to figure out a way to test the strength of different brands of paper towels. As the children work on the problem, the teacher walks about the room, listens carefully to the questions the children ask each other, and observes how they approach the task. The teacher notes who does nothing, who appears to have difficulty, who has trouble measuring, who asks the most interesting questions, and who offers the most interesting ideas.

Systematic observation is guided by a structure; the teacher's observations are focused on specific tasks. These tasks include trying to determine how well the children demonstrate their understanding of the science ideas, how well the children use the science process skills, and what types of scientific attitudes the children demonstrate. Figure 5.13 illustrates an observation form for science skills and Table 5.2 (pages 169–170) defines the attributes of the skills.

Science learning improves when student attitudes are positive (Yager & Penick, 1987). There are dramatic differences between traditional science classrooms and exemplary ones in which teaching and assessment involve all aspects of science. Positive

FIGURE 5.8 Hands-On Assessment: Help MacGyver!

MacGyver is in a jam! Lost in a cave, he is using a small candle that is about to burn out. What he really needs is a flashlight—one that can withstand the drafty and damp cave—to help him find his way out. All he has is:

> 2 size "D" dry cells
> 1 small 3-volt bulb
> 1 thin piece of insulated wire, 30 centimeters long (about 12 inches)
> 1 metal paper clip
> 2 metal paper fasteners
> 1 cardboard tube, 15 centimeters long (about 6 inches)
> 1 roll of masking tape
> 1 plastic bottle cap
> 1 small knife

1. Use the materials to sketch a picture of how these things could be assembled to make a temporary flashlight. Make certain you draw your circuit carefully. (Draw your picture here.)

2. Now help MacGyver. Follow your plan. Did the light work? Keep trying! Now show MacGyver his new light and explain to him how it works.

attitudes about science greatly influence students' achievement levels and process skills, as is shown by research on exemplary science classrooms (Yager & Penick, 1987). These results are now prompting teachers to question the traditional view that attitudes are inconsequential. Figure 5.14 shows one way you can evaluate and record the levels of your students' science attitudes.

Social skills are important to science learning. Karen Ostlund (1992) tells us that we are not born with a set of instinctive behaviors that help us to interact well in social settings. Social skills are learned. If we expect students to work together in cooperative science activity groups or on science projects in smaller teams, then we must assess the extent to which the learners develop those skills. Table 5.3 (page 171) lists important social skills that students can learn if we encourage them. Systematic record-keeping formats (similar to those shown in Figures 5.13 and 5.14, page 168) can help us to monitor the status of students' social skills.

(text continues on page 168)

Student's Name: Raul
Lesson or Unit: Basic Electricity

Concept Number	Description of Activity or Skill	Teacher Rating Low 12345 High	Teacher Comments
1	Open circuit using one bulb, wire, and dry cell	5	Was the first in the group to do it
2	Closed circuit using same materials	3	Had difficulty, needed my help
3	Closed circuit with bulb socket	4	Easily done after I helped with clips
4	Series circuit, 2 or more bulbs	5	Done independently
5	Parallel circuit	2	Having difficulty, made 2 series circuits
6	Short circuit	4	
7	Use a knife switch	5	Easily done
8	Make a paper clip switch	5	Concept easily shown
9	Construct a flashlight	4	No circuit trouble, difficulty with bulb connections only

FIGURE 5.9 Student Progress Report

Unit: Basic Electricity

Children's Names	Objective, Concept, Skill, or Activity Number											Comments
	1	2	3	4	5	6	7	8	9	10	11	
Emerson												
Frankie												
Jaclyn												
Jana												
Jay												
Julie												
Joy												
Marilyn												

FIGURE 5.10 Class Record-Keeping System

Note: This format is easily managed by a spreadsheet program, if a value number is assigned to each object. Some teachers prefer a coding system that shows progress, such as: + for entirely correct, *n* for partially correct, *u* for mostly incorrect, or – for entirely incorrect.

This is a scoring rubric for a learning-cycle lesson on simple circuits. A score of three indicates what the class believes all students should be able to do. A score of four indicates that the students exceeded expectations.

Content scale

0	1	2	3	4
• No work completed	• Few concepts • Models not used in explanation • Some awareness of safety • Some awareness of technology uses	• Some concepts explained • Three common safety examples • Three common technology examples	• Uses circuit model to explain differences • Identifies differences in series, parallel, open, closed circuits • Uses concepts from previous lessons, e.g., conductor, insulator, etc.	• Uses additional concepts to explain differences, e.g., switch, resistance, energy flow • Unusual safety and/or technology examples

Style scale

0	1	2	3	4
• No work completed	• Poor organization • Many misspellings • Punctuation missing or inappropriate	• Clear organization • Very few misspellings	• Appropriate punctuation	• Extremely clear, concise writing

First reviewer's name: _____

Score for content: _____ Score for style: _____

Comments:

Second reviewer's name: _____

Score for content: _____ Score for style: _____

Comments:

FIGURE 5.11   Reflective Questioning Assessment Rubric

Criteria	Exceeds expectations (5 points)	Meets expectations (3 points)	Fails to meet expectations (1 point)
Communication	• Raises relevant questions and shares ideas with peers • Offers clear and concise oral and written presentation of personal ideas and understanding, indicating that time has been devoted to thinking about the topic	• Occasionally participates in group discussions, but rarely initiates or accepts a leadership role in guiding the group • Does not elaborate on his or her understanding • Often does not complete expression of his or her thoughts or ideas	• Provides no oral or written evidence of understanding activity or discussion topics • Never or rarely raises relevant questions • Never or rarely provides oral or written communication
Sharing sources and resources	• Brings sources of information to the class to share with teachers or peers • Brings resources, such as activities, materials, or literature that can be used to extend the learning activities of the class	• Makes reference to outside sources of information and resources, but does not take the initiative to bring them to class to share with others • Is unable to provide evidence that he or she has looked for outside sources and resources	• Never or rarely brings in outside resources that could enhance the learning experiences of others
Openness to learn	• Accepts class assignments and requirements with a positive attitude • Actively seeks (by asking questions or speculating) connections between course requirements and goals	• Reluctantly accepts class assignments	• Rejects or dismisses class assignments as meaningless or boring • Cannot make connections between class requirements and goals of the instructor
Respect	• Listens to others; encourages others to contribute ideas; accepts alternative perspectives; is tolerant of the shortcomings of others; and helps others to succeed in class	• Is tolerant of others, but often dominates the group activity or discussion • Listens to the ideas of others, but generally maintains personal views and ideas	• Dismisses the thoughts and ideas of others; possibly uses rude or abusive language to ridicule • Offers ideas that are limited to his or her personal opinions

FIGURE 5.12   An Assessment Rubric for Class Participation

Source: John A. Craven III and Tracy Hogan, "Assessing Student Participation in the Classroom," *Science Scope* (September, 2001): 36–40.

Criteria	Exceeds expectations (5 points)	Meets expectations (3 points)	Fails to meet expectations (1 point)
Accepts and provides constructive criticism	• Positively accepts constructive criticism and incorporates it in his or her approach to learning • Offers constructive criticism and critiques, including viable suggestions for improvement, to his or her teacher and peers	• Accepts constructive criticism, but does not incorporate it for improving targeted behaviors	• Often or always rejects constructive criticism • Offers no viable alternatives to others' suggestions
Material preparedness	• Makes class materials readily available and accessible without causing interruption of activities or discussions	• Regularly forgets some materials or does not prepare fully; or prepares for class, but is unable to retrieve his or her materials without disruption	• Consistently is unprepared for class
Academic preparedness	• Refers to relevant literature or readings to support ideas and arguments during discussions • Demonstrates awareness of course and teacher expectations	• Refers to concepts or topics related to the activity or discussion topic, but provides incomplete written or oral responses • Expresses opinions that may have merit, but is unable to support them with evidence from classroom work	• Is unable to respond correctly to questions regarding required readings • Offers responses that are consistently wrong or meaningless • Expresses surprise or confusion when probed for his or her understanding
Class Presence	• Frequently volunteers to participate in classroom activities • Demonstrates his or her focus on classroom activities by appropriate eye contact and alert posture	• Occasionally participates in group discussions • Provides ideas or comments that are largely restricted to reiterations of others' ideas or comments	• Sits passively in class • Does not participate in group discussions • Does not pay attention to classroom activities

Score: ____/40

Directions: Circle the number that best represents the skill level you have observed. Number 1 means *having difficulty,* 2 means *fair,* 3 means *good,* 4 means *outstanding.*

Name	Observation	Classification	Communication	Measurement	Prediction
Sam	1 2 3 4	1 2 3 4	1 2 3 4	1 2 3 4	1 2 3 4
Wanda	1 2 3 4	1 2 3 4	1 2 3 4	1 2 3 4	1 2 3 4
Herman	1 2 3 4	1 2 3 4	1 2 3 4	1 2 3 4	1 2 3 4
Kara	1 2 3 4	1 2 3 4	1 2 3 4	1 2 3 4	1 2 3 4

FIGURE 5.13   Recording Science Process Skills

Note: The process skills can be changed and the form expanded to address better the science skills your lessons emphasize.

Check those attitudes or record the number of times each student demonstrates the desired scientific attitudes during the observation period.

Name	Is curious	Cooperates	Persists	Is open-minded	Safely uses materials
Celeste	✓✓✓	✓✓	✓	✓	✓
Jen	✓	✓✓✓✓✓	✓	✓✓✓✓	✓✓✓
Tikara	✓✓✓✓	✓✓✓	✓✓✓✓✓	✓✓	✓✓✓
Jon	✓	✓✓✓	✓✓	✓✓	✓✓
Sara	✓✓	✓✓	✓✓✓	✓✓✓✓	✓✓✓✓

FIGURE 5.14   Evaluating and Recording Science Attitudes

According to Ostlund (1992), science social skills fall into three groups:

1. *Cluster skills*—behaviors that involve a student's ability to move into a science learning group quickly and quietly and get the task started.
2. *Camaraderie skills*—behaviors that help all learners feel better about themselves and about each other as they work together. These skills build a sense of cohesiveness and encourage stable operation of the science group.
3. *Task skills*—behaviors pertaining to management chores, ranging from those necessary for mastering a task to those that use critical thinking to construct a deeper level of understanding.

(text continues on page 172)

TABLE 5.2   Definitions and Indicators of Basic and Integrated Process Skills

Basic Processes

Observation: involves active engagement with the manipulation of objects and the use of the senses, directly or indirectly, with simple or complex instruments. This process

- describes objects' attributes,
- describes changes in terms of actions,
- describes changes with accuracy in terms of patterns and relationships.

Classification: systematically imposing order to data based on observational relationships. This process

- creates groups by using a single attribute and expresses linear relationships,
- creates groups and subgroups using one attribute to express symmetrical relationships,
- creates groups using several attributes together to express symmetrical relationships among different groups.

Communication: exchanging information through a variety of media. This process involves

- expressing opinions;
- explaining using sense data (touch, taste, hearing, sight, and smell);
- explaining causal relationships.

Measurement: describing an event by using instruments to quantify observations. This process

- uses nonstandard instruments, such as paper clips, hands, and feet;
- uses standard instruments, such as rulers, balance scales, and graduated cylinders;
- uses standard instruments with precision, such as measuring within tenths or hundredths when using the metric system.

Prediction: stating future cause-and-effect relationships through manipulation of objects. Accuracy of prediction is based on information gathered through observations. This process includes

- guesses from minimal supportive evidence,
- guesses based on limited observable facts,
- guesses based on an accurate understanding of cause-and-effect relationships.

Questioning: raising uncertainty. This process

- focuses on the attributes of objects,
- focuses on relationships and patterns within an experiment,
- focuses on events and patterns abstracted from an experiment.

Using numbers: expressing ideas, observations, and relationships in figures rather than words. This process

- uses numbers to express ideas without relating them,
- uses numbers to express relationships,
- uses numbers to express relationships in precise terms.

(continued)

TABLE 5.2 Continued

Integrated Processes

Interpreting data: finding patterns or meaning not immediately apparent among sets of data that lead to the construction of inferences, predictions, and hypotheses. This process

- identifies a single pattern among objects within an experiment,
- uses accuracy to identify a single pattern among objects within an experiment,
- uses accuracy to identify multiple patterns among objects.

Controlling variables: identifying and selecting factors from variables that are to be held constant and those that are to be manipulated in order to carry out a proposed investigation. This process involves managing

- one manipulative variable without holding others constant,
- several manipulative variables and holds at least one variable constant,
- several manipulative and constant variables at the same time.

Designing experiments: planning data-gathering operations to determine results. This process involves

- collecting data through trial-and-error processes;
- testing questions and hypothesizing with an attempt to identify and control variables;
- using organized, sequential plans to test hypotheses and interpret results in measurable terms.

Inferring: providing explanations, reasons, or causes for events based on limited facts. Inferences are of questionable validity because they rely heavily on personal judgment. This process

- explains by making guesses,
- explains using observable data,
- explains using quantifiable observable data.

Defining operationally: describing what works. This process

- explains how to measure variables in an experiment,
- states relationships between observed actions to explain phenomena,
- explains relationships by generalizing to other events not observed.

Hypothesizing: tentatively accepting an explanation as a basis for further investigation. Constructing generalizations that include all objects or events of the same class. The hypothesis must be tested if credibility is to be established. This process involves making

- statements based on opinions,
- statement based on simple sensory observations without explanations,
- statements used to create concepts through explanations.

Formulating models: describing or constructing physical, verbal, or mathematical explanations of systems and phenomena that cannot be observed directly. Models may be used in predicting outcomes and planned investigations. This process

- creates one-dimensional explanations,
- creates multidimensional models,
- creates scalar multidimensional explanations.

Source: G. W. Foster & W. A. Heiting, "Embedded Assessment," *Science and Children* 32, 2 (1994): 30–33. Reprinted with permission from NSTA Publications, copyright 1994 from *Science and Children*, National Science Teachers Association, 1840 Wilson Boulevard, Arlington, VA 22201-3000.

TABLE 5.3   Science Social Skills

Science social skills can be observed and recorded by a teacher, or used as a part of a student self-evaluation. As an example, for student self-evaluation you could ask students to rate how often or how well they do the following.

Cluster skills: *How often do you*

- move into groups quietly?
- stay with your group?
- use a quiet voice to speak within your group?
- call the people in your group by their names?
- look at the person in your group who is talking?
- keep your hands and feet to yourself?
- share materials with your group mates?
- wait and take your turn?
- share your ideas?

Camaraderie skills: *How often do you*

- avoid saying "put-downs"?
- encourage others in your group to participate?
- give each person in your group a compliment?
- show your support to others with words or actions?
- describe how you feel when it is appropriate?
- try humor or enthusiasm to help energize your group?
- criticize the idea, not the person?
- allow each person in the group to talk before you talk again?

Task skills: *How often do you*

- ask questions of your group members about the task?
- ask for help from group members?
- ask group members to explain what you do not understand?
- offer to explain things to another group member?
- check for understanding with group members?
- state the purpose of the task and make certain others understand it?
- watch time and let others know when time is short?
- offer ideas about how best to do the task?
- value other group members' contributions?
- summarize the material to help others in your group?
- develop ways to help the group remember important details?
- encourage other group members to share their thinking?
- ask others to plan out loud how they would solve a problem?
- compare viewpoints when there is a disagreement and try to reach agreement?
- combine parts of different persons ideas into a single point of view?
- ask others to explain their reasons?
- help other group members reach a conclusion?
- check your group's work against the instructions?

Source: Adapted from K. L. Ostlund, "Sizing Up Social Skills," *Science Scope* (March 1992): 31–33.

Student Self-Assessments. Student self-assessments are an important part of the authenticity in constructivist science teaching. Self-assessments can range from the informal collections of reflective tape-recorded (for nonreaders) or written journal notes, to more formal efforts, such as self-evaluation ratings. A student portfolio is also a common technique that is used to organize and present the self-assessment.

A *portfolio* is a selection of student work that is collected over a period of time (Hein & Price, 1994). A portfolio's purpose is often to tell a story about the student's science activities. The contents of a portfolio may be focused on illustrating a student's abilities to solve problems, show thinking and understanding, illustrate content and capability of written communication, and reveal science connections that a student is able to make across many lessons, and the views that students have of themselves in science (Glencoe, 1994).

Often times the teacher may get caught up in the *collecting evidence* aspect of the portfolio and miss its use as a tool for learning in itself. With technology now being more readily accessible in the classroom, the focus of portfolio development can easily shift from a collection of student artifacts to an electronic, continuous source of assessment, which represents growth over time. The "electronic portfolios (e-portfolios)—digital collections of student work—are flexible, motivating, and extremely useful teacher tools that can address a range of needs from student assessment and professional development to creating connections between teachers, students, and parents" (Garthwait and Verrill, 2003, p. 22).

Key to making portfolios a tool for learning in themselves is aligning the selection of materials placed within the portfolio with the standards. Identifying the standards for the students and then asking them to select work that they think best demonstrates their understanding of that standard is a great way to find out how that student is interpreting the standard. Asking the students to write and include goal statements for themselves and then to identify how their portfolio meets their personal goal adds to the learning value behind the use of portfolio as assessment.

A student *journal* is a type of self-assessment. A journal can assist the reflective process when students are encouraged to record what they have done and what they have learned. A journal may provide a written summary that is helpful for planning and constructing a portfolio. The following examples are appropriate for a portfolio:

+ written report of a project or investigation,
+ responses to open-ended questions,
+ examples of problems that have been formed or solved,
+ journal excerpts,
+ science art,
+ individual student's contribution to a group report or project,
+ photographs or drawings of science models,
+ teacher check-sheets and recorded observations of student performance,
+ uses of science tools, equipment, and suitable technologies to solve problems or to complete an activity,
+ examples of how science is important to the student,
+ descriptions of safe science practices learned and applied in another setting, such as at home,
+ linkages of science history and how views have changed as a result of study,

✦ examples of how science is used in the community and careers that use the science topics that have been studied.

Portions of a portfolio may be evaluated by the teacher individually or collectively within the portfolio package. Items in the portfolio should invite student self-evaluation. Figure 5.15 provides a format that invites students and teachers to have input into the evaluation in an open-ended way. Figures 5.16 (page 174) and 5.17 (page 175) illustrate specific student self-evaluation approaches that may be used to inform teachers and caregivers about how students perceive their own learning.

Portfolio Topic _____

Student: _____

Teacher: _____   Date: _____

1. Concepts, procedures, process skills explored: _____

   _____

2. Areas of growth in understanding: _____

   _____

3. Unfinished work or work needing revision: _____

   _____

4. Assessment of the following areas:

   (a) Problem-solving work: _____

   _____

   (b) Reasoning and critical thinking: _____

   _____

   (c) Use of language: _____

   _____

   (d) Other: _____

   _____

FIGURE 5.15   Portfolio Evaluation Form

Source: Glencoe Science Professional Series, *Alternative Assessment in the Science Classroom* (1994). (ERIC Document Reproduction Service No. ED 370 778), p. 37.

Student Self-Evaluation Checklist

Name: _____   Date: _____

Did the circuit problems
Finished some   Finished them all

Worked with the materials
Messy   Always careful

Recorded and described in my journal
Wrote a little   Wrote a lot

Practiced important safety rules
Some of the time   All of the time

Discussed ideas and results with the class
Some of the time   All of the time

Worked well with classmates
Some of the time   All of the time

Used time well
Wasted time   Worked hard

Learned from the lesson
Learned a little   Learned a lot

Things I liked or did well: _____

_____

Things I did not like: _____

_____

FIGURE 5.16   Student Self-Evaluation Checklist

Source: Adapted from G. E. Hein and S. Price, *Active Assessment for Active Science: A Guide for Elementary School Teachers* (Portsmouth, NH: Heinemann, 1994).

Self-Evaluation Rating Scale

Name: _____   Date: _____

Directions: Rate yourself. On a scale of one (low) to ten (high), how well did you do each of the following activities?

Making a switch
Didn't understand what to do   Made a great one

| 1 | 2 | 3 | 4 | 5 | 6 | 7 | 8 | 9 | 10 |

Making circuits
Had trouble   Easy to do

| 1 | 2 | 3 | 4 | 5 | 6 | 7 | 8 | 9 | 10 |

Solving circuit puzzles
Had trouble   Easy to solve

| 1 | 2 | 3 | 4 | 5 | 6 | 7 | 8 | 9 | 10 |

Electricity mystery boxes
Did some   Did all

| 1 | 2 | 3 | 4 | 5 | 6 | 7 | 8 | 9 | 10 |

Making the flashlight
Could have tried harder   Did my best

| 1 | 2 | 3 | 4 | 5 | 6 | 7 | 8 | 9 | 10 |

Overall feeling about the electricity lessons
Liked them a little   Liked them a lot

| 1 | 2 | 3 | 4 | 5 | 6 | 7 | 8 | 9 | 10 |

Things I liked or did well: _____

_____

Things I did not like: _____

_____

FIGURE 5.17   Student Self-Evaluation Rating Scale

Source: Adapted from G. E. Hein and S. Price, *Active Assessment for Active Science: A Guide for Elementary School Teachers* (Portsmouth, NH: Heinemann, 1994).

Chapter Summary

When assessment is left for the end of a lesson or unit of study, when it requires the students to rely on habits of recall rather than habits of mind, when it only engages them in lower order thinking skills, which require rote memorization, then it is of no value in the teaching/learning process. Authentic assessment should be used as a means of modeling. It should answer the question of what we want teachers to teach and how, and what we want students to learn and how. Effective assessment becomes a lever for change. It is consistent with the National Science Education Standards and provides a means of collecting data on students about their understanding of the National Science Education Standards.

Tools for authentic assessment include pictorial analysis, hands-on performance tasks, reflective questioning, and systematic observation. Many illustrations show various types of teacher records and student products, including portfolios that verify the types and levels of understanding. These techniques are pragmatically illustrated by supporting a central lesson throughout the chapter.

Discussion Questions

1. Contemporary movements in education usually embrace the preference for students to demonstrate learning outcomes. Performance or behavioral objectives may be used for this purpose. What advantages or disadvantages do you see with this type of objective?

2. How is the idea of *embedded assessment* consistent with the National Science Education Standards for assessment?

3. What is the advantage of having students create a rubric to assess their work over a teacher-developed rubric? What would be the disadvantages?

4. Devise a rubric for scoring a pictorial assessment. To what extent did you struggle with this task? Given your response to the previous question, does it make sense to use only one kind of assessment, such as pictorial assessment, to determine what your students know and are able to do?

5. Create a reflective assessment question and share it with your classmates. Ask them to answer your question without any further prompts from you. Did they respond in the manner you intended when you wrote the question? If not, what do you think you will need to change in the question to get the response you intended?

Build a Portfolio or E-Folio

1. Prepare a lesson plan using the 4–E approach. Does your plan develop an understanding of the concept you identified in the beginning of the lesson? How do you know? What are you expecting the students to do to demonstrate that they can apply their understanding of the concept in a new context? What are you expecting the students to do as an assessment?

2. Construct appropriate ways to evaluate the children's science knowledge, skills, and attitudes for the lesson plan developed in item 1.

3. Prepare the rubrics you will need for assessing the concepts and skills developed in the lesson plan from item 1.

4. How could you use rubrics to help you evaluate science portfolios created by the students in your class? What kinds of things would you require them to place in their portfolios as evidence of their achievements? Use the NSES for assessment to guide your selection.

Introduction

What Is Scientific Literacy?

Science as Inquiry for Literacy

Methods That Use Inquiry to Promote Student Concept Formation and Discovery

✦ 4–E FEATURE LESSON: *Make a Sinker Float: Clay Boats*

Scientific Method: How Can You Use Principles of Scientific Experimentation While Teaching?

✦ VIDEO EXPLORATIONS: *The 4–E Learning Cycle*

✦ WHAT RESEARCH SAYS: *The Science Learning Cycle*

Techniques for Promoting Student Cooperation

✦ TEACHERS ON SCIENCE TEACHING: *What Is a Question Box?*

Recommendations for Enhancing Students' Learning of Science

Chapter Summary

Discussion Questions

Build a Portfolio or E-Folio

Inquiry for Scientific Literacy

Mrs. Myers has loved science since she was very young, and her love is communicated to her students through her positive attitude and enthusiasm. She tries to connect each lesson with her students' experiences by involving each child in a personal way. Her third-grade classroom is an active place. Sometimes her lessons are mistaken by visitors as play. When queried, she always refers to "play" as a way to make an important point. In fact, her young scientists can be overheard asking each other about "the point" because they are accustomed to looking for a focus in each lesson. A "minds-on" focus guides each "hands-on" lesson. Mrs. Myers's classroom consists of individual desks clustered into "research" groups of four. Her classroom walls are alive with brilliant colors, usually the children's artwork and projects, but also commercial posters carefully selected to illustrate a variety of careers and diverse role models for the young scientists as well as to illustrate various forms and uses of technology. Plants and small mammals are positioned in the research corner near the aquarium and the desert climate terrarium.

Mrs. Myers begins the day's science lesson by asking the children to count off from 1 to 4 and reminds each child to remember his or her number. Being of small frame, Mrs. Myers often safely joins the children in the physical activities. She asks:

"OK, scientists. Today we are going to begin an investigation of a very important idea. Would you all please gather in a circle around me?"

In no particular order, Mrs. Myers gently directs the twenty-four children into a tight circle, each standing shoulder-to-shoulder. Humor and gentle prodding accomplish the task and provide a nice link to the geometry lesson learned in math class last week.

"Where are the number 'one's' standing?" asks Mrs. Myers. "All of the 'one's' will represent 'food' during our activity. What does the number 'one' mean for us?"

"Food!" answer the scientists with enthusiasm.

"All of you will represent a special role. Who are the 'two's'?"

Exuberant "me's" identify most of the "two's" and a few gentle jostles of classmates remind the other "two's" to identify themselves.

"The 'two's' will be 'water' " informs Mrs. Myers.

"The 'three's' will be 'shelter.' "

"The 'four's' will be 'space.' " A brief practice session ensures that everyone understands her or his role. Some tightening of the circle and turning in a common direction places all children appropriately, with hands grasping the shoulders of the scientist in front.

"Now for the physical challenge. When I count to 3, our mission is to hold our positions, bend our legs, and gently sit on the knees of the scientist behind us." Mrs. Myers takes some time to offer assurance and make the process clear. The 1-2-3 count is given and success happens fleetingly until pandemonium breaks out when the seated circle breaks apart and children do a controlled fall with enthusiastic exaggeration.

"Everybody up! Let's talk about this. Why do you suppose we had trouble keeping our circle together?"

"I couldn't find Sasha's knees!" quips Sachiko.

"Brent fell down and so did I," offers Jon.

"So what happened to the rest of us when Brent fell?" asks Mrs. Myers.

"We all fell!" responds a chorus of voices.

"That's right. We depend on one another. We have a system of parts, and when one part falls, the others also soon fall. Let's try this again and see whether we can set a record. What do you suppose we could do to make it easier for us to keep our circle together when we sit?"

A number of suggestions are offered and after incorporating them into the arrangement, Mrs. Myers gives the physical challenge again. The children count to 30 before Mrs. Myers gives the signal to stand. Not one child drops out of the circle. Mrs. Myers continues her lesson:

"All animals need a habitat in order to survive, and all habitats contain the food, water, shelter, and space unique for the animal. In today's activity we each play an important role—food, water, shelter, space—and when we keep our circle together we provide a 'pretend' habitat for an animal." Mrs. Myers continues the discussion by asking the children to identify the parts of a habitat needed for a common animal such as a robin, fish, cow, dog, or squirrel.

"What's a habitat?" she asks, testing the young scientists. The children put into their own words their operational definitions and descriptions of food, water, shelter and space as examples for some other animals familiar to them.

"Let's do our activity again, and this time let's pretend we have a drought," offers Mrs. Myers. The children are told that each of the "waters" will leave the circle, one at a time, while all are seated, and try to keep the circle together as long as possible. Some of the children predict all of the "waters" can leave and they can still keep the circle together, while the skeptics don't think any "waters" can leave without the circle falling.

"What do you think we might have to do to keep our circle together?" asks Mrs. Myers. After some discussion, the children offer that they might be able to "adapt" by scooching together to take up the empty space and avoid falling.

The lap sit is repeated. After the first "water" slips out, the strain of the void can be felt around the entire circle, but all adapt and manage to keep the circle together. Mrs. Myers asks the children to think about the effort before the next "water" is invited to leave. Barely successful after the next departure, the circle collapses when the third "water" slips aside.

Introduction

Mrs. Myers led a discussion rich with understanding about the importance of a habitat with all components available in sufficient supply and suitable arrangement. Children were asked to think about how common wild animals and outdoor domestic animals could be affected by a drought or a loss of other essential components of their habitats. Other variations were attempted to simulate stresses placed on human habitats, including famine, overcrowding and shelter lost to natural disasters. Notions of interdependence and the need to adapt or relocate emerged from the ideas. In the days that followed, books were read, videos were viewed, Internet searches were conducted, and information was organized to help the children observe the habitats of local animals and plan suitable habitats for crickets, ants, and earthworms to be placed in classroom terraria.

Mrs. Myers understands that each individual student must integrate a complex mental structure of many types of information in order to construct his or her own understandings of science. She believes her intentions are important in order to help her learners develop a strong foundation for higher learning as one effort to prepare youth for higher levels of achievement. The Third International Mathematics and Science Study (TIMSS) and the National Assessment of Educational Progress (NAEP) have been the objects of many popular press articles describing the science achievement of school youth. General reports of elementary children reveal relatively good performance at achieving basic proficiencies in science. However, a decline is apparent as students move into high school and are expected to meet higher goals. The U.S. science curriculum is described as covering too many topics at each grade without sufficient depth; repetition seems to prevail as children advance through school. The science curriculum is believed to be insufficient and teaching methods are criticized for their failure to prepare learners to meet more rigorous proficiencies.

Mrs. Myers helps her learners strive toward becoming scientifically literate. She encourages each child to explore the ideas of science—looking for relationships among ideas and the reasons for these relationships. Children are encouraged to use their formative ideas to explain natural phenomena and to solve problems. Each lesson is multifaceted and requires each child to make observations, ponder and pose questions, examine books and other sources of information to discern what is already known about a topic, plan investigations, gather data and analyze and interpret data, and suggest explanations and answers for problems and experimental outcomes. Mrs. Myers encourages her learners to be active inquirers in their pursuit of scientific literacy.

"How can you support your learners in becoming scientifically literate as they inquire and construct scientific meaning?" We use this question as the focal point for organizing this chapter: Our response to this question helps you to

1. examine the meaning of scientific literacy,
2. explore several teaching methods that use inquiry to promote student conceptual construction and self-discovery,
3. investigate techniques that promote student cooperation, and
4. identify conditions that enhance students' learning of science.

What Is Scientific Literacy?

A literate person has a fundamental command of the essentials: what one needs to know and be able to do in order to function as a contributing member of a society. Not long ago the standard refrain in education was that a literate person commanded the basics of reading, writing, and arithmetic. But this view is too narrow to provide an education that helps our youngsters survive in a complex world with its wonders of technology and sophisticated social, economic, and political problems. Tomorrow's leaders and policy makers must know more, have a different worldview, and possess an impressive array of skills. What does a scientifically literate person know, and what is that person able to do in a modern society?

Defining Scientific Literacy

Many definitions of scientific literacy have been written. We refer to the definition advocated by the National Science Education Standards set by the National Research Council (NRC):

> Scientific literacy means that a person can ask and find or determine answers to questions derived from curiosity about everyday experiences. It means the ability to describe, explain, and predict natural phenomena. It means the ability to read with understanding articles about science in the popular press and engage in social conversation about the validity of the conclusions. Scientific literacy implies that a person can identify scientific issues underlying national and local decisions and express positions that are scientifically and technologically informed. A literate citizen should be able to evaluate the quality of scientific information on the basis of its sources and the methods used to generate it. Scientific literacy also implies the capacity to pose and evaluate arguments based on evidence and to apply conclusions from such arguments appropriately. (NRC, 1996, p. 22)

Science helps improve our lives.

Promoting Scientific Literacy

The NRC also reminds us that scientific literacy is not an all-or-nothing happening; a person may be scientifically literate in some fields or topics of study but not in others. Furthermore, scientific literacy is developed over a lifetime. Schooling is important, but literacy continues to develop during the adult years. The development of scientific literacy is influenced, as the details of its description suggest, by the attitudes and values of the individual, as well as the habits of mind and conceptual understandings that the individual uses and knows. Very broadly, then, a scientifically literate person has a capacity to use essential scientific attitudes, processes, and reasoning skills, and science types of information to reach reasoned conclusions and use the ideas of science in meaningful ways. This is representative of an ancient proverb's wisdom: "Teach a person how to fish, feed the person for a lifetime." Various reform efforts in science education pursue lifelong learning through efforts that strive to develop attitudes, skills, and knowledge. In other words, educators are encouraged to believe that if they teach a person how to learn, the person will learn for a lifetime.

Scientific Attitudes. Positive scientific attitudes—persistence, curiosity, humility, a healthy dose of skepticism—motivate learners to approach a task or problem with enough interest to find solutions for themselves. There is a relationship between attitudes, interest, achievement, and perception of one's successes, summed up by the saying, "success breeds success." Anyone who has ever persisted with a problem long enough to solve it knows the sweet feeling of achievement and that "can-do" perception that accompanies success. The relationship among these factors appears to be cumulative and conveys the notion that children's achievement increases as they develop more positive attitudes and more interest in science (as well as other subjects). As achievement increases, motivation and desire stimulate the development of new learning skills, and that leads to greater understanding of the information, which is accumulating at a dizzying pace. Therefore, the processes of science are the skills by which observations are acquired and meaning is constructed by the learner. Processes can provide the type and quality of the science experience desired for children where thinking is expanded and improved.

Scientific Skills. Process skills, as literacy-building tools, have tremendous carry-over value in and out of school (see Chapters 1 and 5). They are also vital to adult living. They are the mechanisms by which problems are identified, explored, and solved. Whether the adult mission is to improve or improvise on a recipe; determine the cause of a blown fuse (or tripped circuit breaker); troubleshoot the cause of a car's failure to start; plan the best route to run a new line for an extension telephone; identify evidence and separate it from opinion while listening to a political candidate; or determine how to thread a sewing machine, the processes of science contribute to solving the problem.

Children are naturally interested in science and associated science topics. Surveys done in elementary schools show that children choose science a majority of the time when given lists of school topics from which they can choose. Parents report, too, that their children list science as one of their favored school subjects (Mechling & Oliver, 1983a).

Scientific Knowledge. Like you, children cannot escape the importance of science; it affects every aspect of their lives. However, the intent of scientific information is that it be a means, not an end. Science content can help children become responsible consumers and personally learn how to benefit more from learning science. If science content is applied to real circumstances, scientific information and areas of study provide meaningful contexts for developing literacy skills. Recommendations from science organizations, such as the National Science Teachers Association, urge that children have daily opportunities to relate science to their own lives and that science study not be limited to science time. Other organizations, such as the American Association for the Advancement of Science and the National Research Council, urge that science lessons be focused on meaningful standards that address the historical, social, technological, and interdisciplinary nature of science (see Figure 6.1). The information, attitudes, and skills of science can be used to enrich other school experiences, and times of reading, art, music, social studies, writing, mathematics, discussion, physical education, and so on, can be used to deepen an understanding of science. Science is central to the education of literate citizens.

Science as Inquiry for Literacy

Inquiry means the use of the processes of science, scientific knowledge, and attitudes to reason and to think critically. Inquiry assists in constructing an understanding of scientific concepts, learning how to learn, becoming an independent and lifelong learner, and further developing the habits of mind associated with science. Learning outcomes for inquiry require students to be able to understand inquiry and do a variety of types

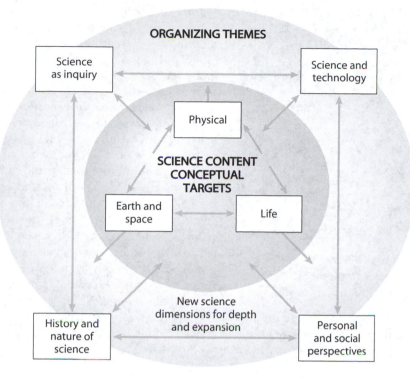

FIGURE 6.1

Traditional Disciplines and New Content Dimensions An appropriate science lesson may be focused on a single concept within a specific science discipline and can expose learners to relationships with all of the new dimensions of science.

of science activities in order to learn the uses and skills of inquiry and develop a greater capacity to inquire.

Inquiry is the process that students should use to learn science. They should be able to ask questions, use their questions to plan and conduct a scientific investigation, use appropriate science tools and scientific techniques, evaluate evidence and use it logically to construct several alternative explanations, and communicate (argue) their conclusions scientifically (NRC, 1996).

The Importance of Scientific Inquiry

The National Science Education Standards (NSES) (National Research Council, 1996, p. 32) list, among specific teaching standards, several points that encourage teachers to

- ✦ focus and support inquiries while interacting with students;
- ✦ orchestrate discourse among students about scientific ideas;
- ✦ challenge students to accept and share responsibility for their own learning;
- ✦ recognize and respond to student diversity and encourage all students to participate fully in science learning;
- ✦ encourage and model the skills of scientific inquiry, as well as the curiosity, openness to new ideas and data, and skepticism that characterize science.

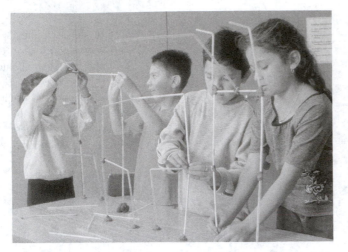

Science goals focus on the interrelationships of learners, their inquiry processes, society, technology, and the history of science.

Inquiry as Cornerstone. Inquiry is the cornerstone of these standards for teaching, and according to the NSES (1996, p. 4) good teachers at all age and grade levels are expected to be able to plan inquiry-based science lessons and science programs, take proper actions to guide and facilitate learning, assess teaching and learning, and develop and maintain classroom environments and learning communities that enable children to learn science. Even so, teachers hold diverse views about what inquiry is (Bybee et al., 1997), and many teachers report familiarity with inquiry, yet their actual teaching practices suggest they do not understand deeply the purposes and processes of inquiry (Lederman & Neiss, 1997; Mullis et al., 1997).

For children, inquiry refers to the activities—the processes—that children experience in which they develop testable ideas and construct understandings of real-world scientific ideas. Inquiry activities usually involve

+ pondering and posing questions,
+ using tools to make and classify observations,
+ examining sources of information,
+ investigating, analyzing, forming answers, and explanations,
+ communicating outcomes and conclusions.

Inquiry Is More Than Hands-On. Hands-on activities alone do not guarantee inquiry. Inquiry is dependent on a set of interrelated processes guided by questions. Inquiry is a process of interrelationships between the object of the inquiry and those who do the inquiring. Inquiry refers to the process of the effort used to explore questions, ideas, and phenomena. The result of the effort is a discovery that is new to the child in school science, but already known by scientists and teachers. Children are able to inquire when they are given hands-on learning opportunities, appropriate materials to manipulate, puzzling circumstances or problems for motivation, enough structure to help them focus or maintain a productive direction, and enough freedom to compare ideas and make personal learning discoveries.

Inquiry methods can take several forms, yet all strive to promote a healthy dynamic between hands-on, minds-on learning processes. This dynamic has been found to improve the spatial ability of children and help to reduce early differences between genders respective to imagining and manipulating objects with moving parts (Solomon, 1997). In this section of the chapter we invite you to explore a learning cycle method, scientific experimental method, Suchman's Inquiry method, playful discovery, and problem-based learning. All of these methods make use of inquiry techniques to stimulate conceptualization and discovery of meaning. As simple as each method appears, you will benefit from cumulative experiences, reflection and self-evaluation, and revision in using these methods.

Methods That Use Inquiry to Promote Student Concept Formation and Discovery

How can you accomplish all that is expected in this age of multiple literacies, curriculum and teaching standards, academic content outcomes, increased public expectations, and expanded calls for accountability? A clearly focused lesson plan, authentic forms of assessment, and sensible teaching tools all help to provide the answer. Chapters 4 and 5 focused on planning and assessment. We devote most of this chapter to illustrating methods that use inquiry to help children discover and understand. Figure 6.1 on page 185 presented the different forms of science content and the multiple interactions to be taught across the primary, intermediate and middle grades. National and state science standards embrace the view that science ought to be learned and understood authentically through inquiry methods.

The 4–E Science Learning Cycle

A learning cycle is a method for planning lessons, teaching, learning, and developing curricula. This teaching method was originally designed for the Science Curriculum Improvement Study and has produced the largest achievement gains of the experimental elementary science programs of the 1960s. These increases are largely a result of the learning cycle as an inquiry teaching and learning method, because the cycle a way of thinking and acting that is consistent with how pupils naturally inquire and make discoveries.

The science learning cycle originally consisted of three phases: exploration, concept invention, and application. Several modifications have been made to the original learning cycle over the past 4 decades and the literature reports several popular iterations. We recommend a 4–E learning cycle, which is specifically designed to accommodate all of the new science goals emphasizing mastery of specific concepts, developing reasoning and problem-solving skills and addressing new dimensions of science and accountability. (See Figure 6.2) The 4–E learning cycle consists of four phases: Exploration, Explanation, Expansion, and Evaluation. Each phase, when followed in sequence has sound theoretical support from the cognitive development theory of Jean Piaget (Renner & Marek, 1988; Marek & Cavallo, 1997) and applies constructivist learning procedures (see Chapter 2). The 4–E learning cycle produced significant gains in pupil achievement, skills and scientific attitudes during the authors' successful Lead Teacher Project for K–6 science funded by the National Science Foundation. Table 6.1 on page 189 presents an overview of the cycle's phases, which are described in more detail below.

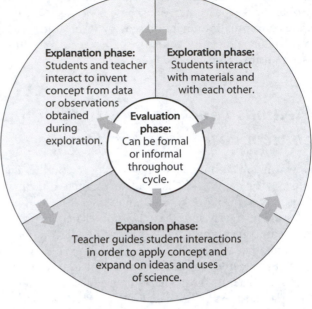

FIGURE 6.2 The 4–E
Science Learning Cycle

Source: Adapted from a figure
by Charles Barman, "The
Learning Cycle: Making It
Work," *Science Scope*
(February 1989) 28–31.

Explanation phase:
Students and teacher interact to invent concept from data or observations obtained during exploration.

Exploration phase:
Students interact with materials and with each other.

Evaluation phase:
Can be formal or informal throughout cycle.

Expansion phase:
Teacher guides student interactions in order to apply concept and expand on ideas and uses of science.

Phase One: Exploration. The exploration phase is student centered, stimulates learner mental disequilibrium, and fosters mental assimilation. The teacher is responsible for engaging the learner curiosity by using inquiry questions, offering sufficient instructions and using materials that help learners to interact in ways that are related to the concept and form intuitive understandings. The teacher's directions must not tell students what they should learn and must not explain the concept; this occurs later. The teacher's role is to

◆ pose the lesson's central question,
◆ engage the learners in the inquiry,
◆ answer students' questions,
◆ ask questions to guide student observations and to cause students to engage in science processes or thinking skills (see Figure 6.3),
◆ give hints and cues to keep the exploration going.

Students are responsible for exploring the materials and for gathering and recording their own information. Teachers rely on questioning skills such as those shown in Figure 6.3 on page 190 to guide the exploring and assisting learners in making observations and collecting data that will be used in the next Explanation phase to construct the concept.

Phase Two: Explanation. The explanation phase is less student centered and provides for learner mental accommodation. The teacher refrains from lecturing or too much telling, but uses this phase to help learners form the conceptual explanation for the

TABLE 6.1   4–E Learning Cycle Summary

Phase	Focus	What Students Do	What Teachers Do	Outcome
Exploration	Inquiry Engaged learning	Hands-on investigations Use process skills and tools Cooperative investigation	Establish the inquiry Interact with student groups Guide exploration Informal assessment	Process skill development Preconceptions formed and explored
Explanation	Convergent thinking for conceptualization Processing the Exploration	Respond to teacher's guidance Examine collected information Respond to questioning Form the concept	Direct investigation of the information Use questioning Coach with explicitness Identify the concept Form operational definition for concept	Concept identified and described
Expansion	Expand understanding of concept Address new dimensions of the National Science Education Standards	Teacher-directed activity Student-directed projects Use concept and skills in new situation Think, reason, apply	Direct additional activity Guide student projects Continue the inquiry Questioning Practical applications Informal assessment	Deeper conceptual understanding Substantive accomplishment of standards
Evaluation	Discern what students know and can do	Respond to teacher Demonstrate understanding Demonstrate skills Express attitudes	Interact with students and groups Focus on what students know and can do Plan next step	Demonstration of conceptual understanding, proficiency in using skills, degree of attitudes

lesson's inquiry question. The main purpose of this phase is for teachers to guide student thinking so the concept of the lesson is constructed cooperatively, not merely given by the teacher. To accomplish this, the teacher selects and sets the desired class environment. The teacher asks students to give the information they have collected and helps students to process and mentally organize the information by using interactive examination of the data and skillful uses of questioning.

Once the information is organized, the teacher introduces the specific language needed for the concept, as Mrs. Myers did in the chapter's opening scenario *after* her students observed and explored what happened to them during the lap sit when different variables were introduced. Teachers help students to identify the lesson's concept and to construct and attach meaning to the concept. Often this action can be simplified by using a sentence starter including the concept and asking the learners to call upon the experiences and intuitive understanding to help form an operational definition for the class.

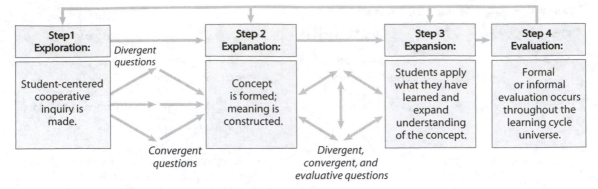

FIGURE 6.3 Using Questions During a Learning Cycle

This phase helps to lead to mental accommodation, as described by Piaget. Here students must focus on their primary findings from their firsthand explorations. The teacher must introduce language or concept labels to assist mental accommodation. These questions may help you think about your mission and help you to guide students' thinking so they construct their own explanations of the concept.

✦ What kinds of information or findings should the students talk about?
✦ How can I help students summarize their findings?
✦ How can I guide the students and refrain from telling them what they should have found, even if their understanding is incomplete? How can I help them use their information to construct the concept correctly?
✦ What labels or descriptions should the students attach to the concept?
✦ What reasons can I give the students if they ask me why the concept is important? This question automatically leads to the next phase, expansion.

Phase Three: Expansion. The expansion phase should be student centered as much as possible and organized to encourage group cooperation. The purpose of this phase is to help learners mentally organize the experiences they have acquired by forming connections with similar previous experiences and by discovering new applications for what they have learned. Constructed concepts must be linked to other related ideas or experiences. The purpose is to take the students' thinking beyond where it is presently, and planning for this part of your teaching can be helped through concept mapping (see Chapter 4). You must require students to use the language or labels of the new concept so that they add depth to their understanding. This is a proper place to help students apply what they learned by expanding examples or by providing additional exploratory experiences for stimulating students' science inquiry skills, encouraging them to investigate science-technology-society interrelationships, and for understanding the history and nature of science. (See goals in Chapter 4 and the science content interactions illustrated in Figure 6.1.) The expansion phase can automatically lead to the exploration phase of the next lesson; hence a continuing cycle for teaching and learning is established. The 4–E Feature lesson shows how to do this.

Teachers help students organize their thinking by relating what they have learned to other ideas or experiences that relate to the constructed concept. It is very important to use the language of the concept during this phase to add depth to the concept's meaning and to expand the range of the children's vocabulary. Consider these questions:

1. What previous experiences have the students had that relate to the concept? How can I connect the concept to those experiences?
2. What are some examples of how the concept encourages the students to see science's benefits to themselves? To help them understand the relationships among science, technology, and society? To help them develop science inquiry skills? To help them be informed about the history and nature of science?
3. What questions can I ask to encourage students to discover the concept's importance? To apply the concept? To appreciate the problems it solves? To understand the problems it causes? To identify the careers influenced by it? To understand how the concept has been viewed or used throughout history?
4. What new experiences are needed to apply or expand the concept?
5. What is the next concept related to the present one? How can I encourage exploration of the next concept?

Phase Four: Evaluation. The purpose of this phase is to overcome the limits of standard types of testing; Chapter 5 presents several tools to use. Evaluation should occur throughout the entire cycle and not be reserved for the end of the lesson. Learning often occurs in small increments before larger mental leaps of insight are possible and frequent assessment nurtures learning. Therefore, evaluation should be continual, not a typical end-of-chapter or -unit approach. Several types of measures are necessary to form a holistic evaluation of the students' learning and to encourage mental construction of concepts and process skills. Evaluation can be included in each phase of the learning cycle. Ask yourself:

1. What appropriate learning outcomes should I expect?
2. What types of hands-on evaluation techniques can the students do to demonstrate the basic skills of observation, classification, communication, measurement, prediction, and inference?
3. What techniques are appropriate for students to demonstrate the integrated science process skills of identifying and controlling variables, defining operationally, forming hypotheses, experimenting, interpreting data, and forming models?
4. How can I use pictures to help students demonstrate how well they can think through problems that require understanding fundamental concepts and the integration of ideas?
5. What types of questions can I ask students to help them reflect and to indicate how well they recall and understand what has been learned?

(text continues on page 195)

Make a Sinker Float: Clay Boats

GRADE LEVEL: **4–6**

DISCIPLINE: **Physical Science**

Inquiry Question: Why can heavy objects float?

Concept to Be Invented: If the upward force of the liquid is greater than the downward force of an object, the object will float because it is buoyed (lifted up or supported) by the water. This concept is called buoyancy, and it explains why some heavy objects, such as steel ships, will float in water.

National Science Education Standards: 4–6 Physical Science—Motion and forces. If more than one force acts on an object, then the forces can reinforce or cancel one another, depending on their direction and magnitude. Unbalanced forces will cause changes in the speed and/or direction of an object's motion.

Science Attitudes to Nurture: Open-mindedness, cooperating with others, avoiding broad generalizations, willingness to withhold judgment

Materials Needed: Small tubs or buckets to hold water, small objects that will sink or float in water, modeling clay (Plasticine), small uniform objects to use as cargo (weights, such as ceramic tiles or marbles) in the clay boats, a container modified like the illustration (Expansion), a small container to catch the water that spills from the modified container, and a scale or balance to measure the weight of the spilled water

Safety Precautions: Have students notify you in case of spills. Use a room with a nonslip floor surface, if possible.

Exploration *Which process skills will be used?*

Observing, estimating, predicting

Have the students examine the variety of objects given to them and predict whether each object will sink or float in the water. Have the students write their predictions on organized data sheets that you provide. Use as one of the objects a lump of clay about the size of a tennis ball. Provide time for the students to test their predictions and then gather the students together to explore what their predictions reveal.

Explanation

If objects of different sizes and weights are used in the Exploration phase, students will discover that heaviness is not the factor that determines whether an object will sink or float. For example, a large piece of 2 × 4-inch wood will be heavier than a glass marble or a metal washer, but it will float while the marble and washer will sink. Explain that

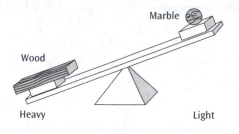

Marble

Wood

Heavy   Light

Archimedes, a Greek philosopher, is credited with discovering that an object immersed in a liquid (water) will appear to lose some of its weight. Ask students to speculate why this seems to be. A suitable explanation may be: If the upward force of the liquid is greater than the downward force of the object, it will float because the object is buoyed (lifted up or supported) by the water. This factor is called buoyancy and is the conceptual focus of the lesson. Steel has been given a special shape (the ship) that gives it a greater volume, which helps to spread its weight across a larger amount (volume) of the water, making it possible for the buoyant upward forces of the water to be greater than the downward force of the ship's weight. How might buoyancy be affected by the amount of cargo a

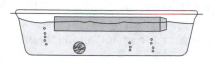

ship carries? Why is it important to keep a ship from taking on water? What were you able to do with the clay to help it to float? What did you do to the clay's mass respective to the volume of the container's water?

Expansion *Which process skills will be used?*

Inferring, hypothesizing, investigating

Weigh the lump of dry clay and the smaller container to be used to catch the water spill; record the measures. Take the lump of clay and use the device as illustrated. Carefully lower the clay into the container of water and measure its weight while it is submerged. Catch the water that spills out of the container and weigh the container again; subtract the dry container weight to determine the weight of the water displaced by the sinking clay. The weight of the submerged clay should be less than the dry weight because of the upward (buoyant) force of the water. Challenge the students to find a way to change the shape of the clay so that it will float in water. Challenge them to see who can make the clay boat that will carry the largest amount of cargo before it sinks. Have students draw pictures of their boats' shapes and/or measure the size of the boats' bottoms. Capable students could calculate the surface area of the boats' bottoms and graph the amount of cargo carried (before sinking) as a function of area. Ask them to observe carefully what happens to make their clay boats sink and to describe later what they observe.

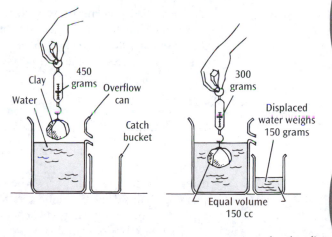

Clay

Water

450 grams

Overflow can

Catch bucket

300 grams

Displaced water weighs 150 grams

Equal volume 150 cc

(continued)

Science in Personal and Social Perspectives

Ask the students why the Coast Guard requires flotation devices on boats and why these devices make it possible for a person who otherwise might sink to float. Why does the Coast Guard set passenger limits on pleasure craft?

Science and Technology

Ask the students to search for other inventions that apply the buoyancy principle. Ask how these uses have had an impact on people. Examples might include floats connected to switches or valves that control pumps or appliances, seat cushions on airliners that are removable and can be used as flotation devices, channel buoys for navigation or to mark danger zones.

Science as Inquiry

+ Ask the students to identify other examples of buoyancy in liquids and to describe differences. As examples, ask the students to redo their sink-or-float tests in denatured or isopropyl alcohol, or a mixture of alcohol and water, or water with different amounts of salt added. (This can lead to another concept and another lesson: specific gravity.)
+ Ask the students to explain why a submarine can sink and float, and how it is possible for a submarine or a SCUBA diver to remain at a particular depth.
+ Construct a Cartesian diver using a 2-liter soft drink container filled with water. Place a glass medicine dropper in the container and put the cap on tightly. Squeeze the sides of the container, release and watch what happens to the dropper. Why does the dropper sink and rise? What is necessary to keep the submarine dropper at a constant depth in the container?
+ Ask the students to explain why it is easier to swim and float in salt water than in fresh water.

History and Nature of Science

As an Expansion assignment, have the students search for pictures and examples of careers that require some knowledge of the buoyancy concept. Examples may include ship builders, navy and marine personnel, fishermen, marine salvage crews, plumbers, SCUBA divers. How have the inventions used by these changed over time?

Read Pamela Allen's *Mr. Archimedes' Bath* (1991) to the class and discuss what the author needed to know about science to write this children's book.

Evaluation

Upon completing these activities, the students will be able to:

+ (with the ball of clay and/or Cartesian diver) demonstrate and explain the concept of buoyancy;
+ draw a picture of what happens when their clay ball is placed in water and when its shape is changed. They will be able to write a paragraph in their own words that explains why and how the clay floats;

+ demonstrate proper use of the balance when weighing the clay, dry and submerged;
+ measure and calculate the area of the clay boats and graph the maximum cargo carried as a function of the surface area of the boats;
+ research the buoyancy inventions used by a single career over a period of time (perhaps fifty years) and explain how different understandings of buoyancy and technical advancement influenced persons in these careers.

Scientific Method: How Can You Use Principles of Scientific Experimentation While Teaching?

Scientific method is defined as the systematic pursuit of knowledge involving the recognition and formulation of a problem, the collection of data through observation and experimentation (the experiential element), the formulation of a hypothesis, and the testing and confirmation (or rejection) of that hypothesis. (Fields, 1989, p. 15)

What went through your mind as you read the definition? If the scientific method was taught in your high school, it was probably taught in a science class apart from actually doing science. Some scientists and educators object to the notion of a scientific method and, justifiably, cite that all scientists do not think or investigate in such a linear way. Often a method is memorized as a series of steps like these:

1. Define the problem.
2. Find out what is already known about the problem.
3. Form a hypothesis or educated guess.
4. Conduct an experiment to test the hypothesis.
5. Use the results to reach a conclusion.

Unfortunately, many textbooks and teachers have treated these steps as a recipe for doing and learning science. The new vision presented by the National Science Education Standards (NSES) encourages inquiry beyond the "science as a process" approach. The principles of scientific experimentation encourage learners to combine science skills (such as observing, classifying, predicting, and experimenting) and scientific knowledge by reasoning and thinking to develop their understanding of science. According to the NSES, students who inquire through scientific experimentation

+ construct understanding of science concepts,
+ "know how we know" in science,
+ develop an understanding of the nature of science,
+ develop many skills necessary to become independent inquirers about their natural world and
+ develop mental habits of using their skills and abilities (NRC, 1996).

Video Explorations — The 4–E Learning Cycle

Video Summary

The learning cycle is a way of planning, teaching, and assessing student learning. This series of videoclips examine the 4–E Learning Cycle: Exploration, Explanation, Expansion, and Evaluation. During the student-centered exploration phase activities should be

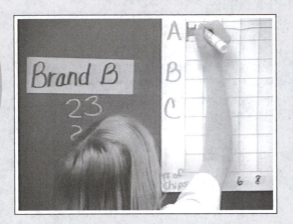

planned that make the students curious about the concept to be explored and engage them in the processes of science. The success of the explanation phase depends upon the teacher's ability to cause the students to reflect on what they did during exploration, to get them to share the data they collected, and to use those experiences to make the concept concrete. The expansion phase is a time to plan experiences, which require the students to apply their understanding of the concept in a new context. The evaluation phase can occur at any time during the lesson.

Tips for Viewing, Objectives, or What to Watch for

As you watch these videos, make note of the following:

- ◆ The phase or phases in which the students are most active,
- ◆ The phase in which the teacher plays a central role,
- ◆ The kinds of process skills the students are engaged in within the lesson,
- ◆ The amount of interaction among students and between students and teacher.

Questions for Exploration

1. Can you identify the roles of teachers during the various phases of the learning cycle lesson?

2. How is the exploration phase in these videos different from the expansion phase?

3. How did the teacher make use of students' experiences from the exploration phase while making the concept concrete in the explanation phase?

4. How do you think the teachers checked for student misconceptions during the learning cycle to deliver their science lessons?

Activity for Application

The use of a learning cycle to plan and deliver science lessons makes sense in that it is consistent with theories of learning proposed by Piaget, and in the research about science achievement done by Karplus as well as Renner and Marek. Since these studies in the 1960s on science achievement, much research has been done on constructivism and its role in learning science concepts. What do you understand about constructivism and how is the use of a learning cycle consistent with that learning theory?

The principles of scientific inquiry and experimentation offer ways to form cooperative problem-solving groups, particularly when the principles are used flexibly to help learners design a procedure they wish to follow. Most children need structure and considerable guidance until they develop the mental habits of thinking like a scientist. Begin simply, perhaps by saying that science deals with answering questions or solving mysteries, or as Fields (1989), says, "Science invents stories and then sees if they are true" (p. 15). Use thoughtful questions to guide classroom discussions and pursue answers to those questions and soon you will find students asking their own questions, inventing their own stories, and pursuing those stories to see whether they are true. These questions usually serve to define the problem and point out what needs to be known and implies how the inquiry ought to occur.

The Principles of Scientific Inquiry as a Teaching Method

The teaching strategy can have five steps that parallel those listed above. Steven Fields's fine article in *Science and Children* (Fields, 1989) provides many practical examples of how the steps you have memorized can be turned into a motivating, interactive, and effective teaching method. We paraphrase his ideas as follows:

Step 1. Have students conclude that experimenting will provide the best answer to the science question.

If a child shows interest in a topic by asking a question, or if children become curious about a topic after you ask a question, look for a way to discover the answer by acting on it. For example, how can you discover the answer to a question like, "If rudders (and flaps) steer an airplane in flight, which rudders steer it in which direction?" (See Figure 6.4.) Problem questions such as this can make good challenges for cooperative group investigations in which each learner has a specific duty to fulfill.

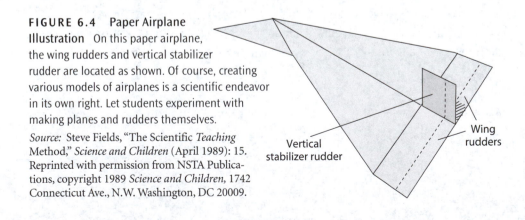

FIGURE 6.4 Paper Airplane Illustration On this paper airplane, the wing rudders and vertical stabilizer rudder are located as shown. Of course, creating various models of airplanes is a scientific endeavor in its own right. Let students experiment with making planes and rudders themselves.

Source: Steve Fields, "The Scientific *Teaching Method*," *Science and Children* (April 1989): 15. Reprinted with permission from NSTA Publications, copyright 1989 *Science and Children*, 1742 Connecticut Ave., N.W. Washington, DC 20009.

Vertical stabilizer rudder

Wing rudders

Step 2. Focus the science question to seek a specific answer.

Try a brainstorming session. Accept all ideas related to the question, then limit the question to the kernel of the problem it poses. Identify a hypothesis from the ideas offered. Help the student groups find out all they can about the problem; then encourage them to make and test predictions. Continuing with Steve Fields's airplane example, some predictions could include:

✦ Wing rudders control up-and-down movement.
✦ Tail rudders control movement to the left and right.
✦ When rudders are set in any given way, the plane will fly up and down or side to side.

Step 3. Guess the answer to the science question and use references to try to find out if the answer is already known.

Individual students and groups can brainstorm and decide the best way to find out the answer. Guiding questions can steer their thinking. Examples include:

✦ "Can you find the answer in a book?" If "yes," what kind of book?
✦ "Who do you know who might already know the answer?" (Other children, teachers, outside resources, experts, and so on.)

If these questions do not help, try "How can you (we) design a test to find out the answer?" For older children, this a good place to discuss variables that can affect the outcome and reliability of an experiment.

Step 4. Follow the procedures suggested by the guiding questions in Step 3 to find the answer to the science question raised in Step 2.

Help children during this stage by limiting their temptation to overgeneralize. For example, if the wing rudders are set up and the plane flies up, guide the students to the conclusion that these settings *probably* affect all planes the same way. One could not know for certain that larger planes are affected the same way unless they also are tested.

Step 5. After experimenting, interpreting, and concluding, have the students use what they have learned.

Focus on everyday experiences and have the children apply the main ideas they have learned—the concepts—to things they can understand. The rudder example applies to paper airplanes as well as kites, model rockets and planes, spoilers on racing cars, and rudder steering on conventional boats and swamp or airboats.

Like most other inquiry approaches, this method requires more time and planning to cover concepts. Equipment is needed, although often simple and inexpensive materials will do. Certain concepts lend themselves to experimentation more easily than others. The emphasis on concepts, however, is precisely what makes student comprehension greater and retention last longer. The cooperative group problem investigation approach helps to leverage the students' ideas by stimulating new approaches to the problem.

The Science Learning Cycle

The learning cycle is an approach to teaching and learning that ensures that students are involved in the types of thinking (inquiry) that constructivists argue is necessary for production learning. Jean Piaget's research on cognitive development helped to establish the first two phases of the learning cycle: exploration and explanation (concept invention). Mental activities in these phases promote what Piaget called *assimilation* and *accommodation*. Imagine the mind as a file cabinet: faced with information, the mind seeks a place to put it. Placing new information in an existing file with similar information would be an example of assimilation, as the mind adds to what already exists. However, when it does not find a file with information similar to that to be stored away, the mind must create a new file.

Robert Karplus, director of the Science Curriculum Improvement Study (SCIS), is credited with adding a third phase to the learning cycle. He named this phase *discovery* and then later changed the name to concept *implementation*. Some science educators prefer to call this the *application phase*. John Renner and Edmund Marek have made improvements and call the third phase *expansion of the idea*. There is considerable research to support uses of the learning cycle for improving children's science achievement and process skill development.

Renner and Marek note that the SCIS program relies on the learning cycle to organize its materials and to guide its teaching methods. Consequently, they have used the SCIS materials to conduct their own research.

Renner and Marek have used Piagetian mental conservation tasks to design experimental studies that indicate what effect the learning cycle may have on the intellectual development of young children. They found that when the learning cycle was used, children in an experimental group significantly outperformed other children who learned within a traditional textbook control group. Number, weight, liquid amount, solid amount, length, and area were the measures of conservation. The researchers believe "the data support the conclusion that the rate of attainment of conservation reasoning is significantly enhanced by the experiences made possible by [the first graders who learned through a learning cycle]." They also claim that the learning cycle enhances the intellectual development of young learners.

The learning cycle has also been used to test the ability of children to use science processes. In a study

Suchman's Inquiry: How Can You Get Students to Think and Question?

Science Magic? Dressed in cape and top hat, Mr. Martinez was ready to deliver his promised special treat to the fourth-grade class. With the theatrical flair of an amateur magician, he proposed to take his very sharp magic wand (the straight steel shank cut out of a coat hanger and filed to a pin-sharp point on one end) and pass it through a balloon without bursting it. Mr. Martinez played the crowd. He blew up a balloon, tied it off, and enlisted the aid of the audience by having them chant, "I believe! I believe!" and then on his signal say the magic words. As the super-sharp pin was about to touch the stretched side of the balloon, several children furrowed their brows and covered their ears. And with good reason: Pop!

The giggles were meant to tell Mr. Martinez "I told you so," but he persisted with remarks about not all of them believing or not selecting the right magic words. "Let's try again," he said as he began working the crowd again. Martinez blew up another

that investigated fifth graders who were controlled (via a matched-pairs design) for intellectual development, chronological age, gender, and socioeconomic level, Renner and Marek found that all differences in the performance of science process skills favored the group that used the learning cycle. They concluded that the learning cycle helped children learn to use the processes of science much better than did a traditional program using a conventional science textbook.

In still another study, Renner and Marek investigated the influence of the learning cycle in a science program on student achievement in mathematics, reading, and social studies. They discovered that children learned *just as much and just as well* from the learning cycle as those who learned from a traditional program on understanding mathematics concepts, learning mathematics skills, learning social studies content, and understanding word meaning. However, they conclude that the *learning cycle was superior* for helping children apply mathematics; master social studies skills that involve interpreting graphs, tables, and posters and assimilation of data for problem solving; and determine paragraph meaning. In yet another study, Renner and Marek discovered that the learning cycle used in the SCIS first-grade program helped children out perform other children in a reading program on reading readiness skills.

The researchers maintain that the learning cycle is a natural way to learn and that it fulfills the major purpose of education: helping children learn how to think. Furthermore, Renner and Marek state that their research provides a rebuttal to school people who say, "We just don't have time or cannot afford to invest in the resources to teach science." They conclude: "The truth of the matter is that any school that teaches science using the learning cycle model is teaching much more than good science; it is also teaching reading, mathematics, and social science. In fact, schools cannot afford *not* to teach science using [the learning cycle model]."

Source: Adapted and quoted from J. W. Renner and E. Marek, *The Learning Cycle and Elementary Science Teaching* (Portsmouth, NH: Heinemann, 1988), pp. 185–199. See also E. A. Marek and A. M. L. Cavallo, *The Learning Cycle: Elementary Science and Beyond* (Portsmouth, NH: Heinemann, 1997).

balloon, tied it, and then remembered that he should add a drop of elixir from an oil can to his magic wand. They all went through the routine again, and this time, to the amazement of the children, the wand pierced one end of the balloon and slowly came out the other—a perfect axis through the top of the balloon and at the bottom near the knot (Figure 6.5). The children clapped and immediately wanted to know how he did it.

Mr. Martinez explained that he was not aware of any magic that really worked; and his build-up was only an act. He emphasized that there are usually scientific explanations for the discrepancies we observe. But he assured the children that the balloon trick was no illusion. To convince them, he passed the balloon around for the children to inspect and then said: "You usually expect me to ask *you* questions, but today is a special opportunity for *you* to ask the questions. Let's pretend you are super sleuths who are going to find out the explanation for this balloon trick. You can ask me all the questions you want, but there are some special rules you must follow. First, you can only ask me questions I can answer with a 'Yes' or 'No.' Second, begin by asking questions to establish the

FIGURE 6.5
Balloon Discrepant Event

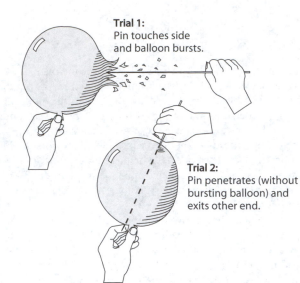

Trial 1:
Pin touches side
and balloon bursts.

Trial 2:
Pin penetrates (without
bursting balloon) and
exits other end.

facts of what you have just seen. Don't take anything for granted: Verify that it was done as you *think* you saw it. Finally, after you think you have all the facts you need, tell me the reason you think this trick was possible. Let's begin. Lucinda?"

"Did you do anything special to the second balloon, like make it stronger?"

"No."

Then other children asked: "Were they the same kind of balloons?"

"Yes."

"Were they the same size? I mean when you blew them up?"

"Yes—I *tried* to have them the same."

"Did you let a little air out of each one?"

"Yes."

"Does the oil make it work?"

"That sounds like an explanation type of question to me. Let's hold that one a while until after we uncover some more facts," said Mr. Martinez. Then the lesson continued until eventually the children discovered the *real* answer, and it wasn't because of the oil. The answer was related to the position, thickness, and strength of the balloon's fabric.

Discrepant Events. This inquiry technique, developed by J. Richard Suchman (1962), relies on the use of discrepant events. *Discrepancies* are differences from what we normally expect, like the sharp pin penetrating the balloon without bursting it. Most often, the human mind is intolerant of discrepancies and needs to maintain consistency. This belief refers to an inconsistency between two cognitions—cognitive dissonance—between what one observes and what one believes. The balloon is a good example: Everyone knows sharp objects cause balloons to pop, but this one didn't!

The Method. Your students' needs for cerebral consistency can motivate even those who are less alert and attentive. Why not use it to your advantage and teach science concepts with it? Suchman's method uses inquiry to help children construct theories (best explanations) for the discrepancies they observe. The approach is student centered and requires children to ask the questions—possibly a difficult task, because it requires considerable thought to ask useful questions and to build the answers into some order that will explain the discrepancy. Take a cooperative approach and divide the class into detective teams to organize questions, conduct research, and form scientific explanations. Use convergent questions, to be answered with either a *yes* or a *no.* (See Figure 6.6 for a visual map of how the inquiry is structured.) These are the phases of Suchman's method:

1. Present the discrepant event.
2. Students ask yes/no questions to verify the events and collect information.

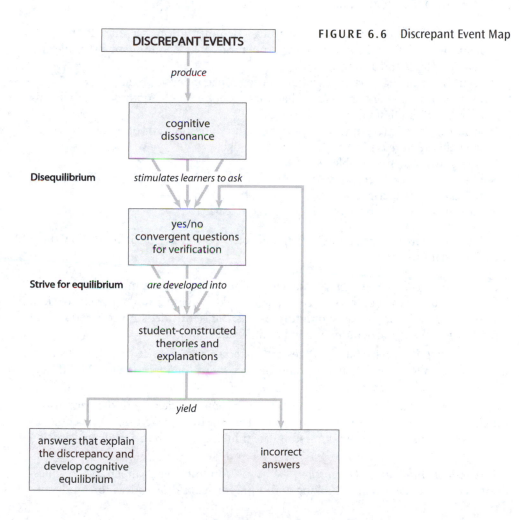

FIGURE 6.6   Discrepant Event Map

3. Students discuss ideas and do library research or further investigations to gather additional information to help them form explanations or theories.
4. The teacher reconvenes the class and leads a discussion to help students give and test their explanations or theories.

Suchman's approach is successful with intermediate and middle-school children, but younger children need more teacher guidance. With K–2 children, we have successfully used versions of the game Twenty Questions to accomplish the same outcome. Familiar objects placed in mystery boxes work well with younger children.

Demonstrations for Inquiry

A little panache can enliven the class, as in the demonstration for Suchman's Inquiry; however, we do not suggest that you must be an entertainer. Demonstrations can be effective teaching tools for stimulating inquiry and can be appropriate if used to

- ✦ avoid putting students in danger by using a demonstration as a safer alternative;
- ✦ help students learn skills, such as the proper ways to use equipment or handle and care for plants and animals;
- ✦ focus on engaging learners in inquiry or for concept development;
- ✦ overcome equipment shortages when there is not enough equipment for all children to benefit firsthand from the exercise;
- ✦ arouse student interest, raise important inquiry questions, or pose learning problems that require critical and creative thinking;
- ✦ help solve academic problems;
- ✦ apply what has been studied to new situations by expanding understanding through new experiences; and
- ✦ encourage slow learners and challenge rapid learners.

Your demonstrations can be safe and effective teaching tools if you follow these recommendations:

1. *Have a specific purpose for the demonstration.* The purpose must *be clear* to all learners. Focus on the point to be learned, and make it evident in the demonstration. Also discuss how it relates to past or future lessons. If it is intended only to entertain and not teach a concept, the demonstration has little value.

2. *Plan carefully.* Collect all the necessary materials and practice the demonstration in advance. Follow the instructions and inspect them for inaccuracies. Modify the demonstration, if necessary, for safety.

3. *Involve the students when possible.* Let the students participate in the demonstrations or permit them to conduct the demonstration. Interactive teaching techniques such as questions and guess-making stimulate thinking, enthusiasm, and participation in the inquiry.

4. *Stimulate thinking and discussion.* "What do you think will happen if . . . ?" questions help stimulate original thinking and bring forth children's ideas for productive

discussion. This technique also releases you from giving away too much information before the demonstration and running the risk of destroying interest.

5. *Repeat the demonstration.* A rapid flash or a loud bang is sure to get attention and will demand a repeat performance. During the repeat, students will pay closer attention, and their powers of observation will be keener. Also, they will be given chances to acquire ideas or form mental connections that seem simple for us but are difficult for them because of their limited experiences.

6. *Use simple materials.* Unfamiliar equipment may distract the students' attention. Familiar objects and equipment will help them focus on the cause of the action or the purpose of the demonstration rather than on the gadgets being used. Students may also choose to try the demonstrations for themselves. Importation of high school equipment for elementary classroom use should be selective and always screened for safety (see Chapter 9).

7. *Keep the demonstration easily visible.* A cluttered demonstration table will distract children from seeing what you intend. Similarly, objects that are too small to be seen by those sitting beyond the first row will frustrate viewers and cause them to lose interest. Use a tall table or counter, gather the students around when feasible (and when safe), or consider using such projection devices as the overhead projector or computer.

8. *Connect with the students' environment.* Interact in order to connect the point of the demonstration with the children's personal interests, community, or social issues to expand the benefits of the demonstration and the scientific concepts or principles.

9. *Rely on quality, not quantity.* Avoid a large number of demonstrations. A single well-designed, timely demonstration can communicate powerful ideas more effectively than an overwhelming number of entertaining shows. Focus on a central concept.

Can Children Learn Science Through Play?

Young children are natural scientists and their time spent at play with common objects helps to reveal their intuitive grasp of simple scientific processes. Sand, water, and block play areas are in demand, suggesting that children usually do not need external motivation to probe into nature. However, teachers and adult helpers can encourage exploratory play and help to nurture a solid foundation of scientific inquiry by providing children with time, place, and simple equipment for investigating the natural world. Ross (1997, p. 35) offers teachers and adult helpers play-based tips that consist of

+ supporting open-ended inquiry;
+ supplying instruments of play;
+ supervising to ensure safety;
+ seizing the moment to capitalize on natural interest;
+ offering inviting places for discovery to occur;
+ providing access to relevant information through tapes, video, picture books and computer programs;
+ sharing respect for life (even the small, innocent insect!);
+ seeking to develop a community for involvement; and
+ celebrating wonder.

The method of playful discovery illustrates how these principles can be put into a simple teaching model. Playful discovery is based on the innate curiosity of very young children, in which play is the method for learning science. The method uses some of the elements of inquiry, but it is much more open-ended. Children are natural investigators. Combine a child's interest with some adult encouragement and opportunities to play around with interesting materials, and playful discovery enables very young children to form initial fundamental science concepts they can build on for the rest of their lives (Lind, 1999; McIntyre, 1984). The method also encourages cooperation among very young learners.

Playful discovery is based on the theories of John Dewey and Jean Piaget, who stated that young children learn best through active involvement with interesting and meaningful materials. Dewey and Piaget, however, reminded us that we as teachers must go beyond simply passing out interesting materials and letting children play with them. Both believed that teachers should direct the hands-on learning through encouragement and guiding questions. Dewey was most concerned about the quality of this hands-on experience, about which he wrote, "Everything depends upon the quality of the experience which is had. The quality of the experience has two aspects. There is an immediate aspect of agreeableness or disagreeableness, and there is an influence upon later experiences" (Dewey, 1937, p. 27).

Versions of playful discovery strive to provide young children with a variety of rich and immediately agreeable experiences. The method is used in childcare centers and preschools with three- to five-year-old children and in progressive kindergarten classrooms. Playful discovery is stimulated initially by teacher-planned experiments that are based on phenomena, substances, and/or materials that are interesting and familiar to the children. For science, the learning activities can promote positive attitudes, lay the foundation for learning simple science concepts, and stimulate development of such process skills as observation, comparison, classification, prediction, and interpretation. The following scenario (Rogers, Martin, & Kousaleos, 1988, p. 21) helps to illustrate the method. Figure 6.7 briefly describes its six stages.

Christopher: A Blossoming Scientist. Mrs. Kousaleos invited her group of four- and five-year-olds to gather by her and experiment with ice cubes in hot and cold water. Five small children were arched over the two containers of water observing and comparing the effects. Christopher suddenly announced with obvious excitement, "Look! The ones in hot water are really getting small." At Mrs. K's suggestion to check the water with their fingers, the children were surprised to discover how very cold the formerly hot water had become.

A week later, after repeating the ice activity, Mrs. K suggested another experiment to find out how to melt an ice cube quickly. Eager children generated ideas, then tested them by several methods. Putting ice cubes into mouths and breaking ice cubes into smaller pieces were by far the most popular methods. Midway through the experiment, however, Christopher, eyes wide open and a "Eureka" tone in his voice, proclaimed, "Let's try hot water!"

After duplicating the ice experiments with slight variations (such as exploring effects of amounts of water, numbers of ice cubes, and sizes of containers), the children began to ask permission to conduct their own experiments, Christopher in particular.

Stage 1: Self-selected teacher-proposed experiment. Encourage children to discover if ice cubes melt at the same rate in hot and cold water.

Stage 2: Repeat experiment with slight variation. Encourage children to
- Vary amount of water used.
- Vary size of containers used.
- Determine if stirring the water makes a difference.
- Vary number of ice cubes placed in water.

Stage 3: Elaborate further on completed experiment. Encourage children to discover how many ways you can break up ice cubes (with hands, feet, teeth, hammer, and so on).

Stage 4: Provide opportunities for and actively encourage children's self-initiated experiments. Make a variety of materials accessible, read books, use teacher questioning. For example:
- Child makes ice cubes in a variety of containers (egg carton, muffin tin, plastic bottle, small bucket).
- Child also explores ways to remove ice from container and uses knowledge from Stage 1 to solve problems.
- Child discovers whether or not magic markers melt in hot water.

Stage 5: Communicate with parents and inform them of child's interest.
- Parent encourages child to experiment at home and while on vacation (exploring ice cubes in bath water, mixing sand and water, discovering effect of jumping in water).
- Parent provides materials as child expresses interest.

Stage 6: Conduct a new experiment.
Encourage
- Children to explore the effect of pressure or force on water.
- Children to explore the effects of adding sand to container of water (e.g., displacement).

FIGURE 6.7 Six Stages of Playful Discovery

Source: D. L. Rogers, R. E. Martin, Jr., and S. Kousaleos. "Encouraging Science through Playful Discovery," *Day Care and Early Education* 16 (1988): 1, 23. Reprinted with permission.

These requests usually meant making ice in some uniquely shaped container, mixing various ingredients together, or adding a variety of materials to water.

During one of Christopher's self-initiated experiments, he noted that pouring salt into a container of water made the water "lift out." Since Christopher seemed intrigued with this phenomenon, Mrs. K planned some activities on displacement.

Later, when Christopher took a vacation, his parents sent a postcard that said, "Christopher is spending much time on the beach experimenting with water, observing changes as he adds shells and sand." Christopher had become fascinated by how the water "came out" when he and his dad jumped into their vacation swimming pool.

When Christopher returned, his class did a displacement experiment, using different sizes of containers and different amounts of water with marbles to assess and extend some of his vacation learning. After exploring the effect of adding marbles to water in narrow and wide containers, Christopher observed, "When the water's up high, the marbles lift the water out." He later concluded in response to a question about the difference between the narrow and wide containers, "In a fat one the water spreads out. In a thin one it goes up to the top."

The Playful Science Classroom. Christopher's response is an example of what can happen when sensitive teacher guidance and well-planned experiences are combined to set the stage for the high-quality "later experiences" John Dewey wrote about. Numerous and different ongoing experiments will be evident in the playful discovery classroom. Many experiences will be based on common activities that use ordinary materials such as sand, water, and blocks.

Playful discovery gives young children opportunities to explore freely and to begin to understand the nature of materials before more structured lessons try to teach them concepts. As shown on page 207, Figure 6.7 outlines the six stages Mrs. K followed. First, she stimulated interest by proposing class experiments; later she stimulated sustained learning and experiential elaboration by permitting children to self-select experiments. Children will function at different stages at different times. For example:

> Some children may not go beyond Stage 1 because of lack of interest or understanding, and the teacher must proceed to Stage 6 for them. Others may spend a great deal of time on Stages 1 and 2, but not be able to make the leap to Stages 3 and 4. In this case it may help to skip these stages and go to Stage 5, so as to promote elaboration and self-initiation [by] suggesting that parents provide experiences in "science experiments" at home. (Rogers, Martin, & Kousaleos, 1988, p. 23)

Is this approach worth the effort? How long do the experiences endure? Perhaps you will find the answer here:

> Even months after the [first ice] experiment, a mother of one of the children [said] that when she was trying to figure out how to get ice cubes in a small-necked thermos, her four-year-old daughter suggested she could melt them a little in hot water first so they would fit. (Rogers, Martin, & Kousaleos, 1988, p. 23)

Playful discovery works best when the experiments chosen deal with phenomena and substances that the children encounter every day. The everyday environment adds a practical aspect to science by showing its usefulness, and it helps the children to construct a better understanding of their own world.

Objects from the everyday environment can be assembled into simple tools or explorer kits. These kits should be built on topics that interest the children and serve the science content recommendations offered by the National Science Education Standards (see the Appendix). Kit materials can be stored in plastic tubs; color-coordinated stickers help children learn to clean up after themselves. Management and storage ideas may be found in Chapter 9. Ross (1997) offers kit ideas such as the following:

+ Exploring light with prisms, crystals, sheets of Mylar or chrome tubes, lenses, kaleidoscopes, and spectroscopes;
+ Creating a disassembly line while wearing goggles and using screwdrivers and pliers to remove loosened screws from broken appliances (electric plugs removed) such as old clocks, radios, computers and modems, VCRs, CD/DVD players, cassette players, toasters, and irons;
+ Digging soil in outdoor or indoor designated areas with various sizes of food containers, cookie cutters, molds, magnets, strainers, trowels, small shovels, or spoons;
+ Investigating (with a respect for life) roly-poly insects—commonly called pill bugs—typically found under rotting logs or leaf litter by using magnifying lenses, soil tubs, watercolor brushes, toothpicks, or pipe cleaners;
+ Seizing the moment by exploring playground puddles and windy days with pinwheels, kites, and vessels made from paper, straws, aluminum foil, or common craft supplies.

Problem-Based Learning

The new age of science teaching recognizes that basic skills are important, yet reformers argue that future citizens must also have a command of key scientific ideas, be able to solve problems, and think critically (National Research Council, 1996). An emphasis on inquiry-based learning methods and student construction of understanding takes time, vision and cooperation, and often interdisciplinary treatment of school subjects. The National Science Education Standards suggest that desirable long-term inquiry activities include formation of arguments, explanation, and communication of ideas to others while using a wide range of procedural, manipulative and cognitive skills (Marx et al., 1997). Problem-based learning approaches are useful for

+ enhancing students' abilities to attend to and store information in closer proximity to what they already know with potential for avoiding misconceptions;
+ situating newly constructed understanding within a realistic experiential context;
+ promoting productive social interaction and learning through collaboration;
+ stimulating the uses of cognitive tools, such as CD learning programs, websites, personal computer simulations, concept maps, and problem-posing/decision-making structures. (Marx et al., 1997)

Marx, Blumenfeld, Krajcik, and Soloway (1997, pp. 344–346) recommend to teachers five important features of their project-based science model, that is exemplary of many problem-based learning approaches in science.

1. Help students form a *driving question* in order that projects have a focus. Driving questions should be worthwhile (connected to a curriculum framework); pose real-world

problems that students find meaningful and feel ownership over; problems that are feasible and within the learners' realms of experience, knowledge, and skills.

2. Engage students in *investigation*—the real work of science—that consists of planning and designing investigations and conducting real-world research to collect and analyze information so that the students may form inferences and conclusions about the driving question.

3. Guide students toward the collection and creation of *artifacts,* which are tangible, real results of an investigation. Artifacts can consist of air- and water-quality samples, documents from corporations and science agencies, multimedia materials obtained from Internet searches, and so on.

4. Help students to *collaborate.* When students labor together to plan and complete tasks, they benefit from the collective intelligence of all members of the group and learn to value the ideas of others.

5. Expose learners to *technological tools.* Investigations become more authentic when students use tools to measure, gather, and process information by themselves. The entire classroom environment becomes more authentic and inquiry becomes more serious through real-time data collection. Students learn to make models and extend their inquiry and collaboration to other groups outside the home base of their classroom.

Figures 6.8 and 6.9 illustrate some of the tools used to nurture the students' cognitive skills and to encourage the formation and analysis of driving questions. A teacher

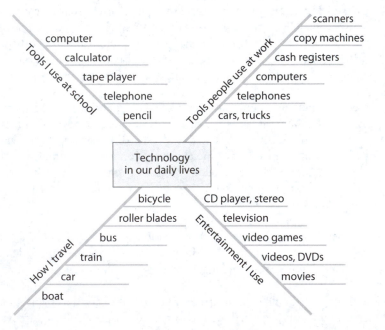

FIGURE 6.8 Spider Map for Investigating Technology's Influence on Our Daily Lives. A spider map can be used to help students list and organize the various ideas they have about a topic. You could draw the basic sketch of the spider and add the legs (we have used just four, but more could be added). You might also suggest the labels for the legs and then ask the children to offer examples, which you list. From the ideas and examples, driving questions may emerge, which can be organized into a framework for investigating a problem as shown in Figure 6.9.

Source: The idea of the spider map is used in *Breakthroughs: Strategies for Thinking* series. Columbus, OH: Zaner-Bloser, 1992.

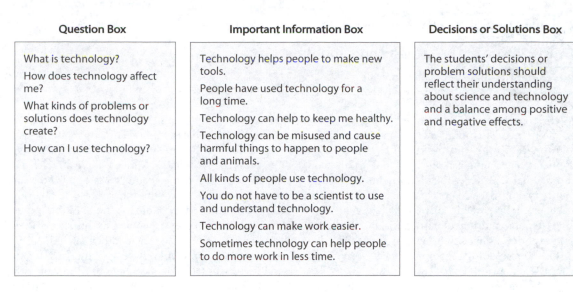

Question Box	Important Information Box	Decisions or Solutions Box
What is technology? How does technology affect me? What kinds of problems or solutions does technology create? How can I use technology?	Technology helps people to make new tools. People have used technology for a long time. Technology can help to keep me healthy. Technology can be misused and cause harmful things to happen to people and animals. All kinds of people use technology. You do not have to be a scientist to use and understand technology. Technology can make work easier. Sometimes technology can help people to do more work in less time.	The students' decisions or problem solutions should reflect their understanding about science and technology and a balance among positive and negative effects.

FIGURE 6.9 Problem-Based Learning Decision-Making Framework

using these tools may consult the National Science Education Standards for content and curriculum framework ideas. The standards help to guide learners in the direction of worthwhile questions and applications to their daily lives. The figures illustrate the investigation of technology, a new science content area included in the standards.

Techniques for Promoting Student Cooperation

Science inquiry encourages learners to construct their understanding from direct physical experiences and guided thinking. The methods have risks and potential difficulties. If all teachers were responsible for only one student at a time, these constructivist, inquiry approaches to science education would be rather simple to manage. Problems arise when two or more learners independently attempt to inquire. That students or a group may pursue several different questions and work on various projects at the same time presents management

Questions from children help motivate further inquiry, encourage discovery, and offer a basis for cooperation.

What Is a Question Box?

by Mary Ann Sloan
Grade 1, Paumanok Elementary School, Dix Hills, New York

My first-grade classroom can best be described as a whole science classroom, where cooperative learning takes place throughout the day. I have found that cooperative learning is a powerful tool. In my classroom, science provides the platform for an interdisciplinary approach. The children raise questions; make predictions; devise plans; obtain, organize, and analyze data; and make many decisions while they gain experiences in using science inquiry skills. All of this is the result of the introduction of a very simple device—a question box!

The question box has helped me to begin the process of transforming the class into groups of cooperative learners. This strategy takes full advantage of the children's natural curiosity and allows them to become active participants in the learning process.

To make the question box, cover a cardboard box about the size of a mailbox with dazzling foil paper. Then cut out five-inch question marks from bright construction paper. Be sure to have one for each child and one for you too. To introduce the question box to your class and to provide a model for the first questions, select an exciting book to read to the whole class. One of the books that I have used with great success is *Papa, Please Get the Moon for Me,* by Eric Carle. After reading the story, I ask the children what questions they would ask Monica, the main character, if she could come to our classroom and visit them. I record the questions they ask. Now I take out the question box. I explain that the question box is the place where they can put any questions they would like to have answered, that they can write their questions on their own or have someone help them, and that I will set aside time each day to work with the question box. I invite each child whose questions I recorded to put his or her question into the box. While we decorate our paper question marks, I move from table to table, modeling the kind of on-task behavior I expect. As I decorate my question mark, I think aloud of questions I might put into the question box and ask them about the questions they may be considering.

After a few days of working with the box—reading the questions aloud and adding more questions—I randomly select a question to be answered. Our first question was: "Are elephants afraid of mice?" The

and organization difficulties for most teachers. Sufficient resources may also be in short supply. Postponing or even canceling lessons are options if the initial difficulties become too much to risk. With encouragement and time to develop the needed skills, students can become confident posing questions and need less help researching their answers. With practice, you too will become more skilled at managing the busy class activities and will know what questions and needs to anticipate. You will also learn many fascinating things about science that you probably never had a chance to investigate. One procedure that can help you manage the inquiry from children's questions is associated with learning teams or cooperative groups.

Cooperative Learning in Science

Science teachers frequently group students during science activities to manage crowded classes and stretch precious materials that always seem to be in short supply. Coopera-

children made a list of what they already knew about elephants. When we reread the list, they decided that they needed to know more. They wanted to know: "How big are elephants and their trunks?" "Why does an elephant have a trunk?" "Had anyone ever seen a mouse attack an elephant?" We made predictions and developed a plan of action. The children began to meet in their cooperative learning groups. Each group worked on answering one of the questions. Now science became what we do to find answers, and the children loved it!

One product that developed from their explorations was a full-size painting of an African and an Indian elephant, with attention to the length and width of the trunk, which demanded measuring with many different devices. Three charts showing objects bigger, smaller, and the same size as an elephant were completed, requiring lots of comparisons. Two world maps showing where elephants and mice are found were drawn using the overhead projector. A diorama, using clay and construction paper, was created to depict an elephant habitat. Drawings of the kinds of foods elephants eat were labeled. Clocks were made to show when elephants sleep, eat, and travel. One group found that elephants don't breathe through their trunks and that it takes lots of food to keep an elephant healthy. This news helped the group that

was working to determine how elephants actually use their trunks. They made paper bag elephant costumes and put on a play. The last group wrote letters to the Big Apple Circus, the Bronx Zoo, the Washington Zoo, and the San Diego Zoo. None of the zoo personnel had ever seen a mouse attack an elephant. In fact, they wrote to say that in their experiences mice seemed to be afraid of elephants. We made elephant T-shirts that the letter-writing group designed. This group was also responsible for keeping a record of money collected. They enlisted a mom to help them buy the shirts. She also helped with the stenciling.

This was just the beginning of the question center. Throughout the year, many questions are answered, and the children have many opportunities to classify, create models, generalize, form hypotheses, identify variables, infer, interpret data, make decisions, manipulate materials, measure, observe, predict, record data, replicate, and use number and language skills. You will know when your class is a community of cooperative learners. I promise this center will never be empty. The children will not want to leave for recess or lunch, and three o'clock will come too soon. They will miss school on weekends and won't be able to wait until Monday mornings, when they can put more questions into or take another question out of the question box.

tive learning, even if used mostly for science management, is more than asking students to group their desks together, however. F. James Rutherford and Andrew Ahlgren, writing in *Science for All Americans*, tell us

> The collaborative nature of scientific and technological work should be strongly reinforced by frequent group activity in the classroom. Scientists and engineers work mostly in groups and less often as isolated investigators. Similarly, students should gain experience in sharing responsibility for learning with each other. In the process of coming to common understandings, students in a group must frequently inform each other about procedures and meaning, argue over findings, and assess how the task is progressing. In the context of team responsibility, feedback and communication become more realistic and of a character very different from the usual individualistic textbook-homework-recitation approach. (Rutherford & Ahlgren, 1990, p. 189)

Scientists and engineers work in an environment that is more cooperative than competitive. Roger Johnson and David Johnson (1991) and Robert Slavin (1995), well-known promoters of cooperative learning methods, maintain that the research base for cooperative learning (in its many forms) indicates that students would learn more science, like it more, and feel more positive about their performance if more of their science experiences were obtained through cooperative learning. In their extensive review of the research on instructional strategies for teaching science, Tobin, Tippins, and Gallard (1994) remind us that cooperative learning should not be viewed as a panacea. Rather, it is valuable because of the potential for students to clarify, defend, elaborate, evaluate, and argue their constructed thoughts with one another. Table 6.2 compares the advantages of cooperative learning teaching and management techniques over those of customary small groups. This comparison illustrates that clear learning outcomes and systematic management procedures are keys to success.

Cooperative Inquiry Groups

Three to five is a functional number for inquiry groups or cooperative learning groups. When each group member has a special job, the group inquiry process can be both effective and functional. The research on this management approach shows that "students who work in groups learn concepts just as well as those who work individually, with the added bonus that students who work together can develop both interpersonal skills and a sense of group responsibility" (Jones, 1985, p. 21).

Form groups, assign roles, and give each child a job description. The *principal investigator* (PI) is in charge of managing the group. Duties are to check the assignment

TABLE 6.2   Benefits of Cooperative Science Groups

Cooperative Groups	Small Groups
Positive interdependence; students sink or swim together; face-to-face verbal communication.	No interdependence; students work on their own, often or occasionally checking their answers with other students.
Individual accountability; each pupil must master the material.	Hitchhiking; some students let others do most or all of the work, then copy.
Teachers teach social skills needed for successful group work.	Social skills are not systematically taught.
Teacher monitors students' behavior	Teacher does not directly observe student behavior; often works with a few students or works on other tasks.
Feedback and discussion of students' behavior are integral parts of ending the activity before moving on.	No discussion of how well students worked together, other than general comments such as "Nice job," or "Next time, try to work more quietly."

Source: P. E. Blosser, "Using Cooperative Learning in Science Education." Columbus, OH: ERIC Clearinghouse for Science, Mathematics, and Environmental Education, 1993, ERIC Reproduction Document No. ED 351 207, p. 4.

and ask the teacher any clarifying questions, then lead the group by conducting the activity for the rest of the group or by assigning duties to the other group members. The PI is also in charge of safety.

The *materials manager* is in charge of picking up and passing out all equipment and materials that are necessary. Inside the classroom, the materials manager is usually the only student who has a reason to be moving around.

The *recorder* is in charge of collecting the necessary information and recording it in the proper form: graph, table, tape recorder, and so on. The recorder works with the principal investigator and the materials manager to verify the accuracy of the data.

The *reporter* is in charge of reporting the results, orally or in writing, back to the teacher or the entire class.

The *maintenance director* is in charge of cleanup and has the power to involve others in this group responsibility. Equipment must be returned and consumables must be cleaned up.

Recorder and reporter can be combined, as can materials manager and maintenance director for groups as small as three. Badges, sashes, headbands, photo IDs, or other role-identifying management devices can be used

Children learn responsibility by sharing tasks in cooperative groups.

to limit confusion. Rotate the roles and form different groups often to promote fairness and group responsibility. This group technique can be used with any inquiry method in which groups are used. Robert Jones provides further tips in Table 6.3.

Successful, problem-free science lessons can occur if each member of the group understands the importance of his or her role. In a cooperative learning environment, the groups purposely comprise boys and girls of different ability levels. Each student realizes that on any given day, he or she could serve in any capacity as a member of the cooperative group. Therefore, each member is responsible for learning the material. The grade earned by participating in the lesson is a reflection of the group effort, not an individual. The group is interdependent; its members will sink or swim together. The students within a group need to communicate to one another problems, observations, and successes before they go to the teacher with them. Courtesy, respect, and encouragement are interpersonal skills needed by each member of the cooperative group.

One useful cooperative method is known as a *jigsaw approach* (Watson, 1992). Use it, for example, when you are teaching third-grade students about the state tree, flower, and bird. Within each cooperative group, a different member will be assigned one of the following tasks:

1. Determine the criteria for becoming the official state tree.
2. Determine the criteria for becoming the official state flower.

TABLE 6.3 Tips for Cooperative Group Inquiry Activities

- Let each group choose a name for itself. It is a good social activity, and the names will help you identify the different groups.

- Change group members from time to time. Try out introvert-extrovert or boy-girl teams; experiment with cultural and racial mixes; form academically heterogeneous groups.

- Talk only to the principal investigators about the activity. This will set up a chain of command and prevent a repetition of questions. The students should discuss questions and problems among themselves so that it will only be necessary for you to clarify points with the principal investigator.

- Employ both indoor and outdoor activities. Badges work well indoors; armbands and headbands are more visible on school grounds. Hand-held walkie-talkies (inexpensive children's type)

are also useful and (if they are available) should be used by the principal investigators.

- Use groups of three when working outdoors or on a field trip. This size group is better for safety.

- To ensure clear communication, post class rules, group names, job descriptions, and any other important information on a bulletin board in the classroom.

- Develop a system for rotating roles.

- Use job descriptions for classroom management and discipline. Most of the time you will simply need to ask which person has which role to resolve problems.

- Develop a worksheet, data recording sheet, or some other instrument for each activity.

- Make yourself a badge and join in the fun.

Source: R. M. Jones, "Teaming Up," *Science and Children* (May 1985): 23.

3. Determine the criteria for becoming the official state bird.
4. Find out who suggested the state tree, bird, or flower, and where these are found in the state.
5. Learn what the state tree, bird, and flower are in one bordering state.

Students in the cooperative groups should decide which student will take on each of the five tasks. Once these students are determined, then all of the students in the class assigned to task 1 should get together to find answers to that task, those assigned to task 2 should do the same, and so on. After a sufficient amount of time has passed (for this topic with third graders, two or three 35- to 40-minute class periods should be enough time) the students should have found answers for their task. They must now return to their original cooperative groups to share their information. The success of the cooperative group will depend on how well the expert gets his or her information across to the members of the group. After two class periods of sharing information from the five tasks, it is time for the quiz. This can be done by student experts for task 1 moving to different cooperative groups. Those experts will then quiz each member of a different cooperative group individually on task 1 information. After task 1 experts quiz the students and record their results, then task 2 experts will do the same, and so on. The success of each student will be reflected by how well his or her cooperative group expert prepared the group for the quiz.

Recommendations for Enhancing Students' Learning of Science

All of the inquiry methods we have presented are student centered to various degrees. They engage children in active thinking and learning and differ only in approach, but despite these procedural differences, each method guides children through inquiry toward making discoveries. The methods are successful when teachers help students to construct understanding. What elements unite these different procedures, which lead to a common outcome (Rakow, 1986)?

1. Successful constructivist teachers *model scientific attitudes*. The scientific attitudes we most wish to develop in children must be evident in the people who teach them. Successful inquiry teachers must be curious, open-minded, tolerant of different viewpoints, skeptical at times, willing to admit when they do not know answers to all questions, and able to view those occasions as opportunities to expand their learning.

2. Successful constructivist teachers are *creative*. Effective teachers find ways to make deficient materials effective. They are masters at adapting others' ideas, and they become comfortable taking risks with the unknown. They encourage creativity in students by being creative themselves.

3. Successful constructivist teachers are *flexible*. Inquiry takes time. Students need time to explore, think, and ask questions. Successful constructivist teachers are patient and use time flexibly to afford children the time they need for effective inquiry learning.

4. Successful constructivist teachers use effective *questioning strategies*. Types of questions used, wait-time, and proper uses of praise, reinforcement, and encouragement are the fodder of inquiry learning.

5. Successful constructivist teachers *focus* their efforts on preparing students to *think* in order to construct meaning. The constructivist teacher wants students to develop an ability to solve problems. Successful problem solving depends on numerous thinking skills that arise from the processes of science that guide all phases of the inquiry. The end result of the inquiry process is the construction of scientific concepts. The end justifies the means, but exclusive focus on the end product does not provide the means for future problem solving.

Take the first step by beginning small. Trying to adapt all lessons into a constructivist approach is an overwhelming task and can be frustrating. If yours is a conventional textbook science program, focus on only one or two chapters at first by mapping the concepts (see Chapter 4). Then develop the material into good inquiry activities or find other supplementing resources. Each year add more, and soon you will develop an effective collection of material. Combine your efforts with those of other teachers (particularly those who teach the same grade level), pool your materials, improve them, and help your program become more effective. Read journals, such as *Science and Children* for elementary teachers and *Science Scope* for middle-school and junior-high teachers. These journals, available from the National Science Teachers Association, contain activities reported by experienced teachers and describe new materials available through government-sponsored programs and commercial publishers.

Chapter Summary

The physical, life, and earth/space science content is an important context for developing scientific literacy. The standards require four new dimensions of science learning to ensure that real progress is made toward helping students achieve literacy in science. These new dimensions challenge us to help students understand science as a process of inquiry, understand the interrelationships between science and technology, benefit from science personally and understand the social perspective of science, and understand and appreciate the history and nature of science. Parts of the many outcomes for these new dimensions predictably overlap and complement learning. The challenge will be to find a way to link all of these dimensions of science learning and literacy to the content context.

Inquiry-based science teaching methods are interactive: Students and teachers investigate together and share many responsibilities that are carried only by the teacher in conventional classrooms. Construction of understanding is encouraged by a family of science teaching methods that promote student inquiry in a hands-on, minds-on way. Inquiry is a process, a way of pursuing learning. The outcomes of its methods are students' discoveries. Discoveries are mental constructions. All constructivist methods are based on a belief about the power of experience. The methods rely on effective questioning to promote concept development.

Several inquiry-based science teaching methods are described in this chapter. The science learning cycle is appropriate for concept development in all grades and is particularly well suited for implementing the new goals in science

education described in Chapter 4. A feature lesson is included in this chapter.

Principles of scientific inquiry help us develop an approach for turning what once were memory exercises into a powerful teaching and learning method. This approach is most suitable for the intermediate through middle school grades and lends itself to cooperative inquiry groups.

Suchman's inquiry makes use of puzzling phenomena—discrepant events—that permit teachers to build on intrinsic motivation and turn children into questioners and pursuers of explanations. Playful discovery is a little-known inquiry method that was developed for very young children. Preschool and kindergarten children benefit from its playful atmosphere, accumulating agreeable and valuable experiences that help them build concept structures for later study. Problem-based learning revolves around children forming and pursuing solutions to meaningful problems. Classroom management can become challenging; therefore, we offer practical recommendations for using cooperative learning groups.

Effective teachers who use inquiry methods demonstrate several common attributes: They model science attitudes, are creative in their approaches to science material and flexible in classroom management, and tend to focus on developing children's abilities to think rather than on mere acquisition of subject matter. Research verifies the superior effects of student-centered constructivist approaches over traditional text-based teaching methods for science achievement, and the attitudes and skills of scientific inquiry.

Discussion Questions

1. What arguments support using inquiry science teaching methods? What barriers seem to limit inquiry's acceptance and use in elementary classrooms? Will you use some of the methods described in this chapter? Why?

2. What are the similarities and differences in the approaches described in this chapter? Under what circumstances would you favor any one approach over the others?

3. Why is it that as children get older and presumably more capable of thinking independently, they appear to rely more on an authority figure for information than on their own experiences for discovering it?

4. Inquiry methods tend to promote greater independence among learners. What are several things you can do to help students become more independent learners?

5. Inquiry teaching strives to accommodate individual student differences. Individual differences do, however, tend to complicate teaching. What are some things you could do to manage the diversity of individuality without losing your cooperative focus?

6. How do inquiry methods help slow and fast learners?

Build a Portfolio or E-Folio

1. Select a teaching method described in this chapter and prepare a lesson for it. Teach the lesson, videotape it, analyze it, and evaluate the effects of the method.

2. How could you modify the method to make it more effective or a better fit for the needs of your learners? Prepare a brief essay describing your experience and your thoughts.

3. Try teaching science lessons a conventional way and then with one of the methods described in this chapter. Determine the extent to which learners obtain and retain the points of the lesson. What does your analysis reveal? Write a summary that describes your "experiment" and your conclusions.

4. Edit a video recording of your teaching to a brief length that highlights the prime features of the method, or prepare still photos showing yourself in action and the reactions of the children as they experience the wonders of science. Share your tape with your supervisor, professor, or prospective employer.

5. Develop original lessons for each of the methods described in this chapter. How do these lessons vary? What aspects of planning are emphasized more and less as the instruction becomes more cooperative among students?

chapter 7

Questioning and Inquiry

Mrs. Barcikowski extended warm greetings to each child as they came running into the lab. A table in the middle of the room was piled with rocks of many different types, colors, shapes, and sizes. Each child was encouraged to pick up several samples and look at them carefully. The children rubbed the samples, held them up to the light, and used magnifying glasses to make closer inspections. The room was buzzing with activity, including the predictable horseplay of a few, and the buzz was punctuated with the exclamations of scientific discoveries. All the while, Mrs. B expressed her interest by asking many different questions that helped the children sharpen their observations.

Then she had the children gather around her. When all were seated, Mrs. B began making conversation with such casual questions as, "How many of you have a hobby? How 'bout your parents or brothers or sisters? What are some of your hobbies?"

After a few minutes of listening and encouraging, Mrs. B said, "It seems that many of you collect different things for a hobby. Right?" Smiles and nodding heads gave her an entry. "I do too. In fact one of my favorite things to do on vacation is to look for unusual rocks to add to the collection I've been sharing with you today. Would you like to see one of my favorites?" Holding up a smoothly polished, quarter-sized sample for all to see, and passing around others for them to hold, Mrs. B said, "We've been studying the concept of *properties* for many of our lessons. Let's use properties to help us study rocks. What kinds of properties do you observe in this rock?" The children's observations were accepted with encouragement and occasional praise. Another key question Mrs. B asked was, "What other rocks from our pile seem like this one?"

After noticing variety in the color, size, and shape of the other samples, a child pointed out that some of them were more different than alike.

"True," Mrs. B confirmed. "I guess we need to focus a bit. What property appears to be the same in each of the samples?"

"Crystals?" offered a child.

"That's right! This type of rock is known especially for its crystals. What kind of rock do you think this is?" Mrs. B reminded the children to refer back to their observations while they tossed ideas around among themselves. She watched them closely and then invited Elizabeth, who seemed unsure, to venture a guess.

"Well, it looks kinda milky so I guess it's called . . . a 'milk rock?' " asked Elizabeth as she groped for an answer. The other children laughed, but Mrs. B reminded them to be polite; then she smiled as she saw how a connection could be made.

"I know you go to the grocery with your parents. What sizes of containers does milk come in?"

Elizabeth thought to herself: gallon? Half gallon? Somehow those didn't seem right. Then an idea came to her. "A quart rock?" Elizabeth hesitantly asked.

"Good try. Almost, Elizabeth, just one more letter," encouraged Mrs. B as she wrote the word *quart* on the lap chalkboard and held it up for all to see. "Let's add a *zzz* sound to this and see what we have. *Q-u-a-r-t-z*. What does that spell, Elizabeth?"

"Quartz!" exclaimed Elizabeth, with emphasis on the *z*.

"Now everyone," encouraged Mrs. B.

For the next several seconds, the class spelled and pronounced the new word like cheerleaders. Then Mrs. B referred them back to the samples and continued her questions, always waiting patiently, and encouraging and building on the children's ideas. She paused periodically to add a point or two of her own. By the lesson's end the children had learned that quartz is a common mineral found in rocks and comes in many different colors. When polished smooth, quartz may be used in jewelry as a semiprecious stone, and quartz crystals are used to manufacture prisms, lenses, watches, computer chips, and other electronic gadgets. They even learned that the scientific name is silicon dioxide, SiO_2.

Introduction

When teaching science through inquiry processes, scientific literacy is not regarded as a collection of facts and recipe-like steps to follow; science is a way of thinking, reasoning and making meaning from essential experiences (Van Tassell, 2001). Within an inquiry-based framework, questions are tools for planning, teaching, thinking, and learning. What do you know about classroom uses of questions and your own questioning skills? It is typical for teachers to use questions intuitively or even out of habit. Some may even achieve satisfactory results. Yet considerable research suggests that many teachers do not realize that modest improvements in their questions can result in substantial gains for their students. In science, the students' questions play an important role in the nature of their inquiry and in their learning; they need to be encouraged. The

National Science Education Standards' Teaching Standard B (NRC, 1996, p. 32) prompts teachers to guide and facilitate learning by

- ✦ focusing and supporting inquiries while interacting with students;
- ✦ orchestrating discourse among students about scientific ideas;
- ✦ challenging students to accept and share responsibility for their own learning;
- ✦ recognizing and responding to student diversity and encouraging all students to participate fully in science learning;
- ✦ encouraging and modeling skills of scientific inquiry, as well as the curiousness, openness to new ideas and data, and skepticism that characterize science.

Effective teachers use productive questions to help students advance in their thinking. Effective teachers use questions to: focus on what is important, orchestrate productive discussions, sharpen process skills, build positive scientific attitudes, and increase understanding (Krueger & Sutton, 2001). Effective questioning enables a teacher to construct a mental framework for helping students to construct their own understandings. How can you develop and use productive questions to promote science inquiry?

The mission of this chapter is to

1. raise questions about questions and report the effects that questions have on students' achievement, attitudes, and thinking skills;
2. explore the different types and uses of questions;
3. investigate how questions can be used to foster inquiry;
4. offer some suggestions you can use to monitor and improve your own questions; and
5. provide a rationale and suggestions for using students' questions as an important part of your teaching for inquiry and discovery.

Questions on Questions

What is a question? We use questions often, but do you know much about their proper uses and effects? Below are seven important questions about questions. Try answering them from what you already know. Then read on to check your answers. How well informed are you about this most potent teaching tool?

1. What kinds of questions do teachers ask, and what kinds of answers do they require?
2. Why do teachers use questions?
3. How do questions affect students?
4. How are teacher questions and student answers related?
5. How do teachers use questions to involve all students?
6. What is wait-time, and why is it important?
7. What types of questions are used most in elementary science books and tests?

What Kinds of Questions Do Teachers Ask and What Kinds of Answers Do They Require?

According to studies of typical science classrooms, most questions demand little of students, and the preponderance of questions are low-level. Examples of low-level questions include: yes/no, guess, remember facts, leading and rhetorical, and questions answered by the teacher (Krueger & Sutton, 2001). Research verifies that elementary teachers use questions more than any other teaching tool. For example, one study reports that third-grade teachers asked reading groups a question every 43 seconds (Gambrell, 1983), while another study found that teachers ask as many as 300 to 400 questions each day; the average being 348 (Levin & Long, 1981). Most agree that the number of teacher questions depends on the nature of the activity. Even so, teachers ask between 30 and 120 questions per hour (Graesser & Person, 1994). Most of these questions are asked in a rapid-fire question-answer pattern. The pattern and extent of question use has changed little in 50 years, with teachers asking about 93 percent of all questions and children receiving little time to respond or opportunity to ask their own questions (Martin, Wood, & Stevens, 1988). This type of limited questioning is ineffective.

Knowledge and comprehension of content make up at least 70 percent of the questions, and questions that require application, analysis, synthesis, or evaluation thinking are used much less often (Martin, Wood, & Stevens, 1988). In the context of the National Science Education Standards teachers who ask for facts appear to be poor role models for productive questions that stimulate inquiry (Graesser & Person, 1994). It has been shown, over time, that teachers asking for answers to facts actually encourage fewer students to ask fewer questions (Marbach-Ad & Sokolove, 2000). However, as students mature, they do ask more questions, but this occurs outside of the classroom (Dillon, 1988). The culture of inquiry that teachers hope to establish is often limited by these uses. Progress toward inquiry can be made by thinking about how we wish to use questions and the impact that our questioning can have on learners.

Why Do Teachers Use Questions?

According to Mary Budd Rowe (1973), a science educator, teachers use questions for three main purposes:

1. to evaluate or to find out what the pupils already know,
2. to control the functions of the classroom: inquisition used as a classroom management strategy or to reduce off-task behavior,
3. to instruct children by suggesting resources and procedures, focusing observation, pointing out differences and discrepancies.

Questions have other uses as the stock-in-trade of teachers, and the potential far exceeds Rowe's three fundamental uses (see Table 7.1).

TABLE 7.1   How Can Teachers Use Questions?

- To arouse students' interest and motivate participation
- To determine students' prior knowledge before a lesson begins
- To determine students' thoughts and other information essential to a problem before it is explored
- To guide students' thinking toward higher levels
- To discipline disruptive students by asking them to explain their behavior

- To provide listening cues for students with difficulties and to focus inattentive students' attention
- To diagnose students' strengths and weaknesses
- To help students develop concepts or see relationships between objects or phenomena
- To review or summarize lessons
- To informally check students' comprehension
- To evaluate planned learning outcomes, such as performance objectives

What other uses can you add to this list?

How Do Questions Affect Students?

Teachers' questions influence students in three areas: attitudes, thinking, and achievement.

Attitudes influence how students participate, think, and achieve. Students with positive attitudes tend to look more favorably on a subject, teacher, or method of teaching. Students with negative attitudes often link them to a subject, school experience, or teacher and tend to resist and perform poorly. From his research, William Wilen (1986) concludes that teachers' uses of questions play an important part in shaping children's attitudes, thinking, and achievement. "Students must develop positive attitudes toward higher-level questioning if instructional approaches such as inquiry are to be effective," Wilen (1986, p. 21) writes. Unfortunately, girls may feel shortchanged because they often perceive that they are given fewer opportunities than boys to answer questions. As well, some classrooms reveal that boys may be treated preferentially by their teachers and are involved more often in higher-level questions than girls. The result can be that boys feel a more positive experience and form a more positive attitude (Altermatt et al, 1998).

Appropriate questions can improve children's attitudes, thinking, and achievement.

Forty years ago, Hilda Taba (Taba, Levine, & Elsey, 1964) discovered that teachers' questions influenced students' levels of thinking. Teachers expected students to think at a certain level (according to Bloom's taxonomy of the cognitive domain), composed and used questions for the expected level, and

Teachers on Science Teaching

How Do Questions Create Independent Thinkers?

by Ursula M. Sexton
Grades 1–5, Green Valley Elementary School, Danville, California

I have moved away from pouring information, most of which students forget, to facilitating discussions, providing opportunities for explorations, and ways to assess our progress and goals. I guess you could say I've gone from being an informational witness to becoming a thinking coach.

I am now defining my teacher role as one who provides the means for my students to make connections with big ideas; guides them through process-oriented activities; demonstrates circumstances that would otherwise be dangerous, foreign, or inaccessible to them; and who is the listener and facilitator. This role works best when students are given situations, open-ended explorations, dynamic roles, and the tools or options to build, to research, to communicate, and to share their thinking. I tell my students our most frequently used questions should be: "Why do you think so?" "How can you support it?" "What do you mean by that?" "How does it work and why?" and "What do you think would happen if . . . ?"

Some ideas foster a climate not only for higher-thinking questions and answers but for inclusion of all students:

• Set the stage like a mystery scene, in which students are given the clues, and they need to prove that these clues are valid to solve the mystery, or they need to use them to find further clues (process skills). They share with the class their approaches and solutions, back them up, and record them on graphs, videotape, illustrations, journals, or portfolios.

• Provide scenarios to visualize, make mental images, or think of characteristics by which they can describe an object, animal, plant, place, person, or situation. We make and brainstorm umbrellas of big ideas for categorization, such as color, weight, time, location, traits, extinct or not, parts, functions, habitats, means of survival, and so on, and hang them around the room for reference.

• Give plenty of opportunities and different materials and means to classify and label their sorting. This one is especially dear to me, because it was my wake-up call to learn to encourage and understand the children's thinking. One day my little first-grade scientists were reviewing the process of classification by sorting ourselves into three groups. I would point to a child and direct him or her to an assigned area in the classroom, within clear sight of the rest of the class. To play, they could not call out the answer to the rule or pattern being sorted, but had to point to the team they thought they belonged to, once they studied it and recognized the rule. If they were correct, they would stand with the team. If not, they would remain seated for a later turn. At the end,

then awaited responses from students that matched their expectations. Teachers can and do control the thought levels of students (Arnold, Atwood, & Rogers, 1973). In fact, Gallagher and Aschner (1963) reported that a mere 5 percent increase in divergent questioning can encourage up to a 40 percent increase in divergent responses from students. Divergent thinking is important for problem-solving tasks and for learning that requires creativity. Also, high-level questions help students to evaluate information better and improve their understanding of lower-level facts (Hunkins, 1970).

How pupils think must match the requirements of teachers' methods if students are to become confident learners. The questions learners ask are indicators of the thinking they are doing and of the impact of teachers' questions.

everyone was standing in one of the teams. As I inquired what their team characteristic or pattern was, most children called out what I, as the chooser, had made for the rule. "We all have turtlenecks," called one. "We all have collars," said the others. Finally, in the third team, the speaker said, "We all have jackets." At that moment, one of the girls in the middle team said, "I thought I was here because we all have red and none of the other teams do." Indeed, she was right! So I decided to capitalize on the thought and asked the rest of the class, "Can you think of any other ways by which we all might be sorted while in the teams we are now?" Oh! it was just wonderful to hear their reasoning! They were very proud of themselves. These are the circumstances that teachers need to act upon repeatedly throughout the day and not in isolated instances. Becoming aware of them takes a little self-training and practice.

- "What ifs . . . ?" are just wonderful, open-ended questions that can be connected to real-life circumstances.
- Have a discovery corner with manipulatives and questions promoting scientific processes.
- Have the children design new questions to go along with the discovery corner boards for another class to try out.

One of the most important elements of science instruction is the teacher's attitude toward science. Your own attitude toward learning will be the underlying gift you pass on to your kids. If and when you need to be the guide, do it with enthusiasm. Facilitate in a motivating, nonthreatening, and enthusiastic manner. If you were asked to write a newspaper advertisement for a science classroom guide and facilitator, what would you write? Check how this description matches the way you teach in the classroom. Take notes on your style if you need to focus more in this direction. You'll probably be pleasantly surprised to see how much you really do to foster the children's previous knowledge and their questions. When you introduce new concepts, ask yourself, "New to whom? To a few? How new? New to me? What questions might they have that will definitely show growth when we are done learning about it? What am I learning from this process?" Listen to their discussions and their questions; take notes. Make comments, bring to light awesome and small achievements, discoveries, questions that foster further questioning. With ownership of their thinking processes, they'll become independent thinkers. As far as assessment, remember that tests are merely a reflection and a tool to tell how well you've conveyed a message and how well they have received it. This is why assessments should be ongoing—by observation, cooperation, participation, and communication.

I have learned so much from my students' attitudes about learning, their questions, their inquisitiveness or lack of it, and their experiences. The gifts they bring on their own are assets to all. It is because of them that I enjoy teaching. They challenge me on a daily basis. I grow with them on a daily basis.

Questions can make the difference between learning from *meaningful* manipulation of materials and *meaningless* messing around. This belief is based on a process-product model of classroom learning, in which specific teaching behaviors provide useful pupil learning experiences. The product of this process is pupil achievement. This model suggests that "increases in the quantity and quality of pupil behaviors should result in concomitant increases in pupil achievement" (Tobin & Capie, 1982, p. 3). The assumed increases are attributed to the quality of verbal interaction. For example, teachers and students are reported to talk about 71 percent of the time in activity-based classrooms, compared to 80 percent of the time spent talking in nonactivity-based classrooms. In average, activity-based elementary science classrooms, 29 percent of the questions are at a high level, while only 13 percent of teachers' questions are high level in average nonactivity-based classrooms (Bredderman, 1982).

Do the changes in verbal interaction make a difference? Apparently, yes. The studies here are limited, but the results show that a teacher's questions can produce pupil achievement superior to levels attributed to written questions found in textbooks and on worksheets (Rothkopf, 1972; Hargie, 1978). Some earlier studies appear to conflict with this conclusion (Rosenshine, 1976, 1979). However, more recent studies suggest that key ingredients of effective verbal interaction may have been missing in the earlier research. For example, Kenneth Tobin (1984) describes increased achievement for middle-school students in science when teachers redirected questions, used probing strategies, and used wait-time to increase student discourse and reaction. Higher-level questions seem to stimulate greater science achievement when combined with a longer wait-time (Riley, 1986).

How Are Teacher Questions and Student Answers Related?

Raising the level of questions is all well and good, but it makes a difference only if students actually think and respond on the level elicited by the questions. Is this what happens?

Greater use of higher-level questions may be a significant difference between hands-on science learning and traditional teaching, according to Ted Bredderman (1984). He reports a direct relationship between the level of questioning and the level of response in elementary science lessons. Bredderman observed specially trained teachers raising the level of questioning in reading lessons. His research suggests that questioning levels "can be raised through activity-based science training, which could have the effect of raising the cognitive level of classroom discourse and could result in increased achievement" (Bredderman, 1984, pp. 289–303). Other researchers found that higher-level questions had a positive influence on the language development of young children and on skills such as analytical thinking (Kroot, 1976; Koran & Koran, 1973). What is the general conclusion? There is a positive relationship between higher-level questions and higher-level student answers (Barnes, 1978). We recommend using more advanced questions to obtain more thoughtful answers from children.

How Do Teachers Use Questions to Involve *All* Students?

Exemplary teachers treat different pupils equitably and are capable of adapting instruction according to student needs, including the levels of questions they use. How equitable is the questioning treatment that is found in typical elementary classrooms?

Studies done in urban classrooms show that teachers call on students whom they perceive as high achievers more frequently than on students they perceive as low achievers. Also, teachers are less likely to react to the responses received from low achievers. Usually, when high achievers hesitate to answer, they are given more time to think. Low achievers often receive less time to think and respond, perhaps out of regard for the students' feelings. High achievers also receive more opportunities to exchange ideas with teachers at higher thought levels (Krueger & Sutton, 2001). Similar data show questioning differences between Caucasian and African American students, with African

American males most deprived of opportunity (Los Angeles Unified School District [LAUSD], 1977).

What is the relationship between where a student sits in a classroom and the number of opportunities the student receives to answer questions? In classrooms with traditional seating arrangements of rows facing the teacher's desk, the students most likely to be asked questions were seated in a T shape, with the top of the T across the front of the room and the stem of the T down the middle (see Figure 7.1). Certainly the shape is not always perfect, yet there are distinct areas usually in the back of the classrooms along the sides where students are seldom involved in questioning and instructive verbal interaction. Who sits in these areas most often? Who needs more opportunities, feedback, and encouragement? Answer: lower-achieving students.

What Is Wait-Time and Why Is It Important?

Pause for a few seconds and think about what happens when you are the student and a teacher asks you a question. Unless you have memorized the answer, you must decode the meaning of the question (no small task if it is unclear or if multiple questions are used); think, "What do I know?" about the question's possible answer; ask, "How can I say the answer without sounding foolish?"; actually form the answer; and then give the response to the teacher. All of these steps take time, as suggested by Figure 7.2.

Wait-time is defined in different ways, but usually two types of wait-time are recognized. *Wait-time 1* refers to the length of time a teacher waits for a student to respond. *Wait-time 2* is the length of time a teacher waits after a student has responded before the teacher reacts to what was said. Several teachers have improved student thinking by

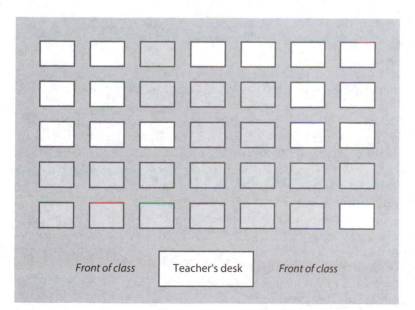

FIGURE 7.1
Where a Child Sits
Can Make a Difference

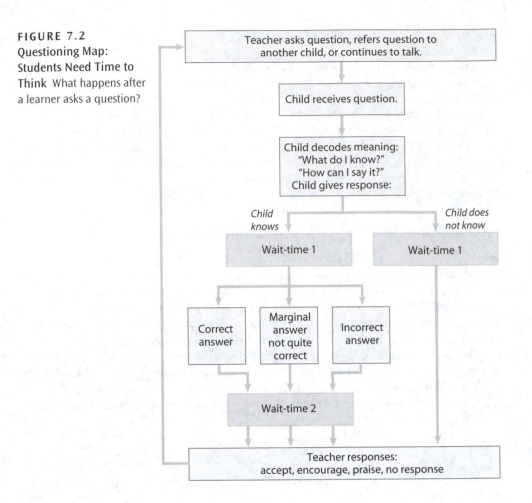

FIGURE 7.2

Questioning Map: Students Need Time to Think What happens after a learner asks a question?

Teacher asks question, refers question to another child, or continues to talk.

Child receives question.

Child decodes meaning:
"What do I know?"
"How can I say it?"
Child gives response:

Child knows

Child does not know

Wait-time 1

Wait-time 1

Correct answer

Marginal answer not quite correct

Incorrect answer

Wait-time 2

Teacher responses:
accept, encourage, praise, no response

". . . practicing quietness through longer wait-times, attentive silence, and reticence" (van Zee, et al, 2001).

How long do teachers typically wait? Rowe (1974) first researched this topic and reported an average for wait-time 1 was 1 second. Wait-time 2 was equally short, with teachers often only parroting the students' answers or providing very low-value feedback, such as, "Okay," "Uh-huh," or "Good." Many teachers wait about 1 second for students to respond without any adjustment for the difficulty of the question and then almost immediately react to what the students have said without giving the response much thought. "Evidently students are expected to respond as quickly to comprehension questions as they are to knowledge-level questions," and teachers believe they can accurately predict what students will say (Riley, 1986). Under what conditions do you think wait-times of 1 second or less *are* appropriate?

There is a growing list of advantages we can expect from increasing the length of wait-times. Kenneth Tobin (1984) reports increases in the length of student responses, increases in student achievement, and changes in teacher discourse. Teachers tend to "probe and obtain further student input rather than mimicking pupil responses" (p. 779). Yet there is a possible threshold effect; a certain optimal length of wait-time exists depending on the type of question, advises Riley (1986). Tobin and Capie (1982) recommend an overall wait-time of about 3 seconds with an approximate mix of 50 percent lower-level questions and 50 percent higher-level questions to produce optimal pupil responses. They advise us to establish the facts first in order to give the students something worthwhile to think about before building on the base of knowledge by using higher-level questions. Tobin (1984) even suggests that an effective strategy is to ask the question, wait, call on a student to answer, wait, then redirect the question or react accordingly (see Figure 7.3).

By allowing appropriate wait time, teachers can encourage students to think carefully before answering.

Some teachers encourage cooperative types of learning by using the think-pair-share approach. A teacher asks the question and waits; students think about possible answers for 10 to 20 seconds; students then pair up and compare answers. A student pair is then asked to share its answer with the class.

Students might find the waiting time awkward at first and misinterpret your intentions. We have had considerable success with learners by telling them about wait-time and why we are going to use it, then cueing them to think before responding. Try waiting at least 3 seconds before you respond, and you may discover the benefits reported by Rowe (1970).

- ✦ Student responses can become 400 to 800 percent longer.
- ✦ The number of appropriate but unsolicited student responses increases.
- ✦ Failure of students to respond decreases.
- ✦ Pupils' confidence levels increase.
- ✦ Students ask more questions.
- ✦ Low achievers may contribute up to 37 percent more.
- ✦ Speculative and predictive thinking can increase as much as 700 percent.
- ✦ Students respond and react more to each other.
- ✦ Discipline problems decrease.

What Types of Questions Are Used Most in Elementary Science Books and Tests?

Textbooks have a profound impact on curriculum, teachers, and instruction because student texts and teacher guides often determine the level of questions. The accuracy and import of texts on learners remain a concern (Budiansky, 2001; Raloff, 2001; Shepardson & Pizzini, 1991). Questions, as we have learned, influence the extent of thinking

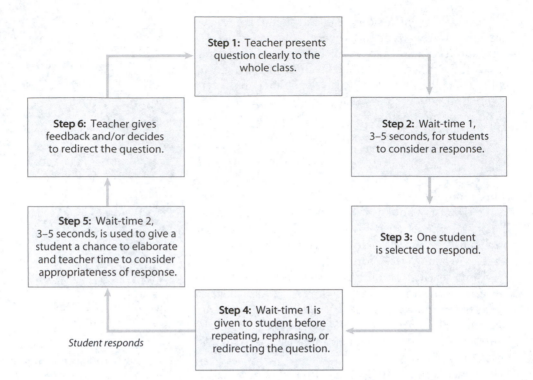

FIGURE 7.3 **A Questioning Strategy for the Whole Class** There are times when questions should be used with the whole class. This questioning strategy can maximize student involvement.

Source: This strategy is based on the research of Kenneth Tobin (1984) as reported in "Effects of Extended Wait-Time on Discourse Characteristics and Achievement in Middle School Grades," *Journal of Research in Science Teaching,* vol. 21, no. 8, pp. 779–791.

and learning that takes place. Low-level questions have been consistently used in textbooks for several school subjects, but high-level questions have seldom been found. For example, of the more than 61,000 questions in history textbooks, teacher guides, and student workbooks, more than 95 percent were devoted to recalling facts (Bennett, 1986). Another researcher found that only 9 out of 144 lesson plans in the teacher guides from the basal readers of four major publishers contained questions distributed over Bloom's various cognitive levels (Habecker, 1976). Overall, elementary science textbooks are no better, but recent improvements are encouraging as publishers enact the science standards. Excellent resource experiment books are also available; they pose questions based on the science processes (see Figure 7.4).

These findings also raise concern for tests and the printed materials they represent. What types of test items are provided? Tests supplied by text publishers appear to be devoted to low levels of thought as well. Gregory Risner (1987) studied the cognitive levels of questions demonstrated by test items that accompanied fifth-grade science

The questions below are representative of those found in books for children. Use these science processes to label the questions: observing, communicating, hypothesizing/experimenting, measuring, comparing/contrasting, and generalizing/predicting.

Process	Question
_____	1. Which plants seem to be sturdier: ones left in the sun or ones left in the shade?
_____	2. Most rain in clouds comes from the ocean; why doesn't it rain over the ocean and nowhere else?
_____	3. Which plant do you think will grow better?
_____	4. Do the creatures react to such things as light or shadows or an object in their path?
_____	5. What was the temperature?
_____	6. Which length works best?
_____	7. What can you move with the air you blow through a straw?
_____	8. Which seeds stick to your clothes as you walk through a weedy field?
_____	9. What happens to the number of breathing movements as the temperature drops?
_____	10. How long does the solution bubble?

Answers: 1. Observing; 2. Hypothesizing/experimenting; 3. Generalizing/predicting; 4. Observing; 5. Communicating; 6. Measuring; 7. Hypothesizing/experimenting; 8. Comparing/contrasting; 9. Generalizing/predicting; 10. Measuring.

FIGURE 7.4   Science Process Questions

*For a complete discussion, see Sandra Styer, "Books That Ask the Right Questions," *Science and Children* (March 1984): 40–42, or W. Harlen, *Teaching and Learning Primary Science* (London: Paul Chapman Publishing, 1993), pp. 83–86. See sources for Figure 7.4 on page 255.

textbooks. Rated on Bloom's taxonomy, Risner found about 95 percent of the test questions were devoted to knowledge or comprehension, about 5 percent used for application, and 0.2 percent used for evaluation; analysis and synthesis questions were neglected completely. All types of questions are important, but consistent overuse of any one type can limit learning. You must be able to identify questions necessary for stimulating desired levels of thought and then build those questions into your teaching.

What Are the Different Types of Questions?

"Many innovative scientists would never have made their most important discoveries had they been unable to think divergently in their pursuit of the new. Through thinking nontraditionally and divergently, scientists like Copernicus, Galileo, Pasteur, and Salk discovered solutions, formulated theories, and made discoveries that revolutionized the modern world. The need for divergent thinking did not die with their achievements." (Pucket-Cliatt & Shaw, 1985, pp. 14–16)

Using Questions in Science Classrooms

One function of teaching science is to help learners develop higher levels of thinking. To do this you must facilitate better communication with and among your students. One way to encourage communication is by asking questions. "Teacher questions can serve a variety of purposes," such as

- Managing the classroom ("How many of you have finished the activity?")
- Reinforcing a fact or concept ("What name is given to the process plants use to make food?")
- Stimulating thinking ("What do you think would happen if . . . ?")
- Arousing interest ("Have you ever seen such a sight?")
- Helping students develop a particular mindset ("A steel bar does not float on water; I wonder why a steel ship floats?")

Science teachers are concerned about helping students to become critical thinkers, problem solvers, and scientifically literate citizens. If we want students to function as independent thinkers, we need to provide opportunities in science classes that allow for greater student involvement and initiative and less teacher domination of the learning process. This means a shift in teacher role from that of information giver to that of a facilitator and guide of the inquiry are learning process.

Few children are able to construct their own understanding from an activity without teacher guid-

ance. Productive questions help teachers to build a bridge between learning activities and student thinking. According to Mary Lee Martens (1999, p. 26), productive questions help learners

- Focus their attention on significant details (What have you noticed about . . . ? How does it feel/smell/sound?)
- Become more precise while making observations (How many . . . ? How often . . . ? Where exactly . . . ?)
- Analyze and classify (How do they go together? How do these compare?)
- Explore the properties of unfamiliar materials, living or nonliving, and of small events taking place or to make predictions about phenomena (What about . . . ? What happens if . . . ?)
- Plan and implement solutions to problems (What is a way to . . . ? How could you figure out how to . . . ?)
- Think about experiences and construct ideas that make sense to them (Why do you think . . . ? What is your reason for . . . ?)

Central to this shift in teacher role are the types of questions that teachers ask. Questions that require students to observe characteristics, recall data or facts have a different impact on pupils than questions that encourage pupils to process and interpret data in a variety of ways.

These scientists learned to think divergently—broadly, creatively, and deeply about many possibilities. They learned how to ask the right questions at the right time. "Wrong questions tend to begin with such innocent interrogatives as why, how, or what" (Elstgeest, 1985, p. 37). Elstgeest provides an excellent example in this brief story:

I once witnessed a marvelous science lesson virtually go to ruins. It was a class of young secondary-school girls who, for the first time, were free to handle batteries, bulbs, and wires. They were busy incessantly, and there were cries of surprise and delight. Arguments were settled by "You see?" and problems were solved with "Let's try!" Hardly a thinkable combination of batteries, bulbs, and wires was left untried. Then in the midst of the hub-

The differential effects of various types of teacher questions seem obvious, but what goes on in classrooms? In one review of observational studies of teacher questioning, spanning 1963–1983, it was reported that the central focus of all teacher questioning activity appeared to be the textbook. Teachers appeared to consider their job to be [seeing] that students have studied the text. Similar findings have been reported from observational studies of teachers' questioning styles in science classrooms. Science teachers appear to function primarily at the recall level in the questions they ask, whether the science lessons are being taught to elementary students or secondary school pupils.

Why doesn't questioning behavior match educational objectives? One hypothesis is that teachers are not aware of the customary questioning patterns. One way to test this hypothesis is to use a question analysis system.

You can do several things if you want to improve your questioning behavior by using a wider variety of questions. First,

> locate a question category system [you] can use comfortably and then apply it, during lesson planning and in post-lesson analysis. Because of the variety of things that go on during a lesson, a post-lesson analysis is best accomplished by tape-recording the lesson or at least those parts of the lesson containing the most teacher questions.

Are the kinds of questions you ask different? What kinds of teacher-student interaction patterns seem to exist? Are some patterns of interaction more effective than others? Compare your written and oral questions. Do they accomplish what you intend? If you use a variety of oral questions to promote different levels of thinking, quiz and test questions should do the same. Students quickly figure out what you value and then strive for it.

George Maxim (1997, p. 42) offers practical suggestions for helping young children improve their thinking through productive questioning:

- Use age-appropriate questions to stimulate children to think about concrete objects in order to form simple abstractions.
- Use questions to help children interpret the sensory information they received by manipulating objects and encourage them to exchange points of view with adults and peers.
- Encourage children who are entering the period of concrete operations (7–11 years) to uncover reflective abstractions by challenging them to answer "Why?" questions.

Source: Unless otherwise cited, excerpted from Patricia Blosser, "Using Questions in Science Classrooms," in Doran, R. (ed.), *Research Matters . . . to the Science Teacher,* vol. 2 (1985) (ERIC document no. 273490).

bub, the teacher clapped her hands and, chalk poised at the blackboard, announced: "Now, girls, let us summarize what we have learned today. Emmy, what is a battery?" "Joyce, what is a positive terminal?" "Lucy, what is the correct way to close a circuit?" And the "correct" diagram was deftly sketched and labeled, the "correct" symbols were added, and the "correct" definitions were scribbled down. And Emmy, Joyce, and Lucy and the others deflated audibly into silence and submission, obediently copying the diagram and the summary. What they had done seemed of no importance. The questions were in no way related to their work. The rich experience with the batteries and other equipment, which would have given them plenty to talk and think about and to question, was in no way used to bring order and system into the information they actually did gather. (pp. 36–37)

Questions can encourage children to develop science process skills.

Elstgeest defines *good questions* as those taking a first step toward an answer, like a problem that actually has a solution. The good question stimulates, invites the child to take a closer look, or leads to where the answer can be found. The good question refers to the child's experience, real objects, or events under study. The good question invites children to show rather than say an answer. Good questions may be modeled after the science process skills in which learners are asked to take a closer look and describe what they find. Try matching the questions and skills in Figure 7.4.

There are several additional ways to classify questions. When presenting information from the research on questions, we have often referred to Bloom's taxonomy of the cognitive domain. It is possible to write questions for each level of the taxonomy. Figure 7.5, which gives examples of each level of taxonomy, is elaborated below.

✦ *Knowledge-level* questions request the memorized facts.
✦ *Comprehension-level* questions stimulate responses of memorized information in the students' own words.
✦ *Application-level* questions cause students to use information while thinking about how to put what they have learned to use in a new context.
✦ *Analysis-level* questions require that students break down what they know into smaller parts to look for differences, patterns, and so on.
✦ *Synthesis-level* questions stimulate children to consider variety, new ideas, or original possibilities.
✦ *Evaluation-level* questions require children to make choices and provide reasons.

The taxonomy suggests that learners cannot make a learned judgment until they know the facts, understand the facts, can apply the facts, can dissect the facts, and can reorganize the facts so that new perspectives are revealed (Bloom, 1956; Morgan & Saxton, 1991).

Educators often disagree about the level at which a question is written. This can make Bloom's taxonomy difficult to use, but it is worth learning. Spreading your questions across the taxonomy's range can make you a more effective teacher.

Gallagher and Aschner (1963) offer a simple and useful method for classifying questions. This method has four types of questions that address all of Bloom's levels and incorporate the science processes. The simplicity of this method makes it useful for all subject areas. Table 7.2 provides a level-of-thinking context; Figure 7.6 provides examples of the following kinds of questions:

✦ *Cognitive memory questions* require students to recall facts, formulas, procedures, and other essential information. This is similar to Bloom's knowledge and comprehen-

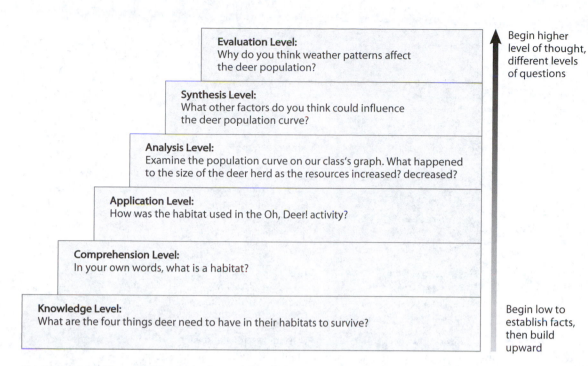

FIGURE 7.5 Bloom's Taxonomy of Cognitive Domain

Source: B. S. Bloom, *Taxonomy of Educational Objectives, the Classification of Educational Goals, Handbook I: Cognitive Domain* (New York: Longman, 1956).

TABLE 7.2 Levels of Thinking Questions Require

Question Type	Level	Type of Thinking Expected
Closed questions	Low	Cognitive memory operations; convergent operations
Open questions	High	Divergent thinking operations; evaluative thinking operations

Source: A comparison of Gallagher and Aschner's questions as adapted from P. Blosser, *How to Ask the Right Questions* (Washington, DC: National Science Teachers Association, 1991), p. 4.

sion levels and helps students establish the facts before moving toward higher levels. Memory questions also assist observations and communication. *Examples:* "Do you see the bubbles rising from the liquid?" "What is the common name for acetic acid?"

✦ *Convergent thinking questions* cause students to apply and analyze information. To do this successfully, children must have a command of cognitive memory types of information. Convergent questions assist in problem solving and are useful for the basic

QUESTION CATEGORY			SAMPLE QUESTION PHASES
Evaluative Thinking	**Bloom's Evaluation Level:** • Make choices • Form values • Overlap critiques, judgments, defenses	**How and Why Reasonings:** • Choose, appraise, select, evaluate, judge, assess, defend, justify • Form conclusions and generalizations	• *What do you favor . . . ?* • *What is your feeling about . . . ?* • *What is your reason for . . . ?*
Divergent Thinking	**Bloom's Synthesis Level:** • Develop own ideas and information • Integrate own ideas • Plan, construct, or reconstruct	**Open-Ended Questions for Problem Posing and Action:** • Infer, predict, design, invent • Hypothesize and experiment • Communicate ideas	• *What do you think . . . ?* • *What could you do . . . ?* • *What could you design . . . ?* • *What do you think will happen if . . . ?*
Convergent Thinking	**Bloom's Application and Analysis Level:** • Uses of logic • Deductive and inductive reasoning • Construct or reconstruct	**Closed Questions to:** • Focus attention, guide, encourage measurement and counting, make comparisions, take action • Use logic, state relationships • Apply solutions • Solve problems • Hypothesize and experiment • Communicate ideas	• *If "A", then what will happen to "B" . . . ?* • *Which are facts, opinions, and inferences . . . ?* • *What is the author's purpose . . . ?* • *What is the relationship of "x" to "y" . . . ?*
Cognitive Memory	**Bloom's Knowledge and Comprehension Level:** • Rote memorization • Selective recall of facts, formulas, instructions, rules, or procedures • Recognition	**Managerial and Rhetorical Questions:** • Simple attention focusing, yes-no responses **Information:** • Repeat, name, describe, identify, observe, simple explanation, compare	• *What is the definition of . . . ?* • *What are the three steps in . . . ?* • *Who discovered . . . ?* • *In your own words, what is the meaning of . . . ?*
Intended mental activity			Key function or science process

FIGURE 7.6 Composing the Correct Level of Questioning: Higher Levels of Thought

science processes: measuring, communicating, comparing, and contrasting. *Example:* "What kind of chart, graph, or drawing would be the best way to show our class's results?"

 ✦ *Divergent thinking questions* stimulate children to think independently. Students are given little teacher structure or prior information; they are encouraged to do possibility thinking by combining original and known ideas into new ideas or explanations. Questions of this type require synthesis thinking and promote creative problem solving and the integrated science processes (hypothesizing and experimenting). *Example:* "Why do you think these seedlings are taller than those?"

✦ *Evaluative thinking questions* cause students to choose, judge, value, criticize, defend, or justify. Often the simple question "Why?" or "How?" propels thinking to this level after students are asked simple choice or yes-no types of questions. Processes stimulated by evaluation questions include making predictions, reaching conclusions, and forming generalizations. *Example:* "What things make a difference to how fast the seeds begin to grow?"

Science for many children, unfortunately, may be an exercise in closed thinking in which memory and convergent questions are emphasized. Children are prodded to seek the so-called right answer or verify the correct results. Teachers should use both open and closed types of questions. *Open questions* are those that encourage divergent and evaluative thinking processes. Because they are traditional and expedient, *closed questions* have been used most often by teachers. Yet there is a danger associated with overuse of closed questions. "Convergent questions sacrifice the potential for many students to be rewarded for good answers, since their focus is a search for one right or best answer" (Schlichter, 1983, p. 10). Because science is a creative process, much more divergent thinking must be encouraged. Try your hand at classifying convergent and divergent questions in Figure 7.7, and experiment with both while you teach. Be advised that there are risks for teachers who use divergent or open-ended questions.

(text continues on page 243)

Convergent questions mean to elicit the single best answer, while divergent questions encourage a wide range of answers without concern for a single correct answer. Use the letters C and D to classify the following questions:

_____ 1. What kinds of food make your mouth water?

_____ 2. What name do we call the spit in your mouth?

_____ 3. What is another name for your esophagus?

_____ 4. How do volcanoes form?

_____ 5. What do you think could be done to make it safer to live near an active volcano?

_____ 6. How many weights do you think you can add to your structure before it falls down?

_____ 7. Are you kept warm by radiation, conduction, convection, or all three?

_____ 8. Why does sound travel faster through solids and liquids than it does through air?

_____ 9. What kinds of uses does a balloon have?

_____10. How does electricity work?

Answers: 1. Divergent, because *how* many different kinds of food make *your* mouth water? 2. Convergent, saliva; 3. Convergent, gullet; 4. Convergent, distinct earth processes; 5. Divergent, numerous creative ideas are encouraged; 6. Divergent, because this question asks for a prediction that depends on several factors that stimulate many different answers; 7. Convergent, because you are asked to select an answer from those given; 8. Convergent, because a specific concept is used to answer the question; 9. Divergent, because who knows the answer to this one? Only your imagination limits the possibilities; 10. Convergent, because descriptions about electron energy transfer rely on a specific concept.

FIGURE 7.7 Indentifying Convergent and Divergent Questions

Investigating Soil

GRADE LEVEL: **5–8**

DISCIPLINE: **Earth/Space Sciences**

Inquiry Question: What is soil and how is it formed?

Concept to Be Invented: Soil is made from finely ground rock and organic material.

National Science Education Standards: Grades 5–8—Earth/Space Sciences. Soil consists of weathered rocks, decomposed organic material from dead plants, animals, and bacteria. Soils are often found in layers, with each having a different chemical composition and texture.

Science Attitudes to Nurture: Activities that investigate and analyze science questions.

Materials Needed: Soil samples from local area, hammers, 1 piece of white construction paper/per student, old newspaper paper/per student, 1 magnifying glass/per student, local sedimentary rock samples (these are easily broken), 1 pair of goggles per student, sand, 2 small transparent plastic jars or containers with lids, organic matter such as leaves or grass clippings, water, soil samples from local area.

Safety Precautions: Students must wear goggles while smashing rocks with hammers. Wrap the rocks in newspaper and then strike them with a hammer. This will prevent rock pieces from flying and causing injury.

If you choose to take the students outside to collect soil samples, be sure proper safety procedures are followed. Pair the students and make sure they know the boundaries for soil sample collection.

Exploration *Which process skills will be used?*

Observing, recording data, classifying

Engage the class by posing the inquiry question and involving the students in predicting answers. Explore by providing the class with soil samples collected from the local area, or if possible, take the students around the school grounds to collect soil samples. Ask the students to cover their desktops with old newspapers and then place the white construction paper on top of the newspaper. Arrange the students in cooperative groups of three to four to make observations of the soil samples. Use the magnifying glasses to make detailed observations of the individual particles. Encourage students to draw or write a description of their observations. Pose divergent questions to stimulate observations using the basic process skills.

After the students have made as many observations as possible, ask them to try to separate their soil samples into different parts. *Divergent question to ask: How many different ways do you think you can use to separate the soil samples?*

Give each cooperative group a hammer and several pieces of local sedimentary rocks like sandstone or limestone. Remind students to *put on and keep on their goggles at all times* during this section of the activity. On top of the newspaper-covered desks, ask the students to wrap the rock samples in newspaper and then pound the rocks with hammers. *How do the rock samples compare to the sediments you separated from the local soil sample? (Open-ended evaluative question to stimulate independent thought.)*

Explanation

Ask the students to share the results of their observations. As they share use the following line of questioning to help the students invent the concept:

+ What kinds of things did you observe? *Convergent question—implies specific answers based on their observations.*
+ How did the components of the soil compare in size? Shape? *Encourages detail observations to respond to the convergent close-ended question.*
+ How many different ways did you separate your soil samples? Suggestions may include size or color; rocklike or plantlike. *An open-ended evaluative question.*
+ What did your rock look like before you crushed it with the hammer? Afterward? *Convergent question—implies specific answers based on their observations.*
+ How do the crushed rock and your soil sample compare? *An evaluative question asking for analysis and synthesis of results.*

Continue using questions, moving from divergent types from the Exploration phase to more convergent and evaluative questions to help the students create a working definition for soil: "Soil is made from finely ground rocks and organic material."

Expansion *Which process skills will be used?*

Manipulating materials, observing, inferring, classifying, estimating, predicting

Provide each cooperative group with two transparent plastic jars with lids. Ask the students to label one jar *local soil* and the second *homemade soil*. Ask the students to fill the first jar halfway with one of the local soil samples. Ask the students to place, in the second jar, some of the crushed rock they just smashed, some sand, and some grass clippings or leaves, so that half of the jar is filled. Into both jars pour enough water to cover all of the solid materials. Place the lids on the jars and shake vigorously. Solicit

(continued)

predictions about what will happen in each jar after it sets for 1 hour, for 3 hours, and overnight. Ask the students to record their predictions and then place the jars where they will not be disturbed for the times indicated.

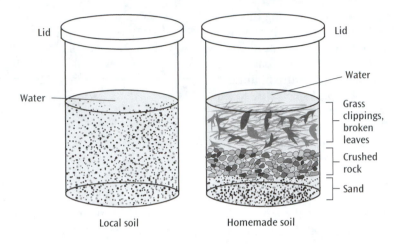

Local soil   Homemade soil

Use the following questions to help the students conclude that the rocks and plants found in the local area will determine the kind of soil formed. Weathered sandstone will create a sandy soil, more finely ground particles will create a silty soil, and very fine particles will create a clay soil. Note the questions start as close-ended, convergent types of questions—this is to help the students to focus on the expansion activity. Next they move into more open-ended divergent and evaluative questions—all designed to help the students create an understanding of the relationship between local rock and the type of soil formed in the area:

+ What did the two samples look like after 1 hour? After 3 hours? The next day?
+ If you did not look at jar labels and just at samples, how could you tell the difference between the soil in the two jars? How are they similar? How are they different?
+ Look at the settled materials. How much of the sample do you estimate is sand? Silt? Clay?
+ Based on your estimates how would you classify the soil?
+ What do you think will happen to the grass or leaves if you let the jar sit for one week, one month, or three months? Solicit predictions and then set the jar in a safe place so that students can observe it over a three-month period.
+ What do you conclude about the local rock found in the area and the soil type after looking at your results and the results of the whole class?

Science in Personal and Social Perspectives

What kind of soil is found around your home? What types of plants would grow well in the soil? Not grow well? How might soil types impact agricultural decisions?

Should people be concerned about farmers using excessive amounts of fertilizers in soils? Why? What can be done to prevent excessive use of fertilizers?

Do you think it is better to have a sandy or a silty soil in your garden? Why? Do you put fertilizers on your soil? If so, why?

Science and Technology

+ As you have discovered, not all soils are alike. Do you think it was important to keep this fact in mind as tractor tires were developed? Why?
+ What do you think *no-till* means, and why would farmers be urged to use this method of farming?

Science as Inquiry

+ What are at least three components of soil?
+ What influence does local bedrock have on the type of soil found in an area?
+ How might the rate of weathering and erosion in an area affect the formation of soil?
+ Where do you think the minerals found in soils come from?

History and Nature of Science

+ What are the responsibilities of a soil agronomist?
+ How important is it for a land developer to understand soil formation?
+ What is organic farming? How do these methods of farming differ from other methods?

Evaluation

Upon completing the activities, the students will be able to:

+ take a soil sample and demonstrate the steps necessary to estimate the amount of sand, silt, and clay in the sample;
+ explain how the type of soil found in a local area is dependent on the local bedrock and ground cover; and
+ write a persuasive argument on why grass is necessary to cover soil, or on how soil is different from dirt.

"The risks for the teachers who ask divergent questions should not be underestimated: an open-ended question can alter the day's schedule, spark discussion on topics the teacher may not be prepared for, and shift the teacher's role from guardian of known answers to stimulator of productive (and often surprising) thinking. But they are risks well worth taking." (Schlichter, 1983, p. 10)

There are risks associated with using *any* type of question. What can you do to limit the risks? How can you learn to use questions more effectively?

What Are the Keys to Effective Questioning?

Plan specific questions. Take the time to write specific questions before you teach. List six to eight key questions that cover the levels of thinking you wish to promote, and then use the questions as a guide for what you teach. The questions should help establish the knowledge base of information and then help build toward higher levels. Avoid yes-no questions unless that is your specific purpose; instead, focus the questions on the lesson topic by building toward the objectives. Open-ended questions can stimulate exploration, and convergent questions can focus concept invention. Both, along with evaluation questions, can contribute to expansion of the lesson's main idea. Pay attention to the types of questions used in children's books; then select books and materials with many different types, and supplement them with your own questions for special purposes.

Ask your questions as simply, concisely, and directly as possible. Make your purpose clear, and use single questions. Build upon previous questions once they have been answered, and avoid multiple, piggy-backed questions. These confuse students and indicate that the question is not well defined in the teacher's mind.

Ask your question before selecting who should answer. This helps keep all learners listening and thinking. Pause briefly after asking the question so everyone can think about it. Then select an individual to respond. Give both high and low achievers a chance to answer, and try to provide equal and genuine feedback. Involve as many different types of students as possible, volunteers and nonvolunteers. The entire class shouting out answers could create discipline problems. Limit rapid-fire, drill-and-practice questions to times when specific facts need to be gathered or reviewed. Avoid parroting the students' answers, but do try to use the students' ideas as much as possible.

Practice using wait-time. Wait-time 1 is often 1 second or less. Practice waiting at least 3 seconds for students to respond to most questions, especially if students are exploring or trying to expand on the lesson's main idea. Wait-time gives the children opportunities to think, create, and demonstrate more fully what they understand. Higher-level questions may require a wait-time longer than 3 seconds.

Wait-time 2 may need to be longer than wait-time 1. Rowe (1974) believes this wait-time is more important, especially when the occasion calls for critical or creative thinking. Quality and quantity of student responses increase, low achievers respond more, and the teacher has more time to think carefully about the questioning sequence.

Listen carefully to your students' responses. Encourage students nonverbally and verbally without overkilling with praise. Make any praise or encouraging remarks genuine. Check to make certain the children's responses match the level intended by your questions, and prompt them if the level is not appropriate. Do not always stop with the right answer. Probing benefits students who are partially correct and helps them construct a more acceptable answer. As a general rule, do not move on to another student before giving the first student a chance to form a better answer. This is a great opportunity to gather clues about students' misconceptions, incomplete information, or limited experiences. A brief questioning sequence may be all that is needed to overcome important learning problems.

Try using questions to produce conceptual conflict. Piaget's research (Wadsworth, 1996) suggests that learners should be in a state of mental disequilibrium to help them adapt or add new mental constructions to their thinking:

- ✦ *What do you think will happen if* we add more weight to the boat?
- ✦ *If* we add a drop of soap, *then* what could happen to the surface tension?
- ✦ *How would you* design a test to determine the effects of fertilizer on plant growth?
- ✦ *What evidence do you have to support* your identification of the limiting factors?
- ✦ *What other ways are possible to* explain the effects of sunlight on plant growth?
- ✦ *How can you explain* to the others what you did and what you discovered?
- ✦ *What do you think causes* newsprint to look larger when viewed through a water droplet?

Talk less and ask more, but make your questions count. Ask, don't tell. Use questions to guide and invite your students to tell you. Work with students by exchanging ideas instead of conducting an inquisition. Try to make discussions more conversational by asking students to share thoughts and react to each other.

Try to use questions that yield more complete and more complex responses. Given consistently adequate wait-time, students should give longer and more thoughtful answers. The effectiveness of any specific question you use is never any greater than the answer you are willing to accept. Establish a base of information first; then build on it by asking questions that require more complex answers. Ask students who give short, incomplete answers to contribute more.

Ask different types of questions to encourage all children. Some learners seem unprepared for or incapable of answering high-level questions. If this is the case, try beginning your questions at a low level before attempting a higher level; build upward. Recalling information with frequent low-level questions for review, recitation, and drill helps children experience success, develop confidence, and establish a reliable foundation to build higher thinking upon. But do not let your questioning stagnate. Begin with closed questions to establish a firm footing, and then move on to more open-ended questions. Use

Listen carefully, ask concise, direct questions, practice wait time, and match the level of the questions to the level of the child.

divergent and evaluative questions less often initially, and increase their use over time if your students have difficulty responding as you desire.

Learners who have already had more successful and satisfying school experiences are eager and appear more capable of responding to higher levels of questions sooner. Reflective discussions that mix convergent, divergent, and evaluative questions can form a strategy for critical and original thinking. Yet despite the type of student, several studies show that lower-level questions promote greater achievement gains for all primary children when learning basic skills.

Several learning theorists and researchers remind us about differences in how primary and upper elementary children think. Each group processes information differently because of differences in mental development. Yet appropriate experiences can help mental development reach its full potential in each group. Questions related to the processes of science provide the momentum for this development.

For younger children in the primary grades (ages 5 to 10), use questions that stimulate.

- ✦ Observation of basic properties. *Example:* "What do you see happening to the Silly Putty?"
- ✦ Classification based on similarities and differences. *Example:* "Which of these animals is an insect?"
- ✦ Communication to show thoughts and increase the value of the experience as well as to develop cooperation and interpersonal relations. *Example:* "What are you observing?" "How do you feel about what you see?"
- ✦ Measurement, using numbers and time. *Example:* "What is the final temperature?" "How much time did it take to reach that temperature?"
- ✦ Prediction to form guesses based on what is known. *Example:* "What do you think will happen to the brightness of the bulb if we use a longer wire?"

For older children in the upper elementary and middle grades (ages beyond 11), use questions that fall into these categories.

- ✦ Identification of variables. *Example:* "What variables did we keep the same?"
- ✦ Control of variables. *Example:* "What variables seemed to affect the size of your soap bubbles?"
- ✦ Formation of operational definitions based on verified information. *Example:* "From what we did in this experiment, how should we define 'force'?"
- ✦ Formation and testing of hypotheses to reach conclusions. *Example:* "Why did the electrical resistance increase in this experiment?"
- ✦ Interpretation of data from experiments. *Example:* "What do the green and pink color changes of the purple cabbage juice indicate?"
- ✦ Formation of models to explain occurrences or represent theories. *Example:* "What kind of relationship between the species is suggested by their population graphs over the same length of time?"

Determine whether the children are providing answers equal to the level of your questions. To do this you will need to monitor your questions and your students' responses.

Realize when not to ask a question. According to Morgan and Saxton (1991), times when it may not be appropriate to ask questions include

- when students have insufficient knowledge and experiences from which to draw an answer (this is a good time to encourage children to ask *their* questions);
- when children are making progress on their own and your question would be an intrusion that impedes productive work;
- when students seem to be despondent or having personal problems. Instead of asking a question to which a student may feel obliged to respond, try making an observation such as "Tina, you seem quiet today" and then become an active listener if Tina chooses to do the talking.

How Can You Improve Your Questioning?

You can improve your questioning with training and practice. One way to improve is to videotape or tape-record a lesson in which you use questions, play back the recording, identify the questions, and analyze them. Observation instruments or checklists such as those in Table 7.3 can be used. A more informative approach is to structure your observation and analysis around these questions.

- What kinds of questions were the most stimulating for learners to engage in the inquiry?
- What questions best nurtured development of process skills?
- How did you use questions to help learners construct conceptual understanding?
- What types of questions sustained or expanded the inquiry?
- How often did you use cognitive memory questions?
- How does this number compare to your use of convergent, divergent, and evaluative questions?
- How are your questions phrased? Do you avoid yes-no questions as much as possible?
- How do you know your questions are at the appropriate level for your students?
- What evidence do you have that you adjust questions to the language and ability levels of the students?
- Are your questions distributed among all learners regardless of ability, gender, socioeconomic status, and where they are seated?
- How often do you call on nonvolunteers? How do you decide which nonvolunteer to call upon?
- How often do you use probing to encourage students to complete responses, clarify, expand, or support a decision?
- How long do you wait? How do you use wait-time? What benefits do you receive from using wait-time? How does your use of wait-time 1 compare with wait-time 2?
- How well do the written questions on your plan match the verbal questions you use in class? Do your test questions represent the same levels as questions used in class?
- How often do children ask questions? What types of questions do they ask? Under what circumstances do they ask questions?

TABLE 7.3   How Effective Is Your Questioning?

Record a lesson and use this checklist to help you examine your questioning skills.
When you teach and question, do you:

_____ 1. plan and record questions when preparing your lessons?

_____ 2. compose and choose different questions for a variety of purposes, such as exploring, observing, clarifying, redirecting, summarizing, explaining, expanding?

_____ 3. begin your lessons with questions to stimulate inquiry?

_____ 4. avoid using Yes-No questions unless that is your specific intention?

_____ 5. focus your questions on searching for student understanding by removing emphasis from correct or incorrect answers?

_____ 6. use wait-time 1 effectively?

_____ 7. encourage students to ask their own questions?

_____ 8. help students improve their own questions?

_____ 9. use wait-time 2 to help you listen carefully to students' questions and answers?

_____ 10. expand on students' ideas?

_____ 11. avoid asking multiple or piggy-backed questions?

_____ 12. avoid answering your own questions?

_____ 13. ask students to clarify, summarize, compose the conceptual explanation?

_____ 14. avoid repeating your questions and rephrase questions that are misunderstood or unclear?

_____ 15. talk less and ask more?

_____ 16. model self-questioning by thinking outloud about a problem?

_____ 17. use good grammar on a level understood by the children?

_____ 18. use questions to punish or embarrass?

_____ 19. stop productive discussions after receiving the correct answer?

_____ 20. avoid repeating student answers and avoid sounding like a parrot?

Why Use Students' Questions?

"The children's questions worry me. I can deal with the child who just wants attention, but because I've had no science background I take other questions at face value and get bothered when I don't know the answer. I don't mind saying I don't know, though I don't want to do it too often. I've tried the let's-find-out-together approach, but it's not easy and can be very frustrating." (Jelly, 1985, p. 54)

Why Bother with Students' Questions?

"Can one black hole swallow another?"

"Why do fireflies light up?"

"How does a steel ship float when it weighs so much?"

"Why are soda cans shaped like a cylinder and not a rectangle?" (Perlman & Pericak-Spector, 1992, pp. 36–37)

Children's questions give precious insight into their world and illustrate topics of interest. Their questions can surprise teachers who might underestimate the ability of particular children and may suggest that certain learners have more ability than is evident from their reading and written work. The questions students ask also give a guide to what they know and do not know, and when they want to know it. These questions give clues about what science content is understood and the level of concept development—if we are willing to listen closely. Questions could also indicate an anxious child, or simply reveal a habit formed by one who has been reinforced to ask questions (Biddulph, Symington, & Osborn, 1986).

Questions help students focus and gain knowledge that interests them. Incessant "why?" questions can be a method of gaining attention, but unlike the two-year-old, the school-age child who asks, "Why?" reveals an area where understanding is lacking and is desired. Questions help young children resolve unexpected outcomes or work through problem situations; they can also be a way of confirming a belief. Children's questions also help them learn more quickly. "When they are following their own noses, learning what they are curious about, children go faster, cover more territory than we would ever think of trying to mark out for them, or make them cover" (Holt, 1971, p. 152).

Children's questions can become the center of inquiry. Children's questions reveal their ideas about a science topic, and they can be used to generate interest. Basing inquiry on children's questions,

- ✦ helps them gain understanding,
- ✦ provides them a powerful incentive to improve their own information-processing skills,
- ✦ helps them learn to interact with ideas and construct meanings for themselves from an interesting situation or topic, and
- ✦ gives them occasional opportunities to learn from their own mistakes.

Encouraging students to ask questions develops a useful habit: reflection. Habits take time to form, and asking questions is a habit that can enrich a school's curriculum. Time spent in contemplation helps form this habit. Asking oneself questions and hazarding guesses about their answers stimulate creative thinking, provide a means for solving critical problems, and can help a child learn "to find interest and enjoyment in situations that others would see as dull or boring" (Biddulph, Symington, & Osborn, 1986, p. 78).

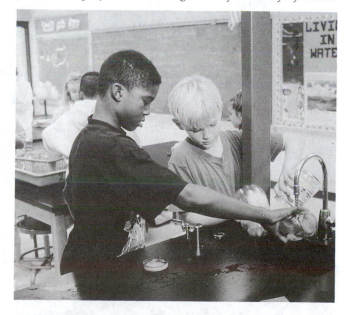

Children's questions can be used to develop interesting problems for science inquiry and to encourage the useful habit of reflection.

How Can You Stimulate Students' Questions?

Four factors stimulate children to ask questions. If you want children to ask more questions, you should provide

Video Explorations Questioning

Video Summary

Questions are universal teaching tools. Good questions can be used to: find out what students know, believe, or can do. Questions can also: motivate, help students organize thinking, interpret meaning, emphasize a point, show relationships, discover interests, provide review, reveal thinking processes, permit expression, and diagnose misconceptions or learning difficulties. Skillful questioning can also help learners to construct and expand their understandings of science concepts.

Tips for Viewing, Objectives, or What to Watch for

Keep in mind the following as you watch these videos:

◆ The first-grade classroom footage is authentic and unrehearsed.

◆ A team of two preservice teachers taught the lesson under the supervision of an experienced classroom teacher.

Questions for Exploration

1. What are the different kinds of ways that teachers may use questions? (Refer to Table 7.1.)

2. What examples of these uses did you see in the video?

3. Consider what you understand about wait-time. What types of wait-time did the teachers use? How long did she wait? Did her wait-time seem appropriate? Why?

4. Consider what you understand about inquiry. In what ways did the teacher help children to inquire? If you were teaching the lesson, what are some things you might have done differently to promote inquiry?

Activity for Application

As seen in the video, what kind of impact on children seems likely when a teacher tries to model good questioning habits? How quickly do you think a teacher could expect to observe the influence of modeling?

Use the effective questioning checklist (Table 7.3) and check those skills you observed in this brief videoclip. Based on this brief observation, what do you conclude about the teacher's skill in using questions? Videotape a lesson that you teach and use the same checklist. What do you conclude about your skills in using questions? What goals will you set for self-improvement?

adequate stimulation, model appropriate question asking, develop a classroom atmosphere that values questions, and include question asking in your evaluations of children.

Stimulation. Direct contact with materials is a first step. What kinds of materials stimulate curiosity in children and provide them opportunities to explore? The best indicator is the materials children bring in spontaneously. The sharing has a built-in curiosity factor and requires little effort to conduct discussion; simply invite them to share and ask questions. The mind will be on what the hands are doing.

Modeling. Teacher question asking is modeling. Learners must be shown how to ask good, productive questions. Showing genuine enthusiasm and consideration for what interests others can show children how to do the same. Consider some of the following ways to bring this modeling into the routine of your classroom (Jelly, 1985).

Share collections and develop classroom displays, much as Mrs. B did in the opening scenario. Link these activities to regular classwork and organize them around key chapter questions. Use one of the question classification systems described earlier in this chapter to help you ask questions at many different levels. Invite children to share their own collections and create class displays while building questions into the discussion the children share with classmates.

Establish a problem corner in your classroom or use a "Question of the Week" approach to stimulate children's thought and questions. These approaches can be part of regular class activity or used for enrichment. Catherine Valentino's (1985) Question of the Week materials could be a good place to start until you acquire enough ideas of your own. Consider one of her examples, "I Lava Volcano," a photo of an erupting volcano, which asks these questions: "Do volcanic eruptions serve any useful purpose?" "Over millions of years, what changes would occur on the earth if all volcanic activity suddenly stopped?" Valentino's full-color weekly posters and questions stimulate curiosity and inquiry.

Prepare lists of questions to investigate with popular children's books. Encourage students to add their own questions to the list.

K	W	H	L
What do I **Know** about _____?	What do I **Want** to know about _____?	**How** can I find out about _____?	What did I **Learn** about _____?
List all ideas in order to document prior knowledge, preconceptions, and possible misconceptions.	List the students' questions here. Their questions give opportunity for engagement and may reveal your oversights.	List all possible sources and resources, e.g., books, Internet, people to ask, etc.	Completed after the inquiry, facts and discoveries listed here may differ from those listed for "K."

FIGURE 7.8   A KWHL Chart

FIGURE 7.9   The Planning House

What did we find out?

How will we make this a fair inquiry?
Let the custodian and helper know about our experiment.
Make sure nobody waters the daisy. We agree that it is
dead when it flops down and the stem does not stand up.

What will we need?
A fully grown daisy in a pot.
A sunny window.

How will we find out?
We will keep the daisy inside in the classroom
window, and we will not water it. We will look at it each
day and draw pictures of how it looks.

What do we want to investigate?
How long can a daisy live without water?

Use questions to organize any teacher-made activity cards that learners may use independently. Encourage children to think of their work as an investigative mission and to see themselves as clue seekers.

Try a KWHL chart. Marletta Iwasyk (1997) describes the importance of modeling curiosity and productive questioning at the beginning of discussions by focusing basic questions on the topic of study and recording the children's answers to four basic questions (Figure 7.8).

For primary-grade learners Neil Dixon (1996) offers the "Planning House" as a concrete metaphor for stimulating children to inquire and to record questions systematically. The roof of the house represents the outcome of the inquiry, which results from the planned steps taken, whereas the lower levels of the house show how children began the inquiry and then worked their way up toward the outcome question (Figure 7.9).

John Langrehr (1993) recommends two additional tools that teachers can use to model effective questioning and help learners improve their thinking and question-asking skills. Figure 7.10 provides sixteen question starters that should help any student to design focused, thoughtful questions. Consider the topic of insects. Using the question starters shown in the matrix, students should be able to expand their inquiry by asking questions such as: *What is* an insect? *How is* an insect different from a spider?

	Object/Event	Situation	Reason	Means
Present	What is ...?	Where is ...?	Why is ...?	How is ...?
Possibility	What can ...?	Where can ...?	Why can ...?	How can ...?
Probability	What would ...?	Where would ...?	Why would ...?	How would ...?
Imagination	What might ...?	Where might ...?	Why might ...?	How might ...?

FIGURE 7.10   Question-Formation Matrix

Source: S. Langrehr, "Getting Thinking into Science Questions," *Australian Science Teachers Journal* 39 (4), (1993): 36.

What can insects do that humans cannot? *Where would* you expect to find insects? *Why might* insects be better able to survive a forest fire than mammals? and so on.

Langrehr also recommends that we show students how to use a *connection map* (Figure 7.11) in order to improve their questioning and construction of mental connections among and between the various ideas that may be illustrated by the map. Less able thinkers tend to think more generally, while more capable thinkers tend to think more abstractly. As a tool, the connection map encourages each student to record several key words in boxes that surround a central idea. Encourage students to write connecting words between the boxes that form simple sentences that make sense. This student-designed map can help you peer inside the thinking of the student. Simple questions such as "Why?" or "How?" can encourage students to construct more thought-provoking questions that stimulate productive experimentation.

Classroom Atmosphere.   Suchman (1971) believes students inquire only when they feel free to share their ideas without fear of being censored, criticized, or ridiculed. Successful teachers listen to children and do not belittle their curious questions. Establish an atmosphere that fosters curiosity by praising those who invent good questions; reinforce their reflective habits. You can provide opportunities for questions by

+ using class time regularly for sharing ideas and asking questions as learners talk about something that interests them,
+ having children supply questions of the week and rewarding them for improvements in their question asking,
+ helping children write lists (or record lists for nonreaders) of questions they have about something they have studied. These questions can be excellent means for review, for showing further interest, and for providing an informal evaluation of how clearly you have taught a topic.

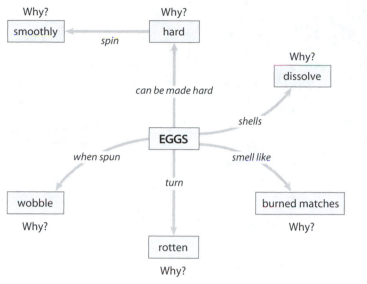

FIGURE 7.11
Question Connection Map
Source: Adapted from J. Langrehr, "Getting Thinking into Science Questions," *Australian Science Teachers Journal* 39 (4), (1993): 36.

Question Asking and Evaluation. Have students form questions as another way of evaluating their learning. This factor can stimulate habits of question asking and is different from if you, as teacher, ask questions children must answer. Include a picture or description of a situation in a test occasionally, and call for children to write productive questions about it. Another approach, is to have students list questions they believe are important for a more complete understanding of the material they have just studied. Lists of their questions can be evaluated for the number and the quality of the questions; quality should refer to the relevance of the question to the topic as well as the thought required to answer it.

How Can You Use Students' Questions Productively?

When children ask, focus your listening on the ideas represented by their questions. You will need to help them clarify their questions until they learn to ask better ones by themselves. Jelly (1985) offers a strategy you can use to turn children's questions into productive learning opportunities. Figure 7.12 is based on Jelly's recommendations.

Sources for Questions for Figure 7.4: 1. Seymour, S. (1978). *Exploring fields and lots: Easy science projects.* Champaign, IL: Garrard Publishing. 2. Bendick, J. (1971). *How to make a cloud.* New York: Parents' Magazine Press. 3. Seymour, S. (1970). *Science in a vacant lot.* New York: Viking Press. 4. Zubrowski, B. (1979). *Bubbles: A children's museum activity book.* Boston: Little, Brown. 5. Seymour, S. (1978). *Exploring fields and lots: Easy science projects.* Champaign, IL: Gerrard Publishing. 6. Renner, A. G. (1979). *Experimental fun with the yo-yo and other scientific projects.* New York: Dodd, Mead. 7. Milgrem, H. (1976). *Adventures with a straw: First experiments.* New York: E. P. Dutton. 8. Selsam, M. E. (1957). *Play with seeds.* New York: William Morrow. 9. Seymour, S. (1969). *Discovering what frogs do.* New York: McGraw-Hill. 10. Zubrowski, B. (1981). *Messing around with baking chemistry: A Children's Museum activity book.* Boston: Little, Brown.

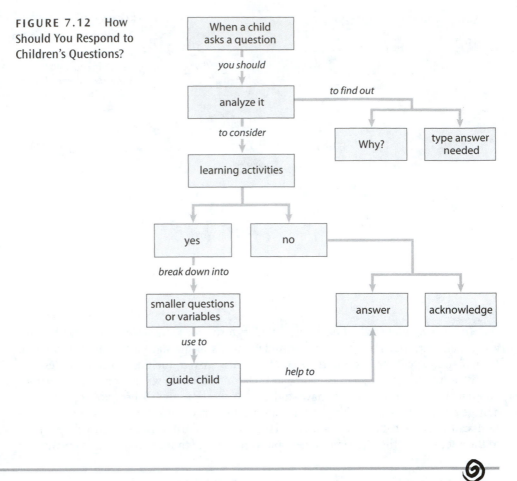

FIGURE 7.12 How Should You Respond to Children's Questions?

When a child asks a question
→ *you should*
analyze it
→ *to find out*: Why? | type answer needed
→ *to consider*
learning activities
→ yes | no
yes → *break down into* → smaller questions or variables → *use to* → guide child → *help to* → answer
no → answer | acknowledge

Chapter Summary

If there is a universal teaching tool, the question is it. Questions provide unique opportunities for teachers and students to become involved in productive dialogue; questions invite both teachers and learners to think and respond in many different ways.

We know that the potential of questioning is underused and that many teachers' questions are closed and stimulate low-level thinking. Questions may be misused if the wrong types of questions are used before children are capable or ready to respond at the level demanded. Know when not to question. Productive questions stimulate productive thinking and curiosity. Effective questions contribute to students' improved attitudes, expanded capability for thinking, and increased achievement.

As teachers, we need to afford all learners equal opportunities to learn through our questioning techniques. Old habits may have to be changed. We must strive to give children adequate time to think by expanding wait-time; screening textbooks, tests, and other print materials for evidence of good questions; and helping them through the habit of inquiring and reflecting to ask their own questions.

All questions are not equal; they come in many different types, such as Bloom's taxonomy, open and closed, science processes, memory, and evaluation. Questions should be selected or composed for specific purposes.

You can question well by using the keys for good questioning described in this chapter. Periodically analyze how you use questions and form a plan for self-improvement. Check your skills against your plan and revise as necessary.

Students' questions provide benefits for teachers, children, and the science program. Teachers can encourage learners' questions if they use materials and activities that stimulate questions, model good questioning skills, provide a supportive classroom atmosphere, and include children's question asking in evaluation techniques.

 ## Discussion Questions

1. Based on your school experiences, what differences have you noticed about how your teachers used questions? How do your elementary, secondary, and college teachers compare on using questions?

2. What types of questions do your teachers usually ask? How well do the questions match with the teachers' intentions? Justify your answer.

3. How do the teachers you have observed use questions to begin a lesson? To focus children's observations? To lead children toward conclusions? To bring closure to a lesson?

4. What priority do you believe teachers should give to children's questions? What strategy should they use?

5. How important is it for teachers to monitor their own uses of questions?

6. Observe a science lesson. Record the number and types of questions asked by the teacher, and try to measure the average wait-time. How do your observations correspond to the average uses of questions and wait-time described in this chapter?

7. If you were writing a letter to the teacher in #6, what suggestions would you offer to help improve the teacher's questions?

Build a Portfolio or E-Folio

1. How well do you use questions? What evidence do you have to support your answer? What do you think you can do to improve your questioning skills? Audio- or videotape yourself using questions when you practice teaching. Use the recommendations of this chapter to focus an evaluation of your questioning skills, and begin by comparing the numbers of closed and open questions you use.

2. Using any of the methods for classifying questions described in this chapter. Write and label samples of two questions for each level. Work within class groups to evaluate the quality of the questions. How well do you avoid yes-no questions, require more than rote memory, and avoid unproductive questions?

3. Use several of the questions you have written to speculate about pupil replies and appropriate teacher responses. List the questions and the replies for the pupil and teacher.

4. Tape-record a class session in which children ask questions. Transcribe these questions, and describe how you could respond to them if you were the teacher. How does your response method compare with Sheila Jelly's suggestion?

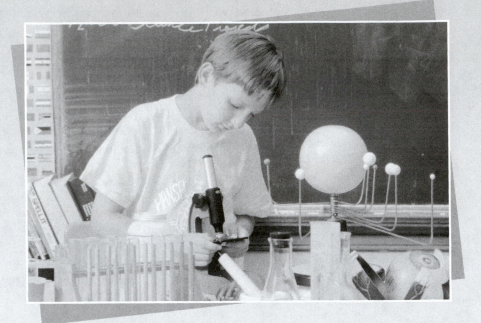

Integration—How Can I Do It All?

Shaundra Lewis is a newly hired first-grade teacher at Wilton Elementary. The day she signed her contract, the principal handed her four thick books of standards for each of the major content areas—science, mathematics, language arts, and social studies. She went home rather bewildered, trying to figure out how she would survive her first year of teaching and meet every standard identified for first grade. Excited about her new position, Shaundra planned to spend the summer determining how she would address each of the standards throughout the school year.

Shaundra started by creating a calendar and marked when she would address each of the indicators for the different disciplines' standards. She soon became overwhelmed with the list of things to cover and called her principal in despair.

"I just can't figure out how I'm going to meet all of these standards within one school year, especially if all of my first graders do not come prepared to begin where the kindergarten standards left off. How do the other teachers do it all?"

"Whoa, Shaundra! I never meant to overwhelm you with the standard guides. I meant for you to review them so that when you met with the other first-grade teachers this summer, you would be up to speed understanding the standards. The other teachers spent the spring quarter looking at the newly adopted state standards for each of the disciplines. Their plan for the summer was to review the standards for overlapping concepts and to determine which units and lessons they could develop integrating the standards across the disciplines."

"How am I going to do that?" Shaundra asked.

"A strategy that we found worked well with fifth-grade teachers was to create a chart of the standards for each discipline and then look for similarities, even when different terms describe the big ideas. For instance, the science standards address science as inquiry. When you read the description for what is meant by inquiry, and examine the specific indicators for your grade level on what inquiry means, you should see an overlap between those descriptions and the problem-solving standard in mathematics. Also, in the language arts standards, for instance, the students are expected to conduct research, pose questions, and gather, evaluate and synthesize data. The fifth-grade teachers saw a link between these skills and what is described as the history and nature of science in the science standards."

"So, basically what you're saying is, the more I can familiarize myself with the individual standards for each of the disciplines, the easier it may be for me to make the links across them," Shaundra said. "Then in our upcoming planning meetings we can begin to write lessons that incorporate standards from two or more disciplines. Wow, I'm so relieved! The idea of integration encourages me. I may just be able to address all of these standards in one year."

Introduction

Being able to "do it all" can be an insurmountable task even for veteran teachers. Teachers are faced with meeting national standards each day for the four major disciplines of science, mathematics, language arts, and social studies and standards for the arts, physical fitness, and technology at least weekly. How can one address the standards for each of the disciplines without treating them like a "to do" list? What does it mean to integrate the disciplines? Is it possible to integrate, and if so, how can it happen so that science is not neglected? In this chapter we help you to

- ✦ explore the meaning of integrated learning;
- ✦ examine two integration methods that support inquiry; and
- ✦ understand the unique challenges of integrated planning, teaching, and learning.

What Is Integration?

It is not uncommon for classroom teachers of the same grade level to plan units together—much like the teachers in our opening scenario. It becomes problematic, however, when teachers are all using the same term, but understand them to have different meanings and intentions. Integration of the disciplines should not be confused with planning topic-based units. At the primary level the problem arises when teachers decide that everyone will use dinosaurs as the topic for the upcoming unit, or when they all try to use a topic like pumpkins when the seasons change from summer to autumn. Using a topic to teach each subject is *not* the same as planning integrated lessons.

Integrated instruction also requires more than a superficial understanding of the standards for each discipline. Shaundra, the teacher in the opening scenario, was correct to begin reviewing the standards documents the principal gave her upon signing her teaching contract. A quick review, however, is not enough. One should be able to understand what is meant by the term "standards" for each discipline and what subdivisions are found under those standards. Does one discipline follow the standards with grade-range benchmarks and then more specific grade-level indicators, or do they simply provide generalizations for grade-level ranges below the standards? Having an understanding of how each discipline organizes their standards helps in looking for recurring big ideas or concepts across the disciplines.

In the literature, integrated instruction is also referred to as *cross-curricular* or *thematic instruction* (Vogt, 1995; Holdren, 1994). Integrated instruction or "thematic instruction seeks to put the teaching of cognitive skills such as reading, mathematics, science, and writing in the context of a real-world subject that is both specific enough to be practical, and broad enough to allow creative exploration" (McDonough, 2001). Therefore, integrated instruction requires choosing a key concept for a theme, which sets a clear focus for all instruction and learning. A good example of a key concept is *pollution. Pollution is considered any contamination of the air, water, or land that affects the environment in an unwanted way.* This key concept is developed in the 4–E Feature Lesson A. It does as Vogt has suggested when describing the use of key concepts in thematic instruction. "This key concept guides all activities and lessons, and the reading selections emerge naturally from it. It is expected, by the end of the theme, that all students will begin to internalize, build upon, and transfer this key concept to their own lives" (Vogt, 1995).

Successfully integrated lessons require the writing of clear and succinct concept statements. A novice teacher may need to work on several lessons within the individual disciplines until he/she has gained experience with the standards for each of the disciplines to make the leap to integration. Planning and delivering lessons for only one discipline helps the teacher personally struggle with the interpretation of the standard, allows the teacher to thoughtfully apply the individual standards within a lesson, and by reflecting on the lessons after they're taught, provides feedback on how the students struggled with the concepts and where the misconceptions may remain. Being aware of children's misconceptions in individual disciplines may help to focus the key concept statement of an integrated lesson and to avoid reinforcing student's misconceptions.

The key to successful integration is not to *force* it. If the links across the disciplines are not evident as the lesson is being developed, do not add an extra task just to address a given discipline's standard if it doesn't fit with the rest of the lesson. This strategy leaves the impression that you're treating the standards like a checklist, something to be covered to force integration. The beauty of creating an integrated lesson is that it allows for revisiting the content that may have been taught in isolation (as just one discipline) to show the links among and between the disciplines.

Approaches to Integration

Across the Standards Approach

Much like the team of fifth-grade teachers mentioned in the opening scenario, one way to purposely plan to integrate multiple disciplines within one lesson plan is to complete a Standards Similarity Analysis (Table 8.1). By first determining what was meant by standards for each discipline, and next, determining the indicators for those standards—what the children are expected to know and be able to do— it became evident that the standards could be classified into five categories: content, skills, technology, the nature of the discipline, and real-world connections.

TABLE 8.1 The Standards Similarity Analysis

Similarity		Disciplines			
	Science	Mathematics	Language Arts	Social Studies	Technology
Content	• Life • Physical • Earth/Space Science	• Algebra • Geometry • Numbers and operations	• Write, speak, and visually represent to create text • Range of materials and purposes for reading	• People, places, and environments • Power, authority and governance • Production, distribution and consumption	• Technology productivity tools
Skills	• Inquiry	• Measurement • Data Analysis and Probability • Problem Solving • Reasoning and Proof	• Research and inquiry • Reading strategies, language use, and conventions	• Individuals, groups, and institutions	• Technology research tools • Technology problem-solving and decision-making tools
Technology	• Technology			• Production, Distribution and consumption • Science, Technology, and Society	• Basic operations and concepts
The Nature of the Discipline	• History and nature	• Communication • Representation	• Purposes for spoken, written, and visual language	• Time, continuity, and change • Civic ideals and practices	• Social, ethical, and human issues • Technology communication tools
Real-World Connections	• Personal and social	• Connections	• Language diversity and competency	• Culture • Individual development and identity • Individuals, groups, and institutions • Global connections	• Technology problem-solving and decision-making tools

Analysis of the standards revealed that each discipline has unique content knowledge. In Table 8.1, the Standards Similarity Analysis, unique content is placed in the first row. Also, found within the standards are skills that at first glance may appear unique to the discipline, but upon careful examination, one may find similarities with the skills developed within another discipline. Overlapping skills can be addressed in an integrated lesson.

In many of the disciplines there is a standard that addressed the link between that discipline and technology. This is not to be confused with computer based technology, rather, technology as a term that is globally defined as: *any manmade invention that alters or changes our environment and/or has impacted the environment in some way.* In mathematics and language arts, technology as defined above is not addressed and is left blank in Table 8.1. These disciplines do, however, as part of their underlying principles behind their standards, address the power of computer-based technology in learning. For instance, the National Council of Teachers of Mathematics (NCTM) states: "Technology enriches the range and quality of investigations by providing a means of viewing mathematical ideas from multiple perspectives" (NCTM, 1991).

A careful examination of the standards for each of the disciplines also revealed that there are concepts, which reflect the history of the discipline; that is, the role the discipline has played in the development of humanity. These standards imply that there is something inherent in the nature of the discipline that should be developed through the experiences and activities we provide our students in our lessons.

The last *similarity category* is the real-world connections emphasized within each of the disciplines. In life, it is rare that we encounter a specific event or phenomenon whereby the standards of only one discipline can be used to explain the event. It is essential when planning an integrated lesson to understand how the disciplines are applied in the real world, and to provide a real-world context for those lessons.

For integration to occur, it is important to dig deeper within each discipline to identify specific benchmarks or indicators that reveal the expectations for each grade level when applying that standard. Using the *Across the Standards* approach to integration, one content area is chosen as the vehicle for addressing standards within each of

Scientists use many different tools.

the disciplines. A concept within that discipline is identified and then the following questions are asked:

+ To what extent will the concept be developed by this lesson?
+ Do I need to build in a discipline-specific activity to develop a rich understanding of the concept, before I apply it across an integrated lesson?
+ Will this integrated lesson develop the understanding of the concept?
+ Is this lesson going to reinforce the student's understanding of a concept previously learned?
+ While I'm teaching this concept within a given discipline, what similar standards will I address from the other content areas?

4–E Feature Lesson A (page 268) models an *Across the Standards* approach for integration. A specific science concept is identified as the *key concept.* However, while developing the key concept *pollution,* standards from mathematics, language arts, social studies, and technology can be reinforced. The *Standards Similarity Analysis* (Table 8.1) selected standards from each of the other disciplines that were addressed within this lesson. These standards are listed in Table 8.2. Before you look at that list, read the lessons and go to the national standards for each of the disciplines provided by the National Council for Teachers of Mathematics (NCTM), the National Council of English Teachers (NCET), the National Council for the Social Studies (NCSS), and the National Educational Technology Standards (NETS). Which standards from those disciplines do you think were used to support concept development through this integrated lesson plan? Did your selection agree with those identified in Table 8.2?

The *Across the Standards* approach used in the 4–E Feature Lesson A explicitly developed the standards for science, while the standards for the other disciplines were implicit. Oftentimes implicit planning leads to disagreements. While the authors of the integrated lesson plan believe the standards identified in Table 8.2 were also reinforced through the lesson, another reader of the written plan may not readily see that link, or may see where a different standard is developed. It is important when using this approach and sharing lessons with other teachers that you walk others through the lesson, clarifying where and how you see the links to the other disciplines within the lesson.

Driving Question Approach

Integrated instruction is an interdisciplinary approach to teaching that combines knowledge from different disciplines and encourages students to: examine a topic deeply, read from a variety of sources and materials, and engage in a variety of activities. Often the topic is presented in an extended time frame allowing students to engage in inquiry that leads the student to a deeper understanding of the topic and its connection to their world. Well-designed, integrated, interdisciplinary units set high standards and expectations for all students (NCREL, 2003).

> It is taken for granted, apparently, that in time students will see for themselves how things fit together. Unfortunately, the reality of the situation is that they tend to learn what we teach. If we teach connectedness and integration, they learn that. If we teach

(text continues on page 273)

TABLE 8.2 Standards Addressed in 4–E Feature Lesson A: Across the Standards Approach

Similarity		Disciplines			
	Science	Mathematics	Language Arts	Social Studies	Technology
Content	• All organisms cause changes in their environment where they live. Some of these changes are detrimental to themselves or other organisms, whereas others are beneficial. • Humans depend on both their natural and their constructed environment. Humans change environments in ways that can either be beneficial or detrimental for other or organisms, including the humans themselves.	• *Algebra* Understand patterns, relations, and functions; represent and analyze patterns and functions, using words, tables, and graphs. • *Geometry* Use visualization, spatial reasoning, and geometric modeling to solve problems—recognize geometric ideas and relationships and apply them to other disciplines and to problems that arise in the classroom or in everyday life.	• *Range of Materials and Purposes for Reading* Students read a wide range of print and non-print texts to build an understanding of texts, of themselves, and of the cultures of the United States and the world; to acquire new information; to respond to the needs and demands of society and the workplace; and for personal fulfillment. Among these texts are fiction and nonfiction, classic and contemporary works.	• *People, Places, and Environments* In the early grades, young learners draw upon immediate personal experiences as a basis for exploring geographic concepts and skills. They also express interest in things distant and unfamiliar and have concern for the use and abuse of the physical environment.	• *Technology Productivity Tools* Students use productivity tools to collaborate in constructing technology enhanced models, preparing publications, and producing other creative works.
Skills	• Scientific investigations involve asking and answering a question and comparing the answer with what scientists already know about the world. • Scientists make the results of their investigations public; they describe the investigations in ways that enable others to repeat the investigations.	• *Measurement* Apply appropriate techniques, tools, and formulas to determine measurements; develop strategies for estimating the perimeters, areas, and volumes of irregular shapes. • *Data Analysis and Probability* Formulate questions that can be addressed with data and collect, organize, and display relevant data to answer them—collect data using observations, surveys, and experiments; represent data using tables and graphs such as line plots, bar graphs, and line graphs; Develop and evaluate inferences and predictions that are based on	• *Research and Inquiry* Students conduct research on issues and interests by generating ideas and questions, and by posing problems. They gather, evaluate, and synthesize data from a variety of sources (e.g., print and non-print texts, artifacts, people) to communicate their discoveries in ways that suit their purpose and audience. • *Reading strategies, Language Use, and Conventions* Students adjust their use of spoken, written, and visual language (e.g., conventions, style, vocabulary) to communicate effectively with a		• *Technology Research Tools* Students use technology to process data and report results.

(continued)

TABLE 8.2 Standards Addressed in 4–E Feature Lesson A: Across the Standards Approach (continued)

Similarity	Disciplines				
	Science	*Mathematics*	*Language Arts*	*Social Studies*	*Technology*
Skills (continued)		data—propose and justify conclusions and predictions that are based on data and design studies to further investigate the conclusions or predictions. • *Problem Solving* Select and use various types of reasoning and methods of proof.	variety of audiences and for different purposes.		
Technology	• Abilities of Technological Design			• *Science, Technology, and Society* Young children can learn how technologies form systems and how their daily lives are intertwined with a host of technologies. Young children can study how basic technologies such as ships, automobiles, and airplanes have evolved and how we have used technology, such as air conditioning, dams, and irrigation to modify our physical environment.	
The Nature of the Discipline	• Although men and women using scientific inquiry have learned much about the objects, events, and phenomena in nature, much more remains to be understood. Science will never be finished.	• *Communication* Organize and consolidate their mathematical thinking through communication. Communicate their mathematical thinking coherently and clearly to peers, teachers, and others; Analyze and evaluate		• *Civic Ideals and Practices* During these years, children also experience views of citizenship in other times and places through stories and drama.	• *Technology Communication Tools* Students use a variety of media and formats to communicate information and ideas effectively to multiple audiences.

TABLE 8.2 (continued)

Similarity	Disciplines				
	Science	Mathematics	Language Arts	Social Studies	Technology
The Nature of the Discipline (continued)		the mathematical thinking and strategies of others. • *Representation Standard* Create and use representations to organize, record, and communicate mathematical ideas. Use representations to model and interpret physical, social, and mathematical phenomena.			
Real-World Connections	• Changes in environments can be natural or influenced by humans. Some changes are good, some are bad, and some are neither good nor bad. Pollution is a change in the environment that can influence the health, survival, or activities of organisms, including humans. • People continue inventing new ways of doing things, solving problems, and getting work done. New ideas and inventions often affect other people; sometimes the effects are good and sometimes they are bad. It is helpful to try to determine in advance how ideas and inventions will affect other people.	• *Connections* Recognize and use connections among mathematical ideas. Understand how mathematical ideas interconnect and build on one another to produce a coherent whole. Recognize and apply mathematics in contexts outside of mathematics.			

Pollution Search: Across the Standards Approach

GRADE LEVEL: 3–4

DISCIPLINE: Life Science Plus Mathematics Language Arts Social Studies and National Educational Technology Standards (NETS) for Students

Concept to Be Invented: Pollution is considered any contamination of the air, water, or land that affects the environment in an unwanted way.

Science Attitudes to Nurture: Curiosity, open-mindedness, cooperation with others

Materials Needed: Dr. Seuss's, *The Cat in the Hat Comes Back* (New York: Random House, 1958), large poster paper, white board or chalk board, clipboard with paper, computer with spreadsheet software, graphing software such as *Graph Master* by Tom Snyder Productions(optional), word processing software (optional).

Safety Precautions: Remind students to sit quietly, keeping hands to themselves during the reading of the story. Be sure proper student-to-adult ratio is followed when taking students on a pollution search in the neighborhood around the school. Remind students to always walk, not run, in classroom and outside in field study area.

Exploration *Which process skills will be used?*

Observing, predicting, communicating, problem solving, designing an experiment

Ask the students to gather around you as you read *The Cat in The Hat Comes Back* by Dr. Seuss. As you read the story, use the poster paper or white board to write the story's events. Ask the children to summarize what happens at each stage of the story.

1. The cat shows up at the house.
2. The cat takes a bath and leaves a bathtub ring of pink stuff.
3. The cat uses a dress to get the pink stuff off the tub and ends up getting it all over the dress.
4. The cat gets the pink stuff on the wall and uses shoes to clean it off.
5. And so on.

Explanation

Use the sequence of story events to have a discussion about how a story like this might be real. Be sure to refer to the list of events as you ask the students questions such as:

✦ Out in the playground when people just throw their trash around, we consider that behavior polluting our environment. What in the story might represent pollution?
✦ Where did the pollution come from?
✦ How did the cat deal with the pollution?

- ✦ Did that help solve the pollution problem?
- ✦ What did the little cats do? Did they help with the pollution problem?
- ✦ Who finally cleaned up the pollution and how did that happen?

Use the students' answers to make a summary statement about pollution. Ask the students to complete this sentence starter: When we put things into the air, water, or land, which affect our environment in an unwanted way, this is considered _____ (pollution); or Pollution is _____.

Expansion *Which process skills will be used?*

Observing, planning an investigation, recording and analyzing data, comparing and contrasting, problem solving, drawing conclusions, communicating findings

Prepare the class to go on a *local pollution sources search.* As a class, the teacher will remind the students about the story and how the "pink stuff" spread, making a mess of the house. Ask them if the pink stuff was pollution, contaminating the house. What might that look like if it contaminated the water? The air? Ask the students that since we don't have to worry about a *Cat in the Hat,* what other ways might *we* pollute our surroundings? Collect a list of these suggestions. Draw two intersecting circles on the board. Label the *inside* circle and the *outside* circle, and label the intersecting area of the two circles, *both.* Ask the children to predict where each of the suggested pollutants may be found—inside, outside, or both—and have a student write that pollutant(s) in the appropriate circle.

Tell the students that this is a Venn diagram and ask them to look at the diagram again. Ask them if there is another way they could group pollution besides inside, outside, and both? Lead them toward these three groups: air, water, and land. Make three new intersecting circles. Label them Air, Water, and Land (see Figure A). Ask the students to take the items from their previous list and now place them in the appropriate new circles. Tell them they will use these categories to search for evidence of pollution—called pollutants—as they work in teams in the neighborhood around the school.

Assign student teams to a field study area within the neighborhood around the school. Have adults supervise each student team. Assign cooperative roles to each of the students (i.e., reporter, recorder, etc.). Direct the student teams to walk around the school neighborhood looking for pollution or pollutants and to record what they see on a data sheet. Figure B is a data sheet to record the field data. When the students encounter litter that can be collected in their neighborhood, instruct them to first record the data, then using rubber gloves and garbage bags, collect the litter for disposal once they return to school.

When the students return to the classroom have them work in the same teams at the computers to record their data into a spreadsheet. The students should be able to graph the data they collect. Figure C provides an example of how that data could be organized for graphing and a sample graph.

Provide the student teams time to log their data into the spreadsheets. If the class is familiar with graphing software such as *Graph Master,* have them use their data to create a bar graph of the pollution types. If no software is available, provide them time to create a bar graph of the pollution types versus number of examples of pollution. Use

(continued)

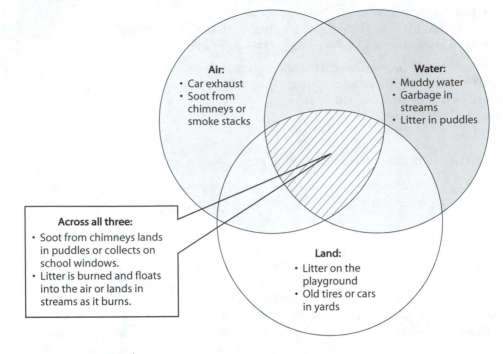

FIGURE A   Venn Diagram

Field Data

Name of Pollution Source	Where It Was Found	Size or Amount	Type
Fast-food wrapper	In playground by swing set	1 wrapper	Land
Soot from chimney	Coming from house on Elm Street	Watched chimney for 5 minutes and soot was coming out entire time.	Air
Oil slick	Floating on the surface of a puddle on Grant Street	Since it was an irregular size, we estimated the area of the oil slick to be about 15 cm x 22 cm.	Water
Candy wrappers	In front of house on Lee Place	5 wrappers	Land

FIGURE B   Field Data

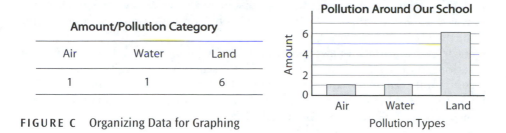

Amount/Pollution Category		
Air	Water	Land
1	1	6

FIGURE C Organizing Data for Graphing

the individual team data to create a bar graph of the entire class data. Discuss with the class the pollution types and the sources for them. Solicit potential solutions to eliminate the pollutant. Have each team write an informational story to be shared in a newsletter that will be distributed to the local community about the data they collected and the results of the data analysis. Be sure each team includes data to back up their story. Ask each team to offer suggestions on what the students in the school can do to reduce pollution and what members of the local community can do as well.

Science in Personal and Social Perspectives

- ✦ What suggestions can you provide members of the local community to reduce the amount of pollution your team found around the school?
- ✦ What kinds of things can you do to eliminate a pollution source around the school? Around your home?

Science and Technology

- ✦ Did you identify any pollution sources that were originally made to make a person's life easier? If so, what were they?
- ✦ Do you think we can live without this technology? If not, do you have any suggestions as to how it can be changed to make less pollution?

Science as Inquiry

- ✦ What other things or events in our life can we collect data on to make informed decisions?
- ✦ Does it help to follow a sequence of events to figure out how to solve problems? Why?

History and Nature of Science

- ✦ Are scientists the only people that collect data and make informed decisions based on the analysis of that data? In what other careers is the ability to collect and analyze data important?

Evaluation

Upon completing these activities, the students will be able to:

- ✦ describe a source of pollution and provide a plan for how that source could be eliminated or at least reduced.

(continued)

+ identify the pollution sources when given a picture of an area with obvious problems due to pollution, or speculate as to possible sources if none are found within the picture.
+ create and distribute a news story to the local school community explaining the various sources of pollution found around the school and what all members of the community can do to reduce the amount of pollution; use graphs and charts that identify the location, the types, amounts, and size of the pollutants found from their *local pollution search* to backup the information in their story.

WHAT Research SAYS

Integration and the Curriculum

Integration of instruction, thematic approach, synergistic teaching, or interdisciplinary curriculum are all terms which relate to a growing understanding of the complexity of today's problems and the need for students to engage in an educational experience that integrates a broad knowledge base. An integrated curriculum is one that links subject areas and meaningful learning experiences to support a greater understanding of conceptual relationships.

The term integrated curriculum is used synonymously with interdisciplinary curriculum. Interdisciplinary curriculum is defined in the *Dictionary of Education* as a "curriculum organization which cuts across subject-matter lines to focus upon comprehensive life problems or broad based areas of study that brings together the various segments of the curriculum into meaningful association" (Lake, 1994). This provides the student with a classroom linked to language arts, social studies, mathematics, science, music and art in such a way that knowledge and skills are developed and applied to solve real life problems. This definition supports the view that an integrated curriculum is "an educational approach that prepares children for lifelong learning" (Lake, 1994).

The debate surrounding curriculum integration has continued well over fifty years. The growth of scientific knowledge, changes in teacher education requirements, and the fragmentation of teaching schedules have made many teachers feel that they will "never be able to teach it all" or that "each year more and more material is added to the curriculum." The increased pace of today's classroom coupled with increased external pressures on schools to provide a workforce with the ability to problem solve in a global environment is one of the motivations behind the development of an integrated curriculum. "More and more schools are coming to an understanding that facts cannot be taught in isolation and are moving toward a more constructivist view of learning, which values in-depth knowledge of subjects" (Lake, 1994).

In the science classroom, an interdisciplinary curriculum may pair the cognitive processes of predicting, classifying, identifying cause and effect, sequencing, inference, and summarizing with similar processes presented in the context of language arts, social studies and mathematics. Greene (1991) found that in the science classroom, an interdisciplinary curriculum motivated learning and improved attitudes toward science. Greene determined that the cognitive processes of science along with student-centered planning for learning created an environment in which students had higher attendance, higher levels of homework completion, and a better conceptual understanding of the connections of science to other content areas.

separation and discontinuity, that is what they learn. To suppose otherwise would be incongruous. (Humphreys 1981, p. xi)

Brain research indicates that to develop long-term memory or a true understanding of concepts, the information acquired must make sense and have real-life meaning to the student. Content integration provides a framework that assists students in making connections between the new information and the previously learned information. This allows for deeper understanding and concept formation. This is not a new idea. John Dewey, in 1938, warned that isolation in all forms is to be avoided and connectedness would better support the processes of learning (McREL, 2001).

Science and language arts provide ample opportunities to interpret and communicate ideas through reading, writing and predicting, inferring, comparing and contrasting, and examining cause and effect relationships. "Many of the process skills needed for science inquiry are similar to reading skills, and when taught together reinforce each other" (Krueger & Sutton, 2001, p. 52). The integration of reading and writing as a component of inquiry-based science has been shown to increase vocabulary not only in science content but in fluency as measured on standard language tests (Krueger & Sutton, 2001). Science journals and reports which communicate observations and data collected through inquiry serve as a natural fit for improving reading and writing competence. The integration of mathematics through the drawing of graphs and charts to represent collected data adds value to the math skills students are learning elsewhere in the curriculum. Integrate the use of technology to access, gather, store, retrieve and organize data, and the teacher is not only able to meet standards for language arts, science and mathematics but technology as well. "Technology can help teachers reach all students with inquiry-based science content and processes that reflect the connected and digital world" in which today's students reside (Krueger & Sutton, 2001, p. 70).

Student success in reading can be a great motivator to stimulate reading, writing, and oral communication as the student pursues science inquiry in greater depth. Teachers should use a wide variety of literature, including trade books, texts, fiction, extensive illustrations and non-fiction to cover science topics in greater detail to motivate and engage students to speak, ask questions, explore and engage in science inquiry. Helping students make connections across the curriculum is an important learning outcome for early childhood and middle grade students. Integration of content can enable students to develop a broader understanding of concepts and improve teaching and learning for all.

Sources: Adapted from K. Lake. *School Improvement Series—Research You Can Use: Integrated Curriculum* (Northwest Regional Educational Laboratory, Office of Educational Research and Improvement (OERI), U.S. Department of Education. #RP91002001.May 1994). Retrieved online October 10, 2003, www.nwrel.org/scpd/sirs/8/c016.html. L. Greene, "Science-Centered Curriculum in Elementary School," *EDThoughts: What We Know about Science Teaching and Learning* (Aurora, CO: Mid-continent Research for Education and Learning, 2001).

Questioning is a basic process of science; it is a basic process of inquiry and a natural result of human curiosity. When we question, we progress into unknowns and uncertainties; we develop hypotheses and test ideas and find solutions. Questioning allows us to extend our knowledge and share similar goals of inquiry, observation, problem solving, experimentation, and communication across content areas.

Planning integrated learning experiences using a problem-based learning model helps students develop scientific thinking for solving problems in real life. The connection of the lessons to the students' real life creates an understanding of the commonalities between and among diverse topics, develops the students' ability to perceive new relationships, and provides a motivational tool for learning (McREL, 2001).

Teachers developing problem-based learning environments often use a *driving question* to help support integration across content areas. A driving question is a single question, which will lead the student to investigate the problem from a variety of viewpoints and through inquiry, build the science concept being studied.

One teacher in a fourth-grade classroom posed the following question to her students: "How do human beings and industry change an environment over time?" In past conversations with her students, the teacher realized that her students did not understand the relationship of the Ohio River to the environment, industry, history, and society of the community in which the students lived. Creating cooperative teams of students to answer the driving question, the teacher provided an opportunity for her students to understand the environmental issues surrounding a large river, and to see the impact the river had historically on the economy of the community as well as the societal impact of immigration to the region. Students were supplied computers and scientific probeware to measure flow rates, pH, and oxygen levels and they maintained a field journal of observations concerning the riverbank area over the course of a school year. Math skills were strengthened as the teams of students charted information from field trips onto posters that described the monthly changes of the river over the school year. During critical points in the school year, predictions were made concerning the anticipated changes in the river and what impact the changes might have on industries, recreational pursuits and families that live downstream.

By planning integrated lessons, teachers provide real-world context for learning.

As a teacher or team of teachers develops the unit, a series of standards-based essential questions should be formed to frame the process of interdisciplinary learning. Assessment goals should align with these essential questions.

The *Driving Question Approach* in the previous example addressed standards from the content areas of mathematics, science, language arts, and social studies. In the *Driving Question Approach* to integration the teachers first identified the driving question. Then teachers used a *Standards Similarity Analysis* (see Table 8.1) to predict from which of the disciplines the students may have to draw on to solve the problem. While writing the lessons, the teachers anticipated which of the standards from each discipline would help solve the problem. They guided the students through the inquiry so that those standards were specifically addressed. Concepts from across the disciplines were explicitly developed.

4–E Feature Lesson B represents a model for the *Driving Question Approach to integration* with slight modifications. This is accomplished by identifying specific concepts from each of the disciplines that the teacher will help the students to understand in the Exploration and Expansion activities. Any questions asked during the Explanation phase should guide students to develop each of the desired concepts. To solve the problem, the students complete their public communication on pollution within the community by considering the driving question. This action also makes specific the knowledge needed for each discipline.

Challenges to Integration

As schools move to a more constructivist view of learning, greater value is placed on in-depth knowledge and less on the teaching of isolated facts. Twenty-first century students will require flexibility in their ability to apply knowledge and manage the complex systems of global interdependence (Damian, 2002). Children do not encounter problems in the real world that can be solved with isolated bits of information. Providing students with learning experiences that require the application of rich, contextualized understanding of content knowledge from across the disciplines should not be planned for in your classroom.

Teachers who use an integrated approach for meeting content standards describe one common barrier—*time*. Planning and teaching an integrated curriculum requires more time. Teachers working together to build integrated lessons need a common planning time to explore themes, locate resources, discuss student needs, and coordinate daily schedules. Locating an effective and coherent theme/key concept on which all agree can be challenging. When teachers work together to identify content knowledge, skills, standards, and themes with appropriate connections to the content areas, the time issue is reduced by the gains found through the division of labor with teamwork. Remember Shaundra in our opening scenario. When working in isolation, she found the task of addressing all of the standards overwhelming. Grade-level teams, working together, can more easily identify the areas of integration that may not be so obvious when working in isolation. The efforts of good planning, flexible schedules, and an empowered team of teachers can produce outstanding lessons that engage learners in inquiry.

When teachers work together in grade-level teams, they can identify areas of integration that may not be so obvious when working alone.

Pollution Search: Driving Question Approach

GRADE LEVEL: 3–4
DISCIPLINE: Life
Science
Plus
Mathematics
Language Arts
Social Studies
and National Educational Technology
Standards (NETS) for Students

Inquiry Question: Does our school neighborhood have a pollution problem?

Concept to Be Invented:

1. Science—*Pollution* is considered any contamination of the air, water, or land that affects the environment in an unwanted way.
2. Mathematics—Data can be communicated through the use of bar graphs.
3. Language Arts—Fictional children's stories can be used to communicate the negative impact man's actions have on the environment.
4. Social Studies—Children can be advocates for social change by the way in which they communicate the analysis of data collected in a walk through their community.
5. Technology—The computer can be used as a tool to communication information.

Exploration *Which process skills will be used?*

Observing, predicting, communicating, problem solving, designing an experiment

Ask the students to gather around you as you read *The Cat in The Hat Comes Back* by Dr. Seuss. As you read the story, use the poster paper or white board to write the story's events. Ask the children to summarize what happens at each stage of the story.

1. The cat shows up at the house.
2. The cat takes a bath and leaves a bathtub ring of pink stuff.
3. The cat uses a dress to get the pink stuff off the tub and ends up getting it all over the dress.
4. The cat gets the pink stuff on the wall and uses shoes to clean it off.
5. And so on.

Explanation

What is the main idea? How will the main idea be constructed? The main ideas are the concept statements listed under Concepts to Be Invented.

Use the sequence of story events for a discussion about how a story like this might be real. Be sure to refer to the list of events as you ask the students questions such as:

✦ When people on the playground just throw their trash around, we consider that behavior polluting our environment. What in the story might represent pollution?
✦ Where did the pollution come from?
✦ How did the cat deal with the pollution?

- ✦ Did that help solve the pollution problem?
- ✦ What did the little cats do? Did they help with the pollution problem?
- ✦ How did the make-believe story show that in reality everyone can be a cause of pollution and everyone can help clean-up pollution?
- ✦ Who finally cleaned up the pollution and how did that happen?
- ✦ What might we do to look for sources of pollution in our school community?
- ✦ What kind of data might we collect on pollution sources and how might we communicate the results of the data we collected?

Use the students' answers to make a summary statement about pollution. Ask the students to complete this sentence starter: When we put things into the air, water, or land, which affect our environment in an unwanted way, this is considered _____ (pollution); or Pollution is _____.

Expansion   *Which process skills will be used?*

Observing, planning, an investigation, recording and analyzing data, comparing and contrasting, solving problems, drawing conclusions, communicating findings

Use the following summary activity to make the integration explicit after the expansion activities have been completed.

Once the public display of the results of the pollution search in the school neighborhood have been completed, reconvene the class and ask the students to reflect on all of their experiences. Suggested questions to ask students to make the connection to each of the disciplines addressed in the lesson include:

- ✦ What is pollution? *(Designed to address the science concept.)*
- ✦ What math skill did you need to communicate or show what you found? *(Looks for an understanding that data can be communicated using a bar graph.)*
- ✦ Who was your audience when writing about the results of your pollution search around the school neighborhoods? Why was it important to keep your audience in mind? *(Designed to address the identified language arts concept.)*
- ✦ In our social studies class we learned that throughout time people will endure great hardships to bring about a social change, such as the pilgrims coming to America to start a new society that would allow them to practice freedoms they did not have while living in Europe. How do you think the activities we just completed show that you can become an advocate for social change? How do you think you might have started some changes in the local community? *(Designed to address the identified social studies concept.)*

As demonstrated in 4–E Feature Lessons A and B, one can "do it all" without making the task overwhelming or insurmountable. Essential to integration is making the decision on whether it will be implicit, as the Across the Standards Approach to Integration suggests, or explicit as explained by the Driving Question Approach.

Video Explorations *Integration*

Video Summary

Science lessons often take a back seat to the teaching of mathematics and reading, which are heavily emphasized in many schools. This does not have to be the case if time is spent in planning teaching units that span the disciplines. This may be done by posing a driving question, with the expectation that students will pull from a variety of disciplines to answer it. Or, one may look across the standards for the discipline, seeking common threads and teaching those within the context of a science lesson. There are many resources available that tie science concepts with literature, social studies and mathematics. Spending some time in planning, before one is ever up in front of the students, makes the task of addressing the standards for *all* disciplines on a daily basis manageable.

Tips for Viewing, Objectives, or What to Watch for

As you watch this video, make note of the following:

✦ The need to make the task of addressing all disciplines within a school day less daunting,

✦ The use of a driving question which requires an understanding of multiple disciplines to solve a problem,

✦ The ability to look across the standards for every discipline to look for similar ideas or concepts that can be addressed in a variety of contexts,

✦ The importance of real-world connections to the classroom content.

Questions for Exploration

1. As was noted in the video, trying to teach every discipline on a daily basis can be overwhelming. What can you do in your planning to eliminate some of this anxiety?

2. What would you consider a good example of a driving question that would cause the students to pull from a variety of disciplines to solve the problem?

3. Do you think everything you teach will have a real-world connection? Why or why not? What strategies might you use to make these connections for your learners?

Activity for Application

Using a lesson you prepared on a science concept, read over your state and/or national standards for two or more other disciplines such as language arts and social studies. Knowing what you expect the students to do in your science lesson, are there any standards within those other two disciplines that you can teach while doing your science lesson? If so, identify those in your lesson. If not, did you see any standards within the other two disciplines that you could build into your science lesson so they are taught as well? Try changing one of your current science lessons so that the standards of two or more disciplines are addressed within the one lesson. Using this newly integrated lesson, develop some questions that you will ask your students as they participate in the lesson so that connections are made between the concepts studied and the real-world application.

Science Comes to Life for Students and Teachers

by Debby Todd

Grade 5, Slate Hill Elementary, Worthington, Ohio

Science in the elementary school needs to leap off of the textbook pages and lab instructions to come in to the lives of the children. Our students need to know science is a continuing story of discovery, inventions, history, art, music, movement, and new theories. Children need to be made aware that science is found in all areas of their life by immersing them in projects that will encompass all of the academic areas.

When a child in my classroom begins to study ecosystems and positive/negative impacts on ecosystems, he/she should be filled with curiosity and wonder. Where did these ideas come from? Who were the people who came up with these ideas? Why did they think about them? How did they use them? How did they impact the world? What is their story?

In the classroom I have found four critical elements that support achievement on science standards and encourage inquiry learning of every child.

1. Make all children think critically.
2. Tell a good story through literature including fiction/nonfiction and writing.
3. Bombard their senses through the integration of all academic and related arts areas.
4. Give them ownership.

Science is definitely an area where all students can be included. Developing lessons with critical thinking components is key to making the lesson flexible enough to·be tiered when integrating math, social studies, reading, and writing. This approach meets the needs of all levels of students. All assignments require every child to meet certain minimum standards. Every assignment integrates two or more of the following areas: math, social studies, reading, and writing. All students then have an opportunity and are encouraged to extend their learning with additional challenges that are provided. These challenges are higher in thinking skills not in the length of the assignment. This component of choice and ownership gives the children pride and a sense of accomplishment when lessons are completed. The students become very motivated to succeed and try another level.

Reading exposes students to science concepts and the people behind those ideas through a story. Here they have an opportunity to experience the hopes, dreams, joys, and disappointments of life. They see conflicting points of view, choices being made, and they think critically. They learn about the impact that science has had on human beings and the integrity of people to use or not use a newly developed idea. They make the idea their own and decide what position to take—pro or con.

Bombarding the children's senses through related arts programs allows me to bring many abstract concepts into the child's real world and creates an opportunity for brain development by making use of the children's multiple intelligences. All the teachers of the school work with the related arts teachers to support and extend many of the lessons throughout the year. Following is one example of how my colleagues and I accomplish this goal.

When the students begin their study of ecosystems and populations, the art teacher presents lessons on animal structure, sculpture, and design; the music department teaches how animal movement and behavior can be represented through music and also shows music of different geographical areas; and the physical education teacher uses physical activities and games that imitate animal movement. The kids use these experiences in class to enhance their study of animal movement, adaptations, and survival in different ecosystems. The children have many personal experiences from these areas to use for discussion/activities in the classroom.

In art class they create an animal sculpture that is displayed in the school and in the classroom. They incorporate music in an assigned hyper-studio research project on ecosystems/adaptations for enhancement. My students have ownership and control of their learning. I have found that these activities increase their motivation to achieve specific goals for the classroom and increase inquiry attitude/enthusiasm in the classroom.

Chapter Summary

Being responsible for teaching all of the disciplines can look like an insurmountable task. Chapter 8 encouraged you to look at it as an asset. Having to teach all of the disciplines provides you the luxury of addressing standards from a variety of disciplines within a single lesson plan. The integration of the standards across the disciplines can be done implicitly through an *Across the Standards Approach,* or explicitly using a *Driving Question Approach.* The differences between the two approaches as defined and modeled in this chapter make our task of having to teach the standards of each discipline within a school year less daunting and quite doable. And most importantly, for the learners, it does not leave the connections among and between the disciplines to happenstance. Purposeful, well planned, contextualized learning allow the learners to confront problems as they see them in the real world.

Discussion Questions

1. How is an integrated lesson different from a topic-based unit?

2. Why do you think it is important to understand how each discipline organizes its standards?

3. Do the different disciplines such as mathematics, language arts, or social studies define the term *standards* differently? Why or how?

4. Examine your state standards for the content areas of science, mathematics, language arts, and social studies. Create a Standards Similarities Analysis. Compare yours to Table 8.1. Did you identify similar categories? Where do your state standards differ from the national standards?

5. Examine your state standards for the content areas of science, mathematics, language arts and social studies. What are the standards within each content area where technology could be used to help meet the content standard?

Build a Portfolio or E-Folio

1. Develop an integrated lesson using either an *Across the Standards* or *Driving Question* approach. Use a learning cycle format and identify the national and/or state standards for each discipline developed within the lesson. Teach the lesson and prepare a critique.

2. Select a science concept. Identify standards in at least two of the other major disciplines (math, social studies, language arts) that could also be developed while acquiring an understanding of the science concept selected. Using the NETS for Students, identify the technology tools that could be used to support the development of the science concept. Explain the relationship between the technology and the science standard addressed and the support for the science concept.

3. Write a position paper that demonstrates your understanding of a topic versus integrated/thematic lesson implementation in your classroom.

Safety: Creating a Safe, Efficient, Inquiry-Based Science Classroom

Nine-year-old Celeste sat reading the current issue of *Science Weekly* magazine. She was intrigued by an article about volcanoes. At the end of the article there was an activity on making a volcano. She read over the list of materials she needed. "Let's see," she said half out loud, "water I can get from the sink; in the bottom cupboard I can find a large baking pan; in the upper cabinet there's white vinegar, red food coloring, baking soda, and dishwashing liquid; in the first drawer on the right I should find the glue, masking tape, and scissors; and in the drawer on the left I can find the tinfoil and teaspoons." Celeste collected the materials from their storage areas and found the clay flower pot and the potting soil stored with the garden supplies. She checked over the materials list once again. "I think I have just about everything I need to make my own volcano," she announced to Sarah, her sister, who was passing by.

Ten-year-old Sarah looked over Celeste's shoulder at the magazine, then took a quick inventory of the materials Celeste had collected. "You forgot an empty tuna can," Sarah proclaimed. Celeste looked pensive for a moment and then shouted, "I know. I'll go to the recycling bin; I'll probably find just what I need in there!"

In a few moments Celeste was back with an empty tuna can. The two girls arranged the materials according to the directions in the magazine. They dumped the baking soda down the vent of their newly formed volcano. They mixed the vinegar, dishwashing liquid, water, and food coloring together. They were just about to pour the vinegar mixture into the vent when they were startled by a command from an adult: "STOP! What do you think will happen to you if you continue to look down that vent as you pour in the liquid? How are you going to protect your eyes and your clothing? And do you think it's a good idea to do that on the carpet?"

A surprised look came over their faces. "Oh, I'm sorry! I forgot about that," exclaimed Celeste. "I guess I was so excited after reading this article, I wanted to try it out as quickly as possible. Come on, Sarah. Let's move this off the carpet and then go get our goggles and put some old sweatshirts on before we make our volcano erupt."

Twanna returned from the supply table of the second-grade classroom with her hands full of materials.

"Did you get the paper, iron filings, hand lens, and magnets?" asked José.

"Yes I did," responded Twanna. "Let's get going."

"First, we need to be sure that we have plenty of room to perform this activity," said José, who was the manager and recorder for the science activity. "Are you sure that you have all the materials now, Twanna?"

Twanna, the materials manager for the activity, ran off to get a box. In a few minutes she returned from the supply table with a shoebox with one end cut out of it.

"Now," stated José, "lay the shoebox flat on the table and place the white paper over it. While I am doing that, Twanna, you need to pour some iron filings onto the second sheet of paper and examine them with your hand lens."

José went about his work while Twanna poured the filings from the glass jar onto the paper. "Wow!" she squealed. "Look at these things! They look like baby fish hooks and spears. Why are they so jagged?"

"Maybe they were simply made using a file on an old piece of pipe," said José. "My father makes them all the time when he puts new pipes in people's houses."

"Okay," said Twanna. "Are you ready for the filings now?"

"Sí," replied José. "Put them on the paper covering the shoebox now."

Twanna poured half her filings onto the paper and leaned forward to watch José, who picked up the large bar magnet and reached under the paper with it. "Watch to see what happens to the iron filings as I move the magnet around under the paper," he stated.

Both students were peering at the shoebox from opposite sides, their eyes on the same level as the filings. Just as José touched the lower right edge of the paper with the magnet, Twanna sneezed. Several of the iron filings sprayed into José's face, with a few of them entering his right eye. "Oowww!" shrieked José as he twirled from his chair, eyes buried in his hands. "Help me, please!!!"

How could this accident have been prevented? Were there any oversights that you noticed?

The Roosevelt sixth-grade class finally arrived at its destination, the old Wilson farm. As the bus rolled to a stop, Mr. J addressed the class: "Please remember our purpose here today. We are visitors to these animals' homes, so do not disturb them or the plants. In science we observe, measure, and record; we don't destroy or disrupt. Let's review our lesson plans for today's environmental science."

Following a five-minute clarification of the outcomes and precautions for the activity, Mr. J answered student questions. "Now for our safety guidelines," he stated. "Are there any questions concerning the safety items on your activity page, such as equipment operation, accident procedures, and the buddy system? Remember to stay with your buddy and never allow yourself to be separated from myself, Mr. P, Mrs. M, or Ms. O by more than 50 meters in this pasture area. If you need help in an emergency, please use your whistles. We adults were here earlier this morning checking out the area and found no hazards to worry about during this mapping exercise. But please be careful, just in case."

Mark and Alicia filed off the bus, confident of their purpose.

"Let's see," said Alicia. "We need to proceed 50 meters to the northeast to pick up our first marker, then 60 meters to the east for our second one. Do you have the map, compass, and whistle ready, Mark?"

"Yes, I do," replied Mark. "Put on your helmet."

As the students proceeded about 20 meters into the trees, they noticed that the terrain became more rugged and difficult to negotiate.

"See these little lines, Alicia?" remarked Mark, looking at the map. "They are the little hills we are walking over now. Another 30 meters and we should spot the first marker."

Just as they came over the next small hill, they both spotted a green plastic lid, partially hidden in the leaves.

"What is that?" asked Mark.

"I don't know. Let's check it out," replied Alicia.

As they cautiously lifted the lid, it broke into several pieces. Before them was a deep hole about 1 meter in diameter. It did not appear to have a bottom, although you could see water down about 2 meters.

"Let's explore it," suggested Alicia.

"No way! Let's get help!" replied Mark.

"Don't be silly," said Alicia. "We can check it out, finish our assignment and return before anyone knows. It could be our secret."

"What if the water is over your head?" persisted Mark. "How long could you stay afloat? I say we get help before some animal or another person falls into it."

"I guess you are right," agreed Alicia. "Use that whistle!"

What was the difference between the safety emphasis in this scenario and those in the first two? Can you credit the judgment simply to the older ages of the students?

Introduction

The first scenario could have taken place in any activity-based science class where the teacher gives the students time to engage in different kinds of inquiry at a science learning center. The girls were able to create the volcano immediately to satisfy their natural curiosity because they knew where the materials were stored and could easily obtain them. The person who reminded them of basic safety rules, however, was not their teacher; it was their mother.

The sisters know where everything is kept in their home. When they want materials for a project, such as building a volcano, they know where to get them. This same familiarity with materials storage that children feel in their homes, including what things they are allowed to touch and those they are to avoid, should occur in the classroom. Teaching children safe science practices and instilling in them a basic safety philosophy, as emphasized in the third scenario, are important for a safe and efficient activity-based science classroom.

This chapter uses two organizing questions: *What are the foreseeable hazards associated with valued educational activities?* and *What materials are necessary for educational activities?* This chapter helps you construct answers to these questions by

1. encouraging you to develop a philosophy of safe science teaching;
2. helping you understand your legal responsibilities;
3. helping you understand when and how to use safety equipment;
4. encouraging you to perform safety assessments of your classroom, lab, field site, or working space;
5. examining the tasks necessary for safe and efficient storage of equipment and materials;
6. suggesting methods for distributing, maintaining, and inventorying science materials.

Recommendations for Safe Science Experiences

The *National Science Education Standards* (NSES) (National Research Council, 1996) states that students at K–4, 5–8, and 9–12 levels should know and be able to "utilize safety procedures during scientific investigations." Teaching Standard D of the NSES states:

> Teachers of science design and manage learning environments that provide students with the time, space, and resources needed for learning science. In doing this, teachers ensure a safe working environment.

These standards provide a blueprint for improving the teaching and learning for *all* students based on an inquiry-based, student-centered curriculum. They also demand a greater understanding of applicable laws, codes, and professional standards for ensuring safety for students. To probe these standards in greater detail, you may wish to review the complete document on line at www.nap.edu/readingroom/books/nses.

With an inquiry-based science program, you are likely to encourage students to experiment, observe, and explore on their own, in addition to following your step-by-step instructions. However exploratory, the work must be done in a safe manner. There can be no experimentation with safety rules. When it comes to safety instructions and safe procedures, you need to be explicit and exacting. While safe practices support inquiry-based science, it is totally inappropriate to let students learn by trial and error when it comes to matters of safety. If you catch your students quoting you—you've succeeded.

For additional elementary science safety information from NSTA's *Exploring Science Safely* booklet (2002), check out this website: www.nsta.org/main/pdfs/store/pb166x1np.pdf. *The National Science Teachers Association Pathways to the Science Education Standards* reinforces the critical nature of inquiry in the learning process of elementary age students.

> The most important tool that children at the primary level use is observation. Curiosity makes students eager to explore by working with objects and asking questions. They learn about objects by grouping and ordering them. Such exploration provides early experiences in organizing data and understanding processes. (Lowery, 1997)

For additional information concerning the pathways document, check out this website: www.nsta.org.

Reasonable and prudent judgment dictates that students who participate in meaningful laboratory and field experiences assimilate the inquisitive spirit of science. Not only are hands-on laboratory and field activities vital for students to learn science, there is a critical minimum amount of time required for these active learning experiences. The National Science Teachers Association (NSTA) recommends minimum amounts of instructional time be devoted to doing science where students are observing, manipulating, measuring, organizing information, reasoning analytically, communicating findings, and conceptualizing scientific phenomena (NSTA Position Statement on Laboratory Science, 1993). Elementary students should spend a minimum of 60 percent of their science learning time doing hands-on activities. Reading about science, computer programs, and teacher demonstrations are valuable, but should not be substituted for hands-on experiences. Middle-school students should spend a minimum of 80 percent of their science instruction time on laboratory-related experience including pre-lab instruction, hands-on activities and a post-lab period involving analysis and communication. High-school science students should spend 40 percent of their time on laboratory-related experiences including pre- and post-lab instruction. Table 9.1 provides the NSTA recommended minimum percentage of time that should be allotted for students' hands-on activities.

TABLE 9.1 Minimum Instructional Time for Laboratory or Field Activities Recommended by NSTA

Level	% of Instructional Time
Elementary	80
Middle school	60
High school	40

Source: National Science Teachers Association, *Position Statement on Laboratory Science* (Arlington, VA: National Science Teachers Association, 1993).

West et al. suggest that there are several patterns in research data that identify factors linked to an increase in the seriousness, the number, and the most prevalent accidents. Safety research findings can be grouped into four areas: 1) overcrowding; 2) state characteristics; 3) district/school characteristics; and 4) teacher characteristics.

Overcrowding and Class Size

"Collaborative inquiry requires adequate and safe space" (NRC, 1996, p. 218). Overcrowding is a complex issue, as well as a serious issue, because adequate and safe space concerns two issues: 1) the class size and 2) the amount of physical space per student. Brennan (1970) found that class enrollment and laboratory space have a significant relationship to laboratory accidents; the higher the classroom enrollment and the smaller the laboratory space, the higher the frequency of accidents. Eliminating overcrowding is the one change that will most affect safety in science classrooms.

There is ample evidence that more accidents occur as the class size or the number of students per teacher in any one class increases (Macomber, 1961; Brennan, 1970; Young, 1972). Teachers consistently rate overcrowding as their number one safety concern (Horton, 1988; Rakow, 1989; West et al., 2001).

Because some research (Young, 1972) indicates that a class size greater than 22 students is a limiting factor for safety, the Texas study (West et al., 2002) also reported data for a class size of 22. As class size increased, so did the number of mishaps (Figure 9.1). The percentage of incidents and accidents increased from 27 percent to 36 percent when class size increased from 22 or fewer to 24 or fewer students. The number of incidents increased to an even more dramatic 58 percent when class size increased to more than 24 students.

Based on the safety research and the experience of science teachers over the years, most American and international professional organizations and states recommend a maximum science class size limit of 24 (see Table 9.2).

The National Science Teachers Association has also provided recommendations for the gross minimum room sizes. The room dimensions are measured wall to wall, and include fastened furniture and other obstructions (Biehle et al., 1999, p. 22). (See Table 9.3.)

FIGURE 9.1 Percentage Comparison of Incident/Accident and Recommended Class Size

Source: S. S. West, J. F. Westerlund, A. L. Stephenson, and N. C. Nelson. "Conditions that Affect Secondary Science Safety: Results from 2001 Texas Survey" (Austin, TX: Texas Education Agency, 2002b). Available at http://bluebonnet.bio.swt.edu.

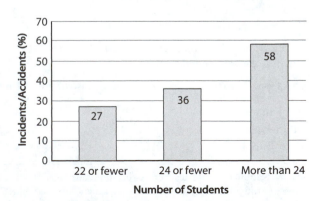

TABLE 9.2   Professional Organizations' Recommendations for Class Size

Organization	Class Size		
	Elementary	Middle School	High School
National Science Teachers Assoc. (NSTA) 1993 www.nsta.org/	22	24	24
National Science Educational Leadership Assoc. (NSELA) 1996 http://nsela.org/size.htm	24	24	24
Council of State Science Supervisors (CSSS) 1999 http://csss/enc.org/position.htm	24	24	24
National Assoc. of Biology Teachers 1994 (NABT) www.nabt.org	24	24	24
United Kingdom Assoc. for Science Education (ASE) 2000 www.ase.org.uk/policy/classf.html	20	20	20

TABLE 9.3   NSTA's Recommendations for Minimum Room Size for a Class of 24

Classroom Type	Room Size		
	Elementary	Middle School	High School
Combination Classroom/Lab	1,080 ft^2	1,440 ft^2	1,440 ft^2
Pure Science Lab	960 ft^2	1,080 ft^2	1,080 ft^2

Source: J. Biehle, L. Motz, and S. West. *NSTA Guide to School Science Facilities.* (Arlington, VA: National Science Teachers Association, 1999).

The issue of building adequate science facilities is so great that the National Science Foundation (NSF) funded a project that established a website (www.labplan.org) that provides a process that can be used to plan and design science facilities.

Teacher Characteristics

The National Science Education Standards recommend that safety become an essential factor for all science teachers, especially in this age of scientific inquiry. The characteristics of these individuals are clearly delineated in their safety premise and is best expressed in this statement:

> Safety is a fundamental concern in all experimental science. Teachers of science must know and apply the necessary safety regulations in the storage, use, and care of the materials used by students. They adhere to safety rules and guidelines that are established by national organizations such as the American Chemical society and the Occupational Safety and Health Administration, as well as by local and state regulatory agencies.

They work with the school and district to ensure implementation and use of safety guidelines for which they (school and district) are responsible, such as the presence of safety equipment and an appropriate class size. Teachers also teach students how to engage safely in investigations inside and outside the classroom. (NRC 1996, p. 44)

It may be overstating the obvious, but individuals who are well prepared in their content fields and who have more experience tend to have fewer accidents.

How Do You Plan for Safety?

Children are natural scientists because they are curious about everything in their physical world. Given the opportunity, they will investigate events and objects of all types and see beauty and intrigue in events that adults accept as mundane. Sometimes it is difficult for children to separate danger from fascination. The teacher's responsibility is to balance these two factors, with information from publishers, science experts, peers, and considerations from their own teaching environment (student abilities and maturities, equipment available) in order to ensure that science learning is effective yet safe.

Natural events provide effective learning opportunities for elementary students. Ice storms, tornadoes, thunderstorms, floods, the first snowfall, a gentle rain, and the changes of the seasons are all natural phenomena which elementary students are curious about. When these events happen around them, students become even more curious about the causes and receptive to learning about what causes the events.

In order to keep students safe while attempting to construct an understanding of science concepts through hands-on science activities, teachers must have a simple yet effective safety philosophy that guides students. It is important to identify appropriate grade-level concepts and worthwhile explorations in order to enact an effective safety philosophy. Once these are clearly identified, the teacher must ask, "What are the foreseeable hazards associated with valued educational activities?" Ask yourself, "Would a respected peer use the same materials or activity I have selected?" "What adjustments might another teacher make to fit the needs of students according to their emotional, social, and academic abilities?" "What group size or class setting would a reasonable teacher use to make the activity effective and safe?"

You must think about any foreseeable hazards your students may encounter as they participate in your activities. Be sensitive to such issues as chemical problems, about which you may have insufficient knowledge, fire hazards, potential eye injuries from sharp objects or flying projectiles, and overcrowding. If the foreseeable hazards exceed the educational value of the knowledge or experience students could gain from direct participation, you have some choices to make:

1. Provide additional safety parameters, such as safety goggles, fire blankets, eyewashes, and additional supervision.
2. Limit the activity to a teacher demonstration, in which you are the only one who manipulates the equipment, and students become active observers. (In many instances this is the most logical and educationally responsible choice.)

3. Eliminate the activity entirely from the curriculum. Unless you have recently performed a detailed assessment of the entire science curriculum across grades, you might be surprised at how many duplicate activities of little value exist in science classes that are taught primarily because of tradition (Gerlovich et al., 2003).

The National Science Teachers Association recommends the following in *Exploring Safely* (Kwan & Texley, 2002):

> Lesson plans often have great continuity but fall short in the real world. Every day there is someone absent in almost every classroom. That means that your safety precautions must consider the consequences of both teacher and student absences.

> Remember that you are responsible for the program offered by your substitute. Because the substitute is unlikely to have your knowledge of the subject matter or the same level of classroom control, it is usually not a good idea to have them conduct complex activities or those with potential hazards. Many teachers have a special substitute folder for one-day unexpected absences containing safe activities that would fit almost any part of the year.

> When students are absent, they often miss safety directions, so it is important to have a written version and to begin every class with a short review. Be sure that all your safety lessons and directions are included in your lesson plan book.

> Students who are absent often need access to the supplies the next day. To save your sanity, you may want to organize these supplies in labeled boxes containing all the supplies for a particular unit. Place a laminated card with the relevant safety rules in the box with the supplies.

In an inquiry-based science program, teachers encourage students to observe, experiment, and explore on their own as much as possible. It is vital, however, that this be guided freedom performed with a safety first attitude. Safety should be explicit and targeted at the scientific investigation being performed. The following lesson plan exemplifies how safety can be planned for and reiterated throughout a lesson.

What Are Your Legal Responsibilities?

Although this section focuses on tort law as it relates to science teaching, the principles and philosophy apply to all school subjects. There are several legal concepts you must be familiar with in order to understand your legal responsibilities.

Tort

A *tort* is a wrong, or injury, that someone has committed against someone else. The injured party generally wants restitution for the injury or damages. The resolution of such conflicts between litigants (*plaintiffs* being those who bring the claim and *defendants* being those against whom the claim has been filed) generally occurs in a court, involving lawyers, a judge, possibly jurors, and witnesses, and is referred to as a *lawsuit*.

(text continues on page 296)

Cooling Crystals

GRADE LEVEL: 5–8

DISCIPLINE: Earth/Space Sciences

Inquiry Question: Why do some rocks, made of the same materials, have different names?

Concept to Be Invented: The rate at which a crystal cools affects the size of the crystal.

National Science Education Standards: Grades 5–8—Structure of the Earth's system. Changes in the solid Earth can be described as the rock cycle. Old rocks are buried, then compacted, heated, and often recrystallized into new rock.

Science Attitudes to Nurture: Curiosity, perseverance, open-mindedness when evidence for changes is given

Materials Needed

3 glass caster cups
3 small test tubes (10-ml)
test tube holder
paradichlorobenzine (PDB) flakes
 (found in supermarkets, hardware
 stores, pharmacies)
1 150-ml beaker
heat-proof glove
hot plate

samples of igneous rocks—rhyolite,
 granite, and obsidian
1 hand lens/per student
grease pencil
crushed ice
2 500-ml beakers
tongs
paper towels

ⓘ Safety Precautions

✦ Review with the students proper use of heating equipment—such as the hot plates used in this activity. Remind them the hot plates purposely have short cords so that they are plugged in close to the wall, NO extension cords should be used. Keep the table/desk that the hot plate is on close to the wall to minimize the risk of someone tripping over the cord.

✦ Extreme care should be used near the hot plate and in handling the hot water and the PDB.

✦ Goggles should be worn at all times, NO excuses.

✦ Be sure the room is well ventilated when melting the PDB.

Exploration *Which process skills will be used?*

Observing, predicting, manipulating materials, recording data, drawing conclusions

As safety is very important with this activity, it is important to conduct this as a *Guided Discovery Activity*. Lead the student teams in a step-by-step process.

Step 1: Ask the students to fill one of the 500-ml beakers with 300-ml of water. Place a caster cup in the beaker. Boil the water on the hot plate. Again, remind the students to place the hot plate flat on the table/desktop as close to the wall as possible to avoid anyone tripping over the cord. Fill the other 500-ml beaker with crushed ice. Place the second caster cup in the beaker. Leave the third caster cup at room temperature.

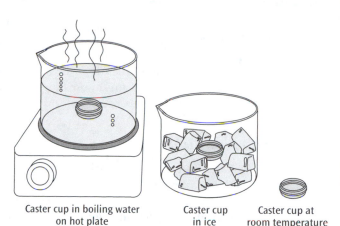

Caster cup in boiling water on hot plate   Caster cup in ice   Caster cup at room temperature

Step 2: Ask the students to observe some PDB flakes. Be sure to remind students that goggles are to be worn at *all* times and that these observations are made in a well-ventilated area of the room. If no fume hood is present, be sure windows are opened. Ask the students to record their observations.

Step 3: Once the water in the beaker begins to boil, ask one student from the group to put on the heat-proof glove and carefully remove the 500-ml beaker from the hot plate. Set it on a heat-proof surface, away from risk of getting knocked over while the students perform Step 4.

Step 4: Again, in a well-ventilated area, ask the students to fill each of the 3 small test tubes with PDB flakes, and to half-fill the 150-ml beaker with water. Place the 3 test tubes in the beaker containing the water. Place the beaker on the hot plate. Heat the beaker gently until the PDB melts. Be sure a team member is carefully watching for the PDB to melt and that goggles are still on *ALL* students.

Step 5: Instruct students to go back to the 500-ml beaker and using the tongs carefully remove the caster cup from the boiling water. Dry the cup and label it *A*. Once the PDB flakes have melted in each of the test tubes, instruct one student from each team to use the test tube holder to carefully remove one test tube from the beaker and pour the liquified PDB into this caster cup. Ask the students to time how long it takes for the PDB to completely become a solid, to record the time, and to record their observations of the PDB when placed in caster cup A.

Step 6: Ask the students to now remove the second caster cup from the beaker with ice. Dry the cup quickly and completely. Label it *B*. Ask another student from each team to use the test tube holder to carefully remove another test tube from the beaker and pour the liquified PDB into the caster cup labeled B. Ask the students to time how long it takes for the PDB to completely become a solid, to record the time, and to record their observations of the PDB when placed in caster cup B.

Step 7: Ask the students to take the third caster cup which was sitting at room temperature and label it C. Then ask yet another student from each team to use the test

(continued)

tube holder to carefully remove another test tube from the beaker and pour the lique-
fied PDB into the caster cup labeled C. Again, ask the students to time how long it
takes for the PDB to completely become a solid, to record the time, and to record
their observations of the PDB when placed in caster cup C.

Encourage the teams to use the hand lens to draw pictures of the now cooled PDB
in each of the caster cups—A, B, and C.

Explanation

Ask the student teams to help create a set of class data on cooling rates for the liquified
PDB in caster cups A, B, and C. Collect student drawings of the cooled PDB from the
caster cups to share with the entire class. Use the following questions to help make the
concept behind the guided activity concrete:

✦ Which caster cup took the longest for the PDB to solidify? Which took the least
amount of time?
✦ Was there a difference in the PDB when it solidified in hot caster cup (A) compared
to cold caster cup (B)?
✦ How does the rate of cooling affect the size of crystals?
✦ Look at the various drawings of the solidified PDB in casters A, B, and C. How are
they different? What caused this difference? What conclusions can you draw?

The students should conclude that the rate at which a crystal cools affects the size
of the crystal formed.

Expansion   *Which process skills will be used?*

Observing, recording data, generalizing, formulating models

This Expansion activity can be completed as an open discovery activity once the students are reminded of the safety issues and proper teacher supervision makes sure that
students follow them. The student teams can be free to explore at their own pace. Remind students to wear goggles during the expansion phase, in case rock samples are
dropped, to avoid getting rock chips into eyes.

Ask the students to observe the crystals in the samples of granite, rhyolite, and obsidian with a magnifying glass. Have them draw the crystals in each sample on paper.
Ask them to compare the crystals in the caster cups with the samples of granite, rhyolite, and obsidian and to respond to this question in their science journals: Which PDB
crystals are most similar to the crystals in the rock samples? (Cup A, granite; cup B, obsidian; cup C, rhyolite.)

Granite, rhyolite, and obsidian are igneous rocks essentially made of the same material. Ask the students to use what they learned in the exploration phase to provide an
explanation as to why they look different. Ask the students to record team responses to
the following questions in their science journal so that responses can be shared once all
the student teams have completed their observations: Where would igneous rocks have

a chance to cool slowly? Where would igneous rock cool rapidly? If you saw a rock that contained large interlocking crystals, what would you say about the way it formed? Some suggested answers are: The more slowly a crystal cools, the larger the crystals are. Granite cooled slowly and crystals were able to form. Rhyolite cooled more rapidly than granite, but more slowly than obsidian. Igneous rocks cool slowly deep in the Earth. They cool rapidly on the surface. Large interlocking crystals form slowly inside the Earth.

As a class, now ask the students to respond to the Inquiry Question: Why *do* some rocks, made of the same materials, have different names?

Science in Personal and Social Perspectives

- ✦ What kinds of crystals do you eat regularly? (salt and sugar)
- ✦ How does the size of a crystal determine its quality? Do you think your knowledge of how crystals form will assist you in determining the quality of precious rocks and gems?

Science and Technology

- ✦ The strength and quality of rocks are important for construction. What is the best type of rock for long-lasting buildings?
- ✦ How has the scarcity of quality gems on the market affected your life, your community, or the world?

Science as Inquiry

- ✦ What kinds of rocks are found in the area where you live? Can you classify them according to their crystal structure?
- ✦ Are crystals found in sedimentary rocks? Why or why not?

History and Nature of Science

- ✦ What kinds of careers would use information on crystal formation? Some possibilities include geologist, geophysicist, volcanologist, jeweler, sculptor, and geographer.
- ✦ Choose one of the career suggestions from the question above and research the skills necessary to enter that career. Provide an oral report to the class.

Evaluation

Upon completing the activities, the students will be able to:

- ✦ (with drawings of crystals of different shapes and sizes) identify where a crystal is cooled (on the Earth's surface or inside the Earth) and at what rate;
- ✦ examine samples of igneous rocks and explain why they have different-sized crystals;
- ✦ and explain how the prices of precious jewels are affected by crystal formation.

Remember, as a teacher you are acting in place of the parents (in loco parentis). The courts point out that you assume these responsibilities because you are a professional educator. *Exploring Safely* (Kwan & Texley, 2002) spells out these responsibilities.

Prepare: Keep up to date with continuing education and activities within professional organizations and school policies and procedures.

Plan: Use best strategies to ensure your students learn effectively and safely and you think ahead to determine how best to work with their strengths and limitations.

Protect: Assess hazards and review procedures for accident prevention and teach and review safety procedures with every student when a hazard is anticipated.

Protect: Check your facilities for the presence and accessibility of correctly operating safety equipment and protective devices, demonstrate their proper use, and maintain these records.

Reasonable and Prudent Judgment

The U.S. legal system does not require educators to be superhuman in the performance of their duties. It is expected only that they be *reasonable and prudent* in their judgment when performing their duties with students. Educators need only do what reasonable

FIGURE 9.2
Request for Correction of Safety Concern

Source: Gerlovich et al., *The Total Science Safety System CD (Kentucky Edition).* (Waukee, IA: JaKel, Inc., 2003). Excerpted, with permission, from The Total Science Safety System software—Elementary Edition 1999 by JaKel, Inc.

Date filed with administrator: _____

Secretary's initials: _____

Request for Correction of Safety Concern

Date: _____   Room: _____

The following is a safety concern in the science area:

_____   _____
(Teacher name)   (Signature)

CC: Teacher, Dept. Chair

---

persons with comparable training and experience would do in similar situations. They must ask themselves whether their peers would endorse these activities being performed with students. Proceed with confidence if questions are answered affirmatively. If not, add more safety features, limit the activity to a teacher demonstration, or eliminate it entirely. As science teachers, we must attempt to anticipate reasonable hazards, eliminate them, or be confidently prepared to address them.

Foreseeability

If you discover something amiss in your teaching environment, you should request corrections, preferably in writing, as soon as possible (see Figure 9.2). Essential items, such as fire extinguishers, fire blankets, eyewashes, or safety goggles, need to be obtained or repaired immediately; less important items, like nonskid floor wax, can be discussed with administrators for future correction. All known hazards and appropriate emergency measures should be explained to students as well.

The foreseeable hazards of all activities, as well as appropriate emergency reactions, should be completely explained to students *prior* to an activity. Field trip sites should be reviewed very carefully by the teacher before students arrive. Ask the owner or proprietor of the field site about any known hazards or potential hazards to students. Any sensitivities to foods the class might be working with should be ascertained before the activity begins. Any phobias should be identified before students are placed in potentially frightening situations. The teacher *must* know about any medical problems that students may have—for example, medication schedules, allergies, fears, and anxieties. Before ever involving students in activities, ask yourself, "What could go wrong with this activity, and am I prepared to address the problem?" If you can answer the questions affirmatively, proceed with confidence.

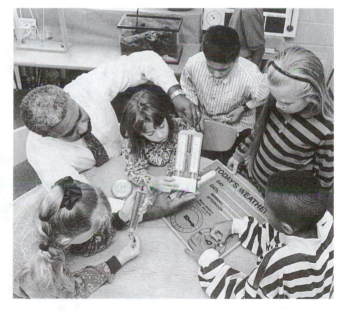

Prudent judgment and proper supervision fulfill most legal responsibilities.

Negligence

Before you can be held accountable for personal injury accidents, it must be proven that you were negligent. *Negligence* has been defined as "conduct that falls below a standard established by law or profession to protect others from harm" (Iowa Annotated Code, 2000). It is sometimes described as failure to exercise due care.

Due Care

Due care may be defined as your duty to protect your students (Iowa Code Annotated, 2000). For younger or disabled students, the degree of care provided must be increased. You must remember that you are the authority in the classroom. You, or an equally qualified adult substitute, must be with students at all times, especially when the potential for injury exists. During science activities, when materials and chemicals are being manipulated, your presence is essential. If you need to leave the room during such activities, you must make certain that an equally qualified person assumes this responsibility. Due care is often summarized in three teacher duties: instruction, supervision, and maintenance (Iowa Code Annotated, 2000).

Instruction. You must ensure that the instruction is appropriate for the physical and mental development levels of your students. Since textbooks form the basis of many science programs, you would be wise to ensure that safety is an integral and conspicuous component. Strive to select textbooks that parallel your safe science teaching philosophy.

All activities which involve students should be weighed for their educational value versus the hazards involved in having students perform them. If the foreseeable dangers outweigh the educational value of the activity, limit the demonstration to the teacher, add more safety features, or eliminate the science activity (Gerlovich et al., 2003). As a service to teachers, newsletters are supplied by safety-conscious scientific supply companies. Many equipment supplier newsletters include safety columns and hints as well as more effective safety equipment ideas for young students.

Rules should be clearly written and explained to students. Copies of the most important rules should be posted conspicuously throughout the room. To help assure the safety of students, the National Science Teachers Association (Kwan & Texley, 2002) recommends that teachers post, in conspicuous places visible to students, General Safety Rules for Students, outlined in Figure 9.3.

Determine the educational value of an activity before doing it.

Seriously consider developing and implementing a *student safety contract* (see Figure 9.4, page 300) for students in the upper grades (4–6). Public Law 94-142, also known as the Individuals with Disabilities Education Act (IDEA), is a federal law approved in 1975 and reauthorized in 1990. It mandates that students receive a free public education that is appropriate to their level of disability. In addition, these students must be educated with peer students who do not have disabilities. The Americans with Disabilities Act (ADA) also prohibits discrimination against persons with disabilities. Teachers must be extra cautious to assure that neither equipment nor facilities discriminate against these students while at the same time keep them

FIGURE 9.3
General Safety Rules
for Students

> (!) Always review the general safety rules with the students before
> beginning an activity.
>
> 1. Never do any experiment without the approval and direct supervision of
>   your teacher.
> 2. Always wear your safety goggles when your teacher tells you to do so.
>   Never remove your goggles during an activity.
> 3. Know the location of all safety equipment in or near your classroom.
>   Never play with the safety equipment.
> 4. Tell your teacher immediately if an accident occurs.
> 5. Tell your teacher immediately if a spill occurs.
> 6. Tell your teacher immediately about any broken, chipped, or scratched
>   glassware so that it may be properly cleaned up and disposed of.
> 7. Tie back long hair and secure loose clothing when working around flames.
> 8. If instructed to do so, wear your laboratory apron or smock to protect your
>   clothing.
> 9. Never assume that anything that has been heated is cool. Hot glassware
>   looks just like cool glassware.
> 10. Never taste anything during a laboratory activity. If an investigation
>   involves tasting, it will be done in the cafeteria.
> 11. Clean up your work area upon completion of your activity.
> 12. Wash your hands with soap and water upon completion of an activity.

Source: T. Kwan and
J. Texley. *Exploring
Safely: A Guide for Ele-
mentary Teachers* (Na-
tional Science Teachers
Association, 2002).

safe. One way that this can be accomplished is through targeted science lesson plans and safety contracts. It is best to check with your state department of education for specific guidelines.

NSTA recommends that teachers develop a safety contract (Figure 9.5, page 301) with their students and have parents read it aloud and review it with their children at home early in the year, and then sign and return the document to the teacher. It might be helpful to everyone to go over the importance and implications of this document with parents at a scheduled parent-teacher conference. It's a good idea to update and repeat the contract process each quarter to semester.

Discipline during science activities should be fair, consistent, and firmly enforced. Safety is so important that no one should be exempt. The only exceptions should be based on a student's obvious physical or mental limitations. Students will support teachers in their activities a great deal more if they feel that everyone is treated fairly. You may also wish to involve students in the safe science and discipline rules for the class.

You are a role model. You set the safety expectations for your class by example. Students cannot be expected to take safety seriously if you do not observe all guidelines. Be especially careful to wear safety equipment items (goggles) and observe all safety rules. Explain all safety considerations and have all safety equipment items available before beginning any activity. Safety should be something that students expect you to enforce.

If you are considering having an outside presenter in your room, you may want to check on the individual's background and follow the guidelines provided by the National Science Teachers Association in their Outside Presenter's Form (Figure 9.6, page 302).

Student Safety Contract

My teacher told me, _____ , about these safety items in my science class.

(student name)

1. Safety rules   _____

2. How to find and use these:

   (a) Fire extinguisher   _____   (g) Heat sources (bunsen   _____
                                                                   burner, alcohol lamp,

   (b) Fire blanket   _____   microwave oven, etc.)

   (c) Goggles   _____   (h) Electrical equipment   _____

   (d) Eyewash   _____   (i) Telephone or intercom   _____

   (e) Drench shower   _____

   (f) Safety can   _____

3. What to do during:

   (a) Fire   _____   (c) Eye emergency   _____

   (b) Chemical splash   _____   (d) Chemical spill   _____
          to the body   (e) Electrical emergency   _____

Date: _____   Teacher: _____

FIGURE 9.4   Student Safety Contract: Sample 1

Source: J. Gerlovich & K. Hartman, *The Total Science Safety System: Elementary Edition,* computer software (Waukee, IA: JaKel, Inc., 1998). Excerpted, with permission, from The Total Science Safety System software—Elementary Edition 1999 by JaKel, Inc.

Consider simulating foreseeable emergencies—for example, a student who receives a chemical splash on his clothing, face, or eyes; a classroom or clothing fire caused by science items; finding another adult to give emergency assistance; evacuating the room—and proper safety responses as part of your daily teaching. Following instructions, you might evaluate students on their proper and expeditious performances. Accent the positive; emphasize what you want students to *do.* Be careful to protect students from any hazards during the simulations.

Should an accident or incident occur, collect as much information as possible from witnesses (student and staff). An accident or incident report (see Figure 9.7, page 304) can help focus the report should legal repercussions arise from the incident. These accounts are powerful, firsthand evidence of what actions were taken and the teacher's commitment to safety. Some states set limits on the length of time, after an incident occurs, wherein legal action can be taken. When the statute of limitations for legal actions passes for the incident, dispose of the materials. These reports can also be very effective learning tools when used with other classes.

I am learning to be a good scientist. I know that I must be organized, neat, and well behaved to learn science best. I promise to:

- Prepare for activities: I will listen to directions and make sure I understand them before I start.
- Care for equipment: I will handle objects carefully and put them away when I am done.
- Follow directions: I will do each step in order, and I will not try unknown things.
- Observe carefully: I will be as quiet and calm as possible so that I can learn more.
- Keep careful records: I will write down my observations.
- Clean up afterwards: I will wash my hands and my workspace.
- Follow all safety rules.

I will share good science safety with students and family so that I can be a good investigator:

(Signed) _____ / (Signed) _____
                         Student   Parent

FIGURE 9.5 Student Safety Contract: Sample 2

Source: T. Kwan and J. Texley. *Exploring Safely: A Guide for Elementary Teachers* (National Science Teachers Association, 2002).

Supervision. The duty of supervision, as part of due care, can be a significant challenge. Teachers should always be in the classroom when scientific equipment or chemicals are accessible to students. The only exceptions to this rule are times of extreme emergencies or when the supervision has been delegated to another equally qualified person. Overcrowding, class size, and field trips are matters that require specific supervisory attention.

There is increasing evidence that *overcrowding* is the root cause of accidents in science settings. Supervision should increase when the danger level of the activity increases, the number of students with disabilities in the class increases, and the learning environment

(text continues on page 304)

Adult volunteers enhance due care through supervision on field trips.

Science safety is an integral part of science education and serves as a preparation for life. Accordingly, the _____ School District encourages teachers to assure meaningful and safe science experiences both inside and outside the classroom. The intent of the safety guidelines that follow is to promote safe science practices at all school-sponsored activities.

The Following Situations May Not Be Part of Any School Science-Related Activity Under Any Circumstances:

1. Parts of the body are not to be placed in danger, such as placing dry ice in the mouth or dipping hands or fingers into liquid nitrogen or molten lead, or exposing the hands and face to microorganisms. Demonstrations such as the following shall not be conducted: walking on broken glass or hot coals or fire with bare feet, passing an electric current through the body, and lying on a bed of nails and having a concrete block broken over the chest.
2. Live vertebrate animals may not be used in demonstrations or for experimental purposes. Such animals may be used only for observational purposes provided the animals have been lawfully acquired, are housed in proper containers, and are handled in a humane way. Any certification papers or vaccination documents shall be made available upon request.
3. Animals are to be used for educational purposes and not for the exploitation of the animal for advertisement, commercial purposes, or sensationalism. This includes use of animals in an exhibit hall.
4. Live ammunition, firearms, or acutely dangerous explosives, such as Benzoyl peroxide, Diethyl ether, Perchloric acid, Picric acid and Sodium azide, may not be used. Commercially available fireworks and blasting caps shall never be used.
5. Plants with poisonous oils (e.g., poison ivy), saps (e.g., oleander), or other plants known to be generally toxic to humans are not to be used.
6. Experiments or demonstrations with human blood/body fluids may not be conducted.
7. Radioactive powders, liquids, or solutions are not to be used except in a laboratory facility designated for the type of radioactive material. Arrange for proper shielding and protection for demonstrations, which involve radiation. Only low-level radioactive sources shall be employed.

Guidelines for Preparing Your Presentation:

1. Practice all demonstrations or workshop procedure BEFORE presenting them to an audience or having participants try them.
2. Research and understand the properties, chemical reactions, and dangers involved in all demonstrations. Plan to use correct handling and disposal procedures for all chemicals and biohazards used. Arrange to have a fire extinguisher available whenever the slightest possibility of fire exists. Be aware of emergency and fire escape routes for your site.
3. Prepare a handout that gives participants detailed instructions about the procedures, safety precautions, hazards, and disposal methods for each demonstration and workshop. Have Material Safety Data Sheets (MSDS) for chemicals and biohazards available upon request.
4. Prepare photographs, slides, videotapes, and so on, that show safe science practices. When preparing these materials, safety goggles and equipment shall not be removed for aesthetic considerations.
5. In planning demonstrations and/or workshops, keep quantities of hazardous materials to a minimum. Use only those quantities that can be adequately handled by the available ventilation system. Do not carry out demonstrations that will result in the release of harmful quantities of noxious gases into the local air supply in the demonstration or other rooms. The following gases shall not be produced without using a fume hood: nitrogen dioxide, sulfur dioxide, and hydrogen sulfide. Volatile toxic substances such as benzene, carbon tetrachloride, and formaldehyde shall not be used unless a fume hood is available.

FIGURE 9.6 NSTA Guidelines for Outside Presenter's Form

Source: National Science Teachers Association Board of Directors. *Outside Presenter's Form* (August 1994; revised July 2000).

6. Make sure your glassware and equipment are not broken or damaged. The use of chipped or cracked glassware shall be avoided. If glassware is to be heated, Pyrex™ or its equivalent shall be used.
7. Thoroughly check motor-driven discs that revolve at moderate or high speeds. Make sure the disc is sturdy, that it contains no parts that may come free, and that the safety nut is securely fastened.
8. Arrange to use a safety shield and/or eye protection for audience members and interpreters for any demonstration(s) in which projectiles are launched or when there is the slightest possibility of an unsafe explosion. Do not allow direct viewing of the sun, infrared, or ultraviolet sources.
9. Make sure any lasers to be used in demonstrations are helium-neon lasers with a maximum output power rating not exceeding 1.0 milliwatt. At all times, avoid direct propagation of a laser beam from a laser into the eye of an observer or from a reflected surface into the eye.
10. Secure pressurized gas cylinders by strapping or chaining them in place or by using proper supports, i.e., lecture bottles.
11. Obtain in advance, the necessary state and/or local permits needed for the firing of model rockets. Activities involving the firing of rockets must be well planned and follow Federal Aviation Agency (FAA) regulations, state and local rules and regulations, and the National Association of Rocketry's (NAR) Solid Propellant Model Rocket Safety Code.
12. Arrange for appropriate waste containers and for the disposal of materials hazardous to the environment.
13. Plan to dress safely for your presentation or workshop.

During the Presentation:
1. Comply with all local fire and safety rules and regulations. Follow the NSTA Minimum Safety Guidelines.
2. Wear appropriate eye protection, an apron, ear protection, and similar protective gear for all chemical demonstrations or when appropriate for other demonstrations. Provide eye protection, aprons, and safety equipment for participants who will be handling chemicals, hazardous substances, or working with flames.
3. Do not select volunteers from the audience. Assistants used in demonstrations shall be recruited and given the proper instructions beforehand.
4. Warn participants or audience to cover their ears whenever a loud explosion is anticipated.
5. Use a safety shield for all demonstrations that involve the launching of projectiles, or whenever there is the slightest possibility that a container, its fragments, or its contents could be propelled with sufficient force to cause injury. Shield moving belts attached to motors. Use caution when motor-driven discs revolve at moderate or high speeds. Shield or move participants to a safe distance from the plane of the rotating disc.
6. Follow proper procedures for working with pressurized gases and when heating all forms of matter.
7. Use appropriate gloves and shields when working with hazardous chemicals and biohazards, cryogenic materials, hot materials, radioactive substances, vacuums, electromagnetic radiation, and when presenting animals for observation.
8. Do not taste or encourage participants to taste any nonfood substances. A food substance subjected to possible contamination or unsafe conditions shall never be tasted.
9. Alert the audience clearly at the beginning of the program to the presence or production of allergenic materials, such as strobe lights, microwaves, "theater"e, lycopodium powder, or live animals.
10. Maintain a clear exit during the demonstration or workshop.
11. Emphasize and demonstrate appropriate safety precautions throughout the presentation or workshop.
12. Distribute a handout that will give participants detailed instructions about the procedure, safety precautions, hazards, and disposal for each demonstration and workshop.

FIGURE 9.6   Continued

FIGURE 9.7 Teacher Accident/Incident Report

Source: J. Gerlovich & K. Hartman, *The Total Science Safety System: Elementary Edition,* computer software (Waukee, IA: JaKel, Inc., 1998). Excerpted, with permission, from The Total Science Safety System software—Elementary Edition 1999 by JaKel, Inc.

1. Staff member completing the report: _____

2. Date of accident/incident: _____

3. Time of the accident/incident: _____

4. Location of the accident/incident:

5. Staff/student(s) involved in the accident/incident:

   (a) Staff (report attached)   (b) Student (report attached)

   _____   _____

   _____   _____

   _____   _____

   _____   _____

6. Teacher description of the accident/incident:

7. Immediate action taken to deal with the emergency:

8. Corrective action taken to avoid a repeat of the accident/incident in the future:

_____   _____
       (Date report completed)   (Signature of person completing report)

differs from the conventional classroom setting. Teachers must be aware of overcrowding and initiate corrections as soon as possible.

The National Science Teachers Association (and numerous other professional science teaching organizations) recommends that the teacher-to-student ratio never exceed 1:24 during science labs and activities (Biehle, 1999). The classroom teaching environment has a significant influence on the safety that can be provided to students. In its 1989 safety guide, the Texas Education Agency recommended two types of floor plans for teaching elementary school science that may provide a model for the nation. Emphasis was placed on safety equipment, a maximum of twenty-four students during science activities, extensive open space leading to at least two exits, and adequate room for students to move about without bumping into each other or equipment. Students need to be easily supervised by the teacher from any point in the room. There must be no blind spots.

For field trips, obtain parent or guardian release forms or waivers for all students and apprise the administration of the event (Figures 9.8 A, B, and C). The activity should be an integral part of the course. Teachers should use only school-sanctioned and insured vehicles. On field trips, increase supervision to one teacher or other qualified adult to ten students. It is imperative that teachers and other assisting adults preview the field site for hazards *before* students are involved. Students should be apprised of any known hazards and appropriate responses in an emergency, such as described in the opening third scenario. Be careful to consider poisonous plants and plants with thorns or other irritating parts, and check for poisonous or biting animals. On the school grounds, look for broken glass, holes, drug paraphernalia, and other unexpected items. Remember to be aware of insects that carry such diseases, such as Lyme disease, encephalitis, and yellow fever. Check with local medical authorities for updates. If an insect repellent is to be used, check that it contains DEET and that no students are allergic to it.

Implement the buddy system on field trips, pairing students and holding them responsible for each other (Rakow, 1989). Buddies can apprise adults of any problem. Very young students (grades K–3) should not be separated from adult supervision at any time. The teacher should arrange for upper elementary students to meet at prearranged times and these times should be adhered to explicitly. Increase adult supervision for young learners.

Maintenance. Maintaining an educational environment is the third teacher duty. It is imperative that you attempt to foresee hazards and expedite their correction. You are not expected to be superhuman in your identification or make the repairs yourself. However, a logical, regular review of the teaching environment is a reasonable expectation. The information available in the safety equipment and safety assessment sections of this chapter can help you with maintenance. For additional information concerning legal concept and case studies, visit the American Association of Law Librarians website at www.aallnet.org/aallnet.web.html.

What must a teacher do to ensure safe field trips?

Federal and State Legislation

A vital state law or statute about which you should instruct students relates to eye protective equipment (safety goggles) (Iowa Annotated Code, 2000). You must

(text continues on page 308)

Field Trips

Item	Date Satisfied
The teacher has visited the field trip site prior to involving students there.	_____
The activity is a well-planned part of the science course.	_____
The activity is appropriate for the mental and physical age of the students.	_____
Transportation is via school or school-sanctioned vehicles only.	_____
Teachers, assistants, and drivers have complete lists of participating students.	_____
Teachers have cell phones, CB-radios, etc, for emergency communications.	_____
Clear, appropriate rules of behavior are established and understood by students.	_____
All field trip dangers are pointed out to students in advance and again when students arrive at the site.	_____
Students are dressed according to the demands of the environment and weather. (Parents are notified of such clothing and supplies to be taken on the trip in advance.)	_____
In tick and mite areas, students' arms, legs, and necks are covered.	_____
Following field trips, in areas where ticks are common, students are checked for ticks when they return to school.	_____
Any field trips to water environments require at least one person in each group to be familiar with lifesaving, CPR, and artificial respiration techniques.	_____
Approved life jackets are available for all students who venture out into the water.	_____
Approved adult/student ration never exceeds 1:10.	_____
Supervision is increased according to the novelty and danger inherent in the field trip environment.	_____
All safety equipment is in proper state of repair.	_____
Equipment is designed for the mental and physical ages of the students using it.	_____
Students know how to use the equipment properly.	_____
Glass collecting equipment is avoided if possible.	_____
The buddy system, pairing students in teams, is used to help ensure safety and mutual responsibility.	_____
The teacher is congnizant of any "known" student medical needs (allergies, medication schedules, phobias, etc.).	_____
Signed parent or guardian permission forms have been received and processed.	_____
Alternative activities are planned for those not attending the field trip.	_____
For extended field trips, appropriate student medical and liability insurance cards have been obtained.	_____
For extended field trips, teacher/supervisors have obtained telephone numbers for contacting parents or designees at any time. A copy of the student's insurance coverage card is also provided to the teacher/supervisor.	_____
Appropriate first-aid kits are appropriately stocked and available.	_____
All safety procedures are demonstrated and understood by students.	_____
The teacher has talked with the landowner or other knowledgeable persons concerning hazards prior to involving students at the site.	_____
The teacher has checked that the weather is safe for student participation.	_____

A

FIGURE 9.8 Field Trip Checklist for Teachers

Source: J. Gerlovich et al., *The Total Science Safety System CD, Kentucky Edition* (Waukee, IA: JaKel, Inc., 2003).

Field Trip Permission Request Form

Date: _____   School: _____

Your child's class is planning a school field trip on (date) _____ to _____ as part of their science class studies. The class will be traveling via school vehicles and departing from the school at _____ and returning to the same location at _____. They will be under the direct supervision of their regular teacher as well as additional "qualified" chaperones.

If you prefer not to have your student participate, please contact me so that alternative activities can be arranged. No student will be allowed on the trip without this signed form returned to me by (date) _____.

If you have questions related to the trip, or specific information concerning your child that would be helpful for the teacher to know (medications, allergies, medical ailments, handicaps, etc.), please contact:

_____ at _____
                      (Teacher)   (Telephone number)

Principal _____

Supervising Teacher _____

B

Field Trip Permission Form

I give permission for my child _____ to participate in the science field trip on (date) _____ to _____, understanding that all foreseeable precautions have been taken to ensure his/her safety.

I have provided my child with the $ _____ recommended to cover meals and other field trip related expenses.

I may be contacted at any time during my child's field trip at the following telephone numbers: _____ (Home)   _____ (Work).

Date _____

Parent or Guardian _____

C

insist that appropriate eyewear approved by the American National Standards Institute (ANSI, 2000) is provided to all students whenever the potential for eye injury exists. These federal equipment criteria were established to ensure minimum quality standards. You must insist that such eyewear meets ANSI standards and that you and your students wear them.

Compliance with these federal equipment standards is ensured when you see "Z87" printed on the goggle. The faceplate will not shatter, splinter, or fall backward into the face of the wearer if hit by a 1-inch ball bearing dropped from 50 inches, or by a quarter-inch ball bearing traveling at 150 feet/per second. In addition, the frame will not burn. The teacher is responsible for insisting that the purchasing agent order only goggles that conform to these standards. Goggles that do not meet ANSI Z87 standards, that do not fit the students, or that have scratched faceplates, missing vent plugs, or damaged rubber moldings or headbands should not be used.

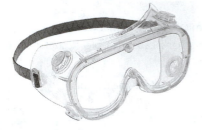

Safety goggles

Require students to wear the goggles whenever there is the slightest chance that someone could sustain an eye injury in your classroom. Remember that injuries can happen even when students are walking about the room while others are performing science activities. Think also about injuries that could happen with simple chemicals, such as salt or vinegar, or with flying objects like rubber bands or balloons. Attempt to foresee such problems and act accordingly.

Most state statutes require that goggles be cleaned before students wear them. Such equipment should be stored in a relatively dust-free environment, such as a box or a cabinet. (Secure a copy of your state's eye protective equipment legislation from the state department of education or school administration, and check for specific details.) Remember, in many states this is the law.

In addition to the eye protective equipment (goggle) legislation for your respective state, you need to investigate and, likely, comply with appropriate federal and/or state Occupational Safety and Health Administration (OSHA) standards that directly impact all school science instruction, such as Bloodborne Pathogens, Right-to-Know legislation, and the Lab Standard—Chemical Hygiene Plan. Each of these are described briefly below; however, for additional information concerning your state, check the OSHA website at www.osha.gov or contact your state department of education for questions.

Bloodborne Pathogens. On December 6, 1991, OSHA issued its final Bloodborne Pathogens Standard. It mandates engineering controls, work practices, and personal protective equipment that, in conjunction with employee training, are designed to reduce job-related risk for all employees exposed to blood. Employers must establish a written exposure control plan that identifies workers with occupational exposure to blood and other potentially infectious material and specify means to protect and educate these employees. Other requirements include hepatitis B vaccinations and applicable medical followup and counseling following personal exposure. The standard became effective May 30, 1992. Under 29 Code of Federal Regulations (CFR), Part 1910.1030, Subpart Z, the

Department of Labor, OSHA released the *Bloodborne Pathogens Standard Summary Applicable to Schools* (1992).

> The intent of this standard summary is to offer schools an overview of the OSHA standard to eliminate or minimize occupational exposure to Hepatitis B virus (HBV), which causes hepatitis B, a serious liver disease; Human Immunodeficiency Virus (HIV), which causes Acquired Immune Deficiency Syndrome (AIDS) and other bloodborne pathogens. Based on a review of the information in the rulemaking record, OSHA has made a determination that employees face a significant health risk as the result of occupational exposure to blood and other potentially infectious materials because they may contain pathogens. OSHA further concludes that this exposure can be minimized or eliminated using a combination of engineering and work practice controls, personal protective clothing and equipment, training, medical surveillance, Hepatitis B vaccination, signs and labels and other provisions. This summary includes scope and application, definitions, exposure control, methods of compliance, Hepatitis B vaccination and post-exposure evaluation and follow-up, communication of hazards to employees, recordkeeping, and effective dates.

Right-to-Know. The OSHA Hazard Communication Standard or Right-to-Know (RTK) legislation, pertaining to hazardous chemicals in the workplace, was originally drafted as Final Rule in 1983 and became effective November 25, 1985. The standard can be found in Title 29 of the Code of Federal Regulations in Subpart 2 of Part 1910 (*Federal Register,* November 25, 1989 and August 24, 1987). Many OSHA regulations have compliance based on national consensus standards from such organizations as the American National Standards Institute (ANSI), National Fire Protection Association (NFPA), and the Department of Transportation (DOT).

All privately financed educational institutions are covered by the federal standard as well as the Right-to-Know laws in force in their respective states. Publicly funded schools must comply with their respective state government statutes. All RTK legislation is designed to help employees recognize and eliminate the dangers associated with hazardous materials in their workplace.

The legislation requires that a *written program* be developed and that all affected employees know its contents. The details of such legislation will vary from state to state. Check with your state department of education, federal (chemical emergency procedures and Right-to-Know questions at 1-800-424-9346) or state OSHA office, or Department of Labor. The program need not be detailed; however, it must include the following items:

1. Written hazard assessment procedures
2. Material safety data sheets (MSDSs) for all hazardous chemicals
3. Labels and warnings
4. Employee training

Laboratory Standard—Chemical Hygiene Plan. As of January 31, 1991, laboratories engaged in activities that encompass the definition "laboratory use" must have in place a written Chemical Hygiene Plan (CHP) outlining how the facility will comply. This is according to *OSHA Occupational Exposures to Hazardous Chemicals in Laboratories Chemical Hygiene Plan,* (29 CFR, 1910.1450). This OSHA standard applies to all employers engaged in the laboratory use of chemicals. "Laboratory use" means

> chemicals are manipulated on a laboratory scale where the chemicals are handled in containers designed to be safely and easily manipulated by one person; multiple chemical procedures are used; procedures are not of a production process; protective laboratory equipment and practices are in common use to minimize employee exposure.

The plan requires that employers, *including schools,* develop a comprehensive plan for identifying and dealing with chemical hazards. The plan must include all employees who could be exposed to these chemicals and it must be updated annually.

The federal government requires that manufacturers of chemicals create Material Safety Data Sheets (MSDS) for all of their products. MSDSs typically provide the following types of information:

- General Material Identification (common name, chemical name, supplier information)
- Ingredients
- Physical and Chemical Information (boiling point, solubility, density)
- Fire and Explosion Hazard (equipment, procedures, flash points)
- Reactivity (conditions to be avoided, etc.)
- Health Hazard (primary routes of entry into the body, acute/chronic reactions)
- Disposal (environmental information, emergency management)
- Special Protection Information (protective equipment, first-aid procedures)
- Precautions (warnings, special hazards, handling)

MSDSs are available not only for exotic chemicals associated with high-school and college-level science courses but also for items common to elementary schools including glues, paints, markers, cleaning supplies, crayons, etc. These documents must be supplied to the school district upon purchase. Be certain to ask your administration for them. Teachers should be familiar with these vital documents and be careful not to use concentrated chemicals, soaps, or cleaners with students.

Be careful to keep all potentially hazardous chemicals under lock and key and out of the sight of students. Do not keep any chemicals that you do not know well. Watch for expiration dates and be certain to dispose of them before that date.

Teachers should consider these ideas for any chemicals they have in school:

- Date all chemicals.
- Anything over two years of age should be purged.
- Do not take used chemicals from others.
- Store chemicals properly.
- Store only essential chemicals—purge others.

- ✦ Watch for changes in the appearance of chemicals and get rid of them if they change.
- ✦ Do not use chemicals that you do not know.

Safety Equipment

Certain safety equipment items are essential when teaching science activities. You should be confident that such items are immediately accessible when needed, that you and students can operate them, and that the items are appropriate for your students. Students should also be taught proper operation and location of all safety equipment items they might need to use, including fire extinguishers, fire blankets, eyewashes, safety goggles, and a telephone or intercom, if available. You might need duplicate safety items in more than one location in the room. Every student should have a set of goggles during science activities when eye protection is needed.

Electrical Equipment

Whenever possible, hot plates with on-off indicator lights should replace open flames. This simple change could eliminate many fire situations from science rooms. You should not have to use extension cords for hot plates, since the room should have sufficient electrical outlets. Extension cords on the floor create tripping hazards unless they are in cord protectors. Do not allow cords to be draped across desks or other work areas in order to prevent students from inadvertently upsetting apparatus. Electrical outlet caps should be in place when the outlets are not in use. In primary grades, outlets should be covered at all times so students cannot stick metal items in the plug holes, which could cause electrocution or burns.

Ground fault interrupter

Elementary classrooms make regular use of electrical power. The science curriculum can increase that need significantly. Teachers should be careful that all outlets are safe for students. The best way to assure this is to check that outlets have ground fault interrupters (GFI) on them. The purpose of a GFI is to shut off electrical power to an outlet in the event that electricity seeks ground through a student, etc. The graphic below provides a visual image of a GFI. Note the three-prongs for grounding and the reset switches in the event the breaker trips.

Heating Equipment

Open flames are periodically necessary; be certain that emergency fire equipment is functioning properly and is immediately available. If alcohol lamps, sterno cans, or candles are used, place them in pie pans filled with damp sand. Should a spill occur, the pie pan will prevent flaming liquids from spreading to clothing, tables, and other items. Alcohol looks like water; be sure to keep it off items where it might be treated like water. If you put alcohol

Alcohol lamp

Safety can

in lamps, add a small amount of table salt so that the flame burns a bright orange color. Large quantities (½ liter or more) of alcohol or other flammable liquids should never be brought into the classroom or lab and students should never have access to quantities of these liquids.

Flammable Liquid Storage

If you are storing flammable liquids, such as alcohol, do so only in small quantities in the manufacturer's original container or in an approved safety can. A safety can is made of heavy-gauge steel or polyethylene. It has a spring-loaded lid to prevent spilling and to vent during vapor expansion caused by a heat source. It also has a flame arrester or heat sump in the throat of the spout to help prevent explosions.

Loose Clothing and Long Hair

Loose clothing (especially sweaters) and long hair should be restricted when students are working with open flames. This seems obvious, yet clothing and hair commonly cause accidents. Be careful to pull long hair back so that it does not hang down over the flame, and restrict loose clothing by pushing up sleeves and securing them with pins or elastic (nonrestricting rubber bands) to keep clothing from falling into open flames.

Fire Blankets

Fire blankets should be of the proper type and size and in the proper location. They should not be so large that students cannot use them in an emergency. Check to be certain that they are placed in conspicuous locations and easily retrievable by all students and staff, including those with disabilities. Unless otherwise recommended by the fire marshal, these blankets should be made of wool. Fire blanket display and storage containers should be carefully checked for proper function. Be sure to eliminate containers with rusted hinges and latches, blankets still stored in plastic wrappers, and blankets made with asbestos fiber. Six-foot vertical standing fire blanket tubes should be avoided since they can result in facial burns. Do not attempt to extinguish torso fires by wrapping a student in the fire blanket. Because of the chimney effect, heat is pushed across the student's face, causing facial burns. The stop-drop-and-roll procedure endorsed by fire departments appears to be the most effective at extinguishing body fires and presents the fewest drawbacks.

Fire blanket

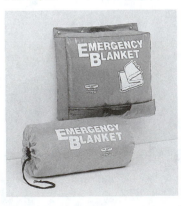

Fire Extinguishers

ABC triclass fire extinguishers are usually preferred by fire departments because they can extinguish most foreseeable fires, such as fires from paper products, electrical items, and grease, that are likely to happen in elementary science. In settings where microcomputers are used regularly, it might be wise to investigate halon extinguisher types. These have been used in aviation for years because their fire-extinguishing chemicals do not foul contacts as dry chemical types will in delicate electronic navigation, communications equipment, and computers. Halon is also preferred over carbon dioxide for extinguishing fires in electronic equipment, such as computers, because it does not cause cold thermal shock to sensitive electronic microcircuits. Teachers should confirm such suggestions with their local or state fire marshal. The major disadvantage to halon is its harmful effect on the Earth's ozone layer. Since such small quantities of this ingredient are in the ABC Triclass fire extinguisher and such emergency tools are used so infrequently, we believe that the benefits outweigh the drawbacks.

It is a good idea to have fire department personnel come into your classroom to demonstrate appropriate fire procedures and equipment to students. You should be confident and comfortable in using fire equipment items. You should also establish the habit of checking the pressure valve on fire extinguishers in or near your room to ensure that they are still adequately pressurized. It is also wise for students to learn to hold or lift extinguishers, unfold and use a fire blanket, and rehearse foreseeable emergencies involving fire.

Fire extinguisher

Eyewash and Shower

It is recommended that 15 minutes (2.5 gallons per minute) of aerated, tempered (60–90 degrees Fahrenheit), running water be deliverable from an eyewash to flush the eyes of a person who has suffered a chemical splash. At the elementary- and middle-school level, eye irritants may include salt, vinegar, sand, alcohol, and other chemicals. You should explore the installation of the fountain fixture type eyewash station (Sargent-Welch Scientific Company). It is not expensive ($60–70) and is easily installed by screwing it into an existing gooseneck faucet. The fixture allows the plumbing to be used as both an eyewash and a faucet simply by pushing a diverter valve. Should traffic patterns or room designs change, fountain fixtures can be moved to other faucets easily. On a temporary basis, you can stretch a piece of

Eyewash station

surgical tubing over a gooseneck faucet in order to deliver aerated, cool, running water to the eyes of a chemical splash victim. In the event of chemical spills on other and/or larger parts of the body, drench showers are recommended. Again, it is critical that such equipment be easily accessible to all staff and students. Be certain that the hot water faucet handle has been removed from any sink's eyewash to prevent accidental burns that could be caused by hot water.

Bottled water stations are not recommended because they can become contaminated, and they cannot deliver 15 minutes of aerated running water. They should be used only when there is no alternative, such as in field settings, and where you maintain strict control of them.

Critical safety equipment, such as fire blankets, fire extinguishers, eyewashes, and drench showers, should be located within 30 steps or 15 seconds of any location in the science room. These vital equipment items should be checked for proper operation every three to six months.

Teachers who work with chemicals must understand the properties, hazards, and appropriate emergency procedures to follow in the event of an accident. Material Safety Data Sheets (MSDS) provide such comprehensive information from chemical manufacturers. They identify the material, listing hazardous ingredients, physical and chemical characteristics, fire and explosion hazards, reactivity with other substances, health hazards, precautions for safe handling and use, as well as control measures. You can secure additional information concerning science equipment and material and MSDSs directly from manufacturers or suppliers such as VWR Sargent Welch. Material safety data sheets should accompany any chemical ordered through the school (not over the counter). If you need MSDSs for other chemicals, they can be obtained via the Internet through the following websites:

www.msdsonline.com
http://chemfinder/camsoft.som
www.chemcenter.org
www.sargentwelch.com
www.umt.edu/research/files/environ/appendic.htm
www.ilpi.com/msds/index.htm

Performing Safety Assessments

Teachers must foresee safety hazards by regularly performing safety inspections (audits) of their room, equipment, and safety techniques. They should learn to document identified problems and inform the administration of necessary changes. This process has been significantly improved through the utilization of the computer. Gerlovich and others have been working for twenty years to automate this process as much as possible. These science education researchers have created an interactive, cross-platform CD-ROM that provides elementary and secondary science teachers with a complete book addressing safety issues, forms and checklists for performing audits, and chemical databases for addressing chemical problems. In addition videos and safety graphics are

(text continues on page 319)

Video Explorations

Safety

Video Summary

Essential to practicing inquiry-based science in an elementary classroom is ensuring that all potential safety hazards have been addressed beforehand. The eight videos provided here take one through the safe use of basic safety equipment. The best advice one could follow is "when in doubt" put them on—goggles that is. Many vendors now make fairly inexpensive goggles designed to fit the faces of young learners. When purchasing, be sure they meet the ANSI standards and carry a Z87 rating.

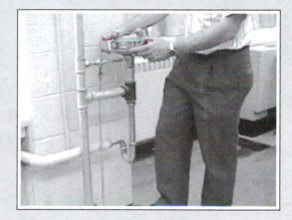

Fire safety means having fire extinguishers available and knowing which type is designed to put out fires started by different sources, such as grease, paper, or electrical. If open flames are used in classrooms, a fire blanket is a must. When using an alcohol burner, a dash of salt added to the burner makes the flame visible. Since open flames are not an ideal source for heating liquids, a more practical item is a hot plate. When purchasing, be sure it has an on/off switch with a light for the on position that is clearly visible. A short cord is advisable so that when the hot plate is plugged in close to the wall, the chance to trip over the cord and pull the hot plate down on the students is avoided.

Young learners are often curious about the electrical outlets within the classroom. Be sure outlets not in use are protected with childproof safety caps and those found near a water source have a ground fault circuit interrupter that can be tripped in the event of a short circuit to avoid serious shock injuries.

(continued)

Video Explorations

Safety (continued)

Safe field trips mean taking the time to visit the site in advance to be sure the facility is accessible for all students. In addition to having the proper permission slips, proper amount of adult supervision, and making sure any special health needs of your students are addressed, it is good practice to bring along a first-aid kit. When purchasing such a kit, be sure it has items, such as scissors, latex gloves, bandages, cold pack, a mouth resuscitation device, and first-aid ointment in the event of an emergency.

Tips for Viewing, Objectives, or What to Watch for

As you watch this video, make note of the following:

◆ The proper way to clean goggles and the safety standards they must meet for purchasing,

◆ Safe use of open flames when using an alcohol burner,

◆ Proper way to hold and use a fire blanket,

◆ Hot plate and electrical outlet safety,

◆ The different kinds of eyewash stations and how they are used,

◆ Safe practices for field trips and essential items in a first-aid kit,

◆ The different kinds of fire extinguishers and the types of fire sources for which they are most effective.

Questions for Exploration

1. As noted in the video, what type of blanket can be safely substituted for an approved fire blanket?

2. Why would one put salt into an alcohol burner?

3. What should one look for when purchasing goggles for the classroom?

4. Is a portable eyewash station effective in removing debris from the eye of a child?

5. What items would you consider essential for a first-aid kit and why?

6. Many hot plates come with a short cord. Is it safe to use an extension cord when operating a hot plate in the classroom?

7. The video identified three types of fire extinguishers. Do a survey of an elementary classroom. Which kind do you find within or closest to the classroom? Would it be effective in extinguishing a fire that started from a computer in the classroom?

Activity for Application

Identify a particular grade level you are most interested in working with. Using the instructions shared in the videoclips, create your own safety poster that can be used by children in that grade level so they know and can demonstrate proper safety procedures. Add any other important safety features that should be followed by children within the identified grade level.

This listing is only representative of teachers' safety duties. Check off these items you are well informed about or prepared for and ask your instructor for more information about the remaining items.

Item	Well Prepared or Informed	Item	Well Prepared or Informed
Teachers understand their teaching duties of		Teachers ensure that all safety equipment is functioning and available.	_____
Instruction	_____	Teachers ensure that all science equipment is of the right size and is appropriate for their students.	_____
Supervision	_____		
Maintenance of the environment, equipment	_____	Teachers ensure that students know how to use safety and other science equipment items.	_____
Teachers attempt to foresee hazards and correct them.	_____	Teachers ensure that the following fire safety equipment is available whenever they are using open flames:	
Teachers' activities are consistent with those recommended by their text-books, professional organizations, state agencies, federal standards.	_____	Fire blanket	_____
		Fire extinguisher	_____
Teachers use student safety contracts with upper elementary students.	_____	Fire alarm	_____
Teachers use only ANSI Z87 approved safety goggles.	_____	Teachers ensure that loose clothing and long hair are confined when students are using open flames.	_____
Teachers insist that students wear safety goggles whenever the potential for an eye injury exists.	_____	Teachers ensure that an eyewash is available and functioning whenever the potential for an eye injury exists.	_____
Teachers ensure that classes are not overcrowded (fewer than 24 students per teacher).	_____	Teachers use only chemicals for which they have MSDS sheets that they have reviewed for hazards.	_____
Teachers ensure that field trips are not overcrowded (fewer than ten students per adult).	_____	Teachers ensure that extension cords are used only when absolutely neces-sary, and then only grounded types.	_____
Teachers review the field trip site before taking students.	_____	Teachers ensure that all electrical outlets are capped when not in use.	_____
Teachers use the buddy system on field trips.	_____		

FIGURE 9.9 Science Safety Checklist

Source: J. Gerlovich & K. Hartman, *The Total Science Safety System: Elementary Edition,* computer soft-ware. (Waukee, IA: JaKel, Inc., 1998). Excerpted, with permission, from The Total Science Safety System software—Elementary Edition 1999 by JaKel, Inc.

provided to address certain safety techniques, and hundreds of web links take teachers to other resources. Figure 9.9 provides an example of one of the checklists. For additional information concerning The Total Science Safety System CD, contact JaKel, Inc. at www.netins.net/showcase.jakel.

What Materials Are Necessary for the Activities?

As foreseeable hazards are addressed, determine materials you will need for the activity. Identify readily available items, and locate where any additional items can be obtained. A good suggestion is to divide the remaining items into categories: items to be purchased through a scientific supplier, items that can be purchased locally through a discount or hardware store, and items that can be made for little or no cost from recycled materials.

A Science Activity Planner form (Figure 9.10) will facilitate your ordering needs. Fill out this sheet at least six weeks before you teach the lesson to allow time for vendor shipping and/or the steps your order must go through for approval of purchase and appropriation of funds in your school district. Figure 9.11 provides an example of how this form can be used.

FIGURE 9.10
Science Activity
Planner Form

Concept to be taught: _____

_____

Material needs: _____

_____

Items available through school inventory: _____

_____

Items available at no cost/recycle: _____

_____

Scientific supplier (indicate vendor name, catalogue number, description, number needed, cost per unit, total cost):

Local store (indicate store name and exact cost):

FIGURE 9.11
Science Activity
Planner Example

Concept to be taught: The circular path electrons follow is called a *circuit*.

Material needs: *For each student:* Battery, flashlight bulb, insulated copper wire, switch, bulb socket, cardboard tube (toilet paper tube), paper clip, two brass fasteners, plastic cap from a gallon milk container or a 35mm film can.

Items available through:

School inventory	Bulbs, switches, wire
No cost/recycle	Cardboard tubes, milk caps, film canister caps
Scientific supplier	Delta Supply, Nashua, New Hampshire
	57–020–9769, Bucket of batteries, 30, $29.95, $29.95
	57–020–5644, Bulb sockets, 30, $4.85/pkg. of 6, $24.25
Local store	John's Dollar Store on Main Street
	1 box of paper clips, 79¢
	2 boxes of brass fasteners, $1.45

Items Purchased Through a Scientific Supplier

Microscopes, slides, cover slips, thermometers, magnets, and electrical bulbs are the typical kinds of materials supplied by many reputable science equipment vendors. Science teachers in your school may already have suppliers they regularly deal with. Talk with fellow teachers about companies they have used in the past. If you are uncertain, request supply catalogs from companies.

Do not be quick to order from the vendor. Be a wise shopper, and compare prices and quality. Ask questions of others who may have previously ordered materials from a particular vendor. "How good is their service?" "Are they willing to meet needs quickly or slow in processing orders?" "What type of return policy do they have?" "Are they willing to take a purchase order or do they need to be paid up front?" A complete listing of science vendors, updated yearly, is available from the National Science Teachers Association.

Does your current textbook publisher supply prepackaged kits to accompany their activities? If so, will it be necessary to replenish materials in these kits? Is there a specific supplier you should order these kits

A variety of materials is necessary for effective science instruction.

from? If your answer to these questions is yes, then determine which items need to be replaced and if it is possible to replace only the used items or necessary to order a new kit. You may often come across prepackaged general science kits, such as one that supplies all materials you will need to do a unit on electricity. Under both circumstances, you must determine your needs. Will you use all of the materials provided in the kit? Will it be less expensive to order the items individually?

Carefully examine the supply catalogs. You may spot items that could enhance a lesson—an item you did not even think of in your original list of materials. Perhaps you found the item in two different catalogs, each at a different price. As you gain experience in ordering, you will find that companies differ in prices on equivalent items. If you are placing a big order with one company, it is usually more economical to purchase the higher-priced item from it along with the rest of your order. The money you may save on the price of the item with a different vendor could be spent on shipping charges.

The task of ordering supplies with school money may appear overwhelming. But if you follow a few easy steps, the work is painless. First, plan ahead. Avoid waiting until the last minute to order supplies. Often district paperwork or supply availability may delay shipment. Live plant or animal specimens can be ordered several months in advance with an indication of when you want them shipped. Once you have determined what items you will need and from which suppliers, you probably will have to obtain a purchase order. Check with the principal or school district treasurer about the proper procedure. Most often this involves filling out the purchase order completely. *Completely* means not only names of items but catalog numbers, quantities, prices, shipping charges, complete name, address, and phone and/or fax number of vendor. Remember that you need only one purchase order per vendor. Once it is completed, you will need to obtain the authorized signatures before you can mail it. If the purchase order form has duplicates, mail the original to the vendor. If it is a single copy, make a copy for the administration and one for yourself.

Local restaurants, grocery stores, or discount stores are usually willing to donate items such as paper cups, containers, or straws to meet your science activity needs.

If you phone in the order, be sure to provide the vendor with all information included on the purchase order, especially the purchase order number. After the initial order is placed, it is customary to write on the purchase order the date and time the order was phoned in. You may be required to send the vendor a copy of that purchase order. If so, make sure to write on the purchase order, "This is a copy of a phone order."

Items Purchased Locally

Consumable items—paper cups, bags, straws—are some of the common items

purchased from local vendors. If you teach in a community that is very supportive of its local schools, you may be able to get donations of consumable items from local restaurants, grocery stores, or discount stores. Even the local lumber yard may be willing to supply a class with yard or meter sticks or scrap lumber.

Discount stores that specialize in overruns are an excellent source for science supplies. As you walk up and down the aisles, scan the shelves thinking about science concepts you could teach with various items. You may be surprised at what you come up with. Simple toys like yo-yos, ball and jacks, paddle balls, and rubber balls can be used to teach a variety of scientific concepts. Paper clips, masking tape, batteries, or wire can start you on the way to a terrific electricity unit (see Chapter 5). Inexpensive bubble gums or chocolate chip cookies can lead to exciting lessons that focus on the scientific method. Never underestimate the science possibilities in a discount store.

Local stores may already have agreements with your school district, such as charge accounts or cash credit accounts. Check with the school district treasurer. You may be able to charge the items at those stores. Other stores may take purchase orders. Occasionally you may have to provide your own money. If this is the case, find out the procedure for reimbursement in your school. Does the principal have a fund from which you can immediately be reimbursed upon turning in your receipt? Is a receipt necessary? Do you need a petty cash voucher from the school before you make a purchase? What kind of information does the vendor need to supply on that voucher? Do you need to supply the vendor with a tax-exempt number from the school so that you are not charged sales tax? Ask all of these questions *before* you go out and spend your own money. You do not want to find out after the fact that since you did not complete the proper paper trail, you will not be reimbursed.

Items Made from Recycled Materials

You've been caught again rummaging through the bin at the local recycling center. Embarrassed? There is no need to be when it's done in the name of science! What was it this time? Looking for cans to paint black for a unit on heat? Was it a plastic soda bottle to make another Cartesian diver? Do you need various size jars for a sound unit? Whatever the science topic, usually one or two items can be found in a recycling bin. Of course, you can avoid those embarrassing moments by encouraging your students to bring in materials they ordinarily throw away. Setting up a recycling area in your classroom will provide a quick source for those necessary items and teach students the importance of recycling.

In the scenario at the beginning of this chapter, Celeste needed a tuna can so she went to the area in her home where recyclables were stored; thus she did not have to hold off creating the volcano for lack of a tuna can. Cans are not the only useful recyclable item. Styrofoam plates from prepackaged meats are useful in many activities. They make great placemats for messy activities that involve liquids. Styrofoam egg cartons can be turned into charcoal crystal gardens in no time, or they can be used to stack small items like rock collections. Toilet paper and paper towel tubes can be used in making flashlights, and aluminum pie plates are useful for heating water. Plastic containers with lids, such as the ones that food comes in at the grocery store, can be used for storage. Your imagination is your only limit when it comes to deciding what to do with recycled materials.

Live Items

The National Science Teachers Association (Kwan & Texley, 2003) recommends that teachers consider these factors when planning for plants and animals in the elementary classroom (Table 9.4):

Plants. Plants should be kept in areas where they can thrive, be readily viewed, and be protected. Be careful to study only plants about which you are knowledgeable. Do not use plants that present hazards from oils (poison ivy, poison oak, poison sumac, poinsettia, and other local plants) or hazards from saps (oleander, stinging nettle, and other local plants). In addition, no plants that are poisonous if eaten should be accessible to students, including those shown in Table 9.5.

For additional information, check the College of Veterinary Medicine & Biomedical Sciences, Dept. of Clinical Sciences, Colorado State University—*Guide to Poisonous Plants,* website: www.vth.colostate.edu/poisonous_plants/. Another excellent database resource for plants and animals of the world can be found on the following Unites States Geological Survey (USGS) website: www.npwrc.usgs.gov.resource.resource.htm. The online guide provides information on more than 100 poisonous plants. Information for

TABLE 9.4 Selecting Organisms for Your Classroom

Type of Organism	Level of Care	Potential Problems
Plants	Low: Need light and water, can be left during vacations	• Molds bother some sensitive students • Some plants are toxic
Aquarium fish, protests (amoebae, paramecia, euglena)	Low: Can be left during vacations	• Slight risk from bacteria in tank • Temperature controls may be required during vacations
Crustacea and snails	Moderate: Simple foods, intolerant of heat	• Moderate risk of bacterial contamination
Insects, butterflies	Moderate: Cultures can become moldy	• Stings • Exotic species endanger the environment
Reptiles (snakes, lizards, turtles)	High: Require live food, intolerant of cold	• Bites • Salmonella infections • Moldy food • Sensitive to temperature change
Rodents and rabbits	High: Can't be left unattended during vacations	• Allergenic dander • Odor from droppings and bedding • Bites and scratches • Human disease carriers

Source: T. Kwan and J. Texley, *Exploring Safely: A Guide for Elementary Teachers* (National Science Teachers Association, 2002).

TABLE 9.5   Plants That Are Harmful If Eaten

Some fungi (many mushrooms)	Daffodil (bulb)	Iris	Nightshade	Sumac
Aconite	Dieffenbachia	Jack-in-the-Pulpit	Oleander	Sweet Pea
Azalea	Elderberry	Japanese Yew	Philodendron	Tansy
Buckeye	English ivy	Jimson Weed	Poinsettia	Tomato
Belladonna	False Hellebore	Jonquil (bulb)	Poison Oak	Virginia Creeper
Bloodroot	Four-O'clock	Lantana	Pokeweed	Wild Tobacco
Buttercup	Foxglove	Lily-of-the-Valley	Potato (sprouts)	Wild Tomato
Caladium	Herbane	Mayapple	Privet	Wisteria
Castor Bean	Holly	Milkweed	Rhododendron	Yellow Jasmine
China Berry	Hyacinth	Mistletoe	Rhubarb	
Croton	Hydrangea	Morning Glory	Scotch Broom	
	Indian Tobacco	Moutain Laurel	Skunk Cabbage	

Source: Gerlovich et al, *The Total Science Safety System CD, Kentucky Edition* (Waukee, IA: JaKel, Inc., 2003). Excerpted, with permission, from The Total Science Safety System software—Elementary Edition 1999 by JaKel, Inc.

each plant includes: common and botanic name; color photograph; description; habitat; animals (including people) affected; toxic principle; gastrointestinal, nervous, integumentary, and other system symptoms; and treatment. The National Gardening Association site, www.kidsgardening.com/hydroponicsguide/toc.asp, provides an excellent overview of hydroponics (growing plants without soil) gardening for kids. Lesson plans are included.

Animals. Whenever animals are used in science activities with students, it is imperative that care be exercised to protect both the animals and the students. It is obvious that animals stimulate learning in many life science and biology classes. They can, however, present some unique hazards to students. Teachers should anticipate such hazards as much as possible so that neither students or animals are injured. Be careful, for instance, not to allow animals to be handled when they are eating.

Do not allow dead animals in the room, as the exact cause of death may not be determinable. Many warm-blooded animals carry and transmit diseases to humans through ticks, mites, and fleas. Be certain that adequately sized and clean cages are provided to all animals. Cages should be kept locked and in safe, comfortable settings. Since most supply houses are required to quarantine animals and check them for disease before sale, it would be wise to obtain study animals only from these dealers. If any are purchased locally, check for general health of all animals before purchase.

Heavy gloves should be used for the handling of animals that might bite.

Students should wash their hands immediately and thoroughly when finished working with animals; this will help prevent students from inadvertently transmitting germs. If an animal dies unexpectedly, have it examined by a local veterinarian. This is cheap insurance in helping prevent disease complications.

Guidelines on the use of live animals in the classroom are available from the National Association of Biology Teachers (NABT). They are well developed and provide the teacher with more depth of understanding in deciding what animals to bring into the classroom and under what conditions. The guidelines can be found on the NABT website at www.nabt.org. For additional information concerning the responsible use of animals in the classroom, you may want to check the *National Science Teachers Association Handbook* (NSTA, 1996) or NSTA's website at www.nsta.org/handbook/animals.html.

Safety/First-Aid Kits

For most elementary programs, a common *Science Safety Kit* should be compiled that addresses all common, foreseeable emergencies. It can then be moved from room to room, within the building, and be used wherever hands-on, inquiry-based science activities are being undertaken by the students. The kit outlined in Figure 9.12 represents the basic necessities. It is imperative that teachers consult with their school nurse or medical authority for specific items that can and cannot be used with students.

The following items should be included in science safety first-aid kit:

- ANSI Z87 approved eye protective equipment (24 sets = 1 per student)
- Prepackaged alcohol pads, or other appropriate sterilizing agent, for cleaning eye protective equipment
- Fountain fixture or other appropriate eye-rinse station
- An approved ABC triclass fire extinguisher
- An approved fire-retardant wool fire blanket
- Surgical mask for addressing bodily fluid splashes
- Rubber gloves for addressing bodily fluid splashes
- Ground fault interrupter (GFI) on electrical outlets near faucets
- Electrical outlet caps—for use when outlets are not being used
- Surgical bandages, surgical gauze, hypoallergenic tape
- Electrical circuit analyzer to check for safe, functioning electrical outlets
- Emergency response telephone numbers (poison control center, hospital, fire department, front office, nurse, etc.)
- Sealable plastic bags for disposal of materials
- Paper towels and kitty litter for absorbing spills
- Lysol and/or bleach/water solution (10% bleach/90% water) for sterilizing hard surfaces
- NFPA chemical hazard labels
- MSDSs for hazardous chemicals
- Safety signs identifying strategic safety equipment
- Scissors

FIGURE 9.12
Science Safety/
First-Aid Kit

Source: Gerlovich et al., *The Total Science Safety System CD, Kentucky Edition* (Waukee, IA: JaKel, Inc., 2003). Excerpted, with permission, from The Total Science Safety System software—Elementary Edition 1999 by JaKel, Inc.

Storage

Central or Classroom Storage Access

The biggest task is over—or so you think. The materials have been ordered and are beginning to arrive. So where do they go? Does your school have a central storage area for science materials? Are the materials you ordered solely for your classroom use, or will you be sharing them with other teachers? Who will be allowed access to the materials? Do you have space in your classroom to store materials? Before you begin stocking your classroom shelves, find the answers to these questions.

Central Storage Area. Some schools designate one room or area in the school to keep all science materials. If this is the case at your school, find out who is responsible for maintaining that area. Careful inventory should be maintained of the items stored there. It is best if one person is responsible for keeping the inventory current. Teachers who borrow materials should be held responsible for their return. One person should have the authority to request the return of borrowed materials after a reasonable time period. Sign-out sheets (Figure 9.13) should be completed by any staff member who uses materials from the central storage.

The teachers should determine who will have access to the central storage area:

+ Will only science teachers be allowed to use it?
+ Will other teachers have access?
+ Will students be allowed to borrow items from central storage?
+ Who will be responsible for disseminating the materials? Will it be done on an honor system?

FIGURE 9.13
Science Equipment
Checkout Form

Science Equipment Checkout Form

Name: _____

Grade and/or subject area: _____

Room number: _____

Date of checkout: Expected date of return:

_____   _____

Items borrowed:

_____

_____

_____

Signature: _____

These questions may appear trivial, but once you count on items for a particular activity only to find that someone has borrowed them without signing them out, you will not be too happy. Often it becomes a wild-goose chase to find out who used the materials last. If the search comes up short, you may end up omitting a valuable lesson for lack of supplies. Some ground rules can avoid any unnecessary searches or hard feelings.

Classroom Storage. If you store materials in your classroom, plan where the materials will be located. The first consideration is who will have access to those materials. Will the students be allowed access to everything, or will safety reasons prohibit total access? Where can you store materials that you consider dangerous to students? Ideally, any hazardous materials should be stored in locked cabinets.

Think about the storage of live specimens. If plants are brought into the classroom, is an area available near windows to facilitate plant growth? Is shelf space available near a window, or will you have to appropriate a table or bookshelf to set up near a window? Can artificial lights be used on the plant? If window space is minimal, where will this designated artificial light be? Should the students have access to these plants? Do they present any potential harm to the students if ingested?

If you know that students will need access to certain materials, arrange materials so that they are on shelves or in cabinets within easy reach. If there are certain materials, such as chemicals or cleaners, that need to be out of the students' reach, a locked cabinet or cupboard is a necessity. Plans to make shelves or cabinets if they do not exist in your classroom. Rather than looking at your classroom negatively and simply deciding that there is no place to put anything, think creatively. Would an unused corner make an ideal storage area? Can you get a local business to donate some unused bookshelves or storage cabinets? Can the school's maintenance personnel make some shorter shelf units for student access? Try to have these problems solved before the materials arrive.

Not all items will be stored. For instance, if you have a learning center that constantly requires the use of a balance, leave the balance out and do not store it. Other activity areas may be set up where materials are always left out. The students should know that they are free to move items from one center to another. For example, going back to the first scenario, if Celeste and Sarah were working on their volcano at school in the science activity center, and realized that they needed red food coloring, which was always out at the food center, they could go over and get the food coloring without having to ask for permission to move it from one center to the next.

Freedom to move materials creates a learning environment that is adaptable to the students' needs. To avoid creating an inventory nightmare, establish some simple task assignments. Most children like to be useful and help the teacher. In the primary grades, the teacher can create a poster for each center with a picture of the necessary items. Older students can have a written supply list for each center. Students can be

Proper materials storage makes preparation and replacement easier.

assigned to the different centers on a rotating basis and be responsible for making sure that at the end of the school day the items for their assigned center are in place. When consumable items are needed, the students should write them on a master list for the teacher, indicating which items are needed at each learning center. The teacher can then use this list to obtain the materials, then give the items to the student responsible for that center to put in their proper place. Gentle reminders to students about returning items to the place where they found them will facilitate the task of taking inventory.

TABLE 9.6   Materials Storage

Materials Stored	Advantages	Disadvantages
As units	All material together Can present lesson at any time without rummaging through shelves for necessary materials	Question of who is responsible for replacing consumable items Scarce resources cause unit to be picked apart and used for other activities
Individually	Ideal storage in schools where resources are scarce Works well when materials are centrally stored, easier to collect	Time needed to pull several items together for each teaching unit Additional storage space necessary to store individual items in classroom
On shelves	Items can be shelved alphabetically for quick and easy retrieval Efficient method for storing glassware and large items	Difficult to determine where one letter ends and the next begins Difficult to store items in multiple quantities With multiple users, need to rearrange shelves frequently
In plastic bags	Sealable bags are ideal for small items Can be labeled with permanent markers Available in a variety of sizes to accommodate various sized materials	If seal not made, items fall out and get lost With extended use, labeling wears off Tear with frequent use
In shoeboxes or cardboard boxes	Inexpensive way to store multiple items like thermometers, magnets, and marbles Easily labeled and can be covered with an adhesive plastic for prolonged use An ideal size for storing on shelves	Since opaque, necessary to open to determine contents Even covered, eventually wear out
In plastic storage bins	Available in a variety of shapes and sizes Clear so items stored are visible Can be labeled with permanent markers Many guaranteed to last at least five years	Better-made containers are costly Lids crack on less expensive containers if heavy things are stacked on top
Using color coding	Ideal for identifying hazardous materials by using orange safety stickers Identify quickly consumed items with one color facilitates reordering needs	Advantages lost if all teachers do not understand or remember color codes If color code key not posted, difficult to locate material

Storing and Dispensing Materials

No matter where materials are stored, you will need to decide how to store them. Will they be arranged according to units, such as electricity, weather, and simple machines, or will the items be stored separately? Once you make this decision, choose from among numerous ways to arrange the items, from shelves to shoeboxes to plastic storage bins. Table 9.6 identifies the advantages and disadvantages of several storage possibilities.

Whether items are kept in a central storage area (see Figure 9.14) or in the classroom, you still need to think about how the students will collect them for a particular activity. When items are stored in a central location, you may want to collect the materials at least a day ahead of time to make sure everything needed for a given activity is still available. Decide how many of what item you will need. Once the items are in the classroom, appoint students to arrange the materials for the various working groups.

In a safe and efficient activity-based science classroom, the teacher does not have to do all of the advance work for a particular science activity. The teacher can appoint responsible students to collect the science materials. A simple way to disseminate the materials is to have a materials list posted for the activity, assign particular students to gather materials, and provide those students with buckets or plastic bins to put the collected materials in for that activity. Each materials manager for the day should be responsible for collecting the correct number of items for his or her group to do the activity and be responsible for counting the materials at the end of the lesson, collecting them in the bucket, and returning them to their proper place. If the materials go back to a central

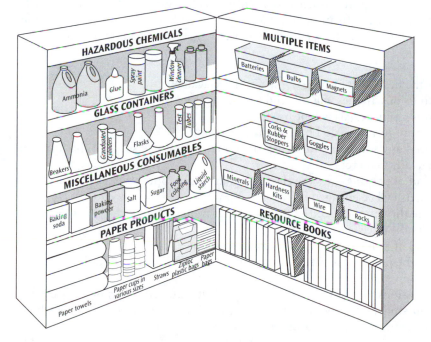

FIGURE 9.14 Central Storage Area Design

storage area, the teacher should make sure they are returned to their proper place as soon as possible. Other teachers may be counting on the use of those materials.

Keep safety concerns in mind when returning used materials. Were hazardous materials used during the activity? (Any material labeled toxic, ignitable, corrosive, or reactive should be considered hazardous.) Many common household items used at the elementary level in science activities could fall into these categories—such items as bleach or ammonia, carpet shampoos, window cleaner, paints, and glues. Does your school have an appropriate system to handle disposal of these wastes? Which materials can be recycled? What procedures should be followed to dispose of used materials? Remember that hazardous waste improperly handled can pollute drinking supplies, poison humans, and contaminate soil and air. The teacher should be responsible for disposing of used hazardous materials. If you are uncertain about disposing of a particular item, check with the local fire marshal or local office of the Environmental Protection Agency. These agencies will be able to instruct you on proper disposal. Many local fire departments are equipped to handle low-level toxic waste. All high schools should have a plan in place for handling waste from chemistry classes. Check to see if your district has one. If it does not, work with local agencies to develop a safe and reliable disposal system.

Room Arrangement

Carefully planned lessons and ample supplies are not enough to carry off a successful inquiry-based science activity. The physical arrangement of the classroom is also an important consideration. Barriers such as classroom size, traffic patterns, blind spots, poles, and walls will require a teacher to be creative about utilizing the available space. Before you begin moving furniture around, draw a scale floor plan of your classroom (see Figure 9.15). Ask yourself the following questions when deciding how to arrange the classroom:

+ What is the best way to utilize the space I have available?
+ What kinds of activities will my students be involved in?
+ What kinds of materials will be used?
+ What type of furniture do I have in my classroom?
+ Will I need any additional furniture, or should I eliminate some of the furniture that is already in there?
+ What kind of flooring does the classroom have? Is it appropriate for the activities my students will be engaged in?
+ Where are the entrances and exits in the classroom?
+ Where are the electrical outlets?
+ What kind of traffic patterns do I wish to develop?
+ What are the potential hazards with the arrangement I have in mind?

The suggestions that follow are designed to help you arrange your classroom to maximize your students' science experiences while allowing you to maintain flexibility to accommodate the teaching of other subject areas.

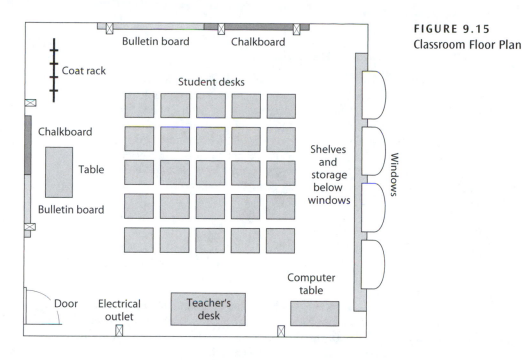

FIGURE 9.15
Classroom Floor Plan

Large-Group Science Activities

Flat surfaces offer the best means of engaging in science activities when working with an entire class. If you are in a classroom with tilted desk tops, you will need to be creative; child-sized tables are one alternative. Another is to designate space on the floor for children to participate in science activities.

Divide the class into small working groups of three or four students each. Current recommendations are that elementary school classrooms should provide at least 30-square feet of space for each student and have no more than twenty-four students for labs and activities. Although elementary science classes are not laboratory based, if all students are to have sufficient feedback and guidance in science projects, twenty-four students is a manageable number. While the physical constraints of your classroom may not allow you this much area or your class size puts you beyond the twenty-four-student limit, whenever possible optimum space should be allocated and ideal class size should be maintained.

Whether the students are working at small tables, several flat-topped desks pushed together to make a larger working area, or on the floor, consider the type of flooring in the classroom. A nonslip tile floor is best but not a necessity. Carefully taping down an inexpensive vinyl floor remnant in the designated science area will save a carpet from messy spills and facilitate clean-up.

Create an area where you can collect materials for science activities before the class uses them. This place should also function as an area where science demonstrations occur. Preferably, this area should be close to the science storage area if supplies are

Class Size and Science Achievement

First, small classes are supported in primary grades. Kindergarten, first, second, and third grade classes should be as small as economically feasible. If cost were not an issue, the limiting factor to reducing class size . . . seems to be the social value of cooperation among very young children.

Second, . . . it seems evident that these changes should be accompanied by research-based changes in teaching methods that take advantage of these changes. One prominent study concludes that reducing class size and proportionally increasing educational expenses by as much as 50 percent might be necessary to increase the student's achievement by a mere 10 percentile points. It may be that reducing class size in itself is not an efficient use of public funds.

Third, the research on teaching and learning (rather than the research on achievement) supports the idea that very large class sizes cannot provide students with reasonable instructional and motivational systems. Safety problems also increase with class size. Small groups make it easier for teachers to monitor problem solving, attempt to improve understanding, and create an atmosphere of scientific inquiry. These factors are among the many that are not measured by most achievement tests.

Fourth, teachers must couple their arguments for smaller classes with requests for other improvements that would help their students achieve. . . . Most science classrooms . . . lack adequate supplies and equipment. . . . Such tools, along with reasonable inservice, might make science truly exciting and academically productive.

. . . Teachers need small classes [to] conduct hands-on laboratory activities and intense follow-up discussions. . . . In large classes, it is unlikely they can prepare and inspire students for tomorrow's world of science.

Source: W. Holliday, "Should We Reduce Class Size?" *Science Teacher* (January 1992): 14–17.

stored within the classroom. Storage space for student projects should also be planned near this area. If possible, choose an area near the sink.

The physical arrangement of the desks and tables should be dictated by the type of activity going on in the classroom on any particular day. If space and furniture availability permit, a permanent science area can be maintained within the classroom. If space is a problem, desks and tables can be moved into configurations like those shown in Figure 9.16, which will facilitate learning. Whenever possible, this area should be near windows to allow the use of natural light. Space should be arranged to eliminate traffic congestion and to provide a clear path to all classroom exits.

Science Learning Centers

When working with the entire class for a science lesson, a teacher committed to the learning cycle and constructivist approaches will find that science learning centers satisfactorily accommodate additional expansion activities for each lesson. You can design the learning center so that it focuses on a particular concept brought out in a class lesson and provides additional experiences to enable a greater understanding of the concept. The center should not simply be a place where the brighter students, or those who finished

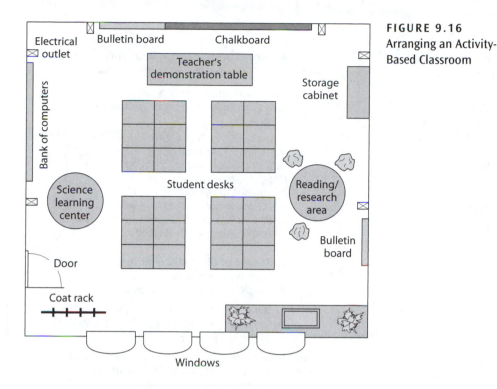

FIGURE 9.16
Arranging an Activity-Based Classroom

their assignments first, get to go. All students should be encouraged to use the learning center at their convenience, to engage in activities that provide additional experiences with a particular science concept. Once all of the students have had sufficient time to participate in the expansion activity, change the activity to address a new concept.

Another approach to science learning centers is to design them so that students gain greater experience in the processes of science. When you present science lessons to a large group of students, the chances that each student has adequate time to make observations, predictions, measurements, and so on, are slim if a more-skilled peer blurts out the answer first. The learning center can be designed so each child has a chance to work in the area, gain experience in solving problems, measuring, predicting, using scientific instruments, and so on. You can change the learning center weekly, with different process skills as the focus (see Figure 9.17).

A science learning center can also be designed as a *discovery area*—a place where children create inventions from a variety of provided materials. The center can be considered challenge areas, where the teacher creates a problem for the week, and using the materials provided, the students work to solve the problem. Science learning centers can be the place where students can play teacher-prepared or commercially prepared science games.

Whatever you decide the focus of your science learning center should be, a few simple rules must be upheld to ensure its success. The guidelines for a science learning center are set out in Table 9.7 (page 335).

1. Obtain light-bulb record books

Process Skill: Recording data

Each student will receive a light-bulb record book. The outer covers are made from yellow cardboard. Several sheets of white paper for students to record their data are stapled between the covers.

2. Page 1 of record book

Process Skill: Observing

On the table is a box with a bulb sticking out of the top. A switch protrudes from one side. A card near the box states:

Make as many observations as possible. Write the word OBSERVATIONS on the top of page 1 in the light bulb record book. Record your observation on that page.

3. Record book

Process Skill: Predicting

A card that is numbered with a 3 and has a drawing of the box with the bulb will be at the center with the following directions:

Label the next blank page in your record book PREDICTIONS. Predict what is inside the box causing the bulb to light. List and/or draw your predictions on that page.

4. Record book, battery, bulb, wire

Process Skill: Manipulating materials

Card numbered 4 near a battery, bulb, and wire, asks the students to do the following:

Label the next blank page of your record book MANIPULATING MATERIALS. Take the battery, bulb, and wire from the table. Using only those three pieces of material, get the bulb to light. Record in the record book drawings of ways you manipulated the materials—whether the bulb lit or not.

5. Record book, battery, bulb, wire, bulb holder, switch

Process Skill: Manipulating materials

At the next station the above materials will be laying near card number 5. The students will be asked to do the following:

Label the next blank page of your record book MANIPULATING MATERIALS. Take the battery, bulb, wire, bulb holder, and switch from the table. Get the bulb to light as you did at station 4. This time wire it so that the switch will turn the bulb on and off. Record in the record book drawings of ways you manipulated the materials—whether the bulb lit or not.

6. Record book, box, battery, bulb, bulb holder, wire, switch

Process Skill: Interpreting data, inferring, formulating models

The above materials will be found at station 6. The students will be asked to do the following:

Label the next blank page of your record book INTERPRETING DATA, INFERRING, FORMULATING MODELS. Using the materials given and your results from activities 4 and 5, try to create a box like the one you observed at stations 2 and 3. When finished go back to your prediction page in the record book. Was your prediction correct?

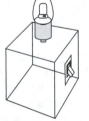

FIGURE 9.17   Process-Oriented Science Learning Center Lesson

TABLE 9.7   Science Learning Center Guidelines

1. The purpose and objectives for the activity are made clear; the students understand what they are supposed to do at each center. The activity is designed so that it enhances the students' understanding of a concept rather than serving to frustrate and confuse.
2. All students have an opportunity to work at the center before the activity is changed.
3. Activities at the center do not interfere with other lessons going on in the classroom. Activities that require darkness, loud noises, or excessive amounts of physical activity are not appropriate for a learning center. The center is in an area where the teacher can readily observe the children in action.

4. At least one 2-feet-by-4-feet table or work area of equivalent size is dedicated to this center. If the activity requires additional space, adequate floor space will be allocated. If audiovisual materials are to be used, electrical outlets are close by.
5. Consumable materials at the centers are replenished frequently.
6. When water is required for an activity, the center is located close to a water source. If this is not possible, care is taken so that children running to sinks or water fountains are not interfering with students engaged in other classroom tasks.

Figures 9.18 and 9.19 provide examples of some typical science learning centers. Centers should be found in an area of the classroom where they are least likely to interfere with normal classroom operations. The information provided on classroom safety should guide you in the placement of the science learning center.

A pegboard or a felt board can be designed so that it will stand on its own atop a table or desk and can easily be stored when necessary. Pockets made from cloth or heavy cardboard serve as areas to hold activity cards, instructions, or small materials needed for the activity. Any material sturdy enough to withstand student wear, without being so heavy

- Outlets should be available when needed.
- Bulletin board contains pertinent science information.
- Center is located near the door to gain access to water from fountain in hall since no water is available in this classroom.

FIGURE 9.18
Science Learning Center

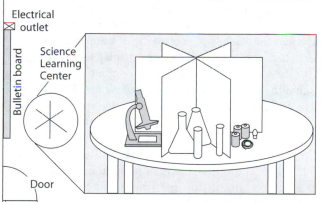

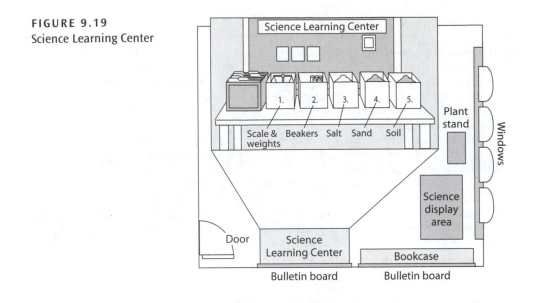

FIGURE 9.19
Science Learning Center

that it topples over, will serve as the backdrop for your science learning center. Appropriate pictures or diagrams should be displayed on this board. If the activity requires a more formal means of record keeping, place record sheets or assessment sheets in a pocket on the board. Figure 9.20 provides an example of a typical science learning center backdrop.

Bulletin Boards and Other Displays

An activity-based science classroom should include a science bulletin board and a science display area. Lettering used for the bulletin board should be no smaller than 4 inches high. Plan the topic to be addressed, and focus on one concept. Don't use too many words. Try to find visuals that will enhance the students' understanding of the concept, but avoid using too much material. If display colors, sizes, and shapes change too frequently, the intended message may get lost.

Science displays should be designed to appeal to the students' natural curiosity. They can be theme oriented and designed by the teacher or a collection of unrelated items provided by the students. For a theme highlighting mammals, the display table could contain pelts of various mammals for the students to touch and to compare and antlers or horns for the students to determine the animal it came from and its age. There may be footprints of various mammals with a challenge to the students to determine which animal left the print. Books or picture of various mammals would be left at the table.

In a hodge-podge approach, the display area may be a catch-all for the various science-related items children bring in that they would like to share. Items on the display table should be ones the students are allowed to touch: household items, like an old radio or clock that can be taken apart to examine the inner works, for example, or unusual rocks or plant parts that may serve to pique a student's curiosity. An item that re-

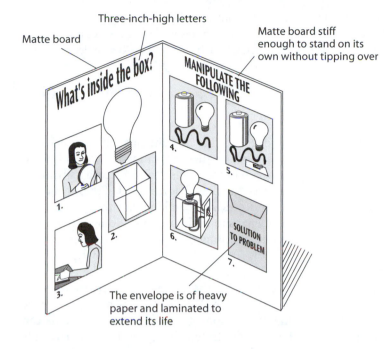

Matte board

Three-inch-high letters

Matte board stiff
enough to stand on its
own without tipping over

FIGURE 9.20
Science Learning Center Backdrop

What's inside the box?

MANIPULATE THE FOLLOWING

SOLUTION TO PROBLEM

The envelope is of heavy
paper and laminated to
extend its life

quires special care, like a geode or a parent's rock collection, that a student brings in may be better suited for teacher-supervised display.

Large-group instruction or small science learning centers? No matter what the mode of instruction is, science learning will be facilitated when careful thought is given to the physical arrangement of the classroom. Allowing the students to travel freely to learning centers implies that certain behaviors are expected of the students. Using instruction time to teach cooperative roles will facilitate class exploration.

One Final Thought

In recent years the United States and the world has become a much less stable global environment. Reasonable and prudent judgment would suggest that educators heed these warnings and act prudently when considering student safety.

The National Science Teachers Association recommends the following concerning Crisis Response Teams (Kwan & Texley, 2003).

It is highly recommended that school systems and individual schools create and train crisis response teams to respond to medical and psychological crises, threats and acts of violence, and the range of circumstances that require immediate action for the welfare and safety of students and others in the schools. Such teams should proactively plan for emergencies that could arise and ensure that appropriate individuals are trained and available to provide first aid, psychological support, physical security, and public information. Such teams should include and/or maintain regular contact with representatives from state and local agencies that provide assistance and emergency response (e.g., police and fire departments, community mental health agencies, local hospitals, state health department).

Chapter Summary

By asking, "What are the foreseeable hazards associated with valued educational activities?" and "What materials are necessary for the activities?" teachers can be successful in creating an efficient, safe environment for activity-based science. Once the concepts to be taught are clearly identified and grade-level-appropriate activities are chosen, decisions about materials needed to teach these concepts, storage of the materials, and safe practices while handling them must be decided upon. Generally storage decisions depend on school building space restrictions and the safety philosophy embraced by the teaching faculty.

Teachers must attempt to foresee problems posed by activities and address them; teach appropriately for the emotional, physical, and intellectual levels of their students; and provide adequate supervision applicable for the environment and the degree of hazards anticipated, in addition to ensuring that the environment and equipment items are properly maintained. Teachers who are sure that they have addressed all of these concerns can proceed with confidence. If they cannot, adjustments should be made—adding more safety features, limiting the activity to a teacher demonstration only, or eliminating the activity.

The physical arrangement of the classroom directly affects the success of the activity-oriented science lesson. When physical barriers impede the completion of an activity, the students can become frustrated. If materials are not readily available to bring a child from a state of disequilibrium to equilibrium, a teachable moment may be lost. A flexible learning environment, carefully planned and designed to promote student exploration, will greatly facilitate science learning.

Discussion Questions

1. You are planning a field trip with your first-grade class to the local prairie ecosystem (or other special local ecosystem) to study plants. All parent and guardian release forms have been returned with the exception of one. Would you allow the student to attend the activity anyway? Give three reasons for your answer.

2. A student in your third-grade class asks you if he can bring his pet northern banded water snake to class to show during your reptile unit. What would be your response? What information would you want to support your decision? Where would you secure such information?

3. You are preparing to do a simple chemistry experiment with your sixth-grade class. A student says that she has new safety glasses provided by her optometrist and would rather wear them than your safety goggles. What would be your response? Why?

4. Ask representatives from the local fire department to visit your classroom and demonstrate the proper procedure for dealing with a personal-clothing fire and the proper use of fire extinguishers. If possible, ask that the fire personnel set small demonstration fires outside in containers and show how the various extinguisher types put out paper, electrical, and grease fires.

5. Visit an elementary school that has a central storage area for science materials. Does this area appear well maintained? Is someone responsible for checking materials in and out? Who keeps the inventory of supplies? How well managed do you think the storage area is? What recommendations would you make?

6. During a unit on insect behavior, several children bring to school both live and dead insects. What

should be done with the dead insects? The live ones? Should the students be encouraged to bring insects into the classroom? Why or why not? What do you believe your responsibility is to the insects and to the students' attitudes toward insects?

7. In 1992, the District of Columbia was offering a summer school program designed to provide hands-on education to gifted and talented eight- and nine-year-old students. Dedrick Howell was a nine-year-old student enrolled in the program. Louis Jagoe, a Ph.D. candidate at the American University, was teaching a class on making sparklers.

The children scooped the chemicals, including potassium perchlorate, out of jars, ground up the mixture in mortars. While they were combining the chemicals, Jagoe ignited three different chemical mixtures at the front of the room with a butane lighter. The children continued to grind the material, while a counselor distributed pieces of metal hangers to be dipped into the mixture at a later time. Dedrick Howell was specifically told not to dip the hanger material until instructed to do so. Moments later the chemicals exploded in front of Dedrick. The chemicals burned at 5,000 degrees Fahrenheit, and Dedrick was burned over 25 percent of his body including his hands, arms, chest and face (*District of Columbia* v. *Howell,* 1992). The jury found the District of Columbia negligent under several alternative theories.

Do you think the court was right? Why or why not? How could the accident have been avoided? What guidelines should teachers follow when having an outside guest presenter in their room for science?

Build a Portfolio or E-Folio

1. Develop a written plan for conducting a safety assessment of a school science classroom in your area. Include all necessary forms and checklists, as well as a time line for its completion.

2. Select an elementary school in your area, and develop a written checklist for performing a safety assessment of its grounds. Be sure to address items that are indigenous to your area, including hazardous plants and animals, automobile traffic, difficult-to-supervise areas, natural hazards (streams, lakes, and so on), and human problems (construction areas, glass).

3. Interview an elementary science teacher responsible for ordering science equipment. Find answers to the following questions:
   ✦ What vendors does he or she use to purchase science equipment and why?
   ✦ How good is the service provided by that vendor?
   ✦ How quick is the vendor to process orders?
   ✦ What type of return policy does the vendor have?
   ✦ Does the vendor take purchase orders or require payment up-front?
   ✦ What procedures does the school follow in placing and paying for orders?
   ✦ If you had to set up an ordering system, would you recommend the one used by the teacher you interviewed? If not, how would you design it differently?
   ✦ What safety features are followed for classroom storage of materials?

4. Identify a grade level range (Pre-K–2; 3–4; 5–6; 7–8) you feel comfortable teaching. Design a science learning center for that grade-level range around a particular theme, such as outer space or the rainforest. Draw a diagram of what it will look like. What kinds of items, activities, and experiments would you place there? What safety precautions should you consider? What if students with special needs who were hearing impaired or in wheelchairs, how would you design this learning space?

Using Educational Technology to Enrich the Classroom

**Scenario 1   Elementary Students with Access
to a Wide Variety of Educational Technologies**

A small group of Ms. Ramirez's fifth-grade students were sprawled on the floor, poring over several pages of data they had just pulled off the Internet from a centralized database on stream quality. Another group was off in the corner near the sink, doing a separation test on a soil sample they took from the bottom of their local stream. A third group was at the computer entering new data and creating colored bar graphs from the data, while a fourth group was transferring digital images of the stream in question from the digital camera to the computer. After 40 minutes had passed, Ms. Ramirez pulled the group together.

"Okay students, I'd like to spend a few moments having each team give me a status report. Kevin, how far along is your team on their stream study project?"

"We just need to check one more source on the Internet to verify these figures and we'll be ready to put our electronic presentation together. We'd like to go to Mr. Hill's room after school some day this week so he can help us edit our video and digitize it for our presentation. Could you find out which night he can work with us?"

"I'm happy to hear how much progress your team has made during the past two weeks. I'll check with Mr. Hill to determine when he's available to work with you. Are there any other groups that need to work with Mr. Hill?"

"Oh, Ms. Ramirez," said Carla, "our team also needs to edit its video. We still need to scan in some still images we took with Sam's camera and add those to our presentation. Our group worked on graphing the data we collected and made graphs that compared our data to data we pulled from that national database you identified for us on the Internet. We're starting to see some interesting comparisons."

"That's great, Carla. What about your group, Ronaldo? How much work does your team have left to complete?"

"We'll probably need a few more days before all of our work is ready to share with everyone. Our team just scheduled a videoconference with an aquatic biologist from the university. We're going to use the desktop conferencing equipment in the library tomorrow afternoon and link to the scientist right at his desk. Mrs. Harp from the library set that up for us and taught us how to make the video phone call at 2 P.M. tomorrow. We're still figuring out how to videotape that session. Charles and Kathy talked to Mr. Hill about it at lunch today. He said he'd have to think about it, but that he'd try to find a way to capture some of the conference on video for us. We'd like to use that in our presentation."

"So, let me see, Kevin, Carla, Ronaldo. Ah, Sally, you've been awfully quiet. What's your group been up to?"

"Well, Ms. Ramirez, our group's been as busy as the others. We're just struggling with one problem. We have some data that seems like it's wrong. We're not sure if it was the pH meter that didn't work right, if the meter wasn't hooked to the computer and calibrated right to give us an accurate reading, or if those of us that read the meter messed up. Do you think if we went out today and got another pH reading that we could just plug that number into our data, or would we have to collect all the other data we're using to make our conclusions as well?"

"Well, you've raised an interesting problem, Sally. I'd like to pose that to the entire class. What do you think about this team's problem? To help them come up with a solution, I'd like all of you to think about that article we pulled off of the Internet last week. Remember the one about the scientists at three different labs, assuming they were doing exactly the same thing with rats in their study and still got different results. What kind of conclusions would they draw from their data if one of the scientists decided to just change one number because it didn't look right. Especially if they didn't inform the others."

A lively discussion ensued in this technology-rich, fifth-grade classroom. The debate ranged from e-mailing several scientists to get their ideas, doing an Internet search on the use of accurate data, to having the students demonstrate to the class exactly how they used the pH meter complete with the computer hook-up, just in case they had done it right and their original data were correct.

Scenario 2 Elementary Students with Access to a Few Educational Technologies

"Mrs. King, are we meeting with your class this afternoon?" shouted three kindergarten students across Marshfield Elementary School's playground to the sixth-grade teacher.

"Of course! If you're ready to share your experiences, my students are ready to listen," replied Mrs. King.

As Kathy King walked back into her sixth-grade classroom, a smile came over her face. All of the planning she did this past summer with the kindergarten teacher, Tom Denton, was paying off. Even after fifteen years of teaching in elementary schools, Kathy King was still excited when she discovered new ways to get students interested in science. This year she collaborated with Tom to help the children in the primary grades move beyond thinking science was just "playing with stuff" to giving them opportunities to explain their understanding of the "science" behind the "play." For her sixth-grade students it was an opportunity for them to review the science they learned over their years of elementary school before taking the statewide proficiency test at the end of sixth grade.

Kathy and Tom developed *kinderpals,* where her sixth-grade students were paired with kindergarten students in an effort to have a "real audience" for the sixth-grade students to share their understanding of the science they learned throughout their years at Marshfield Elementary. The project also gave the kindergarten students an opportunity to share their understanding of what they were learning through their science activities even before they had developed the ability to write down their understandings. The sixth-grade students would "capture" the thoughts of the kindergarten students through what looked like "play and conversation" to the kindergarten students. Prior to their weekly visits to Mr. Denton's class, Mrs. King's class would do the activity Mr. Denton was going to do with his class. Mrs. King would explore with her students the science behind the activity and assign them some additional reading on the given concept or concepts as a refresher for them on previously learned material.

The plan called for starting with the kindergarten and sixth-grade students this year and expanding it up and down the grade levels over subsequent years. As constructivist educators, both Tom and Kathy believed in the value of building on their students' experiences, yet they struggled with getting those experiences into proper conceptual formation. Using even the lowest of education technologies that were available to them in their school—cassette recorders, some old donated computers, and two newer computers with Internet access in the library—proved to be a real asset to their data-collection needs.

Kathy's thoughts were interrupted by her own students' animated conversations as she entered her classroom. Ron was engaged in a heated debate with Sarah and Carmen. "But Jimmy really did get the idea of surface tension after we talked about all the things he did with bubbles," stated Ron.

"I thought you were just supposed to tape the two of you having a conversation about what he did with the bubbles," Sarah said.

"I did do that, but while I was typing up some of his ideas so I could practice my keyboarding skills, something I heard Jimmy say on the tape had me puzzled. The next time we went to Mr. Denton's room, I asked Mr. Denton if Jimmy and I could play over at the water table. I started asking Jimmy some questions about the bubbles he made last week and then I asked him if we could try to make bubbles with just plain water. After stirring up water in a cup, we started playing around to see how many things we could put in a cup of water without it overflowing. I remembered the activity we did in our own class with paper clips in a cup to explore surface tension, so I started telling Jimmy about it. All I know is that when I then took a bowl and shook pepper on the top of the water Jimmy told me it must be surface tension that kept the pepper on top. You should have heard him scream when I put a drop of soap into the bowl and all the pepper fell to the bottom!"

Kathy King could not help jumping in with the comment, "What do you plan on doing the next time you go down to Mr. Denton's class with your *kinderpal* Jimmy? Have you thought about going to the library with him and jointly generating a picture of Jimmy's experiences using the KidPix Software?"

"I didn't think of that, but what a great way to help Jimmy remember what surface tension is!"

At that suggestion other students jumped into the conversation, some wanting to use the Internet connection in the library with their kindergarten charges to find out more information on various topics they were exploring in their class, others wanting to jointly create e-mail letters to community partners with their *kinderpals* that question the partners on how they use, in their jobs, some of the "science" that the kindergarten students were learning. The bell interrupted the enthusiastic sixth graders as they headed over to Mr. Denton's kindergarten class to make good on their plans.

Introduction

The students in Ms. Ramirez's class from the first scenario are not as unique as some may think. Technology initiatives throughout the United States have spent millions of dollars to get educational technology into the K–12 schools, right down to the classroom level. The students at Marshfield Elementary in the second scenario are not as fortunate. However, as evidenced by the *kinderpal* plan of Mrs. King and Mr. Denton, even low-end technology can still offer useful tools for data collection and analysis. Whether you are an advocate of the technology being accessible in the classroom or moving the students down the hall to the lab, there's no doubt about it, the tools available for the twenty-first century classroom will dramatically change the way classrooms function. The artifacts we collect of student work no longer rely on paper, pencil, and chalk. The artifacts created in today's classroom provide the students with multiple opportunities to construct knowledge and to demonstrate what they know.

Those resistant to applying educational technology at the elementary level should reflect on the nature of technology itself and how those applications have benefited society. As an example, for one of this book's authors growing up in the city produced an idealized view of farm life. The "country kids" were envied, thinking it would be like *Rebecca of Sunny Brook Farm* every day, getting up when the rooster crowed to feed the chickens, checking under their nests for eggs, and bring them back in a tidy basket, smiling and humming a happy tune. Many years later good friendships were formed with those "country kids." They laughed at the author's romantic view of farm life. The horror stories they shared about the backbreaking labor were nothing to be dreamed of longingly. On the bright side they talked of how advances in technology actually saved them hours of hard labor. Now chickens are raised in tight quarters in which all food and water are carefully measured. Eggs automatically drop down onto conveyor belts that move them along for easy collection. Egg production is not the only technological advancement on the farm. Baling hay, planting and picking crops, as well as grain storage have changed dramatically with advances in technology.

The lumber industry is another area in which childhood myths were dispelled with the advances of technology. Images of the burly lumberjack were transformed after a visit to some lumber sites in northern Oregon. That burly lumberjack was really teams of average-size humans (females included) using various machines to fell, strip, and drag the pines up the steep hills. Once at the lumber mill, machines using laser scanners and a computer program to determine exactly how many and what kind of boards would be cut from each log. Within a matter of minutes, that log became several strips of lumber of varying widths and thickness.

While for schools we tend to think of technology in terms of computers, just about any artifact of our modern world is really technology. The preceding examples demonstrate the real-world applications of technology. The opening scenarios share some uses of educational technology in the elementary school. This chapter is designed to help you think about how to use

Older learners can become technology mentors for younger children.

education technology in the classroom and apply it in a real-world context, much as the students in Ms. Ramirez's, Mr. Denton's and Mrs. King's classes did. It answers the question of *why* one would use educational technology and *how* one could apply it in the context of science teaching. This chapter does this by examining the National Educational Technology Standards, the varying skill levels for the teacher and student in using educational technology, and by providing examples of how to apply the National Educational Technology Standards to science lessons designed to meet the National Science Education Standards.

Why Use Educational Technology?

Chances are that in a school rich in educational technology a teacher like Ms. Ramirez is given more opportunities to enhance her technology skills and is able to incorporate the available technology into her student's classroom experiences. However, as Mrs. King and Mr. Denton demonstrated, even in a setting in which access to educational technology is difficult, the decision to apply educational technology in the learning environment is often driven by the task at hand, not the available technology.

Educational technology can be seamlessly incorporated into a classroom whether you are a teacher more comfortable using classroom content strictly prescribed by the school curriculum or you are in a school environment in which creating content, based on statewide learning outcomes, is encouraged. Even though you may be an expert at

Video Explorations — *Technology*

Video Summary

Technology can play an important role in helping teachers provide a variety of instructional strategies for teaching science. However, teachers often dismiss the use of technology, seeing the use of technology as an additional subject added to an already full schedule. By examining the National Educational Technology Standards for Students (NETS) and the National Science Education Standards, a teacher can identify areas in which the two standards overlap. The technology can then be used to motivate and support concept development. The ability of technology to provide visual models of difficult to teach concepts creates for the teacher new ways to present science content. Emerging technologies that provide hands-on applications for science concept development can also enhance opportunities for learners. Technology is an engaging and effective tool for increasing deep understanding and appreciation of science.

Tips for Viewing, Objectives, or What to Watch for

As you watch these videos, make note of the following:

1. What types of technology were shown in the video? Can you identify a way in which each technology shown could be used to support concept development in science?

2. We often think of technology as only a computer. What other "technologies" can be used to engage learners in science?

3. What emerging technology is presented in the video? How might this emerging technology meet the needs of students in the science classroom?

4. Create a personal statement about the use of technology in your classroom.

Questions for Exploration

1. How does equitable access to technology in a classroom also support the implementation of quality science education experiences?

2. In Chapter 3, gender issues were discussed in reference to cultural diversity. Do you see any of these same issues affecting the use of technology in a classroom?

3. In the video, the teacher spoke of going to centers. How might a center be used to promote the integration of technology into a science lesson?

4. How might a classroom change if assistive technologies are needed for special needs students?

Activity for Application

Teachers often need to identify websites that are appropriate for student use. What criteria should be used in identifying software that will support science and technology standards? Locate three pieces of software, describe each, and determine which standard the software will support. How does a technology enriched science classroom differ from a traditional science classroom? Observe your college/university professors in the various disciplines. How do your professors use technology to enhance the learning experience?

using one computer application, you may be at a novice level on another. Teachers must overcome the notion that they must be experts at all educational technology before their students are given a chance to use it. As Ediger's (1994) studies on *Technology in the Elementary Classroom* have revealed, applying technology in the classroom does several things to student learning: (1) it increases interest even in rote tasks; (2) it provides purpose for learning; (3) it can attach meaning to an ongoing lesson; (4) it provides opportunities to perceive knowledge as being related, not isolated bits; (5) it allows for individual student differences; and (6) it can impact student attitudes toward learning.

National Educational Technology Standards

The artifacts of student learning—anything created by our students as evidence of their understanding of a given concept—can be created in a variety of formats as teachers provide opportunities for students to use educational technologies in the creation of such artifacts. As shared in the opening scenario, using instructional software on computers is not the only use of educational technology. The International Society for Technology in Education (ISTE) has established National Educational Technology Standards (NETS) for students in grades K–12. These six standards are general enough that students can move from exhibiting novice level understanding to practicing the skills on a

TABLE 10.1 Technology Foundation Standards for All Students (June 1998)

1. Basic operations and concepts
   - Students demonstrate a sound understanding of the nature and operation of technology systems
   - Students are proficient in the use of technology

2. Social, ethical, and human issues
   - Students understand the ethical, cultural, and societal issues related to technology.
   - Students practice responsible use of technology systems, information, and software.
   - Students develop positive attitudes toward technology uses that support lifelong learning, collaboration, personal pursuits, and productivity.

3. Technology productivity tools
   - Students use technology tools to enhance learning, increase productivity, and promote creativity.
   - Students use productivity tools to collaborate in constructing technology-enhanced models, preparing publications, and producing other creative works.

4. Technology communications tools
   - Students use telecommunications to collaborate, publish, and interact with peers, experts, and other audiences.
   - Students use a variety of media and formats to communicate information and ideas effectively to multiple audiences.

5. Technology research tools
   - Students use technology to locate, evaluate, and collect information from a variety of sources.
   - Students use technology tools to process data and report results.
   - Students evaluate and select new information resources and technological innovations based on the appropriateness to specific tasks.

6. Technology problem-solving and decision-making tools.
   - Students use technology resources for solving problems and making informed decisions.
   - Students employ technology in the development of strategies for solving problems in the real world.

Source: International Society for Technology in Education (ISTE), NETS Project, http://cnets.iste.org/sfors.htm.

regular basis and eventually exhibiting mastery with increased experience. Table 10.1 lists the *Technology Foundation Standards for All Students*.

Applying these skills within the context of a science lesson can strengthen the understanding of the science concepts if we recognize and value the experiences students bring with them and then use the technology to clarify any misconceptions and stimulate proper concept formation (Nickerson, 1995). Conceptual understanding will come about when student interaction between the educational technology and the science content is purposeful. Choosing software that promotes active mental processing and student discoveries is vital and must ensure for students a state of mindfulness while they interact with the technology and motivate and engage the students to enable them to form appropriate conceptualizations. Computer software, be it instructional software such as the multitude of titles created to address a specific science topic or application software designed to create a document or draw a picture, is no substitute for active teaching and learning. It can, however, become an essential part of that teaching and learning, a means for creating student artifacts of the concepts studied.

Levels of Use

Utilizing a computer in a science classroom seems like a contradiction of constructivist science teaching. However, as modeled in the opening scenarios, when appropriately used as a learning tool, computers can help learners to construct an understanding of complex concepts. At the most basic or novice level, software applications can be used to observe scientific phenomena directly. The software can provide a concrete example of an object, provide facts, or recall basic information. Novice users of educational technology can easily use drill-and-practice software. As Berger's (1994) study notes, rarely is there mindfulness associated with this type of computer-assisted instruction.

Computers help young children to expand uses of their senses.

A novice when applying the ISTE technology standards would be capable of using software applications that supply scientific information. Information provided in CD-ROM encyclopedias and atlases or software applications that evaluate student performance, keep records, or guide students to resources rarely require anything more than novice-level skills to use them successfully.

As students are given more opportunities to apply the technology in their regular classroom activities, through practice they become more proficient in various computer tools and advance to another technology level. Many of the productivity tools that assist in the creation of multimedia productions require students to have more than a simple working knowledge of the software application. Software simulations typically require more than beginner-level skills as well. Although computer simulations are no replacement for actual experimentation, simulations do "provide a valuable conceptual tool which should be augmented with actual experiments in the classroom," according to McKinney (1997).

Simulation software applications may be a pictorial, verbal, numerical, or graphical representation of reality. Simulations that integrate all four forms of representation appear to offer the best opportunity to stimulate conceptual change. *The Voyages of Mimi I and II* (Bank Street College of Education, 1995) are popular programs that effectively integrate all four representations. This interactive program, designed primarily for middle-school students, makes use of video, print, and computer software to engage students in an interdisciplinary unit centered on the real adventures of the explorer ship *Mimi.*

Computer-based laboratories, which effectively integrate numerical and graphical data as quickly as a probe attached to the computer can record it, often require technology skills beyond the novice level. Using sensors and timing devices attached to a computer, students can do such things as monitor heart rate; detect strength and direction of external forces; determine the strength of magnetic fields; record temperature; record pH of liquids; measure amplitudes of audio sources; sense and record humidity changes; imitate the spectral response of the human eye; sense and record changes in pressure; and use an ultrasonic motion detector to measure distance, velocity, and acceleration (Arbor Scientific, 1996).

Not all simulations require advanced technology skills. Software such as *Amazon Trail, 3rd Ed.: Bring the Rainforest to Life* (MECC, 2001) for students from fourth grade up can participate in a virtual journey to the Amazon rain forest in South America. Many dialogue guides with both text and audio conversations support the interaction along the journey. Other simulations that are attribute mapped do not allow for student-created models of unidentified phenomena (Snir, Smith, & Grosslight, 1995). Some software designed to simulate frog dissection falls into this category; the given attributes are already defined by the software with little room for manipulation of variables. This type of computer simulation may be an insufficient substitute for a certain level of dissection.

Students proficient in all six categories of the National Educational Technology Standards are at a level of technological literacy in which they can use software applications that simulate experiments in which variables may be manipulated and extended beyond ordinary phenomena. At this level, computer models can be created that lead to explorations of unidentified phenomena. This metaconceptual level is one in which a student uses models to explain reality, reflects on those models, and then suggests the manipulation of variables that project far beyond what can be created in the laboratory. This type of software is *structure mapped*. This means that a code is built into the software that allows it to search for laws that govern the behavior of objects (Snir, Smith, & Grosslight, 1995). One such software application is *Thinkin' Science* (Edmark, 2001) for students K–2. When using this software, students have an opportunity to explore a model of the Earth, sun, and moon as well as creating astronomical events, such as solar eclipses or phases of the moon. Simulations involve examinations of Newton's laws of motion and the relationship between momentum and acceleration; the simulations help the student develop a more complete understanding of Newton's laws of motion, phenomena that cannot be accurately observed or understood in the environment of a typical school laboratory.

Microworlds are computer-based laboratory experiences that simulate real-world phenomena. Students can explore undefined phenomena when given proper guidance and intervention by the teacher. Students can be given "what if" predictive situations in order to evaluate and reflect on scientific theories, pose problems that can be solved only through computer-enhanced simulations, and construct the meaning of concepts based on computer-simulated evidence. An inquiring science educator can bring the use of computers to their highest level of application by using microworld environments to give students opportunities to explore and discover scientific theories by using problem-solving strategies to ask, "What is the real problem?" "How do we know it's a problem?" "How can we go about solving the problem?" Microworlds truly embody the spirit of constructivism in its application.

There are many methods that science teachers can use to integrate the ISTE National Educational Technology Standards into their lessons. Some examples are listed.

- Use a digital camera to take pictures each week of a plant's growth and place the measurements of the plant's growth on a bulletin board.
- Classification activities help students increase their vocabulary, observation skills, and critical thinking.
    1. Create a chart (spreadsheet) that shows the characteristics of pets that students in the class have at home.
    2. Use websites (Internet) to locate different animals found around the world and identify these characteristics compared to the students' pets.
    3. Create a chart (spreadsheet) that shows the number and characteristics of trees on the playground.
- Keep a scientist's journal about local habitats.
    1. Use drawings created in KidPix and other drawing software.
    2. Download images from the web or scan from copyright-free pictures.
    3. Write in journal observations concerning their particular habitat and the interaction of organisms in that habitat.
    4. Record activities of organisms in the habitat with a video recorder or digital video camera and share with the class and parents.
    5. Compare and contrast the observations seen in the video at different times of day.

Young scientists enjoy investigating the world around them. Digital cameras and digital video cameras can help improve observation skills and help students become more aware of the world in which they live.

The Networked Classroom—Removing the Walls

Although they are numbered, the National Educational Technology Standards are not linear. One does not have to know all of the basic operations of a computer before beginning to use it as a communication tool. Novice users of technology are capable of using the computer as a communication tool long before they have mastered the use of productivity tools. In fact, using a wide area network (WAN) enables us to expand the boundaries of the classroom walls and to create a virtual classroom with schools across the globe.

For teachers, a network provides increased opportunities to collaborate with other educators over matters of daily instruction or educational reform. Teachers have greater access to additional information, knowledge, and points of view by eliminating barriers of time and place. Networked teachers may discuss issues and access varied resources, including other teachers and resource agencies. A network encourages the development of professional skills: deliberation, collegial consensus building, and development and sharing of ideas related to the profession of teaching.

Future teachers may find that skills in using networked resources such as the World Wide Web (WWW) can provide them with opportunities to link with practicing teachers through sites such as the *Global Learning Co-op* and the *GLOBE Project* www.globe. gov/globe_flash.html. The Web can provide teachers access to standards for science instruction for every state—often an understanding of local standards is expected during job interviews. It can also expose them to teacher grant award competitions and competitions for elementary students, and it can introduce them to various science education associations (O'Brien & Lewis, 1999).

Various national databases exist to support science teaching. Some national services include the National Science Teachers Association (NSTA), the National Consortium for Environmental Education and Training (NCEET), the National Aeronautics and Space Administration (NASA), and the National Park Service. These sources provide websites filled with lessons, resources, and knowledge of various science topics. The Eisenhower National Clearinghouse (ENC) for Mathematics and Science Education is a national database. Like the other sites it provides lessons and lists of resources as well as identifying which print, video, or computer software is available for the teaching of science and mathematics. One added benefit of this site is its extensive software reviews, created by an evaluation protocol that goes beyond the publisher's description of the software or computer operating requirements. It was created in conjunction with the state of Ohio's coordinating agency responsible for providing educational technology funding to all Ohio's K–12 schools, of Ohio SchoolNet. The protocol focuses on interactivity, student engagement, technical characteristics, skills development, and the correlation of the instructional software to state and national standards for science, mathematics, social studies, and language arts. All reviews are posted on the ENC website at www.enc.org and the Ohio SchoolNet website at www.ohioschoolnet.k12.oh.us.

Bringing Students Eureka! Moments

by Louise Sayuk

Grade 4, The Kinkaid School, Houston, Texas

"Robotics was lots of fun! Every day I looked forward to it."

"I really loved learning computer graphing. It was cool how those numbers could turn into a chart."

"What did I like about robotics? Everything . . . cool models, the challenge, racing, and the computer programming was really nifty!"

"Computer graphing was super. I not only learned how to make graphs, but now I am so much better at reading them."

"It was such fun changing the graphics of graphs!"

"Google Images is the best. I can now find pictures of EVERYTHING!"

"I enjoyed programming the robots. After this unit, I tried other programming on my own. It was almost like magic how you could move things from the computer to the Lego brick. Where else could someone my age make something come to life?"

"Eureka! moments" are what science is all about and the quotes above from some of my students show how technology has brought more and more of these moments to our elementary school classroom. Two years ago when our school's technology committee decided to provide computer carts with twenty laptops for classroom use, our world of technology opened considerably. Now all students had their own computer and could connect to the Internet from their desk. There was ample opportunity for everyone to do research, graphing, or robotics. Not being a computer whiz myself, I have to admit I was hesitant. However, after our first exploratory work, the students and I have all been thrilled with the possibilities. Computer graphing, robotics, and Internet research are all standard parts of our curriculum. In addition we use flex cams to show work on our classroom TV and have digital cameras available for recording data.

What value did adding technology contribute to our classroom experience? Students have learned the value of persistence in a project. "Try, try, again" is often the motto when working through how the computer program they have written translates into the movement of the robot. The excitement evidenced by all when it finally responds as planned permeates the classroom. Students from other groups come running to celebrate with the designer, often questioning the strategies used by the inventing group for success.

Girls have learned that they can be just as successful as boys in designing prototypes and programming. Girls working in groups have often become the leaders in writing programs and working on designs. It is evident that they feel very proud of their achievements. What a great boost for self-esteem!

Robotics and graphing seem to offer students success no matter what their learning styles. Some children excel at the programming, some at the designing, and some at embellishing the graphics. All of the projects seem to offer everyone some area where they can make a valuable contribution.

Technology has enhanced the creativity of the students. Once students begin to work on these projects, there is no limit to where their imaginations can take them. The different ways to use robotic sensors and solar panels especially seem to get the creative juices flowing. Availability of the Internet has provided a plethora of information that formally would have been difficult to keep available in the classroom. In addition, sites such as Google Images allow the teacher to show pictures on virtually any science topic. Our computer is linked to our classroom TV screen, giving us the equivalent of a file of millions of classroom posters.

Technology empowers both the teacher and the students to be their best. What a great opportunity for students to coach teachers while teachers are coaching students. Working on these projects not only increases the communication and critical thinking skills of students in the group, but it puts them at ease with technology. When new projects come along in middle school, they will be ready to dive right in!

Several states have developed websites that provide outstanding resources, which have been peer reviewed and evaluated by experts in science and education. Development of web-based sites makes resources readily accessible to the teacher. One such website is the Ohio Resource Center (www.ohiorc.org). The Ohio Resource Center (ORC) for Mathematics, Science, and Reading is a "virtual" best practices center. Materials provided at the ORC site provide web-based content, instruction, and professional resources for science, mathematics, and reading and which exemplify teaching to high standards. The ORC provides a rubric to use when evaluating best practices and contains numerous links to web-based lesson plans on the Internet.

Teachers should critically review any electronically accessed lesson, no matter which website is accessed for science resources. Just because a source is "published" on the Internet does not necessarily mean it is worthwhile. Table 10.2 suggests evaluation criteria for judging the worthiness of electronically accessed lessons. Please use this table to help you sort and separate the safest and most promising resources.

TABLE 10.2   Is This a Worthy Task?

Is the task based on sound and significant content?
- Identify the concepts and/or skills.
- Is the content accurate?

Is the task based on knowledge of students' understandings, interests, experiences, and the range of ways that diverse students learn?
- Identify why the task might appeal to your students.

Are all safety measures properly addressed and followed in any lessons provided? If not, can appropriate safety measures be easily applied to the given task? If you answer no to this second question, do *not* use this lesson.

In your opinion to what extent would the task:

	a lot				not at all
engage students' intellect?	4	3	2	1	0
actively involve students?	4	3	2	1	0
develop students' understandings and skills?	4	3	2	1	0
stimulate students to make connections to other disciplines?	4	3	2	1	0
stimulate students to make connections to the real world?	4	3	2	1	0
call for problem formation, problem solving, and reasoning?	4	3	2	1	0
promote communication/interaction among students?	4	3	2	1	0

For students, networked learning environments provide real-world applications of science concepts. Collecting data that will be shared in a nationwide database, such as the *Everglades Information Network and Digital Library* or the *GLOBE Project*, encourages students to be more careful in applying proper scientific procedures when they collect their data on a local level to be shared nationally.

Parks as Classrooms, an interactive computer-based project funded primarily by the National Park Service, is designed to promote greater understanding and appreciation of the natural and cultural heritage of the United States and to develop sustainable partnerships among parks, schools, and communities. Through this network, data are collected to monitor air, water, and land resources on parklands. This interactive project can simulate landform changes and cycles in populations within the parks (Corporation for Public Broadcasting, 1995).

Technology helps learners to explore and understand social, ethical, and human issues.

The National Geographic Society offers *National Geographic Explorer* a combination of weblinks designed to meet curricular needs, telecommunications' access to classrooms around the world, teacher guides and lesson plans, homework support, and access to activities and experiments (National Geographic Society, 2003). There are various problem-based links to join.

Although national projects can be accessed and joined, having access to a wide area network within the classroom can encourage students and teachers to start their own science research projects and to invite schools throughout the nation to join the research effort. Collaborative projects can be designed to explore bodies of water, landfills, groundwater movement, seasonal changes per latitude, or any local problem or issue that may have global impact. The impact of projects like these is best stated by one teacher who responded to the question, "What are your most compelling reasons for integrating educational technology into the curriculum?" as posed by Randy Knuth on the Internet in September 1995:

> I think we should go beyond integration into the classroom and create a new context for learning that maximizes the learning potential of technology and telecommunications. From my perspective . . . the reason is relevancy. We can extend learning beyond the walls of the classroom . . . to do real stuff with real people for compelling reasons . . . with real results that have real significance. Students are not dumb . . . they know when it matters and when it is simply an exercise. . . . Connect them to their communities through technology! And give them economic viability! (Knuth, 1995)

Using educational technology as a communication tool goes beyond transporting graphics and text. Depending on the connectivity, students can participate in networks that transport voice, video, and data. Schools throughout the nation are linking together to share in scientific explorations with full motion video and voice interface. From the primary level through college, students are linking with content providers to enrich and enhance the lessons studied within the classroom. Zoos, museums, and cultural institutions are revamping the way they present their content to take advantage of the visual medium offered through interactive video networks. Linkages like these promote greater student interaction and discussion of concepts. Providing students with as many opportunities as possible to articulate their understanding of concepts will promote greater conceptual construction and retention. Advancing technologies offer students opportunities on an ever-increasing basis.

Emerging Technologies in the Science Classroom

Emerging technologies are technologies that are at the leading edge; in other words, these are technologies that are just beginning to be found in K–12 classrooms and are being explored as new tools to help students gain a better understanding of science and to improve student achievement. With the recent improvements in wireless technologies, more portable personal computers, and the Internet, schools are examining the use of personal digital assistants in their classrooms. Personal digital assistants are often referred to as PDAs or handheld computers. Many of you will recognize these devices under the brand names of Palm®, PocketPC®, Sony Clie®, and iPaq®.

These small personal computers may be held in the palm of a student's hand, are lightweight, portable, and have enough memory to carry out many of the same functions available on a typical desktop computer. The portability of the handheld computer allows the student to carry a computer to a wide variety of sites for fieldwork and data collection. Word processing, spreadsheet and database software located on most handhelds are similar to that found on a desktop. The student can enter field notes into the word-processor file or collect data into a database file and then transfer the files to their classroom desktop at a later time. The handheld automatically saves all files and stores them in the handheld until they are transferred to the desktop computer.

The limits of emerging technologies are just beginning to be tested in the classroom.

With the advent of the handheld computer, there has been resurgence in the use of probeware in elementary classrooms. Sensor probes allow for the real-time capture and display of data. Using sensory probeware along with handheld devices creates new possibilities for learners to explore and understand the world in which they live. The ability of the handheld device to take the data collected from the probe and display it in a symbolic manner can greatly increase comprehension of difficult to learn concepts (Tinker, 2003).

Creating theories and testing them in the real world are important activities of science. The use of handheld devices and probeware help young students to develop measurement skills and to translate the physical environment in a visual environment that tests conceptual understanding. These small, battery-operated devices give students the freedom to explore their homes, playgrounds, museums, and field environments without being tied to the "electrical outlet" on the wall (Bannasch & Tinker, 2002).

Teachers find that these small handhelds can be used as an assessment tool in the classroom and as a management tool for keeping track of student assignments, lesson plans and organizational needs in the classroom. While some teachers feel it is difficult to integrate handheld devices and probeware into the classroom, many companies which sell handhelds and probeware are developing lesson plans to help teachers overcome their anxiety about this emerging technology. Teachers using handheld devices and probeware are able to integrate technology into a science curriculum that focuses on inquiry, problem solving and conceptual understanding.

How Can Educational Technology Be Applied in the Context of Science Teaching?

The National Science Education Content Standards provide a list of concept statements for the three science divisions, Physical, Life, and Earth and Space Sciences. One would never think of having students simply memorize the concept statements. In fact, the Science Standards provides many suggestions for effective science teaching, all strongly encouraging active student exploration to construct an understanding of the science concepts. The feature lessons in this textbook serve as examples of how the standards can be explored through student-centered inquiry activities within a learning cycle format.

Just as the National Science Education Standards make recommendations for how a science concept may be best learned, so too does the International Society for Technology in Education strongly suggest that the teaching of the National Educational Technology Standards should not take place void of context. In Chapter 10 of the companion website (www.ablongman.com/martin4e) is a section called *Technology Ideas for Meeting the NETS for Students*. This website provides examples of how the National Educational Technology Standards for students can easily be incorporated into each science lesson without an added burden to the teacher and allow the student to develop technology skills while learning a particular science concept.

The lessons in this textbook can be accomplished without the use of educational technology. However, as you read through the tables and recall Ediger's six findings on what educational technology can do to enhance learning, you will discover that by applying a few of these suggestions to the lessons, educational technology can truly enrich the learning experience.

Impact of Light in the Forest

GRADE LEVEL: 5–8

DISCIPLINE: Life Science

Inquiry Question: Does light intensity affect the type of vegetation found in an area?

Concept to Be Invented: Light is a necessary factor for life by way of photosynthesis. The intensity of light varies throughout canopy levels within a forest.

National Science Education Standards: Grades 5–8—NSE Life Science Populations and Ecosystem Concepts:

✦ For ecosystems, the major source for energy is sunlight. Energy entering ecosystems as sunlight is converted by producers into chemical energy through photosynthesis. Energy then passes from organisms in food webs.

NSE Science as Inquiry Concepts:

✦ Activities that investigate and analyze science questions.
✦ Groups of students analyzing and synthesizing data after defending conclusions.

National Educational Technology Standards Met Through Lesson

1. Basic operations and concepts
   a. Use of the Palm® with the ImagiWorks or Vernier Interface to collect light intensity data
2. Social, ethical and human issues
   a. What were the advantages and disadvantages of using the Palm® to collect and analyze data?
3. Technology communications tools
   a. How did you use the Palm® to communicate the results of your field study?

Science Attitudes to Nurture: Open-mindedness, cooperation with others, tolerance for other opinions

Materials Needed: *For each group of 4–5 students:* 1 Palm®, Vernier Light Sensor, ImagiWorks Interface and one-prong interface to sensor adaptor. A computer to download and analyze Palm® data. The software needed on the computer should be LOGGER Pro, Microsoft Word and Excel, and Internet Explorer.

⊘ Safety Precautions: Handle all equipment with care. If any equipment is broken, contact teacher immediately. Do not take equipment near water. Use caution when working in a poorly lighted area. Always walk, do not run, in the classroom and out in field study area.

Exploration *Which process skills will be used?*

Observing, collecting, and recording data, interpreting data, hypothesizing, designing an experiment

Put students into groups and give them Vernier probes and Palm® and ask them to measure the amount of light in different areas of the room with the lights off and only one window with open curtains. Give students three specific areas to measure light in and three areas to choose themselves. Students will collect and analyze data. Results will be portrayed in a model to be put on the chalkboard for whole class review.

As the students maneuver through the introduction activity, they will find that areas away from the window have less light. Wave properties of light will be seen where light is detected even behind obstacles.

- ✦ Where is the intensity of light the greatest and the least?
- ✦ Why is the intensity of light the greatest, the least in these particular areas?
- ✦ How does light get around obstacles?
- ✦ How does light move? (Straight lines? Curves?)
- ✦ Does light bend? Explain.

Begin the next activity once students demonstrate they can use the light probes with the Palm® to collect light intensity data. Divide the students into research groups and provide each team with three growing, potted bean plants. Ask the teams to think about the results of light intensity data they collected while becoming familiar with the probes. Based on the analysis of their data, ask them to select three study areas in which to place their growing plants—(1) the area where they found the light intensity to be the greatest, (2) where they found the light intensity to be the least, and (3) an area where they found the light intensity to be between the greatest and the least. Before they place the plants in the three study areas, ask them to create a data sheet to record the condition of their plants. Allow the teams to pick which variables they will record regarding the *condition* of their plants. Remind them they are manipulating the variable of light only through placement in three different areas. Since they are manipulating the amount of light—all other variables should remain constant, e.g., amount of water provided to each plant, how each plant will be watered, amount of nutrients given to each plant (if any), conditions of the plant that will be recorded (e.g., height, number of leaves, sturdiness of stem). Ask them to record light intensity on their plants and record the condition of their plants on a daily basis. After two weeks, ask the student teams to create a graph that compares the conditions of their three plants over time. Ask them to draw conclusions on the relationship between light intensity and the condition of their plants. They should be able to share their results with the entire class.

Explanation

Ask the student teams to share the results of their data analysis. Ask students to reflect on their exploration activity to answer the following:

- ✦ Was there a difference between the plants grown where the light intensity was the greatest and the plants grown where the light intensity was the least?
- ✦ What did you observe about the growth of the plants in the "in-between" area?
- ✦ Based on the data you collected, what could you conclude about the relationship

(continued)

between light intensity and plant growth? (Students should conclude that too much or too little light intensity would stunt plant growth.)

✦ Once the students can articulate that plant growth depends upon light intensity, then explain to them that light is necessary for plant growth in that it stimulates food production, a process that is called photosynthesis. At this point the teacher can develop a presentation on photosynthesis explaining how light energy is converted to food energy for the plant. Background knowledge on photosynthesis will help the students respond to the inquiry question posed in the beginning of the lesson and explored in the Expansion phase of the lesson.

Expansion   *Which process skills will be used?*

Experimenting, hypothesizing, observing, recording data and analyzing data, cognitive thinking, drawing conclusions

The student groups will be assigned to a field study area within the forested school land lab, in the open prairie area, and in an area right next to the school void of vegetation. On day 1, as a team, the students will go to all three of their assigned study areas and record the type and amount of vegetation found within each area. It is up to the student teams to develop a data table to collect and record this data. A schedule will be set up so that at specific times during the school day, different students within the group will be responsible for going to these three study areas and collecting data on light intensity using the light probes. They will record the light intensity data on their record sheets. (Note: this can be created on the Palm® through Excel or even using the ImagiProbe software on the Palm®.) They will record this data at the same times throughout the day for 5 consecutive days. The inquiry question behind this study is: "Does light intensity affect the type of vegetation found in an area?" Once the students have collected and analyzed this data, the teacher will use that information to get into a discussion on photosynthesis, asking how they think varying levels of light affect the rate of photosynthesis, and how light intensity affects the types of plants found in the study areas.

Science in Personal and Social Perspectives

✦ How will your understanding of light intensity affect where you place the plants you have growing in your homes?

✦ When you see a house plant with yellowed leaves, what do you think the plant is telling you?

Science and Technology

✦ What is the benefit of using the probes with the Palm® in the field or the lab?

✦ Can you come up with any other uses for the light intensity probe other than collecting information on plant growth?

Science as Inquiry

✦ Why do we need plants?

✦ Can we live without plants?

History and Nature of Science

Why is it important when conducting an experiment to manipulate one variable and control all of the others?

Evaluation

Upon completing these activities, the students will be able to:

+ explain the importance of light in the process of photosynthesis;
+ explain why plants found on a deciduous forest floor grow earlier in the spring compared to the trees of the forest;
+ design an experiment that shows the relationship between light intensity and plant growth.

Chapter Summary

Some time in the future, you and your students may pick up a newspaper and read a headline like, "Genetic Engineering Unravels the Aging Process" or "Ozone Hole Increases." The stories following these headlines will be important to both you and your students. They will deal with important quality-of-life issues that you, as citizens, may need to form an opinion about or make a decision about concerning your future. Being able to understand the consequences of your choices is important to you and to your students.

As a teacher, you will need to ask yourself whether you have done your best to provide your students with the skills they need to make these future decisions. Emphasis on student inquiry through questioning, research, issue resolution, and higher order thinking skills must be constantly practiced as much as consistent use of educational technology to create the artifacts that demonstrate the students' ability to perform such skills.

Scientific and technological knowledge are changing so rapidly that it is becoming more difficult to prepare students for this complicated task. Textbooks cannot keep pace with the new discoveries in science; however, as a classroom teacher you can supplement your textbook and your program with experiences and opportunities that are not available through print materials.

Stimulate learning by serving as the bridge between the resources that are relevant and available to you and the students in your classroom. Appropriate applications of educational technology can extend the learning environment beyond the confines of the classroom. Only your imagination and energy limit your uses of educational technology, which can provide inquiry-based learning opportunities that stimulate your students and provide an atmosphere for scientific discovery.

Discussion Questions

1. Review the National Educational Technology Standards provided in Table 10.1. Visit the International Society for Technology in Education website at cnets.iste.org to review the specific performance indicators for each standard at a given grade range. Do you think these are realistic expectations for all students? Why or why not?

2. Defend the notion that the National Educational Technology Standards provided in Table 10.1 are not linear. Do you believe it is possible for your students to be more proficient in some technologies than you are? Would that intimidate you? Explain your feelings. Identify one educational technology tool you'd like to become more proficient in and establish a plan for reaching proficiency.

3. Discuss what criteria you may use to choose instructional science software. Is it enough to make your instructional software purchasing decisions based on the vendor's description? What criteria will you use to make your decision?

4. What are three advantages of accessing information for a given science lesson from the Internet? What are three advantages of having your students access information from the Internet? What criteria do you believe are important to determine the worthiness of a given website?

Build a Portfolio or E-Folio

1. According to the Technology Related Assistance Act of 1988, assistive technology includes "any item, piece of equipment, or product, whether acquired commercially, off the shelf, modified, or customized, that is used to increase, maintain, or improve the functional capabilities of individuals with disabilities" (P.L. 101-407 from McLane, 1998). Identify some assistive technologies that are especially useful in the instruction of students with special needs when using educational technology in your science class. You may find these at the following special education Internet web sites: www.cec.sped.org and www.edc.org/FSC/ASSIST/. Choose one type of special need such as hearing impairment or blindness.

2. Access the National Science Teacher's Association (NSTA) website at www.nsta.org. Research the purposes, fee structure, and service of the association. Identify the NSTA publications that will be useful as you plan science lessons. Locate membership information, meeting schedules, and publications from your state or local science education organization. Add this information to your science portfolio.

3. Select a content area and grade-level range from the National Science Education Standards. Choose a science concept and identify at least three instructional science software applications that will promote greater concept attainment. Identify whether the software is considered drill and practice, a tutorial, a simulation, or a microworld application. Write a summary of what the software was designed to do and your views on how valuable you believe the software will be for students in the grade level you chose.

4. Find a website that serves as a national database for a given science issue. Incorporate the use of this database into a science lesson that ad-

dresses one of the National Science Education Standards.

5. Identify a science concept for a particular grade level from the National Science Education Standards provided in the Appendix. Create a learning cycle lesson plan for a given concept. Include activities that require the students to practice each of the six National Educational Technology Standards for students.

Resources for Best Practices

*P*rofessor Marjorie Becker divided the science methods class into research teams. Each team's purpose was to pick a science topic and locate all the materials available on that topic in the lab, library, and college curriculum collection. The team members were to examine and compare the materials, classify them by intended purposes, and then use their findings to speculate about what makes an effective science lesson. They were told to generalize beyond single lessons because the class would attempt to identify the characteristics of an effective science program. Groans were prompted by the requirement to select and use research-based, practice-proven materials. Those groans subsided when Professor Becker demonstrated the speed and ease of using a free web-based resource center containing professionally reviewed lessons, videos, applets, and simulations (see: www.ohiorc.org).

Professor Becker reconvened the class and asked the groups to report. She listed the features the students found most often among the materials: objectives, suggested teaching methods, materials needed, background information, illustrations, assessment devices, and ideas for extending the activities. Many recent lessons were correlated with the National Science Education Standards and the standards of many host states. These lessons frequently contained references to themes, conceptual frameworks, skills to be developed, ideal group sizes, key vocabulary, lesson rationales, competencies, and subjects with which the lessons could be integrated. When she asked for the groups' ideas about effective programs, she received replies such as: "They [programs] emphasize subject matter most and produce higher test scores," "Effective programs are those that children like," and "You can tell the program is effective if more children take science in high school and if more want to enter scientific careers." These replies fell short of Professor Becker's hopes, so she guided the class into a discussion of the assignment, pressed them to give specific examples of what they found, and repeated the assignment's central question: What are the best practices that compose or support an effective science program?

Introduction

We are likely to repeat mistakes of the past if we are ignorant of the history that brought us to the present. In fact, the National Science Education Standards' history of science content standards encourages a historical development perspective of science. Looking back, we see considerable similarity among the recommendations that arose from several science education reports during the mid-1940s, again during the late 1950s and early 1960s, and still again during the late 1980s and mid-1990s. *No Child Left Behind* and 21st century blue-ribbon panels of experts call for more intellectual rigor, increased standards, elevated expectations, improved student discipline, increased classroom time on task, improved test scores, and enhanced teacher/subject expertise. Indeed, devoting more time to intellectual subject matter in science is a common and worthwhile goal, but when it is the only expectation, it falls short of fulfilling the larger goal of more effective science programs. The key to effective science instruction is selecting and using intellectually engaging experiences with the proper mix of science content and processes.

Calls or mandates for improved pupil achievement and recommendations for producing these improvements may be naively based on uninformed right-wrong perspectives or faulty assumptions about what should be taught and learned and about how children learn and should be taught. But what role are you expected to play? You will be involved, at some point in your career, with science program development. More immediately, your concern is to select the best materials available to plan and teach effective lessons. Can you afford to ignore the lessons of the past? This chapter provides

1. a report of lessons learned,
2. a viewpoint on selecting and using textbooks, and
3. a description of best practices and suggested resources.

Lessons Learned

Legacy of the Past

Biology, chemistry, physics, and *earth science* are common school science curricula. Even in general science and elementary science courses, these subjects persist as topics or units of study. They arose from scientific research disciplines, which were popular during the 1800s. However, since about 1900, these disciplines have not accurately represented the important areas of science. Thousands of diverse scientific journals now report experimental findings from a countless number of new fields of science and technology. Distinctions among the different fields of science are now made more by the type of problem being researched than by the discipline being served. Today, there is simply too much—too many facts of science to be learned in a school science program. The amount of scientific information continues to double about every five years. So what should be taught? At times, this question has been answered with an issues-and-problems approach.

A specific problem in science education has always been to resolve the issue of how the schools could best prepare "citizens to live in a culture most often described in terms of achievements in science and technology" (Hurd, 1986, p. 355). In the 1930s and 1940s, elementary schools tried to resolve this issue by teaching in a "prescribed authoritative manner almost exclusively through single-author textbooks" (Sabar, 1979, pp. 257–269). Basically, science was a reading program that covered a large body of information and used the subtle but powerful force of conformity and consensus to control the direction of American society and to aid citizens as they tried to adjust to society's new directions. The important facts, concepts, and theories of science that were taught were based on the consensus of specialists. Specialists told previous generations of teachers what was important to know and teach.

Past programs prepared children to become scientists.

Teacher emphasis on pupil conformity and learning science by reading is still highly visible today. Another emphasis from the past that is still widely supported is the cry to get back to basics, with emphasis on reading, writing, and arithmetic. This chant began after World War II for the same reasons that can be heard today: the perceived overall low success of high-school graduates as shown by their declining achievement scores and poor job skills and the need for citizens to keep pace with scientific and technological breakthroughs of other advanced countries (Sabar, 1979, p. 258). Ironically, this last factor makes the study of science a basic need for all, a basic literacy subject in the school curriculum, as described in Chapter 6.

Efforts began earlier, but it was the launching of the Soviet satellite *Sputnik* in 1957 that caused the most serious attempts at science curriculum reform. During the twenty-five years after *Sputnik*, $2 billion dollars were spent to support mathematics and science education in elementary and secondary schools. The main goal then, as many believe it should be now, was to prepare future scientists and engineers, mostly out of a concern for national defense. As important as this goal is, we now know that defense issues rise and fall in urgency and that "this is a goal that is appropriate for only 3 percent of high school graduates, and a goal where we have traditionally spent 95 percent of our time, efforts, resources and attention" (Yager, 1984, p. 196).

Alphabet Soup Programs

The decade after *Sputnik* is known for alphabet-soup elementary science programs. Three programs that were developed during this period are worth mentioning now because of their goals, their effects on children's learning, and the eventual improved quality of modern textbooks and other curriculum materials. Several assumptions that the programs were based on have been supported over time by a growing body of research, while other assumptions have fallen from favor. These programs are known as SAPA, SCIS, and ESS.

Science—A Process Approach (SAPA), Science Curriculum Improvement Study (SCIS), and the Elementary Science Study (ESS) were regarded as innovative programs in their day. Designed and field-tested during the 1960s and then revised during the 1970s, these experimental programs had several features in common:

+ They were developed by teams of scientists, psychologists, educators, and professional curriculum specialists rather than written by single authors or single expert specialists.
+ Federal funds were widely available for development, research, field testing, dissemination, and teacher inservice training.
+ Each project was developed from particular assumptions about learning drawn from prominent theories and used to form a specific framework for each project. Behavioral and cognitive-development psychology had major influences.
+ Each project was developed from what were assumed to be the ways children learned best. Specific teaching approaches were emphasized and were used to help children learn the ways and knowledge of science and to develop the attitudes of scientists.
+ Active pupil learning was assumed to be very important. Each project provided hands-on learning experiences for all children because it was assumed that manipulatives help children learn best.
+ The projects did not provide a standard textbook for each child. In fact, a workbook for recording observations was as close as some children came to anything that resembled a textbook.
+ There was no attempt to teach all that should be known about science. Specific science processes or content areas were selected for each project, thus narrowing the field of topics to a specialized few.
+ Attention was given to the basic ideas of science, the concepts and theories, with the intention of increasing the number of citizens who would seek careers in science and engineering.
+ The programs were conveniently packaged. Equipment was included with curriculum materials. This made the programs easier to use and reduced teacher preparation time by eliminating the need to gather diverse equipment.
+ Mathematical skills were emphasized. The programs were more quantitative than qualitative. Emphasis was placed on student observation, careful measurement, and the use of appropriate calculations to form ideas or reach conclusions.
+ Science was taught as a subject by itself and was not associated with social studies, health, or reading. At times, science was treated as a pure subject that was believed to have inherent value for all children.
+ The teacher's role changed. Teachers used less direct methods of teaching such as inquiry and functioned as questioners and guides for students. They avoided lecturing or more didactic forms of direct instruction. The teacher was *not* to be an expert who told children what they should memorize.

Significant Gains

Table 11.1 shows the results of extensive meta-analyses. When compared to comparable learners in traditional textbook-based science programs, students in the three experimental science K–6 programs demonstrated significant gains in achievement, process skills, and scientific attitudes. An important lesson was learned: effective science programs favor a holistic view of science and include features that aim to improve children's science attitudes, science skills, and science content knowledge.

What the three most used programs have in common is an inquiry-based, hands-on curriculum and teaching approach. Despite what is widely believed and practiced, inquiry learning approaches are superior to the traditional direct, textbook-based approach. James Shymansky and his colleagues (1982) tell us that synthesis of the abundant research shows conclusively that children in a hands-on science program achieve more, like science more, and improve their problem-solving skills more than children who learn from traditional textbook-based programs. The hands-on approaches help the minds grow and construct meaning. These conclusions endured resynthesis even though the original statistics have been revised to yield results of greater precision (Shymansky, et al., 1990).

Ted Bredderman (1982) adds support to this view. Bredderman's research arose from *Project Synthesis,* a massive research effort funded by the National Science Foundation to determine the results of past experimental programs so that present and future science education goals could be revised. Bredderman's research collected the results from sixty studies that involved 13,000 students in 1,000 elementary classrooms over fifteen years. He analyzed the results of these studies carefully through meta-analysis procedures to sort out conflicting findings reported in the literature. His conclusion clearly shows what works:

> With the use of activity-based science programs, teachers can expect substantially improved performance in science process and creativity; modestly increased performance

TABLE 11.1   Performance Improvement for Students in Classrooms Using ESS, SCIS, or SAPA as Compared to Students in Traditional Classrooms

Performance Area	Percentage Points Gained		
	ESS	*SCIS*	*SAPA*
Achievement	4	34	7
Attitudes	20	3	15
Process skills	18	21	36
Related skills	*	8	4
Creativity	26	34	7
Piagetian tasks	2	5	12

*No studies reported

Source: James A. Shymansky, William C. Kyle, Jr., and Jennifer M. Alport, "How Effective Were the Hands-On Science Programs of Yesterday?" *Science and Children* (November–December 1982): 15.

Interaction is an important inquiry tool that helps learners to construct meaning from materials and experiences.

on tests of perception, logic, language development, science content, and math; modestly improved attitudes toward science and science class; and pronounced benefits for disadvantaged students. (Bredderman, 1982, pp. 39–41)

Inquiry learning makes the difference. Exploring, investigating, and discovering are essential to meaningful learning and effective science teaching. When children solve problems and make discoveries, they are learning how to learn and constructing meaning for themselves. Jerome Bruner (1961) points out the benefits for children as they make discoveries through active learning:

- ✦ As children's intellectual potency is increased, their powers of thinking improve.
- ✦ Children's rewards for learning shift from those that come from the teacher or someone else to those that are found inside themselves from the satisfaction they feel.
- ✦ Children learn the procedures and important steps for making discoveries and find ways to transfer these to other learning opportunities.
- ✦ What children learn takes on more meaning, and they remember it longer.

Selecting and Using Textbooks

If you had taken a look in a large number of elementary classrooms where science is taught more than a decade after Shymansky and Bredderman's research, what do you think you would have seen? Would you have witnessed a massive change toward the kinds of inquiry-based active and interactive learning? No. Instead, it is likely that you would have observed what Donald Wright reported: "Fifty to 80 percent of all science classes use a single text or multiple texts as *the* basis for instruction. For students, knowing is more a function of reading, digesting, and regurgitating information from the textbook or lab manual than it is of analyzing, synthesizing, and evaluating" (Wright, 1980, p. 144). More than two decades later in the 21st century school science is still largely dependent upon a single text even though texts continue to be criticized for their shortcomings (Holliday, 2002; Kirk et al, 2001; Stern & Roseman, 2001).

Shortcomings and Differences in Textbooks

Although authors and publishers have made dramatic improvements over recent years, science textbooks vary considerably on factors, such as readability, reading and study aids, treatment of race and gender, and emphasis given to vocabulary versus concepts. Readability studies show greater levels of difference mostly for the upper elementary and middle grades. Students' science achievements decline when they use textbooks written above their reading ability levels. Reading and study aids, such as chapter headings, help pupils comprehend and recall, particularly when children are taught to use these features. Gender bias has been reduced, with more balance now seen toward female representation. However, persons who have disabilities and nonwhites often do not receive substantial recognition in textbooks. Science vocabulary continues to be emphasized much more than science concepts, even though researchers report that emphasis on concepts rather than vocabulary results in *increased* science achievement (Meyer, Greer, & Crummey, 1986). In contrast to this finding, Paul D. Hurd (1982) has found science texts often introduce "as many as 2,500 technical terms and unfamiliar words" (p. 12). He notes that a beginning foreign language course attempts to cover only half as many new words.

Who decides what material science textbooks will include and how they will be organized? Recommendations from credible sources such as the National Research Council, the National Science Teachers Association, or the American Association for the Advancement of Science do not always drive the development or revision of printed materials like school textbooks. Authors, teachers, editors, marketing staffs in publishing houses, boards of education, and textbook censors have less influence than you may imagine. Texas, California, Florida, and North Carolina all have statewide textbook adoptions. The combined student population of these states account for 25 percent of the United States' school-age population; the powerful textbook selection committees of these states tremendously influence the content that most publishers choose to put into their books (Kirk et al., 2001). Hence, a few states tend to determine the content and features offered to the rest of the nation. Approaches and material that appear radical or unconventional stand little chance despite their academic merits, origin, or proven effects.

If it seems unlikely that textbooks will be dramatically improved and some errors will be inevitable, what options do you have? You *do* have a choice of programs. The choices you make will influence the direction you use to guide your students and the extent of the positive impact on their interactive learning experience. You can

Student activities can enhance the use of a textbook.

- ◆ enhance the textbook in use,
- ◆ change the sequence of topics to reflect better the concepts to be learned,
- ◆ select the textbook that most closely represents the needs of your students and fulfills the recommendations for effective science teaching and learning.

Enhancing the Textbook

Each teacher can enhance the textbook to include more effective learning activities and interesting information, rather than wait for authors and publishers to do it. You can add enhancements that are timely and that match learner interests and abilities. These are some other ways you can use textbooks to foster constructivism.

1. Combine the best elements from published programs. Use old editions or the most interesting materials from unadopted examination copies of textbooks. Cut out pictures, information, and activities to make mini-books or a resource file by topic.

2. Select relevant supplements from laboratory programs and web-based materials. Experimental programs may have been used by your school in the past and then discarded. Remnants may be found stored away. Conduct an inventory of equipment and teaching materials from the past, and select useful materials relevant to the concepts you are teaching.

3. Identify local resources. School and community professionals, local businesses, parks and recreation facilities, libraries, and museums all provide rich resources for classroom speakers and field trips. These enhancement resources also help to demonstrate the relationship of science and everyday life as well as update or fill in gaps not covered by dated textbooks.

4. Check with your state's department of education. Some states compare commercial materials and keep on file survey-style coverage of important science findings and laboratory programs that make fine enhancements for standard textbook programs.

5. Screen supplementary materials for the appropriate reading level and context accuracy. Deemphasize use of a textbook written on a reading level too high by substituting suitable materials. Use accelerated material if the writing is too simple.

6. Select evaluation devices that reflect the preferred outcomes. If your desire is development of a particular process skill, select performance-based evaluation tasks that require the children to demonstrate the skill. Carefully screen all textbook questions and written exercises and select those that match the intended level of thinking and skills. Adapt project ideas and improve the types of questions used in the textbook or teacher's guide.

7. Work to organize building- or district-level committees in which teachers form supplement teams. More hands make lighter work, and more heads generate a greater number of effective ideas. Teams of teachers can share the research and swap ideas.

8. Attend professional conferences. States have affiliates of the National Science Teachers Association, and large cities have their own science education organizations. Attend their annual conferences and listen to other teachers to get ideas for your own classroom. Adapt these ideas to your science program. Remember, your ideas are just as important as those of others. Why not make your own presentation at a conference or provide a workshop for other teachers?

9. Relearn the concepts and processes of science. Take workshops or courses to learn about the most recent ideas in science and its teaching. This continues your education and professional development; both can help you enhance the science textbook. Request a staff development program for yourself and for helping the other school staff

How Toys Can Enhance Your Teaching

by Michael E. Cawthru
Grade 5, Kyffin Elementary School, Golden, Colorado

There are literally dozens of books out on the market to help teachers bring science demonstrations into the classroom. I know, I'm on the mailing list for all of them. But it is worth it to have an assortment of ideas at your fingertips. Don't let anyone tell you that you must teach the textbook and never vary from it. Textbooks are nice, but you have to be yourself. Go for it!

When you start to do classroom demos, make certain you have practiced and are prepared. Nothing can kill the demo faster than the teacher's leaning over the file cabinet or searching through the closet muttering, "Just a second kids, I'll have what I need. Just sit still." Yeah, right. Before you can turn around, Johnny is all over the room and into everything you had out for the demo. Likewise, nothing can get and hold their attention like all the equipment laid out on the table.

Speaking of equipment, it would be great to have thousands of dollars' worth of glassware, burners, chemicals, and such. But you can also use mason jars and propane torches and check out the chemicals that are sold over the grocery store counter. Ping-Pong balls—I keep at least a dozen on hand for all sorts of demonstrations: atomic structure (color them and give kids colored marshmallows for their set so they can eat them at the end), planets, physics—well, you get the idea. A globe and a ball, the diameter of which is the same as the distance from San Francisco to Cleveland on your globe, will be the perfect model for the earth and the moon. Also include a string that has been wrapped around the globe ten times; that's the distance from the Earth to the moon. And never underestimate the toy department. Oh boy, my wife won't let me go in unescorted. Slinkies, cars, marbles, magnets, and models—models of space shuttles, human bodies, eyes, just about anything.

Yes, I must admit, my room looks like a toy store. But the bottom line is this: Are the kids learning? You bet your atom they are. Because I also don't just sit. When kids with Ping-Pong balls are walking around the room imitating electrons moving about the nucleus, and another kid is trying to hit a ball with a marshmallow, they understand the reason electrons pass through matter without hitting anything, that atoms are mostly empty space. Yeah, they learn. And that is the whole point, the "ah-hah" moment we all live for, when Suzy says, "I get it, Mr. C!"

members relearn and elevate their own levels of scientific literacy. Other teachers will be more likely to enhance the textbook if they feel more confident and informed.

Changing the Sequence

The textbook's chapter order and the organization of the information within chapters may not be what is best for your students. Perhaps some simple resequencing may bring improvement in science achievement, attitudes, and interest and help you to help learners make clearer and stronger conceptual connections.

Cognitive scientists emphasize the importance of anchoring ideas to the learner's mental structure. New information becomes more meaningful when it can be attached to concepts already in the children's minds. Science material is better understood when it interrelates "in such a way as to make sense to the learner" (Hamrick & Harty, 1987, p. 16). Resequencing material so ideas relate in ways that make more sense to the children adds meaning. In a study of sixth graders,

> the findings revealed that students for whom content structure was clarified through resequencing general science chapters exhibited significantly higher science achievement, significantly more positive attitudes toward science, and significantly greater interest in science than students for whom general science content was not resequenced. (Hamrick & Harty, 1987, p. 15)

Concept mapping is a method of sequencing the ideas of a lesson, and a version of it can be used to sequence the text effectively. A concept map shows ideas graphically according to their relationships. (See Chapter 4 for more information.) The relationships communicate important connections that show an intended mental structure to be formed about the map's topic. Consider the following when resequencing:

1. Proceed from the smallest to the largest ideas, or from the simple to the complex, when resequencing a text. Researchers recommend that rearrangements first be made into an interrelated pattern based on the size of the ideas (Hamrick & Harty, 1987). A hierarchy of ideas is formed; perhaps physical science leads to life science topics, which progress to earth and space science concepts. See Table 11.2 for an example of a typical textbook sequence of topics with a revised sequence. You can determine the children's hierarchical views of the material by doing a webbing exercise in which they refer to the table of contents or chapter titles of the text and connect them in a web that makes sense to them. Begin at the chalkboard with a single word such as *science* and have the children refer to the ideas in the chapter titles and sections within chapters to add the ideas of science to the chalkboard. Engage the children in a discussion of how they see these ideas of science connected; ask for their reasons. Your prompts can help them to order material from the simple to the more complex in a way that is more understandable. At the same time, you will be reinforcing higher levels of thinking.

2. Convey the interrelated structure to the students. An overview of the restructured material can be made on a student handout, placed in a notebook, and used for clarification, reinforcement, and review throughout the year. Children can check off the major concepts as they are studied. This serves as a structure of information for learners, gives you an opportunity to teach for concepts, and provides a ready guide for reinforcement.

3. Help learners to clarify the content of the structure. They will not absorb all of the ideas of the resequencing overview at once. Take advantage of any opportunity to discuss the structure of the material you have chosen for your class. Be aware of how many levels of complexity exist once all chapter resequencing occurs and chapters are mapped. Does the textbook take into account the difficulty children may have in developing relationships among and between the concepts? Help learners to paint the big picture and to see how the smaller ideas fit into a pattern with the larger ideas.

TABLE 11.2 A Sample of Textbook Content Sequence and Revised Textbook Content Sequence

Textbook Sequence	Revised Content Sequence
Animals with backbones	Matter (elements and compounds)
Classifying animals without backbones	Sources of energy
Plants	Light
Life cycles	Electricity and magnetism
Matter (elements and compounds)	Communications
Electricity and magnetism	Energy outcomes and the future
Sources of energy	Energy for living things
Light	Plants
Communications	Life cycles
Climates of the world	Classifying animals without backbones
Energy for living things	Animal with backbones
Energy outcomes and the future	Climates of the world

Source: L. Hamrick and H. Harty, "Influence of Resequencing General Science Content on the Science Achievement, Attitudes Toward Science, and Interests in Science of Sixth Grade Students," *Journal of Research in Science Teaching* 24(1) (1987): 20. Reprinted by permission of John Wiley & Sons, Inc.

Selecting the Best Textbook

Teachers are becoming more selective, and it may be that their efforts to identify the best textbooks are having effects on changes. Textbooks are often selected because they offer many activities, worksheets, tests, and programmed teacher's guides. They appear busy or glitzy and may require little more than reading and writing exercises. Such textbooks may fall short of meeting recommendations for effective science instruction and do not support inquiry-based, constructivist learning. What can you do to select a better textbook or to use the one you have in ways that improve the experience for students? As a starting point for screening textbooks, ask yourself:

+ What does the textbook expect my students to do?
+ Does the textbook include important content and related information?
+ What should my students be able to do after they study the textbook that they could not do before?
+ For every student activity, project, or question, ask: "What kind of thinking is required?" "How does this address the National Science Education Standards?"
+ Examine the textbooks for inclusion of the NSES content standards (see Appendix) and ask: "To what extent is each new dimension emphasized?" and "How is it included in the textbook?" "How well do the textbook's concepts represent these recommendations?"
+ Summarize your initial screening by asking: "Will this textbook really help my students reach the goals I have set for them—or is it going to waste their time?"

Look again at the textbooks that pass the initial screening. Now is the time to be more critical. An effective textbook should motivate students; it should involve children in the processes of science by guiding them toward making discoveries. It should include materials that can be adapted to fulfill local needs. How does the textbook help students to experience the history and nature of science within the local context? The activities should not be cookbook recipes that encourage learners to follow the steps mindlessly. Focus on the student activities, sample several from each book, and ask these questions:

◆ Are students required to make careful observations?
◆ Are students encouraged to make inferences?
◆ Is classification a skill used in the experiments?
◆ How often are students asked to make a prediction based on observation or data?
◆ How often are students encouraged to display data in a systematic way that will enhance their ability to communicate?
◆ What kinds of weblinks or enhancements are offered by the publisher and how do those enhancements fulfill your state or national standards?
◆ What resources are offered to assist learners who have special needs?

These questions will help you select a textbook that delivers a strong blend of expository information and productive interaction through sound activity-based learning. Table 11.3 provides a brief instrument for screening textbooks and printed curriculum materials.

The best science textbook will challenge children to improve their thinking.

We cannot force students to learn. We can help them make discoveries and form connections for themselves, and our guidance is an important factor. Go slowly and guide with purpose. Avoid merely covering information without ensuring student understanding. Strive for quality rather than quantity. Remember the maxim: Less is more. Listen to students more and talk less. Try to emphasize student cooperation instead of competition. Blend learning activities to include discovery opportunities, group work, and learning that requires different types of information processing—thinking. Try to concentrate on students doing right thinking rather than getting right answers. If you must use a textbook and teacher-centered approaches, incorporate several of the suggestions offered in this chapter to make your classroom more interactive. Chances for effective teaching will be greater through your efforts, and your reward will be improved student achievement, positive attitudes toward science, and greater interest in school through more student-centered, constructivist teaching practices.

TABLE 11.3   Screening Texts and Other Printed Curriculum Materials

You can learn about the science program by examining the textbooks and other written curriculum materials available.

	Yes	No	?

Science Content

1. Is there a balanced emphasis among the life sciences, earth sciences, and physical sciences?   ____ ____ ____
2. Do the materials include study of problems that are important to us now and in the future? Examples: acid rain, air and water pollution, technology's impact, energy production and availability, medical research, world hunger, population, deforestation, ozone depletion.   ____ ____ ____
3. Do materials require students to apply major science concepts to everyday life situations?   ____ ____ ____
4. Are the materials accurate?   ____ ____ ____
5. Do the materials encourage an in-depth examination of concepts and issues?   ____ ____ ____
6. Other   ____ ____ ____

Science Processes

1. Do the materials include liberal amounts of hands-on investigations and activities that the children can do in order to experience the nature of science?   ____ ____ ____
2. Is scientific inquiry an important part of the materials the children will read? Examples: observing, measuring, predicting, inferring, classifying, recording and analyzing data, etc.   ____ ____ ____
3. Do the materials encourage children to explore, discover, and construct answers for themselves rather than tell them how things should turn out?   ____ ____ ____
4. Do the materials require children to use scientific reasoning, to apply science processes to problem-solving situations, and to construct conclusions?   ____ ____ ____
5. To what extent do the materials help learners to build thinking skills?   ____ ____ ____
6. Other: ____ ____ ____

Other Considerations

1. Are the materials consistent with the science goals of your school? (Or, in the absence of such goals, those of the National Science Education Standards or your state framework of science goals.)   ____ ____ ____
2. Are the materials well designed, clearly written, accurate, up to date, and easy to use?   ____ ____ ____
3. Do the materials proceed from the simple to the complex and are they designed for the children's appropriate developmental levels?   ____ ____ ____

(continued)

TABLE 11.3   Screening Texts and Other Printed Curriculum Materials (continued)

	Yes	No	?
4. Is the information written at the proper grade level?	___	___	___
5. Do the materials for children appear interesting and relevant to their levels?	___	___	___
6. Are there opportunities for children to learn about the history and nature of science and science-related careers?	___	___	___
7. Are valid evaluation materials used or included? Examples: performance demonstrations, pictorial assessment.	___	___	___
8. Is a teacher's guide included and is it helpful for using the materials?	___	___	___
9. Do the materials include enough application of science content and processes to make science meaningful to students?	___	___	___
10. Is technology included and do children have to use appropriate forms of technology to access or process the science material?	___	___	___
11. Are different cultures, races, genders, social groups, ages included with respect and equity?	___	___	___
12. Do the materials promote teaching methods that promote an effective, interactive learning environment?	___	___	___
13. Other:	___	___	___

Source: Originally adapted from Kenneth R. Mechling and Donna L. Oliver, *Characteristics of a Good Elementary Science Program* (Washington, DC: National Science Teachers Association, 1983) and updated by the authors of this text to reflect contemporary expectations and the *National Science Education Standards* (NRC, 1996).

Using Trade Books

Trade books or children's literature is another way to bring content-focused science material to class. While science textbooks focus on the factual and analytical aspects of reading, the trade book can provide an aesthetic or emotional dimension to learning (Rice, 2002). Often this combined approach helps address specific, real-world uses of science, and is an approach that favors the inclusion of females and minorities. The trade book is not a substitute for skills-directed instruction in teaching reading skills or science concepts. However, a trade book can involve a wider audience and offer an applied setting for learning science.

Trade books may include biographies of scientists; reference books on particular types of animals, plants, or environmental issues; natural science concepts; or specifically focused single publications on physical science topics, science theories, or natural causes, such as volcanoes and tornadoes. Trade books may contain fictional characters, but illustrate specific science concepts. Textbook publishers have begun identifying trade books to be used with their textbook series (Rice, 2002). The annual March issue of *Science and Children,* published by the National Science Teachers Association, lists the most outstanding science trade books for children. These books pass scrutiny for having substantial science content; clarity; and freedom from gender, ethnic, and socioeconomic bias.

Teachers must be aware that trade books have their limitations. Some teachers may use trade books to introduce or to complement a lesson, such as during a learning cycle's *Explanation* phase to support the vocabulary and help to develop the concept. Trade books should be scrutinized carefully, just as you would do for a textbook, because some researchers report numerous factual errors and information and illustrations that encourage the formation of misconceptions (Rice, 2002).

Trade books for children help to expand conceptualization and to support habits of scientific literacy.

Best Practices

The field of education is replete with labels containing multiple meanings, and "best practice" probably qualifies for multiple perceptions and meanings. As the label implies, there can be a qualitative distinction between the value of one practice versus another. In science teaching and learning, we use the term *best practice* to convey a clearly defined basis for making an evaluation about a resource's or a practice's impact on learning. A best practice consists of superior teaching materials that are used with effective teaching methods. Choosing and using a best practice should result in a significant impact on student learning.

Identifying Best Practices

The lessons learned from the rich history and research base of science education means that a best practice in science uses effective principles of curriculum design, psychology, cognition, assessment, and teaching. A modern best practice is a teaching resource, such as a lesson, that

- ✦ is aligned with specific content, teaching, and assessment standards,
- ✦ has a research base,
- ✦ has accurate content and is developed in a way that promotes student understanding,
- ✦ implicitly or explicitly supports equity,
- ✦ engages the interests of most students using methods of inquiry and requires active participation for learning to occur,
- ✦ frames the content in a learning context that students find meaningful and significant,

Emphasis on Excellence

The National Science Education Standards provide criteria for excellence in developing K–8 science programs and improving science teaching, learning, and assessment. The standards for excellence are grounded in five assumptions:

1. The vision of science education described by the Standards requires changes throughout the entire system.
2. What students learn is greatly influenced by how they are taught.
3. The actions of teachers are deeply influenced by their perceptions of science as an enterprise and as a subject to be taught and learned.

4. Student understanding is actively constructed through individual and social processes.
5. Actions of teachers are deeply influenced by their understanding of and relationships with students (National Research Council, 1996, p. 28).

Achieving these standards for excellence requires several changes throughout the system of science education. Therefore, the excellent science program must encompass the following changes in emphases (National Research Council, 1996, p. 224):

Less Emphasis On	More Emphasis On
• Developing science programs at different grade levels independently of one another	• Coordinating the development of the K–12 science program across grade levels
• Using assessments unrelated to curriculum and teaching	• Aligning curriculum, teaching, and assessment
• Maintaining current resource allocations for books	• Allocating resources necessary for hands-on inquiry teaching aligned with the Standards
• Textbook- and lecture-driven curriculum	• Curriculum that supports the Standards and includes a variety of components, such as laboratories emphasizing inquiry and field trips
• Broad coverage of unconnected factual information	• Curriculum that includes natural phenomena and science-related social issues that students encounter in everyday life
• Treating science as a subject isolated from other school subjects	• Connecting science to other school subjects, such as mathematics and social studies
• Science learning opportunities that favor one group of students	• Providing challenging opportunities for all students to learn science
• Limiting hiring decisions to the administration	• Involving successful teachers of science in the hiring process
• Maintaining the isolation of teachers	• Treating teachers as professionals whose work requires opportunities for continual learning and networking
• Supporting competition	• Promoting collegiality among teachers as a team to improve the school
• Teachers as followers	• Teachers as decision makers

- may be specifically targeted upon a special need,
- is adaptable to a variety of learning settings and promotes discourse leading to constructed understanding,
- uses appropriate technology in highly effective ways,
- includes tools for helping teachers to conduct assessments of increased student learning, and
- may innovate, motivate, and hold high expectations for learners.

A Site for Best Practices

Fortunately, the list of qualities shown above is built into an evaluation rubric for reviewing web-based science resources www.ohiorc.org/rubric/), which is used to locate hundreds of high quality lessons. The *Ohio Resource Center for Mathematics, Science and Reading* (ORC) is a free web-based center supplying lessons for improving teaching and learning. The ORC resources are used by teachers, school leaders, policy makers and university faculty; children benefit. The ORC provides links to peer-reviewed instructional resources that have been identified by panels of experienced educators. Lessons promote best practices and are correlated to the national standards and Ohio's academic content standards. Correlations with national standards make the resources attractive to educators in any state and may be accessed from any Internet connection any place, any time. The ORC is not a clearinghouse and includes only materials that have passed the most rigorous review. The ORC may be accessed on www.ohiorc.org. The resources may be browsed by topic, grade level, or standard. The resources may also be searched using basic or advanced techniques. An example of a best practice using a learning cycle can be seen by viewing this review record and using the direct link. The ORC record can be found easily by using the search features and searching on key words, topics, or record number.

Supported Beliefs About Effective Elementary Science Programs

A science program consists of more than a collection of individual lessons, even if they are classified as best practices. An effective science program, whether it is based on a single text or multiple resources, will be based on the supported beliefs that have arisen from reputable research and decades of classroom-based impact. According to numerous publications from the National Science Foundation and the National Science Teachers Association, the following list describes the intentions, dispositions and characteristics of high impact programs. Fortunately, numerous resources are available to satisfy the description of this list:

1. National Science Foundations' experimental elementary science programs and new approaches to teacher preparation have been successful, even though a low percentage of schools (30 percent) have used the programs and an even smaller percentage of teachers (7 percent) have received direct training.

2. Effective elementary science programs keep pace with changes in science, society, knowledge, and trends in schooling.

3. Most current elementary school science programs do not serve all children well. Effective programs have meaning for diverse audiences.

4. Effective science programs strive to promote children's personal development; to help children explore the interrelationships among science, technology, and society; to continue academic preparation through inquiry; and to build awareness of the history and nature of science.

5. Effective programs have no single author but are developed by teams with teacher involvement. Extensive classroom testing and program revision are necessary and must be done frequently.

6. Students learn successfully in different ways; multiple views on learning add diversity and help to balance the effective science program.

7. Programs that emphasize conceptual learning appear to be most effective overall and produce the greatest and most enduring gains in achievement when conception is a learner's construct.

8. Multiple teaching methods are useful, and hands-on learning opportunities are necessary for all children. Overall, inquiry methods and learning cycles are useful methods for helping children learn science concepts.

9. What is taught—the substance of science—must be useful and relevant for each child. Publications such as the *National Science Education Standards* help guide content selection.

10. Packaging the program is helpful and reduces teachers' preparation time. New generation science curriculum supplements have several common features that add impact to the materials. They identify relevant themes, define purposes or objectives, give background information, list materials needed, state procedures for teaching, identify essential vocabulary, offer ideas for evaluation or lesson expansion, and so on.

11. The history and nature of science makes it possible to integrate topics into other subject lessons. Science's diversity enriches other parts of the school curriculum and adds to its power as a literacy subject.

12. A less direct, teacher-as-guide instructional role is effective because students are encouraged to assume greater responsibility for their own learning.

13. Conceptual learning takes time and should not be rushed; effectiveness rather than time efficiency should be the driving force of the curriculum.

14. Learners in constructivist science programs achieve more, like science more, and improve their problem-solving skills more than children who learn from traditional textbook-based programs. Innovative newer generations of science textbooks incorporate many of the features of the effective experimental programs.

15. Effective science programs promote children's intellectual development by improving their thinking through inquiry and problem-solving processes.

16. Materials and learning activities must match the child's level of development to have the greatest impact.

17. Students receive intrinsic rewards from the personal discoveries they make through firsthand learning experiences with manipulatives.

18. Science students who learn from effective programs are better able to transfer their learning to other circumstances, obtain more meaning, and remember what they learn longer.

Resources for Best Practices

Lessons from the past have helped to improve the wonderful new resources available to teachers. This exciting era of curriculum and program development has helped to renew interest in science through uses of best practices. Science programs are attempting to keep pace with changes in the fields of science and technology and to investigate the impact of each on our society through the eyes and experiences of children.

The new generation of science programs strives to serve the needs and interests of all learners, not an intellectual elite. New programs often emphasize conceptual development through constructivist techniques, use multiple teaching methods to fill multiple student interests, and incorporate multiple views on human diversity. Many programs promote additional science outcomes, such as students skilled at science inquiry and problem solving; investigations of interrelationships among and between science, technology, and society; awareness of the history and tentative nature of science; and an expanded awareness of career opportunities in science.

The direct and sustained involvement of classroom teachers is one of the greatest factors shaping new science programs, particularly in working to match students' levels of development to appropriate learning experiences and to strengthen the conceptual constructions of learners by connecting learning experiences and central concepts to science themes. Table 11.4 illustrates the thematic similarities and differences among several new science programs. Continual classroom testing of materials and lessons and frequent revision through formative evaluation assist these programs through rapid stages of evolution. Hence, conceptual flaws are reduced, and supported assumptions about learning are expanded.

Although there are numerous small-scale efforts to produce the next generation of science programs, space permits us to share only a sample of the larger efforts that have endured rigorous evaluation and received national (often international) attention.

Programs and Print Resources

AIMS. Activities Integrating Mathematics and Science (AIMS) publishes elementary and middle-school curriculum materials that integrate mathematics and science for grades K–9. These materials are provided in easy-to-use teacher manuals that have been produced and classroom-tested by teachers. Workshops and seminars are available through the AIMS organization, P.O. Box 8120, Fresno, CA 93747, www.aimsedu.org. Titles include *Floaters and Sinkers, Jawbreakers and Heart Thumpers, Primarily Plants, Primarily Physics, Budding Botanists,* and *The Sky's the Limit!* Some are available in Spanish.

TABLE 11.4   Common Science Themes Among Science Programs

Earth Systems	Benchmarks	California Framework	Biological Sciences Curriculum Study (BSCS)	National Assessment of Educational Progress (NAEP)	National Science Education Standards (NSES)	Project Learning Tree (PLT)
Aesthetics	Constancy	Stability	Cause and effect		Order and organization Constancy	
Interaction	Patterns of change	Patterns of change Energy	Change and conservation Energy and matter	Patterns of change	Measurement and change	Patterns of change
	Scale	Scale and structure	Time and scale			Structure and scale
Evolution	Evolution	Evolution	Evolution and equilibrium		Evolution and equilibrium	
Scale & Systems	Systems	Systems and interactions	Systems and interactions	Systems		Systems
Nature of Science			Probability and prediction			
			Structure and function		Form and function	
Careers			Diversity and variation			Diversity
	Models		Models and theories	Models	Models	
Human impact						Inter-relationships

Delta Science Modules. This series of 40 paperback modules ranges from *Air* to *Observing an Aquarium* to *You and Your Body*. Lessons are suitable for intermediate and middle-school grades, provide easy-to-follow instructions that help teachers guide students through constructivist learning opportunities, and offer reasonably authentic assessment devices. Modules may be purchased separately or as a set. Kits of hands-on materials are available at additional cost. Modules are available from Delta Education, P.O. Box 3000, Nashua, NH 03061-3000, www.delta-ed.com, 800-258-1302.

Earth Systems Education. This middle-school science resource guide is a joint product of the Ohio State University and the University of Northern Colorado. Through a K–12 scope and sequence, teachers are urged to use the classroom-tested materials to develop the values of aesthetics and stewardship through practical local learning experiences that help students to explore state, national, and global Earth issues within the context of various science disciplines. Six principles unify the learning experiences. Online activities on environmental decision making are available for students in grades 7–12. Contact the Earth Systems Education Program at the Ohio State University, (614) 292-9826 or the School of Natural Resources, OSU, 221 Coffey Road, Columbus, OH 43210, www2.ag.ohio-state.edu/~earthsys/index.html.

New science programs provide a variety of experiences to help children understand their complex worlds.

FOSS. *Full Option Science System* (FOSS) of the Lawrence Hall of Science in Berkeley, California 94720, is distributed by Delta Education (www.delta-ed.com). For grades K–6, student equipment kits and print materials are accompanied by some of the most innovative assessment alternatives we have seen. Children do science, construct concepts, and perform direct evaluation exercises in the areas of life, physical, and earth science and scientific reasoning and technology. A correlation to NSES can be found on the FOSS website, www.Rhsfoss.org.

GEMS. *Great Exploration in Math and Science* (GEMS) is designed for students in grades K–12. Science and mathematics are integrated in 24 different teacher-activity publications and student project booklets. Available through the Carolina Biological Supply Company (www.carolina.com/GEMS), topics include 50 titles, such as *Animals in Action, Bubble-ology, Buzzing a Hive, Crime Lab Chemistry, Fingerprinting, Mapping Fish Habitats, Oobleck,* and *What Do Scientists Do?* The GEMS website is www.lhsGEMS.org.

Insights: An Inquiry-Based Elementary School Science Curriculum. This K–6 curriculum is designed to develop children's understanding of key science concepts while improving the student's abilities to think creatively and critically; encouraging problem solving through experiences in the natural environment; fostering the development of positive attitudes about science; bridging or linking science concepts to current social and environmental events; and integrating science with the mathematics and language arts curriculum. What is unique about this curriculum is that it was designed to specifically address the needs of an urban student. It was developed by a coalition of Education

Development Center science curriculum specialists and teams of elementary teachers from urban centers such as Baltimore, Boston, Cleveland, Los Angeles, New York, Montgomery County (Maryland), and San Francisco. It is in its second edition. A detailed description of the curriculum can be found at www2.edc.org/cse/products/curricula/insights.asp. The curricular materials can be ordered through Kendall/Hunt at www.insightsk-6.com or at 800-542-6657, ext. 1042.

Kids-Net. *National Geographic Kids Network* of Education Services, Dept. 5389, Washington, D.C. 20036 involves children in a nationwide computer network; learners collect data in their home environments and send the information to the national server. Sharing information helps children to make comparisons and discover concepts about water quality and rain, for example, on a national and global scale. Learners are linked with practicing scientists. The website is www.nationalgeographic.com/kids/index.html.

PEACHES. The Primary Explorations for Adults, Children & Educators in Science (PEACHES) program is another science program developed through the Lawrence Hall of Science at the University of California at Berkeley. This program is designed for children ages 4–6, grades Pre-K–1. Numerous science and mathematics activities and projects as well as professional development opportunities for the early childhood educator are all a part of the PEACHES program. Details on this program can be found at www.lhs.gems.org/peaches.html

Projects WILD and Aquatic. Two different versions of a great idea, these projects emphasize wildlife and aquatic life, respectively. Interdisciplinary and for grades K–12, the materials accommodate major school subjects and skills areas by involving children in direct and simulated wildlife experiences. The purpose is to increase awareness first, then to build toward making personal decisions and taking responsible human actions. The teacher-designed materials make it easy to bring outdoor wildlife concepts into the classroom. Students love the outdoor action sections. The activity guides are available only through training sessions. Information can be obtained by contacting Project WILD, www.projectwild.org.

Project Learning Tree. Perhaps the oldest of the Environmental Education Resource supplements, the Project Learning Tree (PLT) provides a Pre-K–8 guide designed to help learners better understand the forest community and its relationship to the day-to-day lives of people and animals. Each lesson is classroom-tested, linked to a specific science theme, and supported by conceptual story lines. Themes include diversity, interrelationships, systems, structure and scale, and patterns of change. The student pages for each activity, and the glossary pages within the guide have Spanish translations. Modules addressing specific subjects, such as forest ecology and risk are designed for the secondary students. PLT also provides supplemental resources such as the energy and society program which provides formal and informal educators with tools and activities to help students in grades Pre-K–8 learn about their relationship with energy and investigate the environmental issues related to energy's role in society. In addition to hands-on activities, it engages kinesthetic learners through music and dance in energy concepts.

PLT has collaborated with the Department of Interior's Bureau of Land Management and the National Interagency Fire Center to provide workshops on wildland fire education. These workshops make use of Pre-K–8 activities as well as the secondary PLT modules and fire education supplements such as the CD-ROM, "Burning Issues," produced by the Science Education Department from Florida State University. PLT also provides partners for *GreenWorks* grants, specifically designed to encourage student involvement with local community spring initiatives that focus on wildland fire prevention, safety, and restoration. The activity guides are available only through training sessions. Information about Project Learning Tree can be obtained by contacting PLT at the American Forest Foundation, 1111 19th Street, N.W., Suite 780, Washington, D.C. 20036, www.plt.org.

Project WET (Water Education for Teachers).   This program helps teachers explore water issues with learners. One hundred multidisciplinary activities support this resource, which are also supported by such supplements as special topic modules, models, children's literature books, and living history materials. Write to Project WET, 201 Culbertson Hall, Montana State University, Bozeman, MT 59717, www.projectwet.org.

SAVI/SELPH—Science Activities for the Visually Impaired/Science Enrichment for Learners with Physical Handicaps.   The SAVI/SELPH programs were designed to address effective science education for students with disabilities in grades 3–8. The Lawrence Hall of Science at UC Berkeley developed the program as two separate projects: Science Activities for the Visually Impaired (SAVI)—between 1976–79, and Science Enrichment for Learners with Physical Handicaps (SELPH)—between 1980–83. The goal of SAVI was to produce science activities for blind and visually impaired grade 3–8 students. Specialized equipment and new procedures to insure full access to science learning for blind students were also developed. Once field-tested it was found that SAVI materials worked well with students of *all* disabilities. The SELPH Project started out adapting and modifying SAVI materials and procedures for students with orthopedic disabilities and students with learning disabilities. Research on how these materials could be used in full inclusion classes was also conducted. The SAVI/SELPH science enrichment program today is interdisciplinary, multisensory, and found to be effective with blind or visually impaired, physically disabled, hearing impaired, developmentally delayed, learning disabled, and even nondisabled students. The foundation for the FOSS materials, described earlier, came from the SAVI/SELPH programs. Further information on this program and ordering information can be found at www.lawrencehallofscience.org/cml/saviselph/.

SEPUP.   The *Science Education for Public Understanding Program* was developed and produced by the Lawrence Hall of Science in Berkeley, California 94720-5200. The materials are arranged in modules. The original program, CEPUP, emphasized chemical education; new modules address physical, earth, and life sciences as well as science processes. SEPUP emphasizes an integrated approach to teaching issues-oriented science. SEPUP kits are designed for children in grades 6–9 and address topics like pollution, household chemicals, waste, and chemicals in foods. The Chem-2 SEPUP program is designed for grades 4–6. Yearlong SEPUP courses strive to make science concepts relevant to the real world. Further information can be found at www.lhs.berkeley.edu/SEPUP.

(text continues on page 391)

Video Explorations *Science Resources*

Video Summary

Many resources exist to enhance and/or supplement the science textbook. A quality print resource, such as Project Learning Tree, will provide thematic units, constructivist lessons, and inquiry-based activities. The Internet provides ready access to many science resources. One must look for sites that provide activities that focus on conceptual and skill development

while correlating with state and national standards. The Ohio Resource Center of Mathematics, Science, and Literacy is a superior model of such an Internet source.

Tips for Viewing, Objectives, or What to Watch for

As you watch this video, make note of the following:

✦ How resources are different from the science textbook,

✦ The implication that just because something is in print or available on the Internet does not mean it is of high quality,

✦ The criteria a resource must meet in order to be judged as a quality resource.

Questions for Exploration

1. As noted in the video, what criteria must be used to determine if a print resource is consistent with your beliefs about good science teaching?

2. What criteria might you use to determine if an Internet re-source is providing a safe, standards-based lesson for you to use with your students?

3. Do you think quality resources for the classroom teacher can replace the use of a textbook in your science classroom? Why or why not?

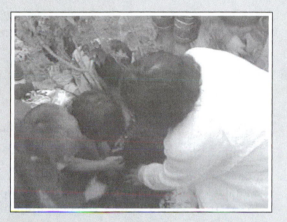

Activity for Application

Many useful print or Internet-based resources exist to enhance our science lessons. The video shared some and this chapter identifies many others. Establish some criteria that you believe are important when choosing and using quality, supplemental resources. Perform a library or Internet search to review some of these resources using the criteria you established. Which resources meet your criteria? Share these with your peers.

Water Cycle

GRADE LEVEL: **5–8**

DISCIPLINE: **Physical Science and Earth/Space Science**

Inquiry Question: Living things need and use a lot of water, so why isn't the Earth's water supply used up?

Concept to Be Invented: The *water cycle* is a system in which the Earth's fixed amount of water is collected, purified, and distributed from the environment to living things and back to the environment.

National Science Education Standards: 5–8 Physical Science—Transformations of Energy and 5–8 Earth and Space Science—Structure of the Earth's System.

Science Attitudes to Nurture: Cooperating with others, obtaining reliable sources of information, avoiding broad generalizations

Materials Needed: See Project Learning Tree (PLT) lesson, "Water Wonders" in Instructor's Manual and on the companion website for this textbook: www.ablongman.com/martin4e.

Safety Precautions: None for Part A. For Part B, wear goggles if making the watering can. Enforce the no eating rule.

Exploration *Which process skills will be used?*

Communicating, predicting, identifying variables, inferring

Modify the PLT lesson into a learning cycle to help students in grades 4–8 experience the fundamentals of a learning cycle. Pose the word "cycle" to the class and ask them to help construct a list of all words they can think of containing the word "cycle." Without drawing special attention to the words Water Cycle, develop a general description of what the word "cycle" means. Use guided imagery and ask the students to imagine they have a glass of water and divide it into its smallest part: a water molecule. Prepare students to take a pretend journey as a water molecule following the instructions and using the water stations' materials as provided in the Project Learning Tree lesson, "Water Wonders." See this information on the companion website (www.ablongman.com/martin4e) or in the Instructor's Manual.

Explanation

Using the chalkboard with the 7 water stations listed in a circular shape, ask the students to describe where they were prior to cloud; where they went after cloud. Do this for all stations and web the chalkboard diagram. Discuss the meaning of the diagram and what it represents: Water Cycle. Ask the children to describe what they think a water cycle is, what it does, and how it functions. Consult the water cycle figure in the PLT lesson. Develop the concept that a water cycle is a system in which the Earth's fixed amount of water is collected, purified, and distributed from the environment to living things and back to the environment.

Expansion *Which process skills will be used?*

Defining operationally, interpreting, modeling

Use Part B of the PLT lesson and the enrichment activity to expand the children's conception of water cycle. Supplement with the discussion questions provided in order to address many of the National Science Education Standards' new dimensions. The expansion can also be supplemented with a video, such as "The Wonders of Weather," commonly shown on PBS or the Discovery or Learning Channel. Also, available from Project Learning Tree is the "Energy and Me" CD or video by Billy B, which demonstrates the water cycle among other energy transfer systems.

Evaluation

Use the PLT assessment opportunity to have the children revise their definitions of the water cycle or to construct a concept map of the water cycle. Students are also challenged to write a scenario about water movement within a water cycle.

TOPS Learning Systems. The Task Oriented Physical Science (TOPS) materials center on physical science concepts. Over forty modules are designed for students in grades K–10. Each module comes with reproducible masters that include detailed instructions for hands-on, concept-based activities around a given theme. A complete listing of the TOPS modules can be found at www.topscience.org or by contacting TOPS Learning Systems, 10970 Mulino Road, Canby, OR 97013.

Windows on Science. This K–6 program is described as a multisensory learning model that combines images and activities to make science come alive for the learner. It contains eleven volumes organized around primary science, earth science, life science, and physical science. Teacher guides with reproducible masters are included with each volume. Students are encouraged to design experiments, create models and apply their understanding in a real-life context. What makes this yearlong program unique is the videodisc that comes with each volume. This videodisc provides numerous visual clips to reinforce the science concepts. A videodisc player is required to use this program. Detailed information including ordering information is provided on the Optical Data Corporation website at www.opticaldata.com/catalog/wos/wosmain.html.

TABLE 11.5 Science Classroom Volunteers

Area of Science	Volunteer
Animals	Zoologist, entomologist, microbiologist, zookeeper, veterinarian, beekeeper, marine biologist, paleontologist, cytologist, animal trainer, physician, forest ranger, physiologist, chemist, ecologist, neurobiologist, wildlife manager, farmer, rancher, geneticist, anatomist, mammalogist, limnologist, nurse, dietitian, x-ray technician, pharmacologist, forensic specialist, pharmacist
Plants	Botanist, paleobotanist, agronomist, horticulturist, farmer, forest manager, chemist, ecologist, geneticist, paleontologist, nutritionist, landscape architect, soil pathologist, soil scientist conservation officer, park ranger, agricultural extension agent
Weather	Meteorologist, ecologist, agronomist, TV weather forecaster, airport flight controller, geologist, oceanographer, climatologist, fisherman, boat captain, farmer, pilot, environmentalist, soil and water conservation agent
Physical and chemical properties	Chemist, biochemist, pharmacologist, architect, inventor, mechanic, carpenter, molecular biologist, physicist, ecologist, musical instrument maker, musician, toxicologist, metallurgist, geologist, photographer, builder, police lab forensic criminologist, materials scientist, technician, water company technician, engineers: chemical, textile, industrial, cosmetics developer, gemologist, acoustical engineer, optical engineer, mechanical engineer, civil engineer, building inspector, potter, nuclear engineer, agricultural engineer, ceramic engineer
Electricity	Physicist, geologist, computer hardware/software designer, electrician, radar technician, amateur radio operator, designer, industrial engineer, electrical engineer, telephone system technician, thermal engineer, mechanical engineer, electronic engineer, electrical inspector, inventor, radio/TV engineer
Earth and space science	Astronomer, geologist, paleontologist, pilot, astronaut, geographer, cartographer, ecologist, physicist, biologist, chemist, surveyor, geotechnical tester, aerial photographer, volcanologist, seismologist, oceanographer, soil scientist, aeronautical engineer, aviation engineer, construction engineer, civil engineer
Behavioral and social science	Animal psychologist, clinical psychologist, marketing professional, business manager, psychiatrist, sociologist, anthropologist, city planner, applied economist, school psychologist, historian, archaeologist, geographer, pollster, market research analyst, demographer, statistician

Source: North Carolina Museum of Life and Science, *Science in the Classroom,* as cited by Triangle Coalition for Science and Technology Education, *A Guide for Planning a Volunteer Program for Science, Mathematics, and Technology Education* (College Park, MD: Triangle Coalition, 1992), p. 59.

Human Resources

A readily available and often overlooked resource are colleagues. Using colleagues as resource persons for instructional guidance and assistance enables us to broaden educational activities and to foster cooperation.

Your colleagues—other classroom teachers, the principal, the school nurse, the resource teacher, the librarian—are all potential sources of assistance. The experienced teacher who is willing to share activities, materials, and support is a natural aide. Teachers in another school or grade level may be able to suggest teaching activities and loan equipment or share materials. Upper-grade-level students are also sources of help because they may be available to provide a demonstration or to serve as a teaching assistant or tutor.

Community volunteers can provide enriching services. Communities may contain engineers, professors, sewage treatment personnel, medical professionals, computer specialists, and mechanics who are interested in education. In addition, parents may offer suggestions. Corporations and institutions may have an educational officer who can assist by providing names of employees who are willing to volunteer their time and talent to assist within the schools. Consider contacting retirement groups; chambers of commerce; local women's clubs; local, state, or national agencies; or even the *Yellow Pages*. Their members are experienced and may have time to volunteer.

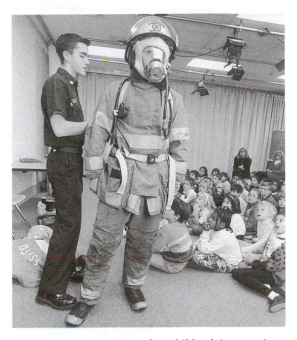

Community resources stimulate children's interests in science and its practical value.

A volunteer can enable you to devote more time to planning, diagnosing the individual needs of students, and prescribing learning activities for these needs. Volunteers may offer other benefits. They extend the number of people available to help the teacher and often bring skills that professional educators do not have, so the educational process maximizes opportunities for all students. Perhaps most important are the positive effects that volunteering can have on the volunteers themselves, and the public relations value is certainly important (Hager-Shoeny & Galbreath, 1982).

Table 11.5 lists vocations that volunteers might have. Look to individuals such as these to help with your school program.

Not all volunteers feel confident to make a presentation to a classroom on their particular area of interest. They may prefer, instead, to be involved in one or more of the following ways:

+ demonstrating scientific concepts
+ serving as a mentor
+ tutoring
+ providing science fair project assistance
+ providing career choice assistance
+ reviewing school safety equipment
+ assisting in science competition instruction
+ demonstrating societal and technological applications of content

- ✦ furnishing specialized equipment
- ✦ assisting in speakers' bureaus
- ✦ spearheading public awareness campaigns
- ✦ encouraging projects for girls and minorities
- ✦ arranging field trips
- ✦ maintaining equipment
- ✦ assisting with special demonstrations

The tips in Table 11.6 may help volunteers feel comfortable in their roles. Volunteers may not always be aware of the relevance of their knowledge and skills for elementary students; explain the benefits the students will receive from his or her assistance. The following advice was adapted from a list of sugges-

Increase interaction and discovery by directly involving children in demonstrations available from community volunteers.

TABLE 11.6 Tips for Teachers Working with Volunteers

1. Take time to talk with the volunteer outside the classroom, explaining class procedures, schedules, expectations, and objectives.
2. Prepare the volunteer with specifics about the assignment, where materials can be found, and what the learning objectives are.
3. Make the volunteer comfortable by explaining the obvious support facilities: where to place personal items, find a rest room, and get a cup of coffee.
4. Keep channels of communication open with the volunteer. Exchange a home number if appropriate and convenient. Plan and follow the schedule developed for the volunteer. Inform the volunteer of a schedule change as soon as possible. Keep in mind that volunteers have additional responsibilities and cannot be expected to wait for an assignment or materials preparation and that their responsibilities may prevent them from fulfilling

their commitment. You will need to be understanding if this occurs.
5. Keep a special folder for regular volunteers with current assignments.
6. Inform volunteers about the students' level of ability, special problems, and students who need assistance.
7. Encourage your volunteer to sign in and to wear a name tag. Other faculty members and administrators will want to acknowledge a volunteer in the building.
8. Let every volunteer know how much you and the class appreciate the help. A thank-you note goes a long way toward making the experience a rewarding one for a volunteer.
9. Evaluate the volunteer encounter. Consider the specific request, the background of the volunteer, and the constraints of the situation.

Source: Project Technology Engineering Applications of Mathematics and Science, Yakima Valley/Tri-Cities MESA, *Tips for Teachers Working with Volunteers,* as cited by Triangle Coalition for Science and Technology Education, *A Guide for Planning a Volunteer Program for Science, Mathematics, and Technology Education* (College Park, MD: Triangle Coalition, 1992), p. 54.

tions for volunteers prepared by the Lane County Juvenile Department in Eugene, Oregon (Hager-Schoeny & Galbreath, 1982):

✦ Invite volunteers to serve as partners.
✦ Clearly define the differences in the tasks and roles of employees and volunteers.
✦ Screen volunteers and accept only the ones who can contribute. Check references and interview each candidate as you would a prospective employee.
✦ Require a specific commitment of time and resources from volunteers.
✦ Provide an orientation program to acquaint volunteers with their functions.
✦ Provide supervision.
✦ Make assignments based on the volunteers' skills, knowledge, interests, capacity to learn, time available, and resources.

Chapter Summary

The rich history of experimental innovation in science education provides us with several dependable lessons about what works, what helps children. The alphabet soup programs illustrate the benefits of inquiry-based experiences: children's achievement, attitudes, and skills improved over traditional text-based programs with teacher-centered instruction. Even so, textbooks remain the most used form of curriculum in elementary- and middle-school science.

Researchers do not suggest that texts be completely abandoned in favor of non-text, hands-on programs. However, researchers and scholars warn of the inherent shortcomings of texts and the extraordinary interests of publishers to obtain adoptions in key states. This chapter offers practical recommendations for selecting, enhancing, and using science texts if that is your choice or only curriculum option.

Best practices have emerged from the research, and extensive experiences gain from classroom use. These best practices are identified, and web-based and print resources that measure up are described. Communities also may abound in high-quality physical or human resources that can strengthen the science program and learning opportunities for children. The chapter concludes with tips for where to look for supplemental human resources and offers practical tips for preparing volunteers and

Discussion Questions

visitors in order to effect a good match for your students' needs.

1. Why do you think most teachers have historically reverted to teacher-centered instruction and authoritarian treatment of science through extensive uses of textbooks even though they may know about more effective alternatives?

2. What characteristics do you think a science textbook must have in order to address all of the National Science Education Standards? What do you consider to be the most important of these characteristics? Why?

3. Why do you think something as simple as resequencing the topics of a textbook is related to increased student science achievement?

4. What signs do you think indicate that a textbook should be avoided or considered?

5. How do you think that reading enhancements typically found in textbooks (such as bold print for special words) could interfere with the goals of scientific literacy? Do you believe that the goals of scientific literacy run counter to the goals of general literacy? Why?

6. What do you think an effective science program would need to look like in order to satisfy the expectations of a best practice? How do you think you might be able to defend your viewpoint to a parent,

teacher, or school administrator who might hold an opposing view?

7. Examine several different science textbooks or print resources for a selected grade level. What evidence do you find that shows inclusion of the criteria for effective programs?

8. Carefully study the course of study or curriculum guide for a school science program. Compare the program against the list of supported beliefs about effective school science programs. How does the program compare to the list?

Build a Portfolio or E-Folio

1. Compose a list of supplemental science resources that you would like to include in your lessons plans on three different topics. Compare your list with that of two more classmates; combine your lists as a resource file for future reference.

2. Locate three inquiry-based resources not mentioned in this chapter that you believe qualify as a best practice. Defend your choices.

3. Identify one resource that may be used to enhance a lesson in each subject matter: environmental education, electricity, digestion, and plate tectonics. You may also choose your own four science topics. Correlate these resources with your state science standards or the National Science Education Standards.

4. Identify resources that may be used to increase your students' skills in observing, questioning, classifying, measuring, and communicating. De-

scribe how you managed to locate resources that match up with these specific skills. What search engines or best practice resource services did you find that made the task a bit easier?

5. Use the ideas from this chapter to develop your own form for reviewing science textbooks or trade books. Try your form and ask two other persons to do the same. How well did your reviews of the same material agree? What revisions may be necessary in your form? Why?

6. Write to your state department of education and ask what information it provides to help teachers and school districts to improve science programs. Does your state have recommended programs or textbooks? If yes, determine how they were selected for recommendation. If no, determine why your state takes no position and what services it does provide to teachers and schools seeking assistance.

National Science Education Standards: Content Standards for K–4 and 5–8

K–4 Physical Science Standards

Content Standard B—K–4:

All students should develop an understanding of:

✦ Properties of objects and materials
✦ Position and motion of objects
✦ Light, heat, electricity, and magnetism

Properties of Objects and Materials Concepts

✦ Objects have many observable properties, including size, weight, shape, color, temperature, and the ability to react with other substances. These properties can be measured using tools such as rulers, balances, and thermometers.
✦ Objects are made of one or more materials, such as paper, wood, and metal. Objects can be described by the properties of the materials from which they are made, and these properties can be used to separate or sort a group of objects or materials.
✦ Materials have different states—solid, liquid, and gas. Some common materials such as water can be changed from one state to another by heating or cooling.

Position and Motion of Objects Concepts

✦ The position of an object can be described by locating it relative to another object or the background.
✦ An object's motion can be described by indicating the change in its position over time.
✦ The position and motion of objects can be changed by pushing or pulling and the size of the change is related to the strength of the push or pull.

✦ Vibrating objects produce sound. The pitch of the sound can be varied by changing the rate of vibration.

Light, Heat, Electricity, and Magnetism Concepts

✦ Light travels in a straight line unless it strikes an object. Light can be reflected by a mirror, refracted by a lens, or absorbed by the object.
✦ Heat can be produced in many ways, such as burning, rubbing, and mixing chemicals. The heat can move from one object to another by conduction.
✦ Electricity in circuits can produce light, heat, sound, and magnetic effects. Electrical circuits require a complete loop through which the electrical current can pass.
✦ Magnets attract and repel each other and certain kinds of metals.

K–4 Life Science Standards

Content Standard C—K–4:

All students should develop an understanding of:

✦ The characteristics of organisms
✦ Life cycles of organisms
✦ Organisms and environments

Characteristics of Organisms Concepts

✦ Organisms have basic needs, which for animals are air, water, and food. Plants require air, water, and light. Organisms can only survive in environments in which they can meet their needs. The world has many different environments, and dis-

National Resource Council. (1996). Science content standards, *National Science Education Standards.* Washington, D.C.: National Academy of Sciences, pp. 123–160.

tinct environments support the life of different types of organisms.

◆ Each plant or animal has different structures which serve different functions in growth, survival, and reproduction. For example, humans have distinct structures of the body for walking, holding, seeing, and talking.

◆ The behavior of individual organisms is influenced by internal cues such as hunger and by external cues such as an environmental change. Humans and other organisms have senses that help them detect internal and external cues.

Life Cycles of Organisms Concepts

◆ Plants and animals have life cycles that include being born, developing into adults, reproducing, and eventually dying. The details of this life cycle are different for different organisms.

◆ Plants and animals closely resemble their parents.

◆ Many characteristics of an organism are inherited from the parents of the organism, but other characteristics result from an individual's interactions with the environment. Inherited characteristics include the color of flowers and the number of limbs of an animal. Other features, such as the ability to play a musical instrument, are learned through interactions with the environment.

Organisms and Their Environments Concepts

◆ All animals depend on plants. Some animals eat plants for food. Other animals eat animals that eat the plants.

◆ An organism's patterns of behavior are related to the nature of that organism's environment, including the kinds and numbers of other organisms present, the availability of food and resources, and the physical characteristics of the environment. When the environment changes, some plants and animals survive and reproduce, and others die or move to new locations.

◆ All organisms cause changes in the environment where they live. Some of these changes are detrimental to themselves or other organisms, whereas others are beneficial.

◆ Humans depend on both their natural and their constructed environment. Humans change environments in ways that can either be beneficial or detrimental for other organisms, including the humans themselves.

K–4 Earth and Space Science Standards

Content Standard D—K–4:

All students should develop an understanding of:
◆ Properties of Earth materials
◆ Objects in the sky

Properties of Earth Materials Concepts

◆ Earth materials are solid rocks and soils, liquid water, and the gases of the atmosphere. These varied materials have different physical and chemical properties. These properties make them useful, for example, as building materials, as sources of fuel, or for growing the plants we use as food. Earth materials provide many of the resources humans use.

◆ Soils have properties of color and texture, capacity to retain water, and ability to support the growth of many kinds of plants, including those in our food supply. Other Earth materials are used to construct buildings, make plastics, and provide fuel for generating electricity, and operating cars and trucks.

◆ The surface of the Earth changes. Some changes are due to slow processes, such as erosion and weathering and some changes are due to rapid processes such as landslides, volcanoes, and earthquakes.

◆ Fossils provide evidence about the plants and animals that lived long ago and nature of the environment at that time.

Objects in the Sky Concepts

◆ The sun, moon, stars, clouds, birds, and airplanes all have properties, locations, and movements that can be described and that may change.

◆ Objects in the sky have patterns of movement. The sun, for example, appears to move across the sky in the same way every day, but its path changes slowly over the seasons. The moon moves across the sky on a daily basis much like the sun. The shape of the moon seems to change from day to day in a cycle that lasts about a month.

◆ The sun provides the light and heat necessary to maintain the temperature of the Earth.

◆ Weather can change from day to day and over the season. Weather can be described by measurable quantities, such as temperature, wind direction and speed, precipitation, and humidity.

5–8 Physical Science Standards

Content Standard B—5–8:

All students should develop an understanding of:

+ Properties and changes of properties in matter
+ Motions and forces
+ Transformations of energy

Properties and Changes of Properties in Matter Concepts

+ Substances have characteristic properties such as density, boiling point, and solubility, which are independent of the amount of the sample. A mixture of substances can often be separated into the original substances by using one or more of these characteristic properties.
+ Substances react chemically in characteristic ways with other substances to form new substances (compounds) with different characteristic properties. In chemical reactions the total mass is conserved. Substances are often placed in categories or groups if they react in similar ways, for example, metals.
+ Chemical elements do not break down by normal laboratory reactions such as heating, electric current, or reaction with acids. There are more than 100 known elements which combine in a multitude of ways to produce compounds, which account for the living and nonliving substances that we encounter.

Motions and Forces Concepts

+ The motion of an object can be described by its position, direction of motion, and speed.
+ An object that is not being subjected to a force will continue to move at a constant speed and in a straight line.
+ If more than one force acts on an object, then the forces can reinforce or cancel one another, depending on their direction and magnitude. Unbalanced forces will cause changes in the speed and/or direction of an object's motion.

Transformations of Energy Concepts

+ Energy exists in many forms, including heat, light, chemical, nuclear, mechanical, and electrical. Energy can be transformed from one form to another.
+ Heat energy moves in predictable ways, flowing from warmer objects to cooler ones until both objects are at the same temperature.
+ Light interacts with matter by transmission (including refraction), absorption, or scattering (including reflection).
+ In most chemical reactions, energy is released or added to the system in the form of heat, light, electrical, or mechanical energy.
+ Electrical circuits provide a means of converting electrical energy into heat, light, sound, chemical, or other forms of energy.
+ The sun is a major source of energy for changes on the Earth's surface.

5–8 Life Science Standards

Content Standard C—5–8:

All students should develop an understanding of:

+ Structure and function in living organisms
+ Reproduction and heredity
+ Regulation and behavior
+ Populations and ecosystems
+ Diversity and adaptions of organisms

Structure and Function in Living Systems Concepts

+ Living systems at all levels of organization demonstrate complementary structure and function. Important levels of organization for structure and function include cells, organs, organ systems, whole organisms, and ecosystems.
+ All organisms are composed of cells—the fundamental unit of life. Most organisms are single cells; other organisms, including humans, are multicellular.
+ Cells carry on the many functions needed to sustain life. They grow and divide, producing more cells.
+ Specialized cells perform specialized functions in multicellular organisms. Groups of specialized cells cooperate to form a tissue, such as a muscle. Different tissues are in turn grouped together to form larger functional units, called organs. Each type of cell, tissue, and organ has a distinct structure and set of functions that serve the organism as a whole. The human organism has systems for digestion, respiration, reproduction, circulation, excretion, movement, control and coordination, and for protection from disease.
+ Disease represents a breakdown in structures or functions of an organism. Some diseases are the

result of intrinsic failures of the system. Others are the result of infection by other organisms.

Reproduction and Heredity Concepts

✦ Reproduction is a characteristic of all living systems; since no individual organism lives forever, it is essential to the continuation of species. Some organisms reproduce asexually. Other organisms reproduce sexually.

✦ In many species, including humans, females produce eggs and males produce sperm. An egg and sperm unite to begin the development of a new individual. This new individual has an equal contribution of information from its mother (via the egg) and its father (via the sperm). Sexually produced offspring are never identical to either of their parents.

✦ Each organism requires a set of instructions for specifying its traits. Heredity is the passage of these instructions from one generation to another.

✦ Hereditary information is contained in genes, located in the chromosomes of each cell. Each gene carries a single unit of information, and an inherited trait of an individual can be determined by either one or many genes. A human cell contains many thousands of different genes.

✦ The characteristics of an organism can be described in terms of a combination of traits. Some traits are inherited and others result from interactions with the environment.

Regulation and Behavior Concepts

✦ All organisms must be able to obtain and use resources, grow, reproduce, and maintain a relatively stable internal environment while living in a constantly changing external environment.

✦ Regulation of an organism's internal environment involves sensing external changes in the environment and changing physiological activities to keep within the range required to survive.

✦ Behavior is one kind of response an organism may make to an internal or environmental stimulus. A behavioral response requires coordination and communication at many levels, including cells, organ systems, and whole organisms. Behavioral response is a set of actions determined in part by heredity and in part from past experience.

✦ An organism's behavior has evolved through adaptation to its environment. How organisms move, obtain food, reproduce, and respond to danger, all are based on the organism's evolutionary history.

Populations and Ecosystems Concepts

✦ Populations consist of all individuals of a species that occur together at a given place. All of the populations living together and the physical factors with which they interact compose an ecosystem.

✦ Populations of organisms can be categorized by the function they serve in an ecosystem. Plants and some micro-organisms are producers—they make their own food. All animals, including humans, are consumers, which obtain food by eating other organisms. Decomposers, primarily bacteria and fungi, are consumers that use waste materials and dead organisms for food. Food webs identify the relationships among producers, consumers, and decomposers in an ecosystem.

✦ For ecosystems, the major source of energy is sunlight. Energy entering ecosystems as sunlight is converted by producers into stored chemical energy through photosynthesis. It then passes from organism to organism in food webs.

✦ The number of organisms an ecosystem can support depends on the resources available and abiotic factors such as quantity of light and water, range of temperatures, and the soil composition. Given adequate biotic and abiotic resources and no disease or predators, populations, including humans, increase at very rapid (exponential) rates. Limitations of resources and other factors such as predation and climate limit the growth of population in specific niches in the ecosystem.

Diversity and Adaptations of Organisms Concepts

✦ There are millions of species of animals, plants, and microorganisms living today that differ from those that lived in the remote past. Each species lives in a specific and fairly uniform environment.

✦ Although different species look very different, the unity among organisms becomes apparent from an analysis of internal structures, the similarity of their chemical processes, and the evidence of common ancestry.

✦ Biological evolution accounts for a diversity of species developed through gradual processes over many generations. Species acquire many of their unique characteristics through biological adapta-

tion, which involves the selection of naturally occurring variations in populations. Biological adaptations include changes in structures, behaviors, or
physiology that enhance reproductive success in a
particular environment.

♦ Extinction of a species occurs when the environment changes and the adaptive characteristics
of a species do not enable it to survive in competition with its neighbors. Fossils indicate that
many organisms that lived long ago are now
extinct. Extinction of species is common. Most
of the species that have lived on the Earth no
longer exist.

5–8 Earth and Space Science Standards

Content Standard D—5–8:

All students should develop an understanding of:

♦ Structure of the Earth's system
♦ Earth's history
♦ Earth in the solar system

Structure of the Earth's System Concepts

♦ The solid Earth is layered with a thin brittle
crust, hot convecting mantle, and dense metallic
core.

♦ Crustal plates on the scale of continents and
oceans constantly move at rates of centimeters
per year in response to movements in the mantle.
Major geological events, such as earthquakes, volcanoes, and mountain building, result from these
plate motions.

♦ Land forms are the result of a combination of constructive and destructive forces. Constructive
forces include crustal deformation, volcanoes, and
deposition of sediment, while destructive forces
include weathering and erosion.

♦ Changes in the solid Earth can be described as the
rock cycle. Old rocks weather at the Earth's surface, forming sediments that are buried, then compacted, heated, and often recrystallized into new
rock. Eventually, these new rocks may be brought
to the surface by the forces that drive plate motions, and the rock cycle continues.

♦ Soil consists of weathered rocks, decomposed
organic material from dead plants, animals, and

bacteria. Soils are often found in layers, with each
having a different chemical composition and
texture.

♦ Water, which covers the majority of the Earth's
surface, circulates through the crust, oceans, and
atmosphere in what is known as the water cycle.
Water evaporates from the Earth's surface, rises
and cools as it moves to higher elevations, con-
denses as rain or snow, and falls to the surface
where it collects in lakes, oceans, soil, and in rocks
underground.

♦ Water is a solvent. As it passes through the water
cycle it dissolves minerals and gases and carries
them to the oceans.

♦ The atmosphere is a mixture of oxygen, nitrogen,
and trace gases that include water vapor. The
atmosphere has different properties at different
elevations.

♦ Clouds, formed by the condensation of water
vapor, affect weather and climate. Some do so by
reflecting much of the sunlight that reaches Earth
from the sun, while others hold heat energy emit-
ted from the Earth's surface.

♦ Global patterns of atmospheric movement influence local weather. Oceans have a major effect on
climate, because water in the oceans holds a large
amount of heat.

♦ Living organisms have played many roles in the
Earth system, including affecting the composition
of the atmosphere and contributing to the weathering of rocks.

Earth's History Concepts

♦ The Earth's processes we see today, including erosion, movement of crustal plates, and changes in
atmospheric composition, are similar to those that
occurred in the past. Earth's history is also influenced by occasional catastrophes, such as the impact of an asteroid or comet.

♦ Fossils provide important evidence of how life and
environmental conditions have changed.

Earth in the Solar System Concepts

♦ The Earth is the third planet from the sun in a
system that includes the moon, the sun, eight
other planets and their moons, and smaller
objects such as asteroids and comets. The sun,
an average star, is the central and largest body
in the solar system.

- Most objects in the solar system are in regular and predictable motion. These motions explain such phenomena as the day, the year, phase of the moon, and eclipses.
- Gravity is the force that keeps planets in orbit around the sun and governs the rest of the motion in the solar system. Gravity alone holds us to the Earth's surface and explains the phenomena of the tides.
- The sun is the major source of energy for phenomena on the Earth's surface, such as growth of plants, winds, ocean currents, and the water cycle. Seasons result from variations in the amount of the sun's energy hitting the surface, due to the tilt of the Earth's rotation axis.

references

AAAS (American Association for the Advancement of Science). (1993). *Benchmarks for scientific literacy.* New York: Oxford University Press.

Adeniyi, E. O. (1985). Misconceptions of selected ecological concepts held by some Nigerian students. *Journal of Biological Education, 19* (4), 311–316.

Alexakos, Konstantinos. (2001, March). Inclusive classrooms. *Science and Children,* 40–43.

Alfke, D. (1974, April). Asking operational questions. *Science and Children,* 18–19.

Altermatt, E. R., Jovanovic, J., & Perry, M. (1998). Bias or responsivity? Sex and achievement-level effects on teachers' classroom questioning practices. *Journal of Educational Psychology, 90* (3), 515–527.

American National Standards Institute, ANSI Z87.1 2000, New York, NY, 10018. www.ansi.org

Antonouris, G. (1989). Multicultural science. *School Science Review, 70* (252), 97–100.

Appleton, K. (1993). Using theory to guide practice: Teaching science from a constructivist perspective. *School Science and Mathematics, 93* (5), 269–274.

Arbor Scientific Company (ASC). (1996). *Arbor Scientific—innovation in science education.* Ann Arbor, MI: Arbor Scientific.

Arena, P. (1996). The role of relevance in the acquisition of science process skills. *Australian Science Teachers Journal, 42* (4), 34–38.

Arnold, D. S., Atwood, R. K., & Rogers, U. M. (1973). An investigation of the relationships among question level, response level, and lapse time. *School Science and Mathematics, 73,* 591–595.

Ausubel, D. P. (1963). *Psychology of meaningful verbal learning.* New York: Grune and Stratton.

———. (1968). *Educational psychology: A cognitive view.* New York: Holt, Rinehart and Winston.

Baker, D. (1988). *Research matters to the science teacher teaching for gender differences.* National Association of Research in Science Teaching.

Baker, L. (1991). Metacognition, reading, and science education. In C. M. Santa & D. E. Alvermann (Eds.), *Science learning: Processes and applications.* Newark, DE: International Reading Association.

Bank Street College of Education. (1995). *The voyages of Mimi I and II.* Pleasantville, NY: Sunburst Communications.

Bannasch, S. & Tinker, R. (Winter, 2002). Probeware takes a seat in the classroom. *The Concord Consortium, 6* (1). [Online: www.concord.org/newsletter/2002winter/probeware.html].

Barman, C. R. (1996). How do students *really* view science and scientists? *Science and Children, 34* (1), 30–33.

———. (1997). Students' views of scientists and science: Results from a national study. *Science and Children, 35* (1), 18–23.

Barman, C. R., & Ostlund, K. L. (1996). A protocol to investigate students' perceptions about scientists and relevancy of science to students' daily lives. *Science Education International, 4* (4), 16–21.

Barnes, C. P. (1978). *Questioning strategies to develop critical thinking skills.* (ERIC Document No. 169486)

Beaton, A. E., Mullis, I. V. S., Martin, M. O., Gonzales, E. J., Kelly, D. L., & Smith, T. A. (1996). *Mathematics achievement in the middle school years: IEA's third international mathematics and science study (TIMSS).* Chestnut Hill, MA: Boston College.

Begley, S. (1996, February 19). Your child's brain. *Newsweek,* 55–62.

Bennett, W. J. (1986). *What works.* Washington, DC: U.S. Department of Education.

Berger, C. F., Lu, C. R., Belzer, S. J., and Voss, B. E. (1994). *Research on the uses of technology in science education.* In D. L. Gabel (Ed.), *Handbook of research on science teaching and learning* (pp. 466–490). New York: Macmillan.

Bergman, A. B. (1993, February). Performance assessment for early childhood: What could be more natural? *Science and Children,* 20–22.

Biddulph, F., & Osborne, R. (1984, February). Children's questions and science teaching: An alternative approach. *Learning in science project* (Working Paper No. 117). Hamilton, New Zealand: Waikato University, February. (ERIC Reproduction Document No. ED 252400)

Biddulph, F., Symington, D., & Osborn, R. (1986). The place of children's questions in primary science education. *Research in Science and Technological Education, 4* (1) 77–78.

Biehle, J., Motz, L., & West, S. (1999). *NSTA guide to school science facilities.* Arlington, VA: National Science Teachers Association.

Birnie, H. H., & Ryan, A. (1984, April). Inquiry/discovery revisited. *Science and Children,* 31.

Bloom, B. J. (1984). The 2 sigma problem: The search for methods of group instruction as effective as one-to-one tutoring. *Educational Researcher, 13,* 4–16.

Bloom, B. S. (1956). *Taxonomy of educational objectives: The classification of educational goals, Handbook I: Cognitive domain.* New York: Longmans, Green.

Blosser, P. E. (1985). Using questions in science classrooms. In R. Doran (Ed.), *Research matters to the science teacher,* 2. (ERIC Document No. 273490)

———. (1993). *Using cooperative learning in science education.* Columbus, OH: ERIC Clearinghouse for Science, Mathematics, and Environmental Education. (ERIC Reproduction Document No. ED 351207)

Bruer, J. T. (1998). Brain science, brain fiction. *Educational Leadership, 56* (3), 14–18.

Bredderman, T. (1982, September). Activity science—The evidence shows it matters. *Science and Children,* pp. 39–41.

———. (1984). The influence of activity-based elementary science programs on classroom practices: A quantitative synthesis. *Journal of Research in Science Teaching, 21* (3), 290–303.

Brennan, J. (1970). An investigation of factors related to safety in the high school science program. Ed.D. dissertation, University of Denver, Denver, CO. (ERIC Document No. ED 085179).

Brown, D. R. (1979). Helping handicapped youngsters learn science by doing. In M. B. Rowe (Ed.), *What research says to the science teacher* (Vol. 2, p. 85), Washington, DC: National Science Teachers Association.

Brown, I. D. (1986). Topic 4: Teacher questioning techniques. *Staff development project—Science Grades K–6.* Jackson, MS: Mississippi Association for Teacher Education. (ERIC Document No. ED 285726)

Bruner, J. S. (1961). The act of discovery. *Harvard Educational Review, 31,* 21–32.

———. (1962). *The process of education.* Cambridge, MA: Harvard University Press.

Budiansky, S. (2001, February). The trouble with textbooks. *Prism.* [Online: www.project2061.org/research/articles/asee.htm]

Bybee, R., & Hendricks, P. W. (1972). Teaching science concepts to preschool deaf children to aid language development. *Science Education, 56* (3), 303–310.

Bybee, R. W., Ferrini-Mundy, J., & Loucks-Horsley, S. (1997). National standards and school science and mathematics. *School Science and Mathematics, 97* (7), 325–334.

Chaille, C., & Britain, L. (1991). *The young child as scientist.* New York: HarperCollins.

Checkley, K. (1997). The first seven and the eighth. *Educational Leadership, 55* (1), 8–13.

Cheney, M. S., & Roy, K. R. (1999). Inclusive safety solutions: What every teacher should know about special education and laboratory safety legislation. *The Science Teacher, 66* (6), 48–51.

Chivers, G. (1986). Intervention strategies to increase the proportion of girls and women studying and pursuing careers in technological fields: A West European review. *Journal of Engineering Education, 11* (3), 248.

CHRIS: Hazardous Chemical Data. (1989). U.S. Department of Transportation, Superintendent of Documents. Washington, DC: U.S. Government Printing Office.

Cleeland, L. (1984). Vistibular disorders—Learning problems and dyslexia. *Hearing Instruments, 35,* 8: 9F.

Coble, C. R., Levey, B., & Matthies, F. (1985). *Science for learning disabled students.* (ERIC Document No. 258803)

Cole, J. T., Kitano, M. K., & Brown, L. M. (1981). Concept analysis: A model for teaching basic science concepts to intellectually handicapped students. In M. E. Corrick, Jr. (Ed.), *Teaching handicapped students science: A resource book K–12 teachers* (pp. 51–53). Washington, DC: National Education Association.

College Board. (1987). *Get into the equation: Math and science, parents and children.* (ERIC Document No. 295785)

Committee on Undergraduate Science Education. (1997). *Science teaching reconsidered: A handbook.* Washington, DC: National Academy Press.

Cooper, H. H. (1979). Pygmalion grows up: A model for teacher expectation, communication, and performance influence. *Review of Education Research, 49,* 389–410.

Corporation for Public Broadcasting. (1995). *The Annenberg/CPB math and science project—the guide to math and science reform; EE toolbox, inter-disciplinary education access (IDEA), parks as classrooms* (Computer disc). Available through the Corporation for Public Broadcasting.

Craven, John A. III, & Hogan, T. (2001, September). Assessing student participation in the classroom. *Science Scope,* 36–40.

Cremin, L. A. (1976). *Public education.* New York: Basic Books.

Czerniak, C. M., & Haney, J. J. (1998). The effect of collaborative concept mapping on elementary preservice teachers' anxiety, efficacy, and achievement in physical science. *Journal of Science Teacher Education, 9* (4), 303–320.

D'Arcangelo, M. (1998). The brains behind the brain. *Educational Leadership, 56* (3), 20–25.

Dalton, B., Morocco, C. C., Tivnan, T., & Rawson Mead, P. L. (1997) Supported inquiry science: Teaching for conceptual change in urban and suburban science classrooms. *Journal of Learning Disabilities, 30* (6), 670–684.

Damian, C. (2002). The power of convergent learning. In *ENC Focus,* 9, 2. Columbus, OH: U.S. Department of Education, Eisenhower National Clearinghouse.

Dean, R. A., Dean, M. M., & Motz, L. L. (1997). *Safety in the elementary science classroom.* National Science Teachers Association, Arlington, VA. Booklet stock number PB 30, ISBN 0-87355-117-6.

Decker, L. E. (1981). *Foundation of community education.* Charlottesville, VA: Mid-Atlantic Center for Community Education.

Demers, Chris. (2000, October). Beyond paper and pencil assessments. *Science and Children,* 24–29, 60.

Denkla, M., Kantrowitz, B., & Wingert, P. (1989, April 17). How kids learn. *Newsweek,* 53–54.

Dewey, J. (1916). *Democracy and education.* New York: Macmillan.

———. (1937). *Experience and education.* New York: Collier Books.

Dillion, G. (1977). Mimeograph. In D. L. Hager-Schoeny et al., *Community involvement for classroom teachers* (2nd ed., p. 27). Charlottesville, VA: Community Collaborators.

Dillon, J. T. (1988). The remedial status of student questioning. *Journal of Curriculum Studies. 20* (3), 197–210.

District of Columbia v. *Howell,* 607 A.2d 501, 503 (D.C. App. 1992)

Dixon, N. (1996). Developing children's questioning skills through the use of a "Question Board." *Primary Science Review 44,* October, 8–10.

Driver, R. (1983). *The pupil as scientist?* Milton Keynes, England: Open University Press.

———. (1994). *Making sense of science.* London: Routledge.

Driver, R., Guensne, E., & Tiberghien, A. (1985). *Children's ideas in science.* Milton Keynes, England: Open University Press.

Duckworth, E., in Kantrowitz, B., & Wingert, P. (1989, April 17). How kids learn. *Newsweek,* p. 55.

Dunn, R., & Dunn, K. (1975). Finding the best fit—learning styles, teaching styles. *NAASP Bulletin, 59,* 37–49.

Ediger, M. (1994). *Technology in the elementary curriculum.* U.S. Department of Education (ERIC Reproduction Document No. ED 401882)

Education Week (1999, October 7). Science group finds middle school textbooks inadequate.

Eggen, P., & Kauchak, D. (1992). *Educational psychology: Classroom connections.* New York: Macmillan.

Elfner, L. E. (1988). *Exemplars: Women in science, engineering, and mathematics.* Columbus, OH: Ohio Academy of Science.

Elliott, D. L., & Carter, K. (1986). *Scientific illiteracy in elementary science textbook programs.* Paper presented at the Annual Meeting of the American Educational Research Association, San Francisco, April, 1986. (ERIC Document No. 269257)

Elstgeest, J. (1985). The right question at the right time. In W. Harlen (Ed.), *Primary science: Taking the plunge.* London: Heinemann Educational Books.

ETS (Educational Testing Service). (1989). *A world of differences: An international assessment of mathematics and science.* Princeton, NJ: Center for the Assessment of Educational Progress.

———. (1992). *National assessment of educational progress.* Washington, DC: U.S. Department of Education.

Fathman, A. K., Quinn, M. E., & Kessler, C. (1992). *Teaching science to English learners, grades 4–8.* Washington, DC: National Clearinghouse for Bilingual Education. (ERIC Document Reproduction Service No. ED 349844)

Fields, S. (1989, April). The scientific teaching method. *Science and Children,* 15.

Flick, L. B. (1989). Will the real scientist please stand up! *Science Scope, 13* (3), 6–7.

———. (1993). The meanings of hands-on science. *Journal of Science Teacher Education, 4* (1), 3–4.

———. (1995). *Complex instruction in complex classrooms: A synthesis of research on inquiry teaching methods and explicit teaching strategies.* Paper presented at the National Association for Research in Science Teaching, San Francisco (April 1995). (ERIC Reproduction Document No. ED 383563)

Fort, D. C., & Varney, H. L. (1989). How students see scientists: Mostly male, mostly white, and mostly benevolent. *Science and Children, 26* (8), 8–13.

FOSS (1990). *Full option science system.* Berkeley, CA: Lawrence Hall of Science.

Foster, G. W., & Heiting, W. A. (1994). Embedded assessment. *Science and Children, 32* (2), 30–33.

Gallagher, J. J., & Aschner, M. J. (1963). A preliminary report on analyses of classroom interaction. *Merrill-Palmer Quarterly, 9,* 183–195.

Gambrell, L. B. (1983). The occurrence of think-time during reading comprehension. *Journal of Educational Research, 75,* 144–148.

Gardner, H. (1983) *Frames of mind: The theory of multiple intelligences.* New York: Basic Books.

Garthwait, A., & Verrill, J. (2003, May). E-Portfolios: Documenting student progress. *Science and Children,* 22–27.

George, R., & Kaplan, D. (1998). A structural model of parent and teacher influences on science attitudes of eighth graders: Evidence from NELS: 88. *Science Education, 82,* 93–109.

Gerlovich J., et al. (2003). *Total science safety system CD* (Kentucky Edition). Waukee, IA: JaKel, Inc.

Gerlovich, J. A. 1997. Safety standards: An examination of what teachers know and should know about science safety, *The Science Teacher, 64* (3), 46–49.

Gerlovich, J., & Hartman, K. (1990). *Science safety: A diskette for elementary educators.* Waukee, IA: JaKel.

———. 1998. *The total science safety system: Elementary, 4th edition* [computer software], Waukee, IA: JaKel, Inc.

Gerlovich, J., Hartman, K., & Gerard, T. (1992). *The total science safety system for grades 7–14.* Waukee, IA: JaKel.

Gerlovich, J. A., Wilson, E., & Parsa, R. (1998). Safety issues and Iowa Science Teachers, *The Journal of the Iowa Academy of Science, 105* (4), 152–157.

Glencoe Science Professional Series. (1994). *Alternative assessment in the science classroom.* (ERIC Reproduction Document No. ED 370778)

Goldhammer, A., & Isenberg, S. (1984). *Operation: Frog* [Educational software]. New York: Scholastic.

Goleman, D. (1995). *Emotional Intelligence.* New York: Bantam Books.

Good, R. G. (1977). *How children learn science.* New York: Macmillan.

Good, R. G., Wandersee, J. H., & St. Julien, J. (1993). Cautionary notes on the appeal of the new "ism" (constructivism) in science education. In K. Tobin (Ed.), *The practice of constructivism in science education* (pp. 71–87). Washington, DC: AAAS Press.

Gorodetsky, M., Fisher, K. M., & Wyman, B. (1994). Generating connections and learning with Semnet, a tool for constructing knowledge networks. *Journal of Science Education and Technology, 3* (3), 137–144.

Graesser, A. C., & Person, N. K. (1994). Question asking during tutoring. *American Educational Research Journal, 31,* 104–137.

Greenfield, S. (1995). *Journey to the centers of the mind.* New York: W.H. Freeman.

Guerra, C. J. (1988, March). Pulling science out of a hat. *Science and Children,* 23–24.

Habecker, J. E. (1976). *An analysis of reading questions in basal reading series based on Bloom's taxonomy.* Unpublished doctoral dissertation, University of Pennsylvania, Philadelphia.

Hager-Schoeny, D. L., & Galbreath, D. (1982). *Utilizing community resources in the classroom: An in-service reference collection.* Charlottesville, VA: University of Virginia, Mid-Atlantic Center for Community Education.

Hallahan, D. P., & Kauffman, J. M. (2000). *Exceptional learners.* Boston: Allyn and Bacon.

Halloran, J. D. (1970). *Attitude formation and change.* Great Britain: Leicester University Press.

Hammrich, P. L. (1997, January). Yes, daughter, you can. *Science and Children, 34,* 21–24.

Hamrick, L., & Harty, H. (1987). Influence of resequencing general science content on the science achievement, attitude toward science, and interest in science of sixth grade students. *Journal of Research in Science Teaching, 24* (1), 16.

Haney, J. (1998, September). Concept mapping in the science classroom: Linking theory into practice. *The Agora, 8,* 1–7.

Hannaford, C. (1995). *Smart moves.* Arlington, VA: Great Ocean Publishing Co.

Hargie, O. D. (1978). The importance of teacher questions in the classroom. *Educational Research, 20,* 99–102.

Harlen, W. (1992). *The teaching of science.* London: David Fulton Publishers.

———. (1993). *Teaching and learning primary science.* London: Paul Chapman Publishing.

Harms, N. (1981). VIII. Project synthesis: Summary and implications for teachers. In N. C. Harms & R. E. Yager (Eds.), *What research says to the science teacher* (Vol. 3). Washington, DC: National Science Teachers Association.

Harris, R. (1981). An audio-tactile approach to science education for visually impaired students. In M. E. Corrick, Jr. (Ed.), *Teaching handicapped students science.* Washington, DC: National Education Association.

Hart, D. (1994). *Authentic assessment: Handbook for educators.* New York: Addison-Wesley.

Haury, D. L. (1993, March). *Teaching science through inquiry.* Columbus, OH: Clearinghouse for Science, Mathematics, and Environmental Education (EDO-SE-93-4).

Hazen, R. M., & Trefil, J. (1992). *Science matters: Achieving science literacy.* (New York: Doubleday).

Hein, G. E., & Price, S. (1994). *Active assessment for active science: A guide for elementary school teachers.* Portsmouth, NH: Heinemann.

Holdren, J. (1994). The Limits of Thematic Instruction. In *Common Knowledge* (Vol. 7, No. 4). Core Knowledge Foundation, Charlottesville, VA 22902.

Holliday, W. G. (2002, January). Selecting a science textbook. *Science Scope,* 16–20.

Holt, J. (1971). *How children learn.* London: Penguin Press, p. 52.

Horton, P. (1988). Class size and lab safety in Florida. *Florida Science Teacher, 3* (3) 4–6.

Howard, P. (1994). *Owner's manual for the brain.* Austin, TX: Leornian Press.

Humphreys, A., Post, T., & Ellis, A. *Interdisciplinary methods: A thematic approach.* Santa Monica, CA: Goodyear Publishing Company, 1981.

Humrich, E. (1988). *Sex differences in the second IEA science study: U.S. results in an international context.* Paper presented at the annual meeting of the National Association for Research in Science Teaching. (ERIC Document No. ED 292649)

Hunkins, F. P. (1970). Analysis and evaluation questions: Their effects upon critical thinking. *Educational Leadership, 27,* pp. 697–705.

Hurd, P. D. (1986, January). Perspectives for the reform of science education. *Phi Delta Kappan,* pp. 353–358.

Iatridis, M. (1981, October). Teaching science to preschoolers. *Science and Children.*

Iowa Code Annotated, Sections 656.1 to 686. End, Volume 51–53, West Group, 1998, plus 2001, Cumulative Annual Pocket Part (laws through 2000 regular session).

Iwasyk, M. (1997, September). Kids questioning kids: "Experts" sharing. *Science and Children,* 42–46.

Jarrett, D. (1997). *Inquiry strategies for science and mathematics learning: It's just good teaching.* Northwest Regional Educational Laboratory. (ERIC Reproduction Document No. ED 413188)

Jegede, O. J., Alaiyemola, F. F. & Okebukola, P. A. O. (1990). The effect of concept mapping on students' anxiety and achievement in biology. *Journal for Research in Science Teaching, 27* (10), 951–960.

Jelly, S. (1985). Helping children raise questions—and answering them. In W. Harlen (Ed.), *Primary science: Taking the plunge.* London: Heinemann, p. 54.

Jensen, E. (1998). *Teaching with the brain in mind.* Alexandria, VA: Association for Supervision and Curriculum Development.

Johnson, F. (1997). New standards show too many students know too little science. *NSTA Reports!, 9* (3), 1, 12.

Johnson, R. T., & Johnson, D. W. (1991). So what's new about cooperative learning in science? *Cooperative Learning, 11* (3), 2–3.

Jones, G. M., Mullis, I. V. S., Raisen, S. A., Weiss, I. R., & Weston, E. A. (1992). *The 1990 science report card, NAEP's assessment of fourth, eighth, and twelfth graders.* Washington, DC: U.S. Department of Education.

Jones, M. G., & Wheatley, J. (1988). Factors influencing the entry of women into science and related fields. *Science Education, 72,* 127–142.

Jones, R. M. (1985, May). Teaming up. *Science and Children,* 21.

Kahle, J. B. (1983). Do we make science available for women? In F. K. Brown & D. P. Butts (Eds.), *Science teaching: A profession speaks.* Washington, DC: National Science Teachers Association, pp. 33–36.

———. (1990). Why girls don't know. In M. B. Rowe (Ed.), *What research says to the science teacher. Vol. 6: The process of knowing.* Washington, DC: National Science Teachers Association.

Kahle, J. B., & Lakes, M. K. (1983). The myth of equality in science classrooms. *Journal of Research in Science Teaching, 20* (2), 131–140.

Kahle, J. B., & Rennie, L. J. (1993). Ameliorating gender differences in attitudes about science: A cross-national study. *Journal of Science Education and Technology, 2* (1), 321–333.

Kahn, S. (2003). Including all students in hands-on learning. *enc Focus 10* (2), 14–17.

Kamen, M. (1996). A teacher's implementation of authentic assessment in an elementary science classroom. *Journal of Research in Science, 33* (8), 859–877.

Katz, L., in Kantrowitz, B., & Wingert, P. (1989, April 17). How kids learn. *Newsweek,* p. 55.

Kinnear, J. (1994). *What science education really says about communication of science concepts* (Report No. CS508-657). Sydney, Australia: Annual Meeting of the International Communication Association. (ERIC Document Reproduction Service No. ED 372455)

Kirk, M., Matthews, C. E., & Kurtts, S. (2001, December). The trouble with textbooks. *The Science Teacher,* 42–45.

Knuth, R. (1995). *Engaging learning through technology.* Paper presented at the IVLA/IAECT Conference, Chicago, October.

Koran, J. J., & Koran, J. L. (1973). *Validating a teacher behavior by student performance* (Report No. FSDE-730-063). Tallahassee, FL: Florida State Department of Education.

Kotulak, R. (1993). Research discovers secrets of how brain learns to talk. *Chicago Tribune,* April 13, section 1, pp. 1–4.

———. (1996). *Inside the brain.* Kansas City, MO.: Andrews and McMeel.

Kroot, N. E. (1976). *An analysis of the responses of four, six, and eight year old children to four kinds of questions.* Unpublished doctoral dissertation, Indiana University, Bloomington.

Krueger, A. and Sutton, J. (Eds.). (2001). *EDThoughts: What we know about science teaching and learning.* Aurora, CO: Mid-continent Research for Education and Learning.

Kuhn, T. S. (1970). *The structure of scientific revolutions.* (1st edition published in 1962). Chicago: University of Chicago Press.

Kwan, T., & Texley, J. (2002). *Exploring safely: A guide for elementary teachers.* National Science Teachers Association.

Langrehr, J. (1993). Getting thinking into science questions. *Australian Science Teacher Journal, 39* (4), 36.

Lederman, N. G., & Niess, M. L. (1998). 5 apples + 4 oranges = ? (Editorial). *School Science and Mathematics, 98* (6), 281–284.

Levin, T., & Long, R. (1981). *Effective instruction.* Washington, DC: Association for Supervision and Curriculum Development.

Levine, D. U., & Ornstein, A. C. (1983). Sex differences in ability and achievement. *Journal of Research and Development in Education, 16* (2), 62–66.

Lind, K. (1999). Science in early childhood: Developing and acquiring fundamental concepts and skills. In AAAS (Ed.), *Dialogue on early childhood science, mathematics, and technology education.* Washington, DC: American Association for the Advancement of Science, pp. 73–83.

Linn, E. (1994). Science and equity: Why it's important. *Mathematics & Science Education, 4,* (1), 1, 4.

Los Angeles Unified School District. (1977). Title IV-D: Effects of teacher expectation on student learning project. In *The Reflector.* Los Angeles: Unified School District Office of Instruction.

Loucks-Horsley, S. (Ed.). (1990). *Elementary school science for the '90s.* Andover, MA: The Network.

Lowery, F. J. (1997). *NSTA pathways to the science standards.* National Science Teachers Association.

Macomber, R. D. (1961). Chemistry accidents in high school. *Journal of Chemical Education, 38* (7), 367–368.

Madrazo, G. M., Jr. (1997, March). Using trade books to teach and learn science. *Science and Children,* 20–21.

Marbach-Ad, G., & Sololove, P. G. (2000, November). Good science begins with good questions: Answering the need for high-level questions in science. *Journal of College Science Teaching, 30* (3), 192–195.

Marek, E. A., & Cavallo, A. M. L. (1997). *The learning cycle: Elementary science and beyond.* Portsmouth, NH: Heinemann.

Martens, M. L. (1999, May). Productive questions: Tools for supporting constructivist learning. *Science and Children,* 24–27, 53.

Martin, R., Wood, G., & Stevens, E. (1988). *An introduction to teaching: A question of commitment.* Boston: Allyn and Bacon.

Martin, R. E. (1984). *The credibility principle and teacher attitudes toward science.* New York: Peter Lang.

Marx, R. W., Blumenfeld, P. C., Krajcik, J. S., & Soloway, E. (1997). Enacting project-based science. *The Elementary School Journal, 97* (4), 341–358.

Matthews, M. R. (1998). In defense of modest goals when teaching about the nature of science. *Journal of Research in Science Teaching, 35* (2), 161–174.

Maxim, G. (1997). When to answer the question "Why?" *Science and Children, 35* (3), 41–45.

McCracken, M. (1986). *Turnabout children.* Boston: Little, Brown.

McDonough, T. (2001). Thematic instruction. On Purpose Associates website. [Online: www.funderstanding.com/thematic_instruction.cfm].

McIntyre, M. (1984). *Early childhood and science.* Washington, DC: National Science Teachers Association.

McKinney, W. J. (1997). *The educational use of computer based science simulations: Some lessons from the philosophy of science.* Boston: Kluwer Academic Publishers.

McLane. K. (1998, Fall). Integrating technology into the standard curriculum: Extending learning opportunities for students with disabilities. *Research Connections in Special Education,* p. 3.

McLeod, R. J. (1979, October). Selecting a textbook for good science teaching. *Science and Children,* 14–15.

McREL: Mid-continent Research for Education and Learning. (2001). In what ways can integrating curriculum enhance learning? In A. Krueger & J. Sutton (Eds.). *EDThoughts: What we know about science teaching and learning.* Aurora, CO: Mid-continent Research for Education and Learning, pp. 56–57.

Mechling, K. R., & Oliver, D. L. (1983a). *Characteristics of a good elementary science program, handbook III.* Washington, DC: National Science Teachers Association.

———. (1983b). *Science teaches basic skills, handbook 1.* Washington, DC: National Science Teachers Association.

———. (1983c). Activities not textbooks: What research says about science programs. *Principal, 43.*

Meyer, L. A., Greer, E. A., & Crummey, L. (1986). *Elementary science textbooks: Their contents, text characteristics, and comprehensibility* (Technical Report No. 386). Champaign, IL: University of Illinois. (ERIC Document No. 278947)

Minstrell, J. (1982). Conceptual development research in the natural setting of a secondary school classroom. In H. B. Rowe (Ed.), *Science for the 80's.* Washington, DC: National Education Association.

Morgan, N., & Saxton, J. (1991). *Teaching, questioning & learning.* New York: Routledge.

Mullins, I. V. S., & Jenkins, L. B. (1988). *The science report card: Elements of risk and recovery.* Princeton, NJ: Educational Testing Service.

Mullis, I. V. S., Martin, M. O., Beaton, A. E., Gonzalez, E. J., Kelly, D. L., & Smith, T. A. (1997). *Mathematics achievement in the primary school years: IEA's third international mathematics and science study (TIMSS).* Chestnut Hill, MA: Center for the Study of Testing, Evaluation, and Educational Policy, Boston College.

Munson, B. H. (1994). Ecological misconceptions. *Journal of Environmental Education, 24* (4), 30–34.

Murphy, N. (1994). Helping preservice teachers master authentic assessment for the learning cycle model. In L. E. Schafer (Ed.), *Behind the methods class door: Educating elementary and middle school science teachers.* Columbus, OH: ERIC Clearinghouse for Science, Mathematics and Environmental Education.

National Association of Biology Teachers. (1990). *NABT guidelines for the use of live animals.* Position Statement of NABT, January 1990.

National Center for Educational Statistics. Homepage for the National Assessment of Educational Progress (NAEP). 2003. [Online: www.nces.ed.gov/nationsreportcard/].

National Curriculum Council. (1989). *Science: Non-statutory guidance.* London: NCC.

National Education Goals Panel. (1997). *The national education goals report: Summary.* Washington, DC: Author.

National Geographic Society. (2003). *National Geographic Kids Network.* Washington, DC: Author.

National Research Council. (1992). *National Science Education Standards: A sampler.* Washington, DC: Author.

———. (1996) *National Science Education Standards.* Washington, DC: National Academy Press.

———. (1997). *Every child a scientist: Achieving scientific literacy for all.* Washington, DC: National Academy Press.

National Science Board Commission on Precollege Education in Mathematics, Science, and Technology. (1983). *A revised and intensified science and technology curriculum for grades K–12 is urgently needed for our future.* (ERIC Document No. 239 847)

National Science Teachers Association. (1982). *Science-technology-society: Science education for the 1980's: Position statement.* Washington, DC: Author.

———. (1983). *Conditions for good science teaching in secondary schools.* Washington, DC: Author.

———. (1993). *Position Statement on Laboratory Science.* Arlington, VA: National Science Teachers Association.

———. (2000, July). *NSTA position statement: Multicultural science education.* Washington, DC: Author. (www.nsta.org/159&psid=21, retrieved August 2, 2003)

———. *NSTA Handbook, 1996–97.* Arlington, VA: Author.

NCREL: North Central Regional Educational Laboratory. Copyright © (1997). *Thematic or integrated instruction.* September 17, 2003, [Online: www.ncrel.org/areas/issues/students/atrisk/at71k12.htm]. All rights reserved. Reprinted with permission.

Nickerson, R. S. (1995). Can technology help teach for understanding? In D. N. Perkins, J. L. Schwartz, M. M. West, & M. S. Wiske (Eds.), *Software goes to school—teaching for understanding new technologies.* New York: Oxford University Press.

North Carolina Museum of Life and Science. (1992). Science in the classroom. In Triangle Coalition for Science and

Technology Education, *A guide for planning a volunteer program for science, mathematics, and technology education* (p. 59). College Park, MD: Triangle Coalition.

Novak, J. D. (1979). *A theory of education.* Ithaca, NY: Cornell University Press.

———. (1991, October). Clarify with concept maps. *Science Teacher,* p. 45.

Novak, J., & Gowin, D. B. (1986). *Learning how to learn.* New York: Cambridge University Press.

NWREL: Northwest Regional Education Laboratory. *Integrated curriculum* by K. Lake. November 3, 2003. [Online: www.nwrel.org/scpd/sirs/8/col6.html].

O'Brien, G. E., & Lewis, S. P. (1999). Connecting to resources on the internet. *Science and Children, 36* (8), 42–45.

Occupational Safety and Health Administration. (1991). *Rules and Regulations* (FR Doc. 91-288886). (*Federal Register* 569235).

Osborne, R., & Freyberg, P. (1990). *Learning in science: The implications of children's science.* In S. Loucks-Horsley (Ed.), *Elementary school science for the '90s.* Andover, MA: The Network, p. 49.

Oskamp, S. (1977). *Attitudes and opinions.* Englewood Cliffs, NJ: Prentice-Hall.

Ostlund, K. L. (1992, March). Sizing up social skills. *Science Scope,* pp. 31–33.

O'Sullivan, C. Y., Lauko, M. A., Grigg, W. S., Qian, J., & Zhang, J. (2003). *The nation's report card: Science 2000.* Washington, DC: U.S. Department of Education. National Center for Education Statistics.

O'Sullivan, C. Y., Reese, C. M., & Mazzeo, J. (1997). *NAEP 1996 science report card for the nation and the states.* Washington, DC: National Center for Education Statistics.

Padilla, M., Muth, D., & Lund Padilla, R. (1991). Science and reading: Many process skills in common. In C. M. Santa & D. E. Alvermann (Eds.), *Science learning: Processes and applications.* Newark, DE: International Reading Association, pp. 14–19.

Pearlman, S., & Pericak-Spector, K. (1992, October). Expect the unexpected question. *Science and Children,* pp. 36–37.

Pert, C. (1997). *Molecules of emotion.* New York: Charles Scribner's Sons.

Peterson, P., & Knapp, P. (1993). Inventing and reinventing ideas: Constructivist teaching and learning in mathematics. In G. Cawletti (Ed.), *Challenges and achievements of American education.* Alexandria, VA: Association for Supervision and Curriculum Development.

Petty, R. E., & Cacioppa, J. T. (1981). *Attitudes and persuasion: Classic and contemporary approaches.* Dubuque, IA: William C. Brown.

Phillips, W. C. (1991). Earth science misconceptions. *Science Teacher, 58* (2), 21–23.

Piaget, J. (1954). *The construction of reality in the child.* New York: Basic Books.

Piburn, M., & Enyeart, M. (1985). *A comparison of the reasoning ability of gifted and mainstreamed science students.* (ERIC Document No. 255 379)

Pollina, A. (1995). Gender balance: Lessons from girls in science and mathematics. *Educational Leadership, 53* (1), 30–33.

Prather, J. P. (1991, April). *Speculative philosophical analysis of priorities for research in science education.* Research report presented at the 64th Annual Meeting of the National Association for Research in Science Teaching, Fontana, WI.

Price, S., & Hein, G. E. (1994, October). Scoring active assessments. *Science and Children,* pp. 26–29.

Project Learning Tree. (1993). *Pollution search: PreK–8 activity guide* Washington, D.C.: American Forest Foundation.

Project Technology Engineering Application of Mathematics and Science. (1992). Tips for teachers working with volunteers. In Triangle Coalition for Science and Technology Education, *A guide for planning a volunteer program for science, mathematics, and technology education.* College Park, MD: Triangle Coalition.

Puckett-Cliatt, M. J., & Shaw, J. M. (1985, November–December). Open questions, open answers. *Science and Children,* pp. 14–16.

Raizen, S. A., & Kaser, J. S. (1989, May). Assessing science learning in elementary school: Why, what and how? *Phi Delta Kappan,* 718–722.

Rakow, S. J. (1986). *Teaching science as inquiry.* Bloomington, IN: Phi Delta Kappa.

———. (1989, November–December). Safety supplement. *Science Scope.*

———. (1989). You spoke and we listened. *Science Scope 13* (3), S3.

Raloff, J. (2001). Errant texts: Why some schools may not want to go by the book. *Science News, 159* (11), [Online: www.project2061.org/research/articles/scinews.htm]

Reichel, A. G. (1994). Performance assessment: Five practical approaches. *Science and Children, 32* (2), 21–25.

Reichert, B. (1989, November–December). What did he say? Science in the multilingual classroom. *Science Scope,* 10–11.

Renner, J. W., & Marek, E. A. (1988). *The learning cycle and elementary school science teaching.* Portsmouth, NH: Heinemann.

Rennie, L., & Parker, L. (1986). *A comparison of mixed-sex and single-sex grouping in year 5 science lessons.* Paper presented at the Annual Meeting of the American Educational Research Association, San Francisco. (ERIC Document No. ED 273 443)

Rice, D. C., (2002, March). Using trade books in teaching elementary science: Facts and fallacies. *The Reading Teacher, 55* (6), 552–563.

Rice, J. R. (1983, January). A special science fair: LD children learn what they can do. *Science and Children,* 15–16.

Riley, J. P. (1986). The effects of teachers wait-time and knowledge comprehension questioning on science achievement. *Journal of Research in Science Teaching, 23* (4), 335–342.

Risner, G. P. (1987). *Cognitive levels of questioning demonstrated by test items that accompany selected fifth-grade science textbooks.* (ERIC Document No. 291752)

Risner, G. P., Skeel, D. J., & Nicholson, J. L. (1992, September). A closer look at textbooks. *Science and Children,* pp. 42–45, 73.

Roberts, R. M. (1989). *Serendipity: Accidental discoveries in science.* New York: Wiley.

Rodriguez, I., & Bethel, L. J. (1983). An inquiry approach to science and language teaching. *Journal of Research in Science Teaching, 20* (4), 291–296.

Rogers, D. L., Martin, R. E., Jr., & Kousaleos, S. (1988). Encouraging science through playful discovery. *Day Care and Early Education, 16* (1), 21.

Rop, C. (1998, December–January). Breaking the gender barrier in the physical sciences. *Educational Leadership, 55,* pp. 58–60,

Rosenshine, B. (1976). Classroom instruction. In W. L. Gage (Ed.), *The psychology of teaching methods.* Chicago: University of Chicago Press.

———. (1979). Content, time, and direct instruction. In P. L. Peterson & H. C. Walberg (Eds.), *Research on teaching: Concepts, findings, and implications.* Berkeley, CA: McCutcheon.

Ross, M. E. (1997). Scientists at play. *Science and Children, 34* (8), 35–38.

Rothkopf, E. Z. (1972). Variable adjunct question schedules, interperson interaction, and incidental learning from written material. *Journal of Educational Psychology, 63,* 87–92.

Rowe, M. B. (1970). Wait-time and rewards as instructional variables: Influence on inquiry and sense of fate control. *New Science in the Inner City.* New York: Teachers College, Columbia University.

———. (1973). *Teaching science as continuous inquiry.* New York: McGraw-Hill.

———. (1974). Wait-time and rewards as instructional variables, their influence on language, logic, and fate control: Part I—Wait time. *Journal of Research in Science Teaching, 13* (2), 81–94; Part II—Rewards. *Journal of Research in Science Teaching, 13* (4), 291–308.

Rutherford, F. J., & Ahlgren, A. (1988). Rethinking the science curriculum. In R. S. Brandt (Ed.), *Content of the curriculum.* Alexandria, VA: Association for Supervision and Curriculum Development.

———. (1990). *Science for all Americans.* New York: Oxford University Press.

Ryan, J, Esq. (2001). *Science classroom safety and the law: A handbook for teachers.* Batavia, IL: Flinn Scientific, Inc.

Sabar, N. (1979). Science, curriculum, and society: Trends in science curriculum. *Science Education, 63* (2), 257–269.

Sadker, D., Sadker, M., & Thomas, D. (1981). Sex equity and special education. *Pointer, 26* (1), 33.

Sargent-Welch Scientific Co. *Equipment catalogue.* Skokie, IL: Author.

Schlichter, C. L. (1983, February). The answer is in the question. *Science and Children,* p. 10.

Schwartz, J. L. (1985). *Sir Isaac Newton's Games* [Educational software]. Pleasantville, NY: Sunburst Communications.

———. (1995). Shuttling between the particular and the general: Reflections on the role of conjecture and hypothesis in the generation of knowledge in science and mathematics. In D. N. Perkins, J. L. Schwartz, M. M. West, & M. S. Wiske (Eds.), *Software goes to school—teaching for understanding new technologies* (pp. 7–22). New York: Oxford University Press.

Scruggs, T. E., Mostropieri, M. A., Bakken, J. P., & Grigham, F. J. (1993). Reading versus doing: The relative effects of textbook-based and inquiry-oriented approaches to science learning in special education classrooms. *The Journal of Special Education, 27* (1), 1–15.

Shakeshaft, C. (1995). Reforming science education. *Theory Into Practice 34* (1), pp. 74–79.

Shapiro, B. (1994). *What children bring to light: A constructivist perspective on children's learning in science.* New York: Teachers College Press.

Shavelson, R. J., & Baxter, G. P. (1992, May). What we've learned about assessing hands-on science. *Educational Leadership,* 20–25.

Shaw, K. L., & Etchberger, M. L. (1993). Transitioning into constructivism: A vignette of a fifth grade teacher. In K. Tobin (Ed.), *The practice of constructivism in science education* (pp. 259–266). Washington, DC: AAAS Press.

Shaw, K. L., & Jakubowski, E. H. (1991). Teachers changing for changing times. *Focus on Learning Problems in Mathematics, 13* (4), 13–20.

Shepardson, D. P., & Pizzini, E. L. (1991, November). Questioning levels of junior high school science textbooks and their implications for learning textual information. *Science Education, 5* (6), 673–682.

———. (1992). Gender bias in female elementary teachers' perceptions of the scientific ability of students. *Science Education, 76* (2), 147–153.

Shrigley, R. L. (1987, May). Discrepant events: Why they fascinate students. *Science and Children,* 25.

Shymansky, J. A., Hedges, L., & Woodworth, G. (1990). A reassessment of the effects of inquiry-based science curricula of the 60's on student performance. *Journal of Research on Science Teaching, 27* (2), 127–144.

Shymansky, J. A., Kyle, W. C., Jr., & Allport, J. M. (1982, November–December). How effective were the hands-on programs of yesterday? *Science and Children,* 14–15.

Silver, H., Strong, R., & Perini, M. (1997). Integrating learning styles and multiple intelligences. *Educational Leadership, 55* (1), 22–27.

Slavin, R. L. (1995). *Cooperative learning.* Boston: Allyn and Bacon.

Smith, D. D., & Luckasson, R. (1992). *Introduction to special education.* Boston: Allyn and Bacon.

Smith, P. G. (1995, September). Reveling in rubrics. *Science Scope,* 34–36.

Snir, J., Smith, C., & Grosslight, L. (1995). Conceptually enhanced simulations: A computer tool for science teaching. In D. N. Perkins, J. L. Schwartz, M. M. West, & M. S. Wiske (Eds.), *Software goes to school—teaching for understanding new technologies* (pp. 106–129). New York: Oxford University Press.

Solomon, J. (1997, September/October). Is how we teach science more important than what we teach? *Primary Science Review, 49,* 3–5.

Spady, W. G. (1994). Choosing outcomes of significance. *Educational Leadership, 51* (6), 18–22.

Starr, M. L., & Krajcik, J. S. (1990). Concept maps as a heuristic for science curriculum development: Toward improvement in process and product. *Journal of Research in Science Teaching, 27* (10), 987–1000.

State of Iowa. (1988). *School code of Iowa.* Des Moines, IA: Author.

Staver, J. R., & Bay, M. (1987). Analysis of the project synthesis goal cluster orientation and inquiry emphasis of elementary science textbooks. *Journal of Research in Science Teaching, 23* (7), 629–643.

Stead, B. R., & Osborne, R. J. (1980). Exploring science students' concepts of light. *Australian Science Teachers Journal, 26* (3), 84–90.

Stefanich, G. P. (1985). *Addressing orthopedic handicaps in the science classroom.* (Educational Resource Document No. 258 802)

Stern, L., & Roseman, J. E. (2001, October). Textbook alignment. *The Science Teacher,* 52–56.

Stone, C. L. (1982). *A meta-analysis of advance-organizer studies.* Paper presented at the Annual Meeting of the American Educational Research Association, New York. (ERIC Document No. 220476)

Styer, S. (1984, March). Books that ask the right questions. *Science and Children,* 40–42.

Suchman, J. R. (1962). *The elementary school training program in scientific inquiry.* Report to the U.S. Office of Education, Project Title VII. Urbana: University of Illinois.

———. (1971). Motivation inherent in the pursuit of meaning: Or the desire to inquire. In H. I. Day, D. E. Berlyne, & D. E. Hunt (Eds.), *Intrinsic motivation: A new direction in education.* Toronto: Holt, Rinehart, & Winston.

Sumrall, W. J. (1995). Reasons for the perceived images of scientists by race and gender of students in grades 1–7. *School Science and Mathematics, 95* (2), 83–90.

Taba, H., Levine, S., & Elsey, F. F. (1964). *Thinking in elementary school children* (U.S. Office of Education Cooperative Research Project No. 1574). San Francisco: San Francisco State College.

Tinker, R. ProbeSight: What are probes? *The Concord Consortium.* September 14, 2003. [Online: http://probesight.concord.org/what/body_index.htm].

Tobin, K. (1984). Effects of extended wait-time on discourse characteristics and achievement in middle school grades. *Journal of Research in Science Teaching, 21* (8), 779–791.

Tobin, K. G., & Capie, W. (1982). *Wait-time and learning in science. AETS Outstanding Paper for 1981.* (ERIC Document No. ED 221353)

Tobin, K., Tippins, D. J., & Gallard, A. J. (1994). Research on instructional strategies for teaching science. In D. L. Gabel (Ed.), *Handbook on research on science teaching.* New York: Macmillan.

Treagust, D. F., Jacobowitz, R., Gallagher, J. J., and Parker, J. (2003, March). Embedded assessment in your teaching. *Science Scope,* 36–39.

Triangle Coalition for Science and Technology Education. (1991). *A guide for building an alliance for science, mathematics and technology education.* College Park, MD: Author.

———. (1992). *A guide for planning a volunteer program for science, mathematics and technology education.* College Park, MD: Author.

U.S. Department of Labor, Occupational Safety and Health Administration. (1990). 29 CFR Part 1910, Occupational Exposures to Hazardous Chemicals in Laboratories. *Federal Register.* Washington, DC: U.S. Government Printing Office.

———. (1991). 29 CFR Part 1910.1030, Occupational exposure to bloodborne pathogens; Subpart Z, bloodborne pathogens: Standard summary applicable to schools. *Federal Register.* Washington, DC: U.S. Government Printing Office.

U.S. Office of Education. (1977, December 29). Education of handicapped children: Assistance to the states: Procedures for evaluating specific learning disabilities. *Federal Register, Part III.* Washington, DC: U.S. Government Printing Office.

Van Horn, J., Nourot, P. M., Scales, B., Alward, K. R. (1993). *Play at the center of the curriculum.* Columbus, OH: Merrill.

Van Tassell, M. A. (2001) Student inquiry in science: Asking questions, building foundations and making connections. In G. Wells (Ed.). *Action, talk & text: Learning and teaching through inquiry.* New York: Teachers College Press.

van Zee, E. H., Kurose, A., Simpson, D., & Wild, J. (2001). Student and teacher questioning during conversations about science. *Journal of Research in Science Teaching, 38* (2), 159–190.

Valentino, C. (1985). *Question of the week.* Palo Alto, CA: Dale Seymore Publications.

Victor, E. (1985). *Science for the elementary school.* New York: Macmillan.

Vogt, Mary Ellen (1995). *Cross curricular thematic instruction,* [Online: www.eduplace.com/rdg/res/vogt.html].

Von Glaserfeld, E. (1993). Questions and answers about radical constructivism. In K. Tobin (Ed.), *The practice of constructivism in science education* (pp. 23–38). Washington, DC: AAAS Press.

Vygotsky, L. S. (1978). *Mind and society: The development of higher mental processes.* Cambridge, MA: Harvard University Press.

Wadsworth, B. J. (1996). *Piaget's theory of cognitive and affective development.* White Plains, NY: Longman Publishers.

Wagner, K. (1998). Unpublished report. Columbus, OH: Ohio Department of Education.

Watson, S. B. (1992, February). Cooperative methods. *Science and Children,* pp. 30–31.

Weiss, I. R., Pasley, J. D., Smith, P. S., Banilower, E. R., & Heck, D. J. (2003). *Looking inside the classroom: A study of K–12 mathematics and science education in the United States.* Chapel Hill, NC: Horizon Research.

West, S. S., Westerlund, J. F., Nelson, N. C., & Stephenson, A. L. (2001). *Conditions that affect safety in the science classroom: Results from a statewide safety survey.* Austin, TX: Texas Association of Curriculum Development.

West, S. S., Westerlund, J. F., Stephenson, A. L., & Nelson, N. C. (2002). *Conditions that affect secondary science safety: Results from 2001 Texas survey.* Austin, TX: Texas Education Agency. Available at http://bluebonnet.bio.swt.edu.

Western Regional Environmental Education Council. (1992). *Project WILD and Aquatic Project WILD.* Golden, CO: Author.

———. (1994). *Project Learning Tree.* Golden, CO: Author

———. (1995). *Project WET.* Golden, CO: Author.

Wheeler, G., & Sherman, T. F. (1983). Readability formulas revisited. *Science and Children, 20* (7), 38–40.

Wilen, W. (1986). *Questioning skills for teachers.* Washington, DC: National Education Association.

Willert, M. K., & Kamii, C. (1985, May). Reading in kindergarten: Direct vs. indirect teaching. *Young Children,* p. 3.

Williams, C. K., & Kamii, C. (1986, November). How do children learn by handling objects? *Young Children,* p. 26.

Williams, I. W. (1984). Chemistry. In A. Craft & G. Bardell (Eds.), *Curriculum opportunities in a multicultural society* (pp. 133–146). New York: Harper & Row.

Williams-Norton, M., Reisdorf, M., & Spees, S. (1990, March). Home is where the science is. *Science and Children,* 13–15.

Willis, S. (1995a, Summer). Reinventing science education. *Curriculum Update.* Alexandria, VA: ASCD.

———. (1995b, Summer). Reinventing science education: Reformers promote hands-on, inquiry-based learning. *Curriculum Update.* Alexandria, VA: ASCD.

Wilson, L. D., & Blank, R. K. (1999). *Improving mathematics education using results from NAEP and TIMSS.* Washington, DC: Council of Chief State School Officers.

Windram, M. P. (1988, March). Getting at reading through science inquiries. *Roeper Review,* pp. 150–152.

Wiser, M. (1995). Use of history of science to understand and remedy students' misconceptions about heat and temperature. In D. N. Perkins, J. L. Schwartz, M. M. West, & M. S. Wiske (Eds.), *Software goes to school—teaching for understanding new technologies* (pp. 23–28). New York: Oxford University Press.

Wolfe, P., & Brandt, R. (1998). What do we know from brain research? *Educational Leadership, 56* (3), 8–13.

Wolfinger, D. M. (1984). *Teaching science in the elementary school.* Boston: Little, Brown.

Wright, D. (1980). A report on the implications for the science community of three NSF-supported studies of the state of precollege science education. In H. A. Smith (Ed.), *What are the needs in precollege science, mathematics, and social science education? Views from the field.* Washington, DC: National Science Foundation.

Yager, R. (1991, September). The constructivist learning model. *Science Teacher,* 52–57.

Yager, R. E. (1984). The major crisis in science education. *School Science and Mathematics, 84* (3), 196.

Yager, R. E., & Penick, J. E. (1987, October). New concerns for affective outcomes in science. *Educational Leadership,* 93.

Young, J. S. (1970). A survey of safety in high school chemistry laboratories in Illinois. *Journal of Chemical Education 47* (12), A828–838.

Zimmerman, B. J., & Pike, E. O. (1972). Effects of modeling and reinforcement on the acquisition and generalization of question-asking behavior. *Child Development, 43,* 892–907.

Page numbers followed by *f* indicate figures; those followed by *t* indicate tables.

Rubrics *(continued)*
    definition of, 160
    for evaluating electronically accessed lessons, 354, 354*t*
    for evaluating web-based science resources, 380
    holistic scoring, for concept maps, 121, 121*f*
    in lab situation, 159
    with reflective questioning assessments, 161, 165*f*
Rudders (lesson), 198–199, 198*f*
Rules, and due care, 298, 299*f*

Safety, 283–338
    assessments of, 318–319
    bloodborne pathogens and, 308–309
    checklists, 306*f*, 318*f*
    and children with disabilities, 298–299
    class size and, 288–289, 288*f*
    clothing and, 312
    correction request form, 297*f*
    Crisis Response Teams for, 337–338
    due care and, 297–305
    of electrical equipment, 311
    eye protective equipment (goggles) and, 305–308
    eyewash station for, 313–315
    on field trips, 296, 305
    fire blankets for, 312
    fire extinguishers for, 312–313
    first-aid kits for, 325, 325*f*
    of flammable liquid storage, 312
    foreseeability and, 296–297, 297*f*
    goggles and, 305–308
    hair and, 312
    of heating equipment, 311–312
    instructions and, 298–300
    legislation on, 305–311
    maintenance and, 305
    negligence and, 297
    overcrowding and, 288–289, 288*f*
    planning for, 290–291
    reflective questioning assessment of, 160*f*
    rules for, 298, 299*f*
    showers for, 313–315
    student contract for, 298, 300*f*, 301*f*
    supervision and, 301–305
    teacher characteristics and, 289–290
Safety can, 312
Safety equipment, 311–315
    eyewash station, 313–315

fire blankets, 312
fire extinguishers, 312–313
goggles, 305–308
Ground Fault Interrupters (GFI), 311
safety can, for flammable liquid storage, 312
safety/first-aid kits, 325, 325*f*
showers, 313–315
Safety goggles, 305–308
Safety kits, 325, 325*f*
Science
    basic values of, 17
    characteristics females bring to, 81*t*
    children's perceptions of, 5–7
    definition of, 10
    essential features of, 12–27
    importance of, for children with physical disabilities, 91–92
    as inquiry for literacy, 184–187
    in integrated instruction, 262*t*, 265*t*–267*t*, 273
    interdisciplinary nature of, 184, 185*f*
    nature of, 10–12, 14–15
    real life applications, 28–29
Science: A Process Approach (SAPA), 368, 369*t*
Science: A Process Approach II, 93
Science Activities for the Visually Impaired (SAVI), 93, 387
Science Activity Planner form, 319–320, 319*f*, 320*f*
Science and Children, 198, 198*f*, 217–218
Science Curriculum Improvement Study (SCIS), 93, 130, 187, 200–201, 368, 369*t*
Science education, aims of standards and research-based reform in, 27–29
Science Education for Public Understanding Program (SEPUP), 387
Science Enrichment for Learners with Physical Handicaps (SELPH), 387
Science for All Americans - Project 2061, 28–29
Science kits, 137, 208–209
Science process skills. *See* Process skills
Science Scope, 217–218
Scientific literacy, 27–29, 124
    defining, 182
    inquiry for, 184–187
    promoting, 183–184
Scientific method
    definition of, 195
    vs. scientific process skills, 16
    shortcomings of, 10–11, 16
    steps of, 10